Maimonides' *Guide of the Perplexed*

Maimonides' *Guide of the Perplexed*

A Philosophical Guide

ALFRED L. IVRY

The University of Chicago Press
Chicago and London

The University of Chicago Press, Chicago 60637
The University of Chicago Press, Ltd., London

Published 2016
Paperback edition 2019
Printed in the United States of America

28 27 26 25 24 23 22 21 20 19   1 2 3 4 5

ISBN-13: 978-0-226-39512-8 (cloth)
ISBN-13: 978-0-226-63759-4 (paper)
ISBN-13: 978-0-226-39526-5 (e-book)
DOI: https://doi.org/10.7208/chicago/9780226395265.001.0001

Library of Congress Cataloging-in-Publication Data

Names: Ivry, Alfred L., 1935– author.
Title: Maimonides' Guide of the perplexed : a philosophical guide / Alfred L. Ivry.
Description: Chicago : The University of Chicago Press, 2016. | Includes bibliographical references and index.
Identifiers: LCCN 2016005826 | ISBN 9780226395128 (cloth : alk. paper) | ISBN 9780226395265 (e-book)
Subjects: LCSH: Maimonides, Moses, 1135–1204. Dalālat al-ḥā'irīn. | Jewish philosophy—Early works to 1800.
Classification: LCC BM545.D35 I97 2016 | DDC 181/.06—dc23
LC record available at http://lccn.loc.gov/2016005826

♾ This paper meets the requirements of ANSI/NISO Z39.48-1992 (Permanence of Paper).

For Joann
Our children, Rebecca, Cliff, Jonathan, Sara, and Jessica
And grandchildren, Molly, Noah, Ben, Talia, Max, Isaiah, and Esti
In love and gratitude

Contents

Preface

Maimonides' *Guide of the Perplexed* is recognized as a classic of medieval Jewish philosophy, its author celebrated for his extensive influence on subsequent thinkers, an influence that extends to the present. Yet for all its acclaim, the *Guide* has been terra incognita for all but a few in every generation. This is as Maimonides would have wanted it, as he wrote the book for a very select audience, one familiar with the science and philosophy of his day. He knew that the unprepared reader would resist his bold reformulation of God's being and of His relation to mankind in general and to the Jewish people in particular. Accordingly, Maimonides deliberately wrote in a guarded and dissembling manner, rendering the *Guide* difficult and exasperating to most readers.

Scholars have worked assiduously over the centuries to plumb the secrets of the *Guide,* creating commentaries and supercommentaries to it. However, these studies of the *Guide,* mostly in Hebrew, remained the province of a select few. Modern translations of the *Guide* into Western languages spurred scholars in the last half-century to reach out to a larger audience with their analyses of the text. As had their predecessors, the more recent commentators on the *Guide* mostly approached it with one eye on Maimonides' great rabbinic compositions, his *Commentary on the Mishnah* and his code of Jewish law, the *Mishneh Torah.* The authors of these studies generally search to find a unifying ideology and perspective in Maimonides' writings, one that can be accommodated ultimately to traditional Jewish beliefs. These studies at best quote key passages of the *Guide,* not requiring or expecting the reader to consult the text itself.

The book before you is not for the few alone, and not meant to substitute for engaging with Maimonides' text itself. It is centered on the *Guide* and abstains mostly from referring to his other work. It provides what is close to being a chapter-by-chapter clarification of Maimonides' text and the concepts and terms he employs. These are often puzzling, even in the generally excellent English translation of S. Pines, to which my paraphrases of the chapters are keyed.[1] Pines wrote a lengthy introduction to his translation but provided very few explanatory notes to it. Moreover, he apparently felt bound to honor Maimonides' wishes to keep his views secret, the translation retaining the ambiguities and ambivalences of Maimonides' writing.

While not wishing to disrespect Maimonides, I feel the time has come to respect the maturity of contemporary readers and their ability to appreciate an unapologetic presentation of his views. My paraphrases are intended to allow the reader to engage with the *Guide* directly and to make his or her own assessment of Maimonides' achievement. At the same time, I offer the reader one person's evaluation of the *Guide,* an evaluation that sees its author as a deeply conflicted and brave figure. This is an interpretation of the *Guide* that should, in the analysis section of each chapter, challenge scholars and nonscholars alike. It shows the extent to which Maimonides was indebted to a philosophical tradition that contradicted his inherited faith, and the extraordinary attempts he made to subvert that impasse.

I assess Pines' translation against the Judaeo-Arabic original of the text,[2] which can offer alternative understandings of Maimonides' intentions. I have strived to present Maimonides' text objectively, though I realize any explication has some degree of interpretation, expressed even merely by relating a particular passage in the *Guide* to other places that either confirm or contradict it. This should, however, help the reader appreciate the subtleties of Maimonides' composition. Extended critiques of major issues in each section of the book are reserved for the analyses that follow the paraphrases given in each unit of chapters.

Among the issues tackled in this book are Maimonides' allegorization of the Bible; his arguments for God's existence, nature, and relation to the world, with particular attention to the issue of creation; the nature of evil and of divine providence; political theory and prophecy; immortality and the attainment of happiness. The secondary literature analyzing these issues is huge, and I draw the reader's attention to the best of it, avoiding duplication of efforts. The references are mainly to works written in English, to enable the intended reader to access them.

This volume is an inquiry into Maimonides' philosophy and theology, an investigation of both separately and together, for they are intertwined in his thought. One of the major goals of this study is to determine Maimonides' priorities, whether his philosophy is handmaiden to his theology, or vice versa.[3]

Put another way, in the conflict between reason and faith, we shall question which takes precedence in Maimonides' mind—and which in his heart.

As this last sentence intimates, I see Maimonides as torn in his loyalties, seeking guidance as much as offering it. In my reading, *The Guide of the Perplexed* is the mature Maimonides' spiritual as well as intellectual autobiography, his discovery of a truth about the nature of God and humanity that he could not fully admit and could not completely deny.

This is not to say that Maimonides held to this position consistently throughout his life, precariously balanced as it is in the *Guide* itself. His adherence to and advocacy of rabbinic law and lore were consistent throughout his life and integral to his personality, the source of most of his creative energy and achievements. Still, the *Guide* stands in marked contrast to most of his rabbinic writings, and should be taken as his definitive position on philosophical issues. This is not to deny that Maimonides delivers significant philosophical pronouncements in his two major rabbinical writings, as well as in his lesser compositions, as we shall see; but he does not argue for them as a philosopher, as he does in the *Guide*. I have therefore kept comparisons with Maimonides' other writings to a minimum, believing that circumstances in his life created a gulf that makes such comparisons conjectural, particularly where he breaks with earlier statements. The *Guide* thus stands alone, in my opinion, as testament to Maimonides the philosopher. That does not make it the definitive depiction of the man himself, whose soul was large enough to contain contraries.

Accordingly, one need not assume any necessary correlation between Maimonides as a theoretician and the practical life he lived as rabbi and communal leader. His philosophical beliefs should not be overridden by possibly contrary positions held in later epistles and legal decisions, heavily colored as they were by political considerations.[4] As we shall see, should he have wanted to, he could easily have rationalized to himself the traditional stance he adopts in his rabbinic writings and epistles with a political philosophy that legitimizes false but necessary assertions by a public figure.

The Maimonides presented in this study, then, appears as a man of many parts, struggling to form a coherent philosophy out of disparate traditions and schools of thought. Where many scholars see him as a finished product and the *Guide* as a work of nearly immaculate perfection, a view he encouraged, I see him as a fallible seeker of truth for himself as well as for others, and the *Guide* as a record of this search.

Accordingly, this book is not a historical biography of Maimonides' life, nor is it a comprehensive survey of all his work. Distinguished works in these genres have recently appeared,[5] so I simply offer a summary, in the first few chapters of this book, of Maimonides' life and of those writings of his, and of others, that bear upon his philosophical outlook. Essentially, I place in the reader's hands a work of intellectual inquiry, concentrating in the analysis sections of the book on those issues of the *Guide* that I find philosophically challenging. I particularly attempt to identify and explain the underlying metaphysical and epistemological structures of Maimonides' beliefs, knowledge of which is essential to a proper appreciation of his work.

I also attempt to isolate the substantive issues that Maimonides addressed in the *Guide* from the exegetical subtleties with which he posed them, though Maimonides would have objected strongly to such a procedure.[6] For him, as for his fellow Jews, the Bible was a virtual reality competing with the natural world, and he saw his task as synthesizing these worlds. He did this primarily by treating the biblical stories as philosophical parables. Yet for all the subtle ingenuity of his use of parables, I do not believe they fundamentally subverted the message Maimonides conveyed prosaically, the message being sufficiently radical and compelling in itself.

I take careful note of Maimonides' linguistic choices, the possible meanings of Arabic words and sentence constructions that are occasionally misleading in the generally fine Pines translation. Similarly, I attend to Maimonides' probable sources among the Muslim philosophers, through whom he also became familiar with Greek philosophy. The Muslim sources include the Arabic legacy of Neoplatonic texts and the generally overlooked theologian-philosophers of Shīʿī Islam.

It will become clear that Maimonides vacillates between Aristotelian and Platonic positions, or more precisely, neo-Aristotelian and Neoplatonic views (all duly, if succinctly, described). He is strikingly naturalistic in his physics and metaphysics, even with the addition of a decidedly nonempirical emanative scheme whereby God's presence and providence are affirmed. Maimonides is skeptical and ambivalent in his attitude toward metaphysics, aware of the problematic status of many of its proofs. He is ambivalent also toward political philosophy, advocating both participation in and a qualified retreat from society. His ideal political and social stance is Stoic, though he had no direct contact with Stoic philosophers. While adapting some tenets of Islamic theology (*kalām*), Maimonides tries to disengage from its kind of radical voluntarism, as well as from a complete skepticism of philosophy's affirmations.

The questions Maimonides asks of God (about His nature and relation to the world and to evil) and of man (about his status as a political and rational animal) are those we still ponder, and his responses—and doubts—can still guide, as well as challenge, our lives.

This book is the culmination of many years spent in thinking and writing about Maimonides' philosophy, years in which I have had the good fortune of being indulged in this endeavor by colleagues, friends, and family. I studied with two of the last century's great masters of Maimonidean scholarship, the late Professors Alexander Altmann and Shlomo Pines, and learned much from the cohort of Maimonides scholars and friends who appear in the notes to this book. I owe a special debt of gratitude to Seymour Feldman, who commented on an early draft of this manuscript, and to the late Michael Schwarz, the immensely erudite scholar whose fine modern Hebrew translation of the *Guide* is also a mine of annotated information.

Shem Tov ibn Falaquera (ca. 1225–95), apparently of Spain, was one of the first commentators on the *Guide*, calling his book *Moreh ha-Moreh*, "A Guide of the *Guide*."[7] Many commentaries and studies on the *Guide* have been written since then, all assuming a level of familiarity with the subject that is beyond the grasp of most readers today. Without simplifying the material, my study attempts to make Maimonides' text, in Shlomo Pines' fine translation, fully comprehensible and offers the reader an interpretation of the *Guide* that is largely challenging and original. It is thus, in many ways, a new Guide to the *Guide*.

Salisbury, CT
August 2015

Introduction

Moses Maimonides is the name by which the West, and more precisely the English-speaking and -writing West, knows the great medieval Jewish rabbi, philosopher, doctor *cum* medical authority, and community leader whose given names were Abū ʿImran Mūsā ibn Maymūn ibn ʿAbdallah al-Qurṭubi al-Andalusī al-Isrāʾīlī in Arabic and Moshe ben Maimon in Hebrew. It is from the Hebrew "son of Maimon" that the Greek "Maimonides" is derived. His Arabic name identifies him as a Cordovan and Andalusian, and it is thus that he signed his name, proud of his Spanish heritage.

It is the Spain of the "Golden Age" of the tenth and eleventh centuries with which Maimonides was proud to identify. The period was one of cultural and scientific efflorescence and of relative economic and political security for Jews (and Christians) who lived in the Iberian peninsula, easing their integration into the larger society and culture. This period of "convivencia," as it has been called (and interrogated),[1] had come to an end by Maimonides' time, if not before, and Maimon and his family, including the young Moses, endured living under repressive and coercive regimes. Nevertheless, Maimonides remained attached to the accomplishments of the Spanish school of (Muslim) philosophers and scientists and sought to find his own voice among them.

The acronym of Maimonides' Hebrew name is *Rambam,* which stands for Rav (Rabbi) Moshe Ben Maimon, and it is as "The Rambam," and often just as *Rav* or *Ram* (Rabbenu Moshe, i.e., Moshe our Rav), that he is known to a Hebrew-reading public. That audience at first had "just" his monumental code of Jewish law, the *Mishneh Torah,* to read in Hebrew, but soon the Arabic compositions of his other rabbinic and philosophical works were translated into Hebrew,[2] and the extraordinary range of his oeuvre was revealed to his Ashkenazi as well as Sephardi co-religionists.

The impression made by Maimonides' organization and mastery of the talmudic corpus in his Code earned him the sobriquet of a "second Moses." The first Moses has pride of place also in the *Guide,* Maimonides' philosophical magnum opus, though in that work he is guided as much by Aristotle as by Moses. Despite this foreign influence, many (though not all) Jewish readers acclaimed the *Guide* as *the* preeminent work of Jewish philosophy. Its fame and reputation have grown through the ages, and many readers see it as a bold defense of Jewish belief, a response along philosophical lines to the challenge of Graeco-Muslim philosophy.

All things considered, then, it is no wonder that Maimonides is generally considered the greatest intellectual that Jewry produced in the Middle Ages, and perhaps in all times. Be that as it may, Maimonides was certainly a man of his time, thoroughly immersed in the scientific, religious, social, and political currents of his age. As a Jew, he was a minority member of the Islamic society that surrounded him, while within his own community he laid claim to a lofty pedigree of rabbinical ancestors. His father was a *dayyan* or communal judge, author of an important epistle encouraging the Jewish community in Spain to stand fast in the face of religious persecution.[3]

In his turn, Maimonides also sought ways to offer solace and advice to a people threatened with forced conversion or exile.[4] His identification with the people of Israel was complete, with their God, complex. As a leading interpreter and codifier of the talmudic tradition, Maimonides sided with the majority "Rabbanite" tradition and was opposed to the challenge to the oral law (i.e., talmudic authority) and to Jewish society posed by the fundamentalist Karaites.[5] However, many of his political and personal struggles were with other recognized leaders of the Rabbanite community, particularly the Geonim of "Babylonia" (present-day Iraq). Most of our information on Maimonides' personal life is gleaned from the vast correspondence he maintained, a good portion of which has remained extant.[6]

Maimonides arrived in Egypt with a commanding expertise in Jewish law and in medicine. It may be equally obvious that he was also deeply learned in the philosophical and intellectual currents of his day.[7] If we are to believe the epistle that Maimonides prefaces to his introduction to the first part of the *Guide* (and there is little reason to doubt its veracity), he wrote the book following the unanticipated departure of a prize pupil, Joseph ben Judah ibn Simeon, whose education in mathematics, astronomy, and logic had commenced under Maimonides' guidance. Joseph's original desire was to study theoretical subjects, metaphysics and theology, but Maimonides thought it necessary to proceed systematically with more basic subjects. Now that Joseph was ready for the more advanced disciplines, though, he had to leave and take a rabbinic position elsewhere.

Joseph's departure, Maimonides writes him, "aroused in me a resolution that had slackened. Your absence moved me to compose this Treatise, which I have composed for you and those like you, however few they are. I have set it down in dispersed chapters. All of them that are written down will reach you where you are, one after the other."[8]

As we know from later correspondences, Joseph, as well as others, indeed received the chapters in various installments as they were written. This puts in some question Maimonides' claim, in his introduction to the first part of the *Guide,* that the work as a whole, even each word, was written "with great exactness and exceeding precision,"[9] such that any apparent inconsistencies or contradictory remarks are to be deemed intentional.[10]

There are in fact a considerable number of misleading statements in the *Guide.* Maimonides was writing not only for Joseph and a few others, but also for a larger audience. One of the indications of this is that there are large sections of the book that do not require the mathematical, scientific, and logical skills that Maimonides claims in the preface are necessary propaedeutics to the study of metaphysics and theology. Much in the book is devoted to biblical exegesis and apologetics that are philosophically inconclusive. Maimonides would have been aware that his audience would be larger and less sophisticated than he would have liked, and many sections of the book accommodate this *jumhūr,* unsophisticated mass of readers. At the heart of the book, though, Maimonides wrestles with the very real challenges of a Neoplatonized Aristotelian brand of philosophy on the one hand, and a voluntaristic, *kalām*-inspired theology on the other, and these are challenges that he meets with philosophical sophistication and craftiness.

Broadly speaking, scholars have attempted to resolve Maimonides' contradictory positions in a number of ways. A common path is to adopt the exoteric-esoteric bifurcation of meaning that Maimonides alerts the reader to in his opening introductory remarks, a path usually culminating in the view that Maimonides was a committed philosopher and dispassionate elitist.[11] Scholars have differed, however, over just what Maimonides as a philosopher was committed to, be it metaphysics or political philosophy, orthodoxy, skepticism, or agnosticism.[12] Other scholars believe Maimonides underwent a change of heart before or while writing the *Guide,* emphasizing certain themes more than before.[13]

I agree with those who understand Maimonides as writing consistently on two levels, the exoterically "apparent" (*ẓāhir*) and the esoterically "hidden" (*bāṭin*), and I see him as struggling to affirm those axioms of Jewish belief that affirm a special relationship between God and the Jews. I believe Neoplatonism is the bridge that allows Maimonides to present Judaism philosophically. In this, he follows the lead of the Muslim philosophers and the Ismāʿīlī theologians, doing for Judaism what they had done for Sunni and Shīʿī Islam, respectively.

Notwithstanding Maimonides' prefatory remarks, I believe, as mentioned, that Maimonides wrote the *Guide* for himself, as well as for Joseph. As is the case with the author of every major work of literature and philosophy, Maimonides was attempting to resolve issues that had challenged, and probably bedeviled, him. The summary and essentially dogmatic presentations of metaphysics that he included in his rabbinical treatises no longer satisfied him; he wanted to think and write now as a philosopher, to present arguments and defend them as strongly as possible, using philosophical criteria of proof. Joseph's departure presented an opportunity to do so, in writing.

As we shall see, however, Maimonides was unable to present conclusive, demonstrable, and irrefutable proofs for the most important propositions he addressed, those concerning God, creation, and revelation. On other issues, such as God's relation to the world and human immortality, Maimonides reached conclusions he could barely express.

He may have realized the quandary he was in as a philosopher before he began working with Joseph, but it is more likely that Maimonides was initially sure of his abilities to philosophize conclusively. The introduction to the first part of the *Guide* breathes confidence in the discipline. Soon enough, however, it would have become clear to Maimonides that he had to settle for less than conclusive proofs, that his arguments with Aristotle and the Muslim theologians, the *mutakallimūn,* were indecisive at best.

This realization would have perplexed and disappointed Maimonides, given his previous endorsement and appropriation of philosophy where suitable in his rabbinic writings and the confidence with which he embarked on Joseph's education. Consequently, I contend that Maimonides is one of the perplexed for whom the *Guide* is written; his writing the book is his attempt to work his way out of conundrums he shared with the best minds of his time.

Maimonides' methodology is to map the Bible and rabbinic *midrashim* onto philosophical paradigms, offering a comprehensive interpretation of biblical terms and parables, the first and second "purposes," respectively, for writing the book.[14] He claims, and presumably believes, that the early rabbis knew (what is usually regarded as Greek) physics and metaphysics, and that they treated them as great secrets to share with the very minimum of persons. Maimonides honors the rabbis' tradition by disguising the most daring of his convictions, though his philosophically oriented exegesis of the Bible reveals the direction of his thoughts.

For Maimonides, the various teachings of philosophy were public knowledge, at least for the few who had access to teachers and books. However, the majority of Jews, including the rabbis of his day (and later), were ignorant of the subject, and Maimonides was aware of their potential opposition to it. His tactic to disarm these critics was to tease out the Jewish roots of philosophy, to show its inextricable relation to Scripture and rabbinic teachings.

Maimonides does not generally acknowledge the impasse to which philosophy brought him, but his philosophical acumen was such that he had to realize it, and he intimated it to Joseph and those like him who were trained properly. Some scholars have recently turned Maimonides' failed quest for certain knowledge into a bold acceptance of a skeptical posture,[15] viewing his purpose all along as essentially heuristic, to teach the limits of philosophy. Such a reading distorts the significance of the preface and introduction to the first part of the book, denying Maimonides' confidence in his ability to disclose the secrets of physics and metaphysics and to reveal that they are present already in the Bible. The skeptical view also does not appreciate the fact that Maimonides never abandons the components of the metaphysical structure whose scientific validity he doubts, accepting it on less than demonstrable grounds. This reading also undermines Maimonides' belief in the perfection and happiness that are available to man ideally through intellectual conjunction with the divine realm.

Other scholars see Maimonides as adopting an orthodox posture in his vigorous criticism of philosophy's belief in an eternal universe, and his endorsement of the notion of creation from nothing.[16] This view has to contend, however, with alternate readings of these issues such as are offered in this book, as well as with Maimonides' introductory pleas to the reader not to publicly divulge his teachings. If Maimonides believed he was defending a traditional view of divine creation and providence, he need not have been so concerned with the reaction to his work.

Had Maimonides been fully conscious of the limitations of philosophy when he began to work with Joseph or when he began to write the *Guide,* in all likelihood he would not have striven to show that the Bible and Jewish tradition utilize the discipline. He could simply have referred his student to Judah Halevi's critique of philosophy in part 5 of his *Kuzari,* or to the extended exposition and critique of philosophy that the great Islamic theologian and mystic Abū Ḥāmid al-Ghazālī (d. 1111) had offered.

A century before Maimonides, Al-Ghazālī had defended his faith against what he regarded as the heretical views of the philosophers in general, and of Avicenna in particular. He called his book *Tahāfut al-Falāsifa,* "Incoherence of the Philosophers," and in it he critiqued in detail the tenets of the philosophers' beliefs.[17] To enable his readers to follow his critique, Al-Ghazālī felt obliged to present the philosophers' views objectively first, so he wrote a volume meant to precede the *Incoherence* and called it *Maqāṣid al-Falāsifa,* "Intentions of the Philosophers."[18]

Al-Ghazālī's two volumes, the fame of which could not have escaped Maimonides' attention, would have sufficed for Maimonides if he wished to acquaint his readers with both the imposing edifices of philosophy and their weak foundations. Instead, Maimonides goes to great length to show the compatibility of the Bible with Aristotle (not pursued by Al-Ghazālī with the Qur'ān), and he then brings both support and supposed rejection of the philosophers' metaphysical beliefs together in one volume, challenging the reader to discern his final position.

If a reader chooses to believe that Maimonides' professions of doubt and skepticism of philosophy's metaphysical teachings are his last word on the subject, then Maimonides would have held out cruelly false expectations to Joseph and all his readers. Indeed, Maimonides would appear to have played the Pied Piper in the *Guide,* to have led Joseph and his brothers away from the certainties they sought to the unfamiliar postures of the skeptic or agnostic; the putative philosophers could not be expected to embrace the idea that they would reach a state of psychic bliss in pursuing a hopeless quest. Consequently, viewing the *Guide* as advocating for recognition of the essential limitations of metaphysical knowledge, and for the spiritual tranquility that purportedly comes with such recognition,[19] appears counter to the main thrust of the book, and to the desires of its author.

It is nevertheless possible that Maimonides, in the course of writing this book, resolved his doubts by accepting them, becoming convinced of the inability of the intellect to prove philosophy's metaphysical assertions. It is questionable, however, that Maimonides would have felt obliged to so disabuse Joseph of his faith in philosophy, or to so "enlighten" him, without providing convincing counterarguments in support of those beliefs he does accept, of both a political and a theoretical kind. The admittedly inconclusive arguments Maimonides does offer on behalf of tradition would not have impressed Joseph, if he truly was the prize pupil Maimonides believed him to be.[20] Joseph would have seen that, given his teacher's reservations about the possibility of any true knowledge of metaphysics, Maimonides would have had little justification for his affirmation of the spiritual value of observing the commandments. Moreover, Maimonides accepts in fact if not in principle the architecture of the philosophers' cosmos, providing him with the mechanism to explain God's governance of the world.

Maimonides' awareness of the limitations of philosophy should not, therefore, be taken as his last word on the subject. However qualified his faith in the truths philosophy could offer, Maimonides does not reject them essentially. They lead him to a modified form of deism that offers the possibility of intellectual immortality and ecstatic communion with the divine.

Background

1

A Concise Biography

Maimonides was born in 1138[1] in Cordoba, Spain, which was then part of the Almoravid empire.[2] The Almoravids were Moors from North Africa who originally invaded Spain with the declared intention to establish a more strict observance of Islam among the faithful. This led them to attempt to rid the country of Jews and Christians, formerly tolerated as fellow monotheists. Those who persisted in their original belief were persecuted and ostensibly had to choose between exile and apostasy. Maimonides' father, Maimun ben Joseph, a leader of the community, wrote a "Letter of Consolation"[3] urging his fellow Jews to observe as much of the Law as possible, even if it had to be kept secretly. It may be inferred from this that many Jews chose to remain in Spain and publicly professed allegiance to Islam, while privately retaining their ancestral faith.

In 1148 the Almohads, another Berber group from the Atlas Mountains, overran Andalusia with the same rationale as the Almoravids, the latter's religious zeal ostensibly gone lax. The Almohad rulers again forced non-Muslims either to convert or to leave the country without their possessions. Many in the Jewish community again chose a third way, that of dissembling their allegiance to the Prophet of Islam. It is possible that Maimonides' father chose this path, for we hear nothing of him or his children for twelve long years, despite his position of leadership in the Jewish community. When they emerge it is in Fez, the Almohad capital, so it is likely they passed as Muslims for that period of time, a period in which Maimonides concentrated on his studies, mastering the texts of both the Jewish religious tradition and the Graeco-Muslim philosophical and scientific tradition.

An early indication of Maimonides' absorption in philosophy is to be found in his *Treatise on the Art of Logic,*[4] a handbook of key terms and definitions that form the basis for scientific reasoning. Maimonides' information is taken from the treatises on Aristotelian logic compiled by Alfarabi, the Muslim philosopher whom Maimonides most admired.[5] Maimonides writes allegedly at the request of a traditionally educated but philosophically innocent patron, apparently Muslim, who wishes to have the technical language, categories, and divisions of logic briefly explained to him.

Herbert Davidson has challenged the claim that Maimonides wrote this treatise, both because his name does not appear on some extant early manuscripts, and because in one place the author brings Moses and Jesus into a temporal relationship in order to exemplify a logical point.[6] Now, while the Jew Maimonides might not have chosen to adduce the Christian messiah as an appropriate figure in a treatise intended for a Jewish reader, as Davidson argues,[7] a dissimulating Muslim Maimonides would not have had to be that sensitive, especially for a Muslim reader. Nothing else is decisively Jewish, or Muslim, in this treatise.[8] It is thus highly likely that Maimonides composed the treatise in Spain or the Maghreb, while posing as a Muslim.

Another early work, written in 1157–58 while Maimonides was still somewhere in Andalusia, is a treatise on the calendar,[9] intended to assist people in understanding the vagaries of the rabbinically calculated lunar year. Maimonides here shows an early grasp of mathematics and astronomy that he was to expand upon in the chapter "Laws of the Sanctification of the Moon" in his law code, the *Mishneh Torah.*[10]

At the time of his initial scientific forays in print, Maimonides was also absorbed in writing preliminary commentaries on portions of both the Babylonian and Jerusalem Talmuds.[11] As well, he began then to comment on the Mishnah, a neglected text usually subsumed within commentaries that focus more on the later talmudic stratum of the Gemara.

The first major public statement that Maimonides put his name and Jewish identity to is "Letter on Apostasy" (*Iggeret ha-Shemad*), also known as "Treatise on Martyrdom" (*Ma'amar Qiddush ha-Shem*), which he wrote while still in Fez.[12] In it he assured those of his co-religionists who had "converted" to Islam that they would be welcomed back to Judaism if they chose to return. He urged that they should make every effort to do so, though it meant leaving their homes and wealth.

Maimonides wrote in response to a French rabbi's more severe, though legally/*halachically* correct, edict that ruled against those who committed apostasy (however nominally), denying them the right of return. This put those who wished to remain Jewish in Spain in the position of having to accept martyrdom, should they be put to the test.

In his statement, Maimonides implies that the reality of life under the

Almohads is not what it might seem to an outsider, that after their Islamic "confession of faith," the *Shahāda,* nothing further is asked of the Jews, and they are able to pursue their own religion discreetly. In a highly daring and innovative ruling, Maimonides distinguished speech acts from other actions that testify to the adoption of another faith, claiming that these oral confessions are understood by everyone to be disingenuous and hence do not sever the individual's tie to his ancestral faith.[13] In so writing, Maimonides may be seen as following his father's pragmatic approach in responding to threats to Jewish survival, bending the law to accommodate a frightening reality.

It is not surprising that having gone public in a matter that required discretion, Maimonides with his family—father, brother, and presumably mother and sister (or sisters)—soon thereafter emigrated from the lands of Almohad rule. They traveled east, first sailing to Palestine and then overland to Egypt. In leaving the land of Israel after having set foot in it, and in settling in Egypt, Maimonides violated injunctions that he was to endorse later in the *Mishneh Torah,*[14] not the first or last inconsistency life and his public responsibilities demanded of him.

The Maimon family's departure from the Holy Land, after brief visits to Jerusalem and Hebron, was a realistic decision, given the bleak economic and social conditions of the small and impoverished Jewish community in Palestine and the political turmoil and danger there caused by the ongoing fighting between Crusaders and Saracens. By contrast, Egypt was home to a sizable Jewish community that benefited from a long-standing, relatively tolerant Fatimid regime. The safety of the Jewish community was not affected by Saladin's overthrow of this regime shortly after the Maimon family arrived in 1165, nor by Saladin's installation of an Ayyubid Sunni regime to replace the Shīʿī confession of the Fatimids.[15]

The Maimon family chose to live in Fustat, adjacent to the new capitol of Cairo, where Maimonides' services as a physician were sought by the court. He had studied medicine in the course of his education prior to coming to Egypt, arriving as both an accomplished rabbinic scholar and a medical practitioner, eventually to become an author and authority in both genres. Maimonides' medical treatises were mostly written later in his life. Some were of a comprehensive sort intended to serve as a primer for physicians; others were dedicated to a particular person and medical problem. Galen was his mentor, and most of the material in Maimonides' *Medical Aphorisms* and other works is taken from the translated writings of that sage of Pergamum.[16]

We know of Maimonides' life in Egypt primarily from his extensive correspondence, in some of which he speaks very personally.[17] He was quickly recognized as an authority in halakhic matters for the Rabbanite community, and was apparently appointed *ra'īs al-yahūd,* "head" of the entire Egyptian Jewish community, soon after Saladin's assumption of power. He held that fiercely contested office for a year or two in the period 1171–73, and possibly again in the 1190s.[18] Maimonides' reputation spread, and with or without an official title he was inundated with legal questions bearing on all aspects of life from all over the Jewish world.

Maimonides' stature as a halakhic "decisor," that is, a person qualified to issue legal rulings, was based primarily on two monumental compositions: his *Commentary on the Mishnah* (finished in 1168, though often revised) and a code of Jewish law, called in Hebrew *Mishneh Torah* (completed in 1177).[19] In what follows I focus mainly on presenting the philosophical components in the *Commentary on the Mishnah,* and will do the same for the *Mishneh Torah* in the next chapter. The opinions he presents in these two books often serve as background for views he presents or assumes are known in the *Guide.* While scholars often interpret the *Guide*'s statements in light of these earlier works, and attempt to resolve all apparent conflicts between them, I have largely avoided this methodology, for reasons given in the preface.[20]

The *Commentary on the Mishnah* covers all sixty-three tractates of the Mishnah, a second-century (CE) work edited in Palestine. Maimonides concisely synthesizes the Mishnaic discussion of a particular issue, stresses the normative interpretations given, and often provides the methodological rule or rules whereby a particular decision is to be inferred.[21] He contextualizes the original material within the discourse and perspectives of the later Amoraim of the Talmud. As he implies in the introduction to his commentary,[22] Maimonides does the work of the reader for him: a person would no longer have to study the Gemara in order to understand the Mishnah.

This could be seen as a (possibly unconscious) first step in Maimonides' vision of reforming the curriculum of Jewish studies, devoted nearly in its entirety to study of the Talmud. The second step was that taken in his law code, the *Mishneh Torah.* There Maimonides restructured the entire body of rabbinic law, organizing it topically in a presentation free of the dialectic found in the Talmud. As Maimonides announces in his introduction to this work, one would need to study only the Torah and Maimonides' *Mishneh Torah* to know the Law and be able to follow it.[23]

In addition to synthesizing the Mishnaic material in his commentary on that work, Maimonides composed three essays in the form of introductions that introduce extralegal themes into that work. The first introduction, at the beginning of the commentary, purports to be historical.[24] Maimonides traces an unbroken line of transmission of the oral law from Moses to Judah HaNasi (second century CE), the final redactor of the Mishnah.[25] That book (and its fifth-century companion, the Gemara) is the heritage of rabbinic Judaism, passed on by the Geonim, the religious leaders of post-talmudic times, to Maimonides. In his view, he is the recipient of the Law in all its fullness and authority, a law that will never be altered or surpassed. This position expresses the view of Rabbanite Jewry, faced with internal challenges from Karaites who rejected the oral law in its rabbinic formulation, and from external supersessionist challenges of both Christians and Muslims.

Maimonides' second introduction, called *Ḥeleq*, prefaces his commentary to the tenth chapter of the Mishnah tractate Sanhedrin.[26] It is so called since the Mishnah opens with the statement (soon qualified) that "all Israel has a portion [*ḥeleq*] in the world to come." Maimonides takes this opportunity to introduce something that was common among Muslim jurists, but largely foreign to Jews: a set of fundamental principles of the faith. Maimonides counts thirteen such, a number much disputed by later rabbis, but one that came to have near universal popularity and that entered into the liturgy in the poetic *Yigdal* hymn sung on Sabbath eve.

Maimonides presents these principles dogmatically, offering immortality to those who accept them, and threatening death to those who doubt even one of them. In terms often borrowed from a philosophical lexicon that would have been foreign to many of his readers, Maimonides' principles include belief in the existence of a being that is perfect; the cause of all else; uniquely one and eternal; incorporeal, creating the world "after" absolute nothingness (literally, absence or "privation" of being, *ʿadam* in Arabic); and alone deserving worship and obedience, all worship of others being prohibited and considered idolatry.

Belief in prophecy is the sixth principle, described in terms of a union or "conjunction" with the Agent Intellect and emanation from it, concepts that would have mystified many of Maimonides' readers then (and still do now), but which would have been familiar to those readers who had some philosophical training.[27] The preeminence of Moses as a prophet is another principle, as is the belief that the Torah was revealed to him by God and will never be abrogated or changed.

The tenth principle proclaims God's knowledge of the actions of human beings,[28] followed by the assurance that reward and punishment are attuned to a person's observance of the Law. The great reward is life in the world to come, even as the most dreaded punishment is exclusion from that, i.e., the loss of immortality. The afterlife envisaged is purely spiritual, as Maimonides explained earlier in the chapter.[29] Maimonides concludes with affirming belief in the advent of the Messiah, for whom one should wait patiently, and with a two-word (!) affirmation of the principle of resurrection.

This decision to write a catechism of Jewish belief was part of Maimonides' desire to present Judaism in as clear and explicit a manner as possible, theologically as well as legalistically. As a rationalist, he believed it important to have a clear idea of the essential beliefs of one's faith, even if the philosophical style of his presentation would have been less than clear to most of his nonphilosophical readers.

Maimonides' third introduction in the *Commentary on the Mishnah* is in its way also revolutionary. He writes it in eight chapters preceding his commentary on the tractate Avot, "Fathers," and it therefore came to be known as *Eight Chapters* (*Shemonah Peraqim*).[30] "Fathers" itself is a collection of *gnomoi,* wise sayings of a moral and pietistic kind, charmingly unsystematic. In his introduction, Maimonides largely ignores the following Mishnah and imposes a mostly Aristotelian ethic upon Judaism, adopting Alfarabi's earlier appropriation of Aristotle's *Nicomachean Ethics.*[31]

Maimonides does not accept everything Aristotle has to say about human nature and society. As Aristotle himself saw ethics and politics as conditioned by particular circumstances and conventions, and thus not subjects given to universal pronouncements or demonstrative proofs, Maimonides was free to modify his sources in accordance with the particular mores of his society. At the same time, Maimonides felt, as did his predecessors, that civilized human beings share a large body of values and that most virtues and vices are universally "well known" as such, allowing (quasi-scientific) categorization. Thus, in chapter 6 of *Eight Chapters,*[32] he identifies murder, theft, robbery, fraud, injuring the innocent, ingratitude, and disrespect toward parents as well-known vices. Later, in his *Mishneh Torah,* Maimonides considers the seven Noahide *mizvot* (treated here as laws) in a similar near-universal light.[33]

In the first chapter of *Eight Chapters,* Maimonides describes the human soul in terms discussed by Plato, Aristotle, and Galen. The originally Platonic division of the soul into reason, spirit, and appetite is mentioned, followed by a brief outline of the five faculties Aristotle first delineated: the nutritive, sensory, imaginative, rational, and appetitive faculties.[34] These are all seen as part of a single soul, and the relation of the other faculties to the rational faculty is considered that of matter to form. Though Maimonides does not elaborate further, in the *Guide* he will apply this analogy literally and treat all the faculties of the soul other than the intellect as materially conditioned and hence perishable.[35]

As the form of the soul, the rational faculty is meant to govern the other faculties, particularly the sentient and appetitive ones, which are prone to succumb to temptation. It is these faculties, and particularly the appetitive one, to which the Law addresses commandments, and it is to these faculties that the moral virtues are directed. It is inconceivable to Maimonides that one would willfully disobey a commandment to which the rational faculty assents, whereas physical desires, as perceptions, have no such innate check. A person's soul must therefore be acculturated toward virtue and become aware of the corresponding vices.

The moral virtues Maimonides first mentions include acts of moderation, liberality, justice, gentleness, humility, contentment, and courage in terms that mostly derive from Aristotle.[36] The vices, Maimonides says, are simply deviations in one direction or the other from an assumed mean in each virtue. He identifies some of these excesses in chapter 4, adding at the same time the classical virtues of wit and generosity. As Maimonides treats the latter, it differs from Aristotle's *megaloprepeia.* That is a "magnificence" of an ostentatious sort, whereas Maimonides views generosity as consisting of acts of charity that are accessible to everyone.

Absent in Maimonides' list of virtues is Aristotle's notion of a person who possesses "greatness of soul," *megalopsychia,* a trait that would have seemed to Maimonides to entail snobbery and condescension, for all its show of public generosity.[37] Maimonides' ideal person here is characterized rather as following Moses in possessing humility, being a (moderately) pious sage, rather than an aristocratic gentleman.[38]

The model of a pious sage combines moral and intellectual perfection, in which the rational faculty dominates all others. Education of this faculty entails exposing it to scientific knowledge, a necessary step for Maimonides in the perfection, and ultimate happiness, of the soul. This would have surprised many of his readers then, as well as now.

Maimonides is more attuned to his readers in the last or eighth chapter of *Eight Chapters,* where he expounds upon the traditional Jewish belief in free will.[39] In remarks that he was to repeat years later in his *Letter on Astrology,*[40] Maimonides rebukes those who believe actions are the result of either astral determinism or blind chance. The world is governed by a divine will that has granted human beings the freedom to choose how to conduct their lives. The Torah with its system of rewards and punishments is predicated on the assumption of free choice. The passages in the Bible that appear to have God determining human behavior, as when God is said to harden Pharaoh's heart (Exodus 14:4), need to be interpreted to show that the deity is responding to man's actions, not causing them.

Maimonides feels compelled to respond to the question of God's foreknowledge, though "I did not want to speak about it at all."[41] Maimonides assumes divine foreknowledge, without which God's knowledge would not be "true knowledge," i.e., knowledge worthy of the omniscience that is uniqely

His. The nature of that omniscience is beyond human understanding, however, and Maimonides can only say that God's knowledge is identical with His essence, as are all His attributes.

Maimonides refers to these remarks approvingly in his commentary on 3:15 of the Mishnah Avot, explaining briefly the enigmatic statement attributed to Rabbi Aqiba that "All is foreseen, yet authorization [for free choice] is granted."[42] Maimonides again insists that though God's knowledge is all-encompassing, He does not determine man's actions, having given him agency over his deeds. Maimonides leaves the issue here, and will return to it in his later writings.[43]

The *Mishneh Torah* is a compendium of Jewish law, arranged in fourteen books, which are then further divided into treatises, chapters, and smaller units.[44] As the numerical equivalent of the Hebrew letters composing the word *yad* (hand) is fourteen, the *Mishneh Torah* is also known as "the strong hand," *ha-yad ha-ḥazaqah* (alluding to Exodus 13:9, Deuteronomy 6:21, and elsewhere).

The Bible and rabbinic tradition view the exodus from Egypt, achieved by God's "strong hand," as a transition from slavery to freedom, where freedom is construed as obedience to the dictates of God's law. So too Maimonides meant his Code to facilitate Jewish freedom. It both guided the observant reader through the thickets of rabbinic law with resolute authority and clarity, and freed him from the task of studying the Talmud constantly, as the rabbinic ideal urged.

Though not the first code of Jewish law, Maimonides' *Mishneh Torah* surpassed previous attempts in its comprehensive and logical organization of all areas of Jewish law, including those rendered inapplicable by historical circumstances.[45] The Code is comprehensive also in the sense that it takes into account the rulings of all major rabbinic sources from talmudic times to his day, not just the Babylonian and Jerusalem Talmuds, however prominent their role. Maimonides was interested in the rulings deemed normative, not in the arguments and counterarguments that preceded the ruling, and he took it upon himself to give only the ruling to be followed, not citing his sources. In this way, Maimonides did more than reiterate the Law, he reshaped it, both structurally and substantially. In distilling the normative rulings of the Law, he was discarding the surrounding body of discourse, study of which for ages past had been a prime expression of Jewish scholarship and religiosity.

The books of the *Mishneh Torah* range over the entirety of life's circumstances for a person living within a rabbinic framework, promulgating laws that are presented as invested with moral and philosophical perspectives.[46] The very first book, the "Book of Knowledge," opens with a dogmatic philosophical presentation of the principles of Jewish belief, and there follows a discussion of ethical virtues. It then proceeds to specifically "Jewish" issues of Torah study, idolatry, and repentance. Subsequent books cover such issues as prayer; observance of the Sabbath and holidays; marriage, divorce, and permitted and illicit sexual relations; oaths, vows, and the giving of charity; states of physical and dietary impurity; torts, commercial, civil, and criminal law; and laws of inheritance.[47]

Maimonides devotes two and a half books to issues his readers would have found to be of essentially theoretical interest, namely, laws concerning the sabbatical and jubilee years and laws relating to the Temple ritual and sacrifices. As these issues found expression in the liturgy and recitations of the Torah, they were not absent from popular consciousness and were believed to be part of a restored sovereignty in messianic times. Maimonides' inclusion of these laws in his Code was thus an indication of his desire to keep faith with the faithful, an oblique sign of his commitment to the messianic ideal. His own, more qualified attitude toward sacrifices and the reconstruction of the Temple may be inferred from the historical rationale of sacrifices he offers in the *Guide*, and from his comment in the *Mishneh Torah* that one should not interrupt instructing children in Talmud in order to rebuild the Temple, even upon hearing word of the Messiah's advent.[48]

The last book of the *Mishneh Torah*, the "Book of Judges," deals mostly with specifically political matters, laws considering the composition of the (once and future) supreme court, or Sanhedrin, as well as of other courts; the responsibilities of judges and kings; witnesses and evidence; disbelievers in the oral law; mourning and the conduct of war. Maimonides here also discusses a traditional Jewish standard of nominal universal morality, known as the seven Noahide commandments;[49] and concludes with a vision of messianic times that is strikingly naturalistic. Maimonides is generous here to Christianity and Islam, which serve, he says, to accustom people to the essential message of Judaism and the worship of God.[50] He thus closes his code of law on a utopian and somewhat ecumenical note. In this he may be affirming belief in a better future for his people.

Maimonides' schedule in the years he wrote his rabbinic masterpieces was apparently less taxing than later, allowing him to concentrate on these large projects. He was economically involved with and assisted by the mercantile activities of his beloved younger brother, David. David's death at sea in 1178 precipitated a yearlong depression in Maimonides. It also propelled him to earn his livelihood as a physician, since he refused to accept remuneration as a rabbi.[51] His son Abraham was born in 1184, when Maimonides was forty-six years old. Abraham eventually followed in his father's footsteps as a leader of the community, though he differed in his spiritual affiliations, being inclined to Sufi-like mystical practices.

Maimonides wrote the *Guide of the Perplexed* in the years 1185–90, beginning it eight years after finishing the *Mishneh Torah,* and seven years after his brother's death. The *Guide* breathes an essentially different spirit than his earlier rabbinic work, even though both the *Commentary on the Mishnah* and *Mishneh Torah* have philosophically oriented chapters. Maimonides was called a "second Moses," owing to his organization and elucidation of Jewish law in those two books, and particularly in the *Mishneh Torah.* As we shall see, this title is no less apt for Maimonides' efforts to transform Moses' biblical legacy.

Both before and after writing his major studies on the Law, Maimonides composed a number of monographs that testify to his commanding position as the leader of his people, the "Great Eagle" (*ha-nesher ha-gadol*), as he came to be known. Besides receiving letters of a personal nature involving the correspondent and immediate family or litigants, Maimonides received communications from rabbis about issues confronting their entire community. In 1172, when thirty-four years old and apparently serving as *ra'īs al-yahūd,* "head of the Jews," Maimonides responded to a plea for guidance from a leading figure in Yemeni Jewry. The community there was under siege on many fronts. The regional government was in the hands of a religious zealot who was prepared to kill those who did not convert to Islam; an apostate was quoting Scripture to argue that it foretold the coming of Muhammad and Islam; and a Jew was parading around, with some success, as the Messiah. What were the Yemeni Jews to do, and what to believe, given that their plight could well have fulfilled the conditions of disaster, the "birth pangs" (*ḥevlei leidah*) that were supposed to precede the messianic advent?

In his *Epistle to Yemen,*[52] Maimonides assured the communal leaders that everything was happening according to a divine plan foretold in the Book of Daniel. Islam, he says, is the fourth and last empire alluded to by the prophet, so that the redemption and restoration of Israel are relatively imminent. Maimonides even breaks a rabbinic taboo that he was later to endorse, revealing what he claims is a family tradition that says prophecy, a forerunner of the messianic advent, will be renewed in the year 1209–10, some 37 or 38 years hence.[53] The end is nigh, but in the meantime the Yemeni community is to hold fast to the Law[54] and wait patiently for the true Messiah.

Maimonides' insistence on observing the Law encompasses the "oral law" (that based on the Talmud) as well as the "written law" (that found in the Pentateuch). He calls the Karaites heretics (*minim*) and is prepared to forfeit their lives.[55] He is more sympathetic to the messianic pretender, whom he considers mentally sick, not evil. He should be taken into custody to show the authorities that the Jews are not in a messianic ferment, and then he may be released. In general, Maimonides counsels the community to bear their humiliations silently, not to make waves.

Maimonides is not silent, however, in his indictment of Islam, and of Christianity too, as religions founded by false prophets in imitation of the one true faith and its incomparable prophet, Moses. Maimonides thus turns the epistle into a lengthy polemic against the supersessionist claims of Christianity and Islam. The Bible is his proof text, the prophets his guide to history.

Anticipating a theme that he develops in the *Guide,* Maimonides claims that Jewish law has a unique inner dimension, an esoteric side, that distinguishes it from the *shari'a* of Islam. This secret teaching is for the intellectually elite, those who can comprehend philosophical ideas. Judaism, Maimonides states, provides a perfect and unsurpassable blend of practical and theoretical teachings.

Maimonides' *Treatise on Resurrection* (1191)[56] and *Letter on Astrology* (1195)[57] were also written to affect public attitudes toward issues on which the community held strong views. In the former, Maimonides attempts to correct the impression inadvertently given in his *Commentary on the Mishnah* that he did not believe in resurrection of the body, despite having listed it there among the principles of the faith.[58] The problem he created, which he acknowledges and is at pains to resolve, is that he simply *listed* the belief in resurrection, without any discussion whatsoever, thus giving the impression of not really believing it.[59]

Since this treatise was written just one year after he finished *The Guide of the Perplexed,* it is hard to believe Maimonides is not being disingenuous in protesting his loyalty to a doctrine absent from that work and opposed to its spirit. In the *Guide,* Maimonides minimizes the significance of the corporeal aspect of life and sees immortality in intellectual terms solely. While apparently accepting the theoretical possibility of miracles contrary to nature, he seems to believe that with the exception of creation and revelation at Sinai, God allows nature to take its course, it being a course of His design.

In the *Treatise on Resurrection,* however, Maimonides affirms his fidelity to a belief that he finds in only one chapter in the Bible, namely, in Daniel 22, verses 2 and 12.[60] He contends that belief in resurrection is binding on a Jew and states that it is not susceptible of metaphorical interpretation, owing to its unanimous acceptance in the tradition.[61] He is completely candid in admitting this fact, though probably less than candid in insisting that he always firmly believed in this principle. Indeed, it is more likely that he simply was deferring to tradition in the *Commentary on the Mishnah* in citing resurrection as a principle of the faith, and in condemning those who deny it in the *Mishneh Torah.*

In the *Treatise on Resurrection,* Maimonides considers resurrection a test case for the belief in miracles, which he sees as central to the Jewish belief in creation and revelation. Here Maimonides is revisiting a central issue in the *Guide,* though treating it more superficially than in that other work. The challenge to natural philosophy presented by Islamic theology, fully discussed in the *Guide,* is all but ignored here, and it is not clear that Maimonides' position is essentially different from that of the Muslim theologians, the *mutakallimūn.*[62] Maimonides is giving the people what they want, a world of miraculous possibilities, in which all the biblical miracles can be taken literally. Maimonides' *Treatise on Resurrection* thus shows the lengths to which he was prepared to go to avoid arousing the anger of the multitude and their leaders on issues they considered central to their belief.[63]

The *Letter on Astrology,* on the other hand, denying the planets autonomous power, is entirely consistent with Maimonides' attitude in the *Guide.* The planets, he believes, have no independently irreversible effect upon human beings and should not be seen as determining their destinies. People are free to act as they choose, and should know that whatever happens to them is decreed—though not *in itself* predestined—by God.[64]

In viewing human events as occurring under God's direction, even if mediated through the motions of the planets, Maimonides differs with what he regards as the philosophers' view of chance as a decisive factor in life. So too does he distinguish his view of creation from nothing from that of the various views of the philosophers that affirm an eternal universe.

In taking these positions, Maimonides reiterates positions expressed previously in the *Mishneh Torah* and *Guide.* This might be seen as confirmation of the views expressed there, as well as an expression of Maimonides' strategy in addressing a nonphilosophical, traditionally inclined audience. His denunciation of astrology as a pseudoscience, like his praise of astronomy as a true science, is written sharply but superficially, and even the more elaborate discussions of the differing views on creation and eternity, and on whether and in what sense human behavior is free, are presented briefly and dogmatically.[65]

In his famous letter to Samuel ibn Tibbon, who was translating the *Guide* into Hebrew, Maimonides recounted his exhausting schedule as physician to the court in Cairo as well as to his own community in Fustat. In his last years he bemoaned the lack of time and energy to write the rabbinic commentaries he had started years before. He had, however, written two works in that genre that established his lasting eminence as an interpreter and decisor of Jewish law: the *Commentary on the Mishnah* and the *Mishneh Torah.*

2

The *Mishneh Torah*

In 1168 Maimonides produced his first major writing in the rabbinical tradition, a commentary on the Mishnah, briefly discussed in the preceding chapter. He followed this in 1170 with a book that identified and organized the 613 commandments of rabbinic law, called simply *Sefer ha-Miẓvot,* "Book of the Commandments."[1] In the ensuing ten years, Maimonides worked on organizing the vast talmudic corpus into a coherent and systematic code of law, the *Mishneh Torah.*

This can be translated as "Reiteration of the Torah," for in it Maimonides presents the commandments of the Torah, as augmented by the rabbis. Their work is known as the "oral law," and it was—and is—considered in the rabbinic tradition to be as divinely sanctioned at Sinai as was the written law. Study of the Talmud, *talmud torah,* was the ideal pursuit of rabbinic scholarship; equivalent, in one pronouncement, to observance of all the other commandments. The *Shekhinah,* or divine presence, was said to envelop those engaged in talmudic argument, an ongoing dialectic that probed beyond the letter of the law to its ever-expanding and entailing spirit.

Maimonides now dared to curtail and summarize the rabbis' work, stating that the Torah and his *Mishneh Torah* could substitute for study of the Talmud.[2] He claimed that the level of rabbinic scholarship had diminished among his peers, and that there was need for a definitive book of Jewish law, a legal code. Be that as it may, his goal was also to open the syllabus of Jewish studies to encompass new subjects, those formerly regarded as foreign. Study of the *Mishneh Torah* was not meant to be a lifelong occupation, as study of the Talmud was conceived. Jewish law was now to be researched primarily for its dictates guiding the lives of its practitioners, rather than for intellectual and spiritual inspiration.

Maimonides did not succeed in these bold goals. Historically, the *Mishneh Torah* did not displace study and veneration of the Talmud among the vast majority of the Jewish people. Maimonides' work did, however, confirm his authority as a master decisor of Jewish law, the greatest rabbinic mind of his age, and perhaps ever since. In time, his Code became an authoritative appendage to talmudic study, the challenge it presented ignored and largely forgotten.

Maimonides' appeal, in effect, to open the hearts and minds of Jews to the scientific study of the natural world did not go unheeded, however, and a small but significant number of Jews took up his challenge in the following centuries, often using Maimonides' *Guide* as their lodestone. It is in the *Guide* that Maimonides exhibits the familiarity with the scientific legacy of Greece for which the *Mishneh Torah* was in part intended to make room.

Not that the *Mishneh Torah* itself is void of scientific statements, particularly in the first chapter of the opening treatise in the "Book of Knowledge."[3] Here Maimonides presents as accepted wisdom a cosmological précis rooted ultimately in Aristotle. He appears committed to the scheme adopted by most philosophers in the Peripatetic tradition, and feels it incumbent to teach it dogmatically, even as part of sacred law (*halakha*), to his fellow Jews.

Thus, Maimonides says that the very first of the "laws pertaining to the principles of the Torah" (*hilkhot yesodei ha-torah*), the "principle of principles and foundation of the sciences," is to "know that there is a First Existent [*mạzui ri'shon*] that brings every being into existence, and that none would have existed were it not for its existence."[4]

Maimonides has here adopted the impersonal language of Avicenna (eleventh century) to describe God, which could well have puzzled his traditional readers.[5] It is only a few paragraphs later that Maimonides identifies this "Necessary Existent," as Avicenna called it, with the more recognizable "God of the universe, master of the whole earth" (*elohei ha-'olam adon kol ha-'arez̩*).[6] It is this God, Maimonides says, who governs the (outermost) sphere with a force that has no limit, end, or interruption; for the sphere circles continuously and could not do so without a cause responsible for that motion. "It is He, blessed be He, who without hand or body causes [this] circular motion," Maimonides concludes, having offered a truncated Aristotelian proof for the existence of a first mover/God based on the eternal circular motion of the heavens, and particularly that of the outermost, all-encompassing sphere.

This knowledge, Maimonides then says, should be considered a positive commandment, attested by nothing less than the first of the Ten Commandments, even as anyone who believes in a God other than this (cause of perpetual motion) transgresses the second of the Ten Commandments and denies the principle upon which all else depends.[7]

This deity, Maimonides continues, is uniquely one and incorporeal, having no finite dimension that would necessarily compromise its infinite power. Knowing this is also a positive commandment, expressed in the scriptural injunction of Deuteronomy 6:4 that proclaims "the Lord is our God, the Lord is one."

This verse is the archetypical statement of Jewish allegiance, central in the liturgy and in critical existential moments of a Jew's life. The verse begins with the famous declaration of *Shema' Yisra'el,* "Hear O Israel," which particularizes it in a way that Maimonides apparently chose to avoid. He believes the Torah is teaching universal truths, the most important being the incorporeal nature of the necessarily one God. Maimonides considers the biblical statements that present God in physical terms to be concessions to conventional views, the Torah condescending to popular speech and opinion. It is an axiom of his faith, buttressed by his reason, that God, in His singular incorporeality, has no physical attributes or affect, is not in time or space, and does not change. All prophetic statements to the contrary, Maimonides is convinced, should be taken as metaphorical or allegorical expressions.[8]

In this way, Maimonides both universalizes the concept of God and threatens to sever the personal relation that his readers felt they had with their God, the God of Israel. It may well be to ameliorate this threat that Maimonides begins the second chapter of this first book of fundamental principles with the commandment to love and fear God. Fear, *yir'ah* in Hebrew, may also be translated as "awe," and it is in awesome appreciation of the wondrous works and creations of God and of the incomparable wisdom to which they attest, and in recognition of one's own insignificance, that Maimonides would have one turn, in love, toward God.[9] For Maimonides, then, deeply religious feelings can be elicited by a God who is beyond human understanding and who is unrecognizable to His worshipers except through the wondrous works of nature.

While mortal beings have but a very limited knowledge of God, the intellects of the spheres—the existence of which Maimonides accepts, treating them as synonymous with angels—have more, more than we can ever know.[10] God's knowledge, on the other hand, is all-encompassing, for everything exists "by virtue of His essence" (literally "truth," *mi-koaḥ amito*), an ambiguous phrase that does not specify the nature of God's creation of the world or His relation to it.

Nor is Maimonides unambiguous as to the type of knowledge God possesses. While he says that nothing is hidden from God, he says too that God knows everything inasmuch as He knows Himself.[11] His knowledge is not extraneous to His essence, indeed, "the Creator, His knowledge and life are one in every aspect."[12] In a striking phrase that he uttered before in the eighth chapter of *Eight Chapters* and that he will repeat in *Guide* 1.68, Maimonides says that God is the knower, the known, and the knowledge itself, all one and the same.

Maimonides says that the mouth is unable to say this, the ear to hear it, and the heart to fully comprehend it. The danger of misconstruing the radical unity of God's nature by distinguishing His essence from such presumed attributes as life and knowledge leads Maimonides to this position. He emphasizes again that God knows created objects not as such, by virtue of themselves (*me-ḥamat ha-beru'im*), as we know them, but by virtue of Himself (*me-ḥamat aẓmo*). "Thus, inasmuch as He knows Himself He knows everything." While Maimonides does not elaborate on these rather cryptic formulations, he apparently felt they adequately conveyed notions of God's omniscience and singular unity of being.

Chapter 3 of book 1 outlines the natural world as understood by most philosophers in Maimonides' day. The heavens are conceived as composed of nine planetary concentric spheres, in eight of which other lesser spheres reside. The outermost, diurnal sphere is free of any celestial body other than itself. The spheres differ in position, direction, and rate of motion, but otherwise are weightless and unchanging. Each has a soul as well as an intellect with which they recognize God, themselves, and the intellects/angels in the spheres above them.[13]

Maimonides next speaks of God's creation of earth's prime matter and the four elements—fire, air, water, and earth—that inform it, each functioning unconsciously or according to a "regimen" (*minhag*) that it cannot alter. As Maimonides relates in chapter 4, all sublunar objects are composed of a mixture of these four elements, constituting the form and matter combination that is ubiquitous in all earthly being. All, that is, except the intellectual aspect of man's soul, which is the essence of his form.[14] It is this physically unencumbered intellect that, in knowing God and the separate intellects of the spheres, is vouchsafed immortality.

Important as this last subject would be to his readers, Maimonides claims that knowledge of astral and terrestrial physics, called *ma'aseh bere'shit* (the account of creation), is not as profound[15] as the metaphysical teachings of the first two chapters of this book. Following tradition,[16] Maimonides says that instruction in physics should be conveyed privately to a single individual and not taught in public, while metaphysics, known as *ma'aseh merkavah* (the

Account of the Chariot) can be taught only obliquely, with "chapter headings," and only to an exceptionally intelligent individual. Maimonides will repeat this teaching in the *Guide,* though committing the sciences as he understood them to writing, however guarded, effectively undermines the tradition he was supposedly honoring.

Maimonides then says that the specific commandments that inform Judaism (and their observance), however "small" in comparison with the "large" truths of metaphysics, take priority over them, since they are a civilizing force[17] for the individual and society. The commandments, moreover, enable one to inherit life in the world to come, and everyone, young and old, man and woman, can know them. This statement is geared toward the intended audience of this book, whereas in the *Guide* Maimonides makes the possibility of realizing immortality contingent upon intellectual achievement.[18]

In chapter 7 Maimonides asserts that it is a principle of the faith to know that God grants prophecy[19] to certain individuals, those with distinguished intellectual, moral, and physical traits, particularly the ability to control one's desires. Maimonides' prophet is ascetically inclined, turning away from the vanities and temptations of life to be sequestered with God. This takes the form of contemplating God's wisdom as manifested in all of nature.

Such a person experiences the presence of the Holy Spirit (*ru'aḥ ha-qodesh*), which causes his soul to mingle with those angels who are called *Ishim* (literally, "men"), so called because they communicate with prophets; in the *Guide,* though, Maimonides makes it clear these are imaginative representations that substitute for the Agent Intellect.[20] This commingling, which is more properly elsewhere called "conjunction," *devequt,* is a transformative experience for the prophet; he becomes "another person," *ish aḥer,* superior to other men.

Maimonides detects gradations among the prophets, distinctions that he will elaborate upon in the *Guide.*[21] Here he simply distinguishes between Moses and all other prophets. Moses alone is said to have had direct and constant communication with God, an intellectual relation that dispensed with imaginative representations. Moses also dispensed with conjugal relations, being always in God's presence, "as holy as the angels."[22]

Maimonides thus elevates Moses to superhuman levels, a daring though not unusual feature in rabbinic lore. Equally striking, though, is his relegation of the other prophets' revelations to the status of allegories (*derekh mashal*), stories not to be taken literally, however inspired. The prophet understands the meaning of the allegory vouchsafed him, sometimes explaining it, sometimes not.

Moses' superiority for Maimonides is not based on the miracles that he performed, even as the test of any prophet's authenticity does not depend on the miracles he is alleged to perform. The public revelation at Sinai, the giving of the Torah, witnessed by the whole people, is the linchpin of the trust in Moses' prophetic status for Maimonides, proof of Moses' calling.[23] As the Torah can never be altered, so no other prophet can supplant Moses and change his teachings.

In this way, Maimonides defends Judaism, his rabbinic Judaism, against all challenges, even as he proceeds to interpret the Torah in a radically philosophical manner. This is true equally for Maimonides' treatment of moral and ethical behavior, which largely he ties to Aristotle's doctrine of the golden mean (without ascribing it to Aristotle). This emerges in the first chapter of the second part of the "Book of Knowledge," known as *Hilkhot De'ot,* which may be translated as "Laws concerning Character Traits."[24]

Maimonides gives his evaluation of positive and negative character traits the weight of law, and ties them to religious belief, in the opening sentence of the chapter, when he outlines the contents of the treatise and their purpose. The very first purpose is to "resemble [God's] 'ways,'" *le-hiddamot bederakhav*;[25] the deity for Maimonides appearing to endorse Aristotle's prescriptions for ethical conduct. One may strive to imitate the divine attributes of mercy and compassion best by practicing moderation in all things.

Maimonides thus matches rabbinic prescriptions for considerate and sociable behavior with a standard of virtue articulated by Aristotle, supplemented with medical advice taken largely from Galen and Arab physicians.[26] Only a person with the proper set of character traits and virtues can hope to understand God's ways, having already imitated Him, to a degree. The conduct Maimonides prescribes is thus a necessary condition for the spiritual/intellectual experience that ensues. The "laws" or *halakhot* concerning character traits are thus similar in purpose to all the other *halakhot* in the *Mishneh Torah:* they have mainly instrumental value in shaping a character toward an extraneous end and have less value in themselves.

Thus, Maimonides endorses a healthy lifestyle, though not for its own sake and not for the physical pleasures it offers. Only one who first satisfies his needs for food, drink, and sex is able to transcend the corporeal dimension of life and concentrate on the spiritual. Maimonides is against extreme acts of an ascetic sort, even as he deprecates the pleasure to be had in the physical realm as such.[27] In this, he is following the rabbinic practice of enveloping every physical response to life within a matrix of blessings and directives that temper absorption in the act itself. Where the rabbis concentrate upon observance of the *miẓvot* or commandments that surround an action, and (unlike the mystics) have no clear program other than increased devotion and religious study with which to attain communion with God, Maimonides is convinced that the study of nature and knowledge of science can bring one close to God. As Maimonides later makes clear in *Guide* 3.51, the pleasure to be had in that proximity is infinitely greater than physical pleasures, even as the passionate love for the divine that the wise person experiences is incomparably greater than love for another person.

Maimonides' general injunction is for moderation in behavior, though his idea of moderation may be more abstemious than many would wish today. Anger and arrogance are the exceptions to the rule, Maimonides seeing them as cardinal sins, to be extirpated by extreme antithetical behavior: apathy instead of anger, self-abasement instead of arrogance.[28] This is the technique he discerns the rabbis of former days used, being extreme in their behavior only for therapeutic purposes, to restore a needed equilibrium in some trait of character.

Maimonides does allow a *show* of anger for those in charge, in order to intimidate others and assist them toward proper behavior, the person showing anger being aware that he is playing a role, and not allowing himself to be carried away by his presumed anger. This too is an imitation of God's supposed behavior, to which Maimonides refers in the *Guide*.[29]

As in the *Commentary on the Mishnah*'s *Eight Chapters,* Maimonides here too distinguishes between normative behavior, the behavior he recommends for the average person as well as for the wise man, the *ḥacham,* and the more extreme behavior of the pietist, the *ḥasid*.[30] The latter engages regularly in ascetic acts that others are to perform only as occasional therapy. Maimonides does not approve of the hasidic form of piety; he believes one can achieve proximity to the divine presence without physical deprivation. He also may have been wary of the mystical freight that the pietists were likely to carry, their deluded notion, as he saw it, that one could reach God without acquiring the intellectual wisdom that Maimonides thought necessary. God, for Maimonides, was to be found, at least initially, in an engagement with life, not in retreat from it. This attitude does not, however, encourage an aggressive approach to others, and twice Maimonides follows talmudic injunctions and urges his readers to "be among the oppressed and not the oppressors, among the insulted and not those who insult."[31]

The engagement Maimonides recommends is both with the family and community, and intellectually with the life of the natural world, as given to the scientist to study and admire. It is the scholarly life that attracts Maimonides, the life of the mind, while his commitment to the social and political dimensions of life is out of a sense of duty and responsibility.[32] The latter also is a religious obligation, another expression of walking in God's ways. One should thus marry, but not engage in much talk with one's spouse, or derive pleasure from the conjugal act as such; be active in earning a living, but be content with a modest wage. In these ways, and by combining moral and medical advice, Maimonides attempts to mold the character of his readers.

The full nature of that character is succinctly revealed in a letter written to Saladin's son Al-Afḍal, who ruled Egypt briefly, and who had written Maimonides for his opinion on a number of medical issues. After dispensing his advice as a physician, Maimonides offered his royal patron counsel as a moral philosopher. His advice to Al-Afḍal is to curb his passions and adopt what amounts to a Stoic attitude toward life, not allowing himself to be much affected by whatever life may bring.[33] A person should cultivate a positive attitude, neither dwelling on past misfortunes that cannot be altered, nor dreading the future. That which is feared may not occur, and since everything is possible, one should anticipate the best, and not the worst, occurrence. Writing to a Muslim interlocutor, Maimonides does not go so far as to say that the future is undetermined, or that a person may affect it through the use of his free will, as he does in *Eight Chapters*[34] and, as we shall see, in the *Mishneh Torah.* Yet his advice is the same for both Muslim and Jew: there is a shared moral ideal that Maimonides wishes to encourage, and that is to keep one's passions and emotions in check, realize one's mortal destiny, and meet one's spiritual challenge.

In the final section of the "Book of Knowledge," dealing with the laws of repentance, Maimonides declares his belief in free will, a necessary condition for holding man responsible for his actions and for the imposition of a just legal system.[35] God wills that man have free will, Maimonides declares, even as He has foreknowledge of everything, including man's actions. Maimonides then poses the obvious conflict in holding both positions: either God's knowledge compels human behavior, or God is not omniscient and man has free will.

Maimonides responds to this conundrum by referring to his earlier statement in the *Mishneh Torah* describing God's knowledge as identical with His essence; as the one position cannot be comprehended by mortals, neither can the other.[36] Yet we know "beyond doubt," Maimonides says, that man is the author of his own actions, and that God does not determine his behavior. Moreover, this knowledge is based not only on religious tradition but on "clear scientific proofs" (*re'ayot berurot me-divrei ha-ḥokhmah*). Unfortunately, Maimonides does not even hint at what these proofs may be, and it is only later, in the *Guide,* that a possible solution may be inferred from his remarks there.[37]

The rest of the *Mishneh Torah* covers the entire spectrum of life, as framed by Jewish law, including instruction for institutions that history had rendered defunct, such as the Temple worship and sacrifices, the Sanhedrin, and monarchy. Maimonides' incorporation of these laws testifies to his belief in their future validation, contingent, presumably, on a messianic advent.

Maimonides largely naturalizes the figure of a messiah, insisting that he will neither work wonders nor alter the Law in any way. He will rebuild the Temple and restore the people to its land, where peace and plenty shall flourish. The nations of the world will accept the "true religion," and all will seek to know God.[38]

Maimonides concludes the *Mishneh Torah* with this peaceful vision for Israel and the world, having instructed the people throughout the book how they must live in a far different reality, the commandments offering structure and solace in a hostile world. That world will not have changed when Maimonides sets out to write the *Guide,* but he will be looking at it through a different lens.

3

Maimonides' Graeco-Islamic Philosophical Heritage

Before proceeding with an analysis of the *Guide,* we must clarify some of the terms and underlying concepts we have mentioned in the previous chapter and get an idea of the main influences upon Maimonides' thought as a philosopher and theologian. These two terms need to be looked at closely before we proceed, for in one respect the distinction between philosophy and theology would have been foreign to Maimonides. For him, as for his philosophical mentors, the primary subject of metaphysics was an investigation into the nature of immaterial, intelligible being, which meant God and the separate intellects of the heavens.[1] In that sense, philosophy was theologically oriented, and much of the *Guide* may be seen as a study in philosophical theology. The theology is often controlled by philosophical, logically structured arguments that are based largely on physical principles, so it is a metaphysics that is in good part in the Aristotelian tradition.

There was another type of theology with which Maimonides had to contend, however, that practiced by the mostly Muslim adherents of *kalām,* the *mutakallimūn,* and Maimonides strongly contests its legitimacy. This is a complex, logical theology divorced from empirical principles, with God considered the sole and immediate cause of all that transpires.[2] In a less formally developed way, rabbinic Judaism held to this form of theology as well, affirming divine involvement in every event, with little scientific argument. Maimonides, while opposed as a philosopher to this approach to theology, adopts it at critical moments in the *Guide,* thereby allowing us to distinguish between his philosophical and theological selves, between the philosophical theology that is reasoned philosophy and the theology that is rooted in dogma and conventional tradition.

As Maimonides was philosophically indebted to Aristotle and Alfarabi,

Plato and Ibn Bājja, Plotinus and Avicenna, among others, a brief synopsis of their views is in order. The *Guide* is a compendium of medieval philosophical views between which Maimonides navigates, accepting some, critically modifying others, with few specific references. All his statements should be viewed as deliberate responses to the accepted wisdom of his time, a wisdom that is the legacy of Graeco-Islamic philosophy. That legacy is a closed book to most readers today, but we must become familiar with it, even in summary form, to appreciate Maimonides' bold adventure.

Maimonides introduces Jewish sources, both biblical and rabbinic, into this legacy, creating a Jewish philosophy *cum* theology. That is, the *Guide* is not a work of philosophy only, but mingles rigorous philosophical argument with theological assertions that lack such structure. Islamic philosophy tried to steer clear of theological entanglements for the most part, though Maimonides' contemporary Averroes could not avoid them, however much he tried to do so.[3] Maimonides, however, set out in the *Guide* to marry Judaism to philosophy, attempting at the same time to avoid writing as a theologian. The *mutakallimūn* are his declared opponents, as much for their method of reasoning as for their well-articulated beliefs. Maimonides devotes the better part of *Guide* 1.69–76 to delineating his view of the core tenets of their theology, called *kalām,* and then to critiquing them (perhaps influenced by Al-Ghazālī's strategy vis-à-vis the *falāsifa*). As he is explicit in his presentation (discussed in our chapter 5 below), we need not expand upon their views here except to note that for all his opposition to the *mutakallimūn,* Maimonides has more in common with them than he wishes to admit.[4]

Maimonides is indifferent to and dismissive of the work of his Jewish predecessors,[5] giving him a free hand to bend to his philosophical purposes the theologically inclined statements that appear in the Talmud and midrashic corpus. The philosophy to which Maimonides was attracted was not all of one piece, as stated, but Maimonides wanted to be seen primarily as a disciple of Aristotle, so it is with him that we begin.

Aristotle is quoted a number of times in the *Guide,* and Maimonides could have read him directly in Arabic translations originally made in the ninth century, as well as in commentaries on his work made by both Greek and Muslim philosophers.[6] In a letter to the Hebrew translator of the *Guide,* Samuel ibn Tibbon, Maimonides recommends reading Aristotle with the commentaries of Alexander of Aphrodisias (second–third century CE), Themistius (fourth century), and his contemporary, Averroes.[7]

Aristotle stood as the fount of scientific knowledge for Maimonides, even though it was an Aristotle modified by later disciples and critics. Aristotle's logical treatises, as well as his writings in physics, metaphysics, psychology, and ethics, established criteria of that which was considered scientific knowledge. Aristotle's *Politics* did not share this distinction, however, probably eclipsed by Plato's *Republic* and *Laws,* as echoed in Alfarabi's political writings.[8]

Little else of Plato's work, except for his *Timaeus,* was transmitted to the Arabs.[9] His metaphysics was systematized and widely transmitted through the Neoplatonic writings of Plotinus (third century CE) and Proclus (sixth century). Maimonides does not mention them in his letter and studiously avoids recommending anyone with Neoplatonic leanings.

Maimonides respected Aristotle's teachings in that he believed they conformed to and accurately represented reality. It was Aristotle's teachings that explained coherently the sensible world, providing Maimonides with a sense of order and necessity in nature, vital concepts in his battle with the *mutakallimūn.* Thus, in Aristotle's view, both the heavens and the earth are subject to the same overarching physical principles, adjusted to each realm. The same four causes—material, formal, efficient, and final—are employed, in whole or part, to describe all objects, the same framework of species and genus to define them. Potentiality and actuality are the ontic poles between which change occurs, with allowance for the state of uninterrupted actuality found in heavenly bodies. They do not suffer change, and hence have no potentiality, other than that found in the locomotion of their planetary bodies.

For Aristotle, this circular movement of the spheres is eternal, due to an unmoved (uncaused) mover of each sphere.[10] Later philosophers were to posit a single ultimate mover and first cause, or god, understanding it with Aristotle[11] as an immaterial or mental entity, an intellect (*nous*) that solely thought itself, a purely self-reflexive being that nevertheless attracted the movements of the heavens and through them exerted its power over the species on earth. The world was purposively structured, with a final cause part of each object's nature, ultimately traceable to a god who was conceived as providential in a nonintentional, impersonal sense.

Hylomorphism is a hallmark of the Aristotelian system, as all objects are conceived as combinations of matter (*hyle*) and form (*morphē*), the body and soul of living beings. Aristotle's *On the Soul* identifies five aspects of the human soul: the nutritive, sensitive, imaginative, rational, and appetitive faculties.[12] Aristotle considered the rational faculty initially potentially rational, able to receive imaginative intentions in their (attenuated) materiality. Its intellectual potentiality is assured it by the co-presence in the faculty of an active rational agent or, in short, an active intellect, *nous poiētikos.* For Aristotle, then, the human intellect is innate in both its potential and its active aspects. The active intellect is the aspect of the rational faculty that abstracts the essential aspect of the sensed and imagined datum and conceives it as a universal intelligible form.

Aristotle's description of the faculties of the soul and their interrelations formed the basis of widely accepted later epistemological theories.[13] His understanding of the intellect as having passive and active aspects offered later thinkers a way to conceive not only of cognition, but of immortality. Aristotle opened the door to this belief in considering true cognition to be an identification of the knowing subject with its immaterial intelligible object,[14] and in remarking elsewhere that there is a divine intellect external to the body of an individual that enters into it.[15]

Within the Aristotelian scheme no immaterial entity, not even the god referred to as the unmoved mover, is permitted total or absolute separation from matter, a completely independent existence. Ontically, this god is thought to be totally immaterial; phenomenologically, however, it is intimately related to the physical world. However much the proof for God's existence that Maimonides brings in *Guide* 1.72 requires the deity to be unmoved and unaffected, totally impassive, in order to be a genuine first, uncaused cause, this ultimate and seemingly self-contained being is also, for both Aristotle and Maimonides, the cause of the motion of the universe. Indeed, for Maimonides, God is the cause of the very existence of the universe.

Aristotelian logic anchors Maimonides' philosophy; he was familiar with it either directly or, more probably, through the logical writings of Alfarabi, which he praises highly. As mentioned above,[16] the *Treatise on Logic*, which tradition has ascribed to Maimonides, is heavily indebted to an Alfarabian work, and its teachings are faithfully reflected in the *Guide*. Maimonides would have wanted the well-educated reader of the *Guide* to be at least as well-informed as the (anonymous) patron for whom the *Treatise on Logic* was written. Maimonides had there provided concise definitions of words, sentences, and propositions, the various kinds and modalities of syllogisms, and the names and nature of Aristotle's logical categories. Maimonides distinguished homonyms from synonyms and defined univocal, equivocal, and amphibolous terms, clarification of the biblical use of which he adduced later as his first purpose for writing the *Guide*.[17]

Logic itself is an equivocal term, Maimonides says at the commencement of the last chapter of this treatise. It applies to the (rational) faculty whereby one identifies particular thoughts, disciplines, and moral judgments; to the "internal" logic, or reason (*al-nuṭq al-dakhīl*) involved in thinking the intelligible thoughts themselves; and to the "external logic" (*al-nuṭq al-khārij*) of words that correspond to the mental thoughts. We thus have an ability to think and speak logically, and while our thoughts are couched in words normally, they can exist independently of spoken expression. The distinctions Maimonides draws here will play an important role in the *Guide* in his belief in the "silent speech" of the celestial spheres as well as in the perfect man's silent striving for communion with the divine.[18]

In his *Treatise on Logic,* Maimonides also delineated the differences between demonstrative, dialectical, and rhetorical proofs, explaining that while both premises of a demonstrative argument are universally recognized as necessarily true, dialectic has one or both premises based on conventional wisdom that is generally—though not universally—accepted, while rhetoric has one or both premises based purely on tradition.[19]

Thus, in the *Guide,* we can be sure that Maimonides makes his assertions aware of the syllogistic structure of his arguments, even though he frequently does not present them formally. Aristotle called the knowledge had by means of demonstrative premises "science" and "truth," and the knowledge acquired by dialectic and rhetoric "opinions."[20] This distinction is accepted by all who follow Aristotle and becomes a commonplace. Maimonides alludes to it in the eighth chapter of his *Treatise.*[21] The highest degree of knowledge, the only truly scientific knowledge, is considered to be that which yields certainty, viz., theoretical knowledge, which comprises mathematics, physics, and metaphysics.

Aristotle and his medieval followers conceived of nature as composed of indispensable elements and principles that could be fully categorized and defined, such that consequences of natural acts could be predicted and necessary inferences drawn as to their effects. Nature, if only it could be fully known, was thought to be able to yield knowledge as precise and certain as that of mathematics or logic. Aristotelian concepts were the necessary tools for organizing knowledge. Maimonides expresses this thought in the *Treatise:* "anyone who cannot distinguish between the potential and the actual, between *per se* and *per accidens,* between the conventional and the natural and between the universal and the particular, is unfit to reason."[22]

It is this extended body of knowledge which offers certainty, according to Maimonides in the eighth chapter of the *Treatise;* and it is acquired via both immediate and accumulated sensations, as well as by primary and secondary "intellections," i.e., concepts. Yet, though dialectic and rhetoric cannot presume to "scientific" truth, i.e., to incontrovertible certainty, they too have an important role to play, both in the development of man's reasoning powers and in relation to those many areas of human concern for which by definition absolutely certain knowledge is not obtainable. These include propositions of a particular or contingent sort, relative to the time and place of a person or given group.

Such propositions of course form the majority of utterances in the fields of politics and the arts, law and religion. It is not so much a failing of these propositions that they do not yield truth in the strict necessary sense; rather is it a necessary consequence of their condition. Anyone working in these fields of inquiry must be content with the varying degrees of probability offered, and be sensitive to the applicability—or lack thereof—of particular assertions to universal propositions.[23] Maimonides, like all the philosophers, wanted to establish demonstrative propositions, but the premises of many of his—and their—arguments lacked that self-evident, necessary truth which would have qualified them as such. Maimonides' various assertions in the *Guide,* including those related to metaphysics, thus often have to be accepted as probabilistic at best.

Scholars have long been critical of Maimonides' claims to certain knowledge that lacked demonstrable proof, and believe he made such claims deliberately, as part of his esoteric writing strategy. Some scholars have concluded that in disavowing "scientific" knowledge of metaphysics, Maimonides denied knowledge *tout court,* entirely, in that area, discounting the cognitive significance to him of assertions made on a probabilistic, dialectical basis.[24] It is my contention that Maimonides, like his predecessors, was more disposed to accept the broad outlines of metaphysical claims than his "scientific" criteria allowed, in order to give his religious beliefs a structure that appeared possibly true. These beliefs meant something to Maimonides; he considered them to be "true," if not demonstrated.

As mentioned, Maimonides recommended reading the work of Alexander of Aphrodisias, and his presence is felt in the *Guide* when Maimonides discusses providence, the validity of Aristotelian metaphysics, and other topics.[25] Alexander may have been responsible as well for putting Aristotle's remarks on the soul into a coherent system that established a link between a person's rational faculty and an Active, or Agent, Intellect that was now taken to be external to the person and divine.[26]

That link is the last stage in a process that Aristotle identified as beginning usually with sensory perceptions of an object. These external senses transmitted their particular impressions to a common sense that unified them. The imaginative faculty could conceive of these impressions and remember them correctly or fancifully, freed of their presence. It transmitted these imagined impressions, later known as "intentions" (*maʿnān/ʿinyanim*), to the rational faculty, which abstracted the universal form contained in the particular impression. The rational faculty then combined these intelligible intentions into propositions that expressed universal truths, the stuff of scientific discourse.

Alexander superimposed upon this scheme a now transcendent, hypostatized Agent (or Active) Intellect in the heavens, which he identified with God. Most medieval philosophers, however, considered the Agent Intellect to be the last of the separate, immaterial intellects that Aristotle assigned to each sphere as the formal cause of its motion. They saw this universal Agent Intellect in Aristotelian terms as enabling the potential intellect, now called the "material intellect," *nous hylikos,* to become active, abstracting the universal species that were present in nature. Avicenna, however, understood the Agent Intellect both as endowing nature with its specific forms, and as emanating knowledge of them upon a person's intellect when it is prepared to receive them.

Alexander saw the material intellect as a pure disposition to think, and discerned an intermediate stage of cognition in which the intellect had accumulated some knowledge, but was not presently active, saying it was *en heksei,* an "intellect *in habitu*" (*bi'l-malaka*). To the intellect when in act, the Muslim philosophers added a further and last stage of advanced knowledge, the "acquired intellect," which Avicenna thought conjoined with the Agent Intellect and was synonymous with it.[27] Maimonides, we will see, was strongly influenced by these views.

Though Maimonides expresses a negative attitude toward Neoplatonic writing in his letter to his translator, its undeclared presence in the *Guide* is highly significant.[28] His silence as regards his debt to Neoplatonism may be due to rejection of its cosmology, the positing of a universal Mind and Soul. He could, however—and did—accept certain key concepts of Neoplatonism that passed by his time as part of the Aristotelian heritage. Thus Plotinus's concepts of the One, of emanation, matter and evil, all figure critically in Maimonides' philosophy, without being attributed to that Greek sage.

Maimonides would have been familiar with Neoplatonic texts from a variety of sources. Plotinus (205–70 CE) and Proclus (ca. 410–85), the major Neoplatonists, were absorbed into Islamic and medieval Jewish philosophy through Arabic paraphrases of the *Enneads* and *Elements of Theology,* respectively.[29] Isolated statements of theirs, sometimes attributed to others, circulated and had their impact.[30] The earliest expressions of Islamic philosophy, the "Encyclopedia" of the "Brethren of Purity" and the compositions of the first philosopher of Islam, the ninth century Al-Kindī, already exhibit familiarity with various aspects of Neoplatonism.[31] This is a philosophical movement that had roots in both Platonic idealism and Gnosticism, offering pathways to communion with a spiritual realm and salvation from a devalued physical world.

The major premises of Neoplatonism as absorbed in Islamic and Jewish thought assume the existence of a divine transcendent One, a single undifferentiated source of all being, itself beyond being and time.[32] This unknown and unknowable God is yet the ultimate source of the good (equated with being)[33] and of a providence that envelops individuals insofar as they are members of their species (thus leaving individuals free of absolute determinism).[34] Plotinus regards this process as eternal and necessary and also as freely willed,[35] a combination of opposites that was emulated by later thinkers, for all its (or because of its) illogical assertion.

The Neoplatonic doctrine of creation within an eternal universe is expressed through a concept of emanationism.[36] Emanation is understood as an outpouring or effulgence of being that moves in reified stages from the pure simplicity of the One to the unified totality of forms in Intelligence (or Mind, *nous* in Greek), and then to the discrete appearance of these forms in Soul (*psyche*). These ideal forms are recognizable to us owing to their imperfect replication in bodies, the material foundation for which proceeds from the lowest stratum of Soul, thereby forming our physical, natural world.

Given that matter changes and perishes, it is at the lowest level of "real" being, virtually equivalent to nonbeing in its impermanence and indeterminacy.[37] As such, it is considered the cause of both evil (as the absence of actuality and form) and chance or accidentality.[38] The good is that which endures forever, happiness achieved when a person's intellect (re)joins with the immaterial substances or "hypostases" of the supernal intelligible world.

These themes and attitudes are strongly represented in the *Guide*,[39] and though they reached Maimonides in part through various Muslim philosophers, including Alfarabi and Avicenna, they should be recognized for their Neoplatonic provenance. Maimonides' indebtedness to this perspective is especially reflected, as we shall see, in his image of God and His relation to the world via emanation, and in his view of matter and divine providence.

Shīʿī, particularly Ismāʿīlī, theologians gave a more mystical and theosophical interpretation to Neoplatonic views than that found among their Sunni counterparts and the philosophical, mostly Sunni, community.[40] Fatimid Shīʿa dynasts had ruled Egypt for over two hundred years until shortly before Maimonides arrived there, and he would have known the writings of their thinkers.[41] Shīʿī theologians like Abū'l-Ḥasan al-Nasafī (d. 943), Abū Ḥātim al-Rāzī (d. 933/34), Abū Yaʿqūb al-Sijistānī (d. 975), and Ḥāmid al-Dīn al-Kirmānī (d. ca. 1021) adapted Neoplatonic philosophy to their theology. God is often understood as the ultimate source—through His "word" (*kalima*) or "command" (*amr*)—of the "origination" (*ibdāʿ*), i.e., creation, of the world from nothing, establishing Universal Mind, Soul, and the natural world.[42] The individual strives to unite his soul with the universal Soul (*nafs*) or even Mind (*ʿaql*), assisted by appealing to the immortal prophets and imāms of Shīʿī belief.[43]

Shīʿī thought contains certain elements peculiar to its own tradition that would not have attracted Maimonides. Thus, Maimonides would have objected to the Ismāʿīlī mythical depiction of heaven, with a universal Adam and angels in its various strata. Likewise, Maimonides would have rejected the Ismāʿīlī veneration and divinization of their imāms. Seen as successors to the prophets, seven such persons were believed to culminate in the return of the last, occluded imām, closing the present historic cycle and inaugurating a period of resurrection. Maimonides certainly would have opposed the Ismāʿīlī strain of ecumenicism, in which each prophet of the monotheistic tradition is seen as affirming the message and *shariʿa* of his predecessor, understanding that the esoteric essence of their revelations is the same.[44]

Other elements of Ismāʿīlī thought, however, would have appealed to Maimonides. He would have responded favorably to the Ismāʿīlī insistence on God's total otherness, beyond all attribution, even denying the negation of predicates lest they be taken as affirming something of God in their very denial. Maimonides might have thought the Ismāʿīlīs went too far in denying God direct causal agency for creation, giving it to a reified Word (*kalima*) or Command (*amr*) that is synonymous with the divine will.[45] Yet Maimonides himself will have the Will of God act in a way that God cannot, on Maimonides' understanding of His nature.

Moreover, Maimonides could not have objected, in principle, to the Ismāʿīlī reliance on allegory in using the Qur'ān for their doctrines. The Shīʿa in general were known as supreme esotericists, the laws of Islam having meaning for them on both the literal level, commanding observance, and on a deeper spiritual level that was known only to the educated initiates. Maimonides may have faulted the Shīʿa for excessive allegorization of their tradition,[46] but his approach to Scripture is very similar to theirs.

Maimonides would have found the last major Ismāʿīlī theologian, Al-Kirmānī, particularly attractive, for he added the spherical cosmic structures of the Aristotelian philosophers to his predecessors' triadic scheme of Neoplatonic hypostases.[47] Al-Kirmānī also held, as did his predecessors, to the idea of both creation from nothing, and a universe that is everlasting though created, ideas close to Maimonides' heart, as we shall see. Moreover, Al-Kirmānī expresses his opposition to predicating attributes to God in the same language that Maimonides later adopts.[48] Though Avicenna is thought to have influenced Maimonides' view of negative theology, Al-Kirmānī may also be a main source for it.[49]

Lastly, though Maimonides would have been uncomfortable to admit it, his understanding of Moses as a unique individual with superhuman intelligence, a prophetic lawgiver combining both intellectual and political skills, has many similarities with the teachings of revered Ismāʿīlī prophets and imāms.[50]

As mentioned above, the Muslim *falāsifa* were familiar, in varying degrees, with Plato's *Republic,* and Maimonides could have received Plato's political philosophy also as filtered through a number of Alfarabi's writings, such as his magnum opus, *The Opinions of the People of the Virtuous City,* or his *Political Regime,* which Maimonides knew and praised highly as *Principles of Beings.*[51] Alfarabi taught of the philosopher's duty to lead his society toward the truth, a truth that may need to be accommodated to the conventions and myths of his people's faith.[52] The ideal philosopher, who is (or should be) the ruler of his community, knows the unvarnished truths of metaphysics, but must translate them to the people in imitations of those truths. He cannot turn his back upon the people, and must present his teachings in language comprehensible to them, while conveying philosophical truths in metaphorical and allegorical fashion discernible to an educated person.

Alfarabi wrote extensively on the allegedly historical, politically normative roles of dialectic and rhetoric. As does Aristotle, he too saw demonstrative knowledge as surpassing them and being the acme of human achievement. There are, though, demonstrably true propositions that, with proper translation, may be rendered dialectically or rhetorically. Religion is an area in which this type of cognitive translation is constantly going on. In his *Book of Religion,* Alfarabi describes religion as a way to approach the truth both directly and through likenesses of it (*mithāl al-ḥaqq.*)[53] Sometimes the truth can be grasped immediately; at other times it is approached through demonstrative proof. Religion as such does not work out these proofs, being content merely to accept them. Religious teachings take the form of dialectical and rhetorical assertions based on conventional and traditional opinions. While not able to claim more than strong probability, these assertions are compatible with the notions held by the masses and strengthen their religious views.[54] Such views encompass the beliefs and actions of the people, their organization and society. Religion in the highest sense is thus the key element in bringing about civic and personal satisfaction.[55]

That religion has both theoretical and practical concerns, conveying certain as well as probable truths, is also part of the message of Alfarabi's *Book of Letters.*[56] Religion is seen as first entering history after the appearance of the various stages of reasoning. The final religion in this scheme is that which is based upon a complete awareness of theoretical and practical truths.[57] The original lawgiver of the faith, and those leaders and jurists who follow and imitate him, would have understood these truths.

In this manner, Alfarabi (as well as Avicenna after him) appreciates the role of dialectic and rhetoric in religion, and emphasizes the need for those practical observances and beliefs that compose the religio-cultural and politico-legal mores of society. Such observances of society's practices are ultimately an individual necessity for man as a political animal, though the particulars of each action may not in themselves be grounded in necessity. Alfarabi knows that the particular circumstances of societies vary, and that their requirements cannot be legislated universally.[58] While some actions may relatively easily be put in the form of universal propositions, others may not. These latter need extensive reformulation, to the point where presumably they would lose their specific identity and appear as arbitrary expressions of universal principles.

All this is surely understood by Maimonides as well,[59] and we can be quite certain that he agreed with Alfarabi's view of the role of the ideal religious leader, as well as with his view of religion in general.[60] The role of the jurist is also something on which they would both agree, seeing him as continuing the teaching of the lawgiver, as known through tradition and widespread opinion. Finally, Maimonides would easily find himself in agreement with Alfarabi's teachings concerning the lawgiver himself, for Alfarabi explicitly refers to divine revelation of the law to the virtuous first ruler.[61]

Alfarabi figures prominently in the *Guide* and is referred to when the subject is logic, *kalām,* the eternity of the world, the intellect, or providence. As we have seen, Alfarabi is the author of a number of works extolling political philosophy as the path to human fulfillment and happiness, a path that requires astute and manipulative leadership by philosophers.[62] He portrays religious law as a philosophically inspired human instrument by which a society is organized, and regards the narratives of the canons of religion as symbols and parables of philosophical truths, conveyed in the conventional beliefs of a given society. Seen in this light, the *Guide* appears to explicate Alfarabi's teachings. It also, however, goes beyond the political to address metaphysical issues differently from Alfarabi.

In one of his compositions, his *Commentary* on Aristotle's *Nicomachean Ethics,* Alfarabi is reported to have denied that human beings, whose intellects are conditioned by imagination and sense perceptions, are capable of knowing purely immaterial beings, i.e., God and the separate intellects. Humans cannot therefore conjoin with the Agent Intellect and thereby achieve immortality; the happiness or felicity of mastering metaphysics is denied them. A person must seek satisfaction rather in understanding the sublunar world and in striving to establish a just political order.[63]

Alfarabi's *Commentary* is lost, known through quotations supplied by Ibn Bājja, Ibn Ṭufayl, and Averroes, as well as by Maimonides.[64] Maimonides' quotation, however, is not relevant to Alfarabi's daring claim, and he does not address or renounce it directly, unlike his Muslim predecessors. Nevertheless, it is highly probable that he gave Alfarabi's thesis serious consideration, given Maimonides' near contemporaries' attention to what they saw as an audacious and philosophically disturbing claim, and given Maimonides' high regard for Alfarabi. It may well be that the denial of metaphysical knowledge allegedly maintained in this commentary may have influenced some of his views on the difficulty of attaining knowledge of metaphysical truths.[65] Alfarabi, however, wrote many treatises in which he affirmed the possibility of achieving perfection through mastery or near mastery of metaphysics,[66] and Maimonides would have been very familiar with them as well. Maimonides, as we shall see, vacillates over this issue, as he does on many others.

Alfarabi is important for Maimonides also in that he synthesized Aristotle's unmoved mover and Plotinus's One in a way that explained the causal relations that obtained in the spheres and the mechanism—emanation—by which God governed the world. For Alfarabi, God, while eternally thinking himself, somehow produced an equally eternal intellect, or "intelligence," that is the first of such heavenly beings. That first intellect, unlike God, has two thoughts, of itself and of its cause, God. In thinking of itself, it produces a heavenly body, the matter to its form, while in thinking of God, it produces a second intellect. The process is repeated through the nine spheres of the heavens, culminating with the Agent Intellect. That intelligence actualizes not one but all the potential intellects on earth, given that terrestrial matter and the forms it takes are not uniform.[67] Matter is produced last in this scheme, emanated somehow by the celestial bodies.

The emanations of the Agent Intellect affect people differently, depending on their innate faculties and the cultivation of their intellect.[68] The emanations can take universal or particular form, and can be received awake or in dream states.[69] The imaginative faculty receives or imitates them in symbolic form as necessary, to communicate them to others, but the acquired intellect of the person receiving these emanated forms understands them in their essential, universal truth. The person who reaches this level of cognition is the ultimate philosopher, and to the degree that he receives emanations that pertain to the future, i.e., revelations, he is also a prophet. Moreover, in his capacity as public leader, that person is also the imām of his community.[70] In this manner, Alfarabi offers a unified theory that brings together the philosophical, religious, and political traditions of his society. Whether his choice of the term "imām" was meant to signify partiality toward Shīʿism is debatable, but historically the imām functions for Shīʿīs as a figure possessing the intellectual, mantic, and political skills that Alfarabi identifies.

As mentioned, Maimonides was particularly fond of Alfarabi's *The Po-*

litical Regime. In that treatise, Alfarabi contends that with the assistance of the Agent Intellect a man who develops his intellect acquires a will that can make good or bad choices. The good choices further develop the person's intellect until it joins with the Agent Intellect, which is the ultimate happiness that can be desired. The emanations a person in this perfected state receives from the Agent Intellect can be called revelations from God, in that He is their ultimate cause.[71]

Alfarabi then speaks of the community of "virtuous, good, and happy people," whose souls after death "form as it were a single soul." Though intending that part of the soul that is not encumbered with matter, i.e., the rational faculty, and particularly its acquired intellect, Alfarabi refers to the soul in general terms at this point, claiming its perfected state grants it immortality and awareness of the presence of other such souls, increasing its happiness indefinitely.

These sentiments of Alfarabi may not be his last word on the issue of conjunction with the Agent Intellect or the state of immortal souls,[72] but it may well be that Maimonides was taken with these formulations and selectively borrowed them.

Maimonides gives high marks, in his letter to Samuel, also to Abū Bakr ibn Bājja (Avempace to the Scholastics), an earlier-twelfth-century Andalusian philosopher (d. 1139). He is mentioned in the *Guide* a number of times and figures as one of the conduits through which Maimonides formed his opinions upon the intellect and conjunction, as well as upon astronomy and the challenge it then posed to Aristotelian cosmology.[73] Unlike Alfarabi, Ibn Bājja had a negative attitude to political life and sought happiness solely in personal intellectual perfection, expressed in terms of conjunction with the universal Agent Intellect.[74] In this conjunction, Ibn Bājja held, as did Averroes after him, that man loses his personal individual immortality. Though Maimonides is reluctant to discuss this subject in any depth, he does in passing agree with Ibn Bājja on this sensitive—and highly controversial—point.[75]

Another Andalusian, Abū Bakr Muḥammad ibn Ṭufayl (ca. 1110–85), wrote a novelistic treatise in which he despaired of efforts to educate the public toward a philosophical understanding of religion, seeking solace in the mystical annihilation of the self in communion with God.[76] Maimonides had to have known of Ibn Ṭufayl and his treatise, and the *Guide* may be seen as a complete rejection of its rejection of political philosophy, and a less than complete rejection of Ibn Ṭufayl's mysticism.[77]

While Maimonides' relation to Shīʿī theologians is generally unacknowledged in the scholarly literature, his (highly selective) indebtedness to Avicenna is widely recognized. Nevertheless, Maimonides does not recommend

Avicenna enthusiastically in his letter to Samuel ibn Tibbon. It may well be that Maimonides viewed Avicenna's philosophy as too inflected with Neoplatonism, or that he objected to drawing attention to the body of Avicenna's work, which included allegorical fables and quasi-mystical treatises.[78] Avicenna is a powerfully original thinker, challenging Aristotelian doctrines in metaphysics and psychology, and Maimonides, perhaps for that reason, was not interested in engaging him fully.[79] Al-Ghazālī (eleventh century) did just that, first articulating Avicenna's philosophy and then critiquing it,[80] and Maimonides ignores him too, for the most part.[81]

By his own admission, Maimonides did not set out (as did Avicenna repeatedly) to write a complete philosophical exposition in the *Guide;* he was content to adopt and adapt the views of others, sometimes with acknowledgment, usually without. His purpose was to establish a philosophically coherent religion, picking and choosing the criteria of philosophical coherence, often without announcing them.

Maimonides was very taken with Avicenna's proof of God's existence, based upon the non-Aristotelian distinction between essence and existence; that is, the belief that existence is a predicate theoretically separate from the essence to which it is "accidentally" attached, rendering the essence a "possible existent" in itself.[82]

One of Maimonides' proofs of God's existence is based upon this idea, depicting God as the only being in whom there is no discrepancy between essence and existence, in that His very essence is existence.[83] God is therefore a "Necessary Existent," in contrast with all other beings that are themselves only "possible existents," their essences not existing necessarily. The contingent nature of all beings is rendered necessary, however, by the action, via emanation, of the Necessary Existent, the source of all existence. Every being on earth, therefore, whose existence is only possible "in itself," *bi dhātihi,* is rendered necessary "by another," *bi ghayrihi.*

The contingent nature of a possible being, the possibility that it may or may not be realized, is altered once it is affected by an external cause. Its modality then ceases to be that of an indeterminate, possible being and becomes that of a necessary being, having a determinate nature. In the causal sequence of events that Avicenna traces through the process of emanation, God is the ultimate and original necessitating cause of all being. The entire actual world of existent beings, all caused, is therefore considered necessary by Avicenna. This encourages the belief that Avicenna denied the reality of contingent possibilities and ultimately embraced a universally necessitated determinism.[84]

This is stronger than the Aristotelian belief in a ubiquitous causality, for Avicenna appears to have affirmed the Islamic belief in a God who has foreknowledge of all events, determining the actualization of a possible action before it occurs. Accordingly, one may assume that man does not have the freedom to choose which possible course of action to adopt, i.e., his behavior is predetermined.

This reading of Avicenna is supported by statements scattered throughout his writings to the effect that God has complete knowledge, including foreknowledge, of everything in the world.[85] Elsewhere, however, Avicenna writes of man's native ability to acquire knowledge and to perfect himself (or to choose not to), and in his commentary on Aristotle's *De interpretatione* he follows Aristotle in assuming the contingent nature of future possibilities, enabling man to have free choice.[86]

Avicenna's understanding of divine providence (*'ināya*) foreshadows much that is found in Maimonides' *Guide.*[87] The world is suffused by an ordered goodness that emanates from God's very being. Evil, which takes many forms but is essentially a privation of the good intended for a given object, is relatively rare and insignificant in its effect upon the species to which the affected individual belongs. The changeable matter of earth is a prime cause of evil, having the potentiality to deviate from the good. Matter is necessary, nevertheless, for the actualization of the desired form, and thus serves God's beneficent purpose.

For Avicenna, as for the Shīʿī theologians, creation via emanation is voluntary, i.e., a willed action, however much this will is identical with the necessity of God's singular being.[88] Moreover, creation is understood as an "origination" (*ibdāʿ*) not from a previously existent something, and is therefore tantamount to creation from nothing, even though the world is considered eternal.[89]

Moreover, the Necessary Existent is the acme of intelligible perfection and goodness, refractions of its being. Avicenna believes the Necessary Existent has knowledge of particulars insofar as they are subsumed within universal intelligible ideas, these ideas contained somehow within the self-knowledge of its singular, uncaused essence.[90]

Notwithstanding the above assertions, Avicenna believes that the Necessary Existent, as God, is unknowable and (inadequately) described by negative attributes, predications that deny their relation to Him.[91] Avicenna shared this idea with Shīʿī thinkers,[92] and Maimonides was attracted to it too.

Avicenna took Alfarabi's cosmogony and modified it, differentiating the activities of the soul and intellect within each celestial sphere, the intellect apprehending its source in the separate intellect of the preceding sphere, and the soul moving the sphere in an attempt to realize that apprehension. The "separate" intellects attached to but separate from the heavenly bodies serve as final causes for the next sphere's intellect, in the astronomical system of concentric spheres to which Maimonides also subscribed. The intellects are inconceivable apart from the heavenly bodies that they inform; they have no purpose by themselves. The same can be said of the "souls" of these bodies, which serve as the efficient cause of their spherical motion.[93]

Like Alfarabi before and Maimonides after him, Avicenna sees prophecy as a natural phenomenon, the Agent Intellect emanating its intelligible, universal forms upon a person with suitable imaginative and intellectual endowments.[94] The imagination of a prophet also receives particular impressions, Avicenna believes, via emanations from the souls of the celestial bodies.[95] In this construal, the prophet need not translate into popular terms the abstract truths received in his intellect; he receives them as such in his imagination. In making this claim, Avicenna applies to medieval epistemological theory the generally accepted Aristotelian notion that the heavens influence the composition of the earth; however, he goes beyond Alfarabi in identifying a cause beyond that of the Agent Intellect that emanates particular images.

It is the Agent Intellect, however, that is the main emanating source with which the prophet's intellect conjoins, and that intellect can receive true propositions intuitively and suddenly, without prior empirical or logical preparation. Avicenna probably was thinking of the prophet of Islam in making this claim, an impression strengthened by the examples Avicenna then draws from the Qur'ān to illustrate universal truths in particular forms. In two of his writings on prophecy, Avicenna gives an elaborate philosophical exegesis of verse 35 of the Sūra of Light (Qur'ān 24), a passage that was utilized by Al-Ghazālī and others in mystical modes.

In this manner, Avicenna anticipates Maimonides' more extended exercise in biblical hermeneutics in the *Guide*. Unlike Maimonides, however, Avicenna cautions against admitting that one has knowledge that should be kept from the masses, urging they be taught the basic beliefs of the faith in comprehensible (and traditional) "symbols and similitudes" (*rumūz wa amthila*).[96] Additionally, it should be noted that Avicenna employs imagery that Maimonides adopts to express the intuitive immediacy with which a prophet can grasp true propositions.[97] Moreover, Avicenna's privileging meditation over verbal prayer and his philosophically facilitated passionate devotion to God also resonate with Maimonides.[98]

As contrasted with these Avicennian sightings in Maimonides' writing, there are noticeable absences in the *Guide* of significant Avicennian themes, as well as significant modifications.[99] Maimonides lacks the elaborate epistemological scheme that Avicenna describes,[100] and does not share his view that cognition is a process that merely prepares an individual's intellect to receive emanations from the Agent Intellect, that universal substance thereby ultimately preempting the abstractive capability of the individual's intellect.[101] Similarly, Maimonides does not follow Avicenna in propounding individual immortality of the soul, based on its assumed autonomous substantiality.[102]

Daringly, Maimonides opts for a view of immortality that in effect obliterates the individual consciousness of it, with the universal truths that a person has intellectually acquired becoming assimilated into the one universal Agent Intellect, their eternal source.[103] This view, known as monopsychism, is associated famously (or infamously) with Averroes, but it was adapted before that twelfth-century philosopher by Alfarabi and Ibn Bājja.

Though Maimonides recommends reading Averroes' commentaries on Aristotle, their influence on his own thinking is conjectural. Both Averroes and Maimonides had strikingly similar professional careers, writing in a variety of genres, and Maimonides has been seen as responding to Averroes' theological works particularly.[104] Philosophically, there are significant similarities between Averroes and Maimonides in their God-centered view of metaphysics, their concern over the beleaguered status of Aristotelian celestial physics, and the use of equivocal, if not contradictory religious statements.[105] Maimonides was not as thoroughgoing an Aristotelian as was Averroes, and it is not apparent that he read the *Incoherence of the Incoherence,* Averroes' response to Al-Ghazālī and indirectly, through him, to Avicenna. Maimonides does, however, express an attitude toward the will of God that is similar to the position Averroes, for all his strict Aristotelian leanings, adopts in the *Incoherence.*[106]

Strikingly, Maimonides does not lay before the reader of the *Guide* the epistemological principles upon which his belief in cognition and conjunction depends, as Averroes did repeatedly.[107] Maimonides apparently regarded the subject as well discussed already and assumes familiarity with it. He treats the theory of emanation similarly, that is, superficially, for all its centrality in his system. The stages of cognition and intellection, culminating in conjunction with the Agent Intellect, have to be gleaned from disparate passages in the *Guide.*[108] The presence of emanation is ubiquitous in the book, being the basis for Maimonides' theory of providence and divine governance of the world. Not treating these two topics explicitly is Maimonides' way of protecting his text from unprepared readers.

The *Guide of the Perplexed*:
Paraphrases and Analyses

4

Wrestling with Language (*Guide* Part I, Introduction and Chapters 1–68)

Paraphrase

The *Guide* is composed of three parts, each part having an introduction. The theme Maimonides presents in the first introduction, reprised in the introduction to the third part, is that it is his intention to "explain what can be explained" of the "Account of the Beginning" (*ma'aseh bere'shit*) and the "Account of the Chariot" (*ma'aseh merkavah*).[1] He identifies these rabbinic terms with "natural science" and "divine science" respectively, i.e., physics and metaphysics ("divine" in that it deals with God and beings of the celestial realm).

In the third introduction, Maimonides acknowledges that this inquiry is the "chief aim" of his work, while in the first introduction he subsumes it within the category of allegorical explanation or exegesis, "the explanation of very obscure parables occurring in the books of the prophets." Maimonides deems this explanation of parables "not explicitly identified as such" to be the "second" purpose of the book, the first being "to explain the meanings of certain terms occurring in books of prophecy."[2]

Maimonides thus intends the *Guide* to be a lexicological as well as philosophical study, the former intended to pave the way for the latter. His study of the multiple usages a term may convey, and of the parabolic or allegorical interpretations scriptural pronouncements may harbor, legitimates the philosophical inquiries he wishes to pursue. In both introductions Maimonides is careful to say he intends to examine terms and parables in the books of the prophets, not in the Torah itself, though he does both.[3] He may have wanted initially to ease his readers' anxieties about what they might have viewed as tampering with Holy Writ. As we will see, he has no compunction about insulting those who engage primarily in the study of Talmud, even though that too was highly revered as expressive of God's will.

The first introduction, then, alerts the reader to what will be an exegetical tour de force that will transform the Bible into a philosophical text. Maimonides knows that not everyone will be satisfied with his interpretations of the words of Scripture, and that it is best for him (politically and personally) to be brief (employing "chapter headings" rather than full disquisitions) and discreet, scattering his true views within different contexts. He justifies this with a talmudic injunction not to transmit knowledge of the secrets of the Account of the Beginning and the Account of the Chariot to the public at large, actually, not to more than one or two persons at a time.[4] The *Guide* is meant for a very restricted audience, though Maimonides knew it would be read by many whom he considered unprepared for it. He thus deliberately makes it difficult to digest, and in a special request (*waṣiya*)[5] commands the reader not to divulge—or critique—any of the novel ideas he may have encountered in the book. Maimonides pleads for people who are put off by the book to ignore it or give it a positive assessment, even if that involves a "far-fetched interpretation."[6]

Yet Maimonides is prepared to risk a negative reaction to his book for the sake of the truth and for the enlightenment of the select (and philosophically alert) few. Maimonides is sure this kind of reader, a person devoted to the Law yet perplexed, will benefit from the book, finding "rest" from his doubts and achieving perfection (*yakmal wa yaṣtariḥ*). For the moment he does not spell out exactly what he means by "perfection," but it will become clear that it is the *summum bonum* of both the philosophers and the adherents of religion: a state of knowledge that becomes a state of being, an intimacy with the true nature of being and its author, and the inexpressible joy that ensues.

Maimonides concludes his untitled introduction to part 1 of the *Guide* with an explicit "Introduction" (*muqaddama*), in which he lists seven kinds of contradictory or contrary statements, at least one of which can (supposedly) be found in any written work. The causes for these conflicting statements include (1) references to diverse but unidentified sources; (2) unstated authorial changes of opinion in the same composition; (3) unstated changes in the style of the work, shifting registers between literal and allegorical meanings; (4) claims not made explicit and not in their proper place, due to a "certain necessity" (*li-ḍarura mā*); (5) the difficulty of the material, causing the subject to be taught simplistically and illogically at first; (6) the inattention of the author to the fact that a contradiction exists, due to the number of premises needed to make it evident; (7) the necessity to reveal only part of the discourse of "very obscure matters" (*umūrun ghāmidhatun jiddan*), where "obscure" can also mean secret. In this case, necessity dictates using contradictory premises when discussing the issue in different places, the common person[7] to be unaware of the contradiction.

Chapters 1–30—with the exception of chapter 2—and chapters 37–45 of part 1 of the *Guide* are given over to reframing the anthropomorphic depictions of God that abound in the Bible. Maimonides' first target is scriptural references to the body of God, His eyes and ears, hands, feet, and face. These cannot be understood literally, Maimonides insists, for His God, by a definition he has yet to spell out here, is incorporeal.

God, therefore, can neither see nor be seen, neither hear nor be heard, i.e., speak, at least not physically, not as these terms are used in a literal sense.[8] They are to be understood as metaphors denoting God's apprehending presence and His providential regard. A similar meaning is to be attached to all scriptural images that capture God in any particular state of being, whether sitting, standing, rising, coming, or going.[9] Motion of any sort—as well as rest from motion—is foreign to God's nature for Maimonides, in that it can occur only to a body that has magnitude.[10]

Paradoxically, Maimonides believes the Bible's dynamic depictions of the deity are meant to convey the image of an unchanging, stable, and permanent state of being. This is a function of God's incorporeal and perfect nature, where perfection is measured by a totally uncaused and unaffected singularity of being. The providence God shows the world, like His apprehension of it, is not, therefore, for Maimonides an ad hoc response to particular individuals or circumstances. Rather, providence is expressed by the presence of permanent species that ultimately owe their being to God.[11]

Surprisingly, given Maimonides' soon to be revealed aversion to positive predication of God, he identifies Him in the very first chapter of part 1 with intellectual apprehension (*idrāk ʿaqlīy*), His essence being what we could best understand as an active intellect. This is also the feature that distinguishes *homo sapiens* from other animals and explains for Maimonides why man is said, in Genesis 1:27, to be created in the "image" (*ẓelem*) of God. Though Maimonides says the apprehensions of the two intellects are dissimilar, he claims, based on the biblical passage, that they are "conjoined."[12]

Maimonides does not dwell on this issue here, however important it is; rather he devotes much effort in the following chapters to denying the literal meaning of every other term predicated of the deity in the Bible. He sees each as carrying with it the stigma of corporeality and thus regards it as compromising the pure unity of God's being.

The second chapter of part 1 is also somewhat anomalous, in that it again introduces a topic that Maimonides does not develop until much later, and that is theodicy, the defense of divine justice. Maimonides broaches this issue through a dazzling exegesis of the third chapter of Genesis, the story of Adam and Eve in Eden, their fall and expulsion.[13] As Maimonides tells it, he was challenged to justify God's apparent act of creating man initially without his noblest and defining feature, the intellect and the intellectual ability to distinguish between good and evil, God actually forbidding man to acquire this knowledge, only to grant it as part of his punishment for disobeying Him.

Maimonides' response, couched in unusually vituperative terms to an anonymous challenger,[14] reveals much of Maimonides' attitude toward mankind, the human condition, epistemology, and politics. It also reveals his ability to disguise his negative attitude toward depicting God in human terms, for he seems to accept the terms of the biblical story literally.

Accordingly, Maimonides distinguishes between Adam before the fall and after it, i.e., between prelapsarian and postlapsarian man. For Maimonides, it is inconceivable that God would have made man without the feature that is his ultimate perfection, with which he was created in the image of God. Thus, Maimonides says that originally Adam had a perfect intellect, which is to say an intellect devoted solely to questions of truth and falsity, what the philosophers described as a speculative or theoretical intellect. Though Maimonides does not say so here, it was a given among philosophers that such an intellect can entertain only propositions subject to demonstrable proofs requiring universally acceptable logical premises and undeniable conclusions. Prelapsarian Adam was thus created to be an ideal (and socially disinterested) scientist/philosopher.

The intellect that man acquired after the fall, for Maimonides, is generally referred to (though not by Maimonides here) as the practical intellect. It is that faculty which considers propositions for which no universal scientific judgment is possible, the premises being based on commonly accepted views that may be true or false, but that must be considered from the viewpoint of their social or moral utility as good or evil, or as Maimonides calls them, "fine and bad," *al-ḥasn* and *al-qabīḥ*.[15]

This is the punishment Maimonides would have us believe God meted out to Adam and his descendants: to wallow in moral and political issues for which no necessarily true or false judgment is possible; to construct a society in which judgments of good and bad are based on conventions the truths of which are probabilistic at best. For Maimonides, this is the human condition for which man and not God is responsible, the political and moral sphere that God had intended to spare Adam.

The logic of Maimonides' exegesis here raises questions, both within the chapter itself,[16] and in relation to Maimonides' later insistence on a God who is unchanging and unaffected by human behavior. Maimonides must, therefore, consider the entire story as a parable devoted to distinguishing between the theoretical and the practical intellect, and to assigning responsibility for each to God and man, respectively.[17] For Maimonides, the most that God could be said to have done for man is to have given him the potentiality to create his own social and moral universe, a potentiality that Maimonides imagines God ideally had not wanted man to develop. Where this leaves the Torah and its laws, and the entire sphere of ethics and politics for Maimonides, remains to be seen.[18]

Chapters 28–36 of part 1 contain abbreviated remarks on a variety of topics, foreshadowing more expansive and reasoned expositions later. In chapters 31 and 32 Maimonides makes the point, often reiterated elsewhere, that there are limits to what the human intellect can apprehend, assertions about things concerning which demonstrative proofs cannot be given. Maimonides is thinking mostly of metaphysical propositions and, relying on a cryptic talmudic passage, praises Rabbi Aqiba for recognizing the limits of such speculation.[19] Though he enumerates various reasons why most people do not make sufficient use of their intellects, Maimonides does not want to impugn the integrity of the intellect itself and closes chapter 32 with reference to later chapters[20] in which he will give a "precise account" (*taḥrīr*) of the essence of the intellect.

In chapters 33 and 34 Maimonides emphasizes the danger and difficulties inherent in embarking on the study of metaphysics without proper training and natural aptitude. Reflecting the biases of his time, Maimonides believes all young people and women, as well as most men, are naturally incapable of understanding the subject, and that is one reason the Torah presents scientific truths in popular, nonscientific terms. As Maimonides puts it, "the Torah speaks in the language of man."[21] This is necessary for most people, however much a literal reading of the text may mislead them. It is necessary too, to tolerate false beliefs in order to keep the "secrets" of physics and metaphysics, *ma'aseh bere'shit* and *ma'aseh merkavah,* inviolate.

Maimonides, however, draws the line at statements that attribute corporeal attributes to God. Everyone—"children, women, stupid ones, and those of a defective natural disposition"—must be compelled to disavow that belief, as well as the concomitant belief in a deity that is affected by anything (and thus subject to change). Children (as well as everyone else) must be "made to accept on traditional authority [*taqlīd*] the belief that God is not a body; and that there is absolutely no likeness in any respect whatever between Him and the things created by Him."[22] Such terms as "existence," "life," and "knowledge" mean something entirely different when predicated of God and of man. As Maimonides says of existence, it "can only be applied equivocally to His existence and to that of things other than He."[23]

Maimonides is very insistent on this issue: the belief in divine corporeality and its entailments is a cardinal sin for him, one that warrants death to the person holding the false belief.[24] Such a person is an infidel in Maimonides' opinion, worse even than an idolater who uses a statue as an image of, and an intermediary to, the one God.

The vehemence of Maimonides' belief in the necessity of negating God's corporeality, using as a proof text the genocidal command of Deuteronomy 20:16, is striking. It is a sign of the critical importance this principle has in Maimonides' philosophy and faith, extending beyond theoretical tenets to practical and political ramifications. Clearly, he felt not only that the monotheistic idea was threatened by misunderstanding the nature of God, but that the Jewish people, Maimonides' own flock, were exposing themselves to corruption and ruin with this misapprehension. As Maimonides says, "necessity" (*aḍ-ḍarūra*) required that the masses (*al-jumhūr*) be "guided" to the belief in the existence of God and in His possessing all the perfections, particularly life, power, and knowledge.[25] This necessity for Maimonides is as much a political imperative as it is a metaphysical one.

So agitated was Maimonides over the infidelity, as he saw it, of those who believed in a corporeal God that he threatens them with God's anger, jealousy, and the "fire of His wrath," forgetting, as it were, that these were part of the package of attributes and actions that he wanted everyone to deny God has.[26]

In chapter 34, Maimonides, following what he regards as an accepted, demonstrated truth, asserts that "the moral virtues are a preparation [*ṭauti'a*] for the rational virtues,"[27] and that it is impossible to achieve perfect rationality without moral training, itself suitable only for those with a tranquil and placid temperament. The moral sphere is the political arena, and for Maimonides the perfect individual is one who has mastered knowledge of "the varieties of political regimes" as well as of the theoretical sciences, particularly metaphysics.[28] In a nod to his doctrine of prophecy, which he has not as yet developed in this book, Maimonides adds that such a person has to have the ability "to communicate notions in flashes,"[29] i.e., both receive and transmit truths in cryptic, allusive fashion. Asserting mastery of the moral sciences as a condition of achieving theoretical perfection is important for Maimonides' subsequent emphasis on law.

Maimonides throws out passing references to other important issues in this section, all which he develops later in the book. Thus, in *Guide* 1.17, he refers to the three physical principles of mortal beings: matter, form, and "particularized privation," *al-'adam al-maḥṣūṣ*.[30] He refers to Plato's designation of matter as female,[31] an association Maimonides also identified, in the introduction to the first part of the *Guide*, as the allegorical import of King Solomon's tale, in Proverbs 7, of the seductive wiles of a married harlot.[32] Maimonides, it is clear, held both women and matter in low esteem philosophically, an attitude that was reinforced by his belief in an emanative outpouring of essential being that terminated at the lowest level in a surreptitiously problematic relation with matter.[33]

That God's relation to matter is "problematic" is not immediately apparent from Maimonides' allegorical exegesis of Exodus 24:10, in *Guide* 1.28. There, Maimonides identifies the object that seemed like white sapphire, which Moses and leaders of the people saw under God's feet, as prime matter, with God the cause of its existence. As Maimonides proceeds to explain, prime matter has no form of its own and is therefore capable of assuming any form, and in this sense it is the "first among the things [God] has created that necessitates generation and corruption."[34] Maimonides concludes this sentence by saying God is the *mubdi*ʿ of first matter, which Pines translates as "creator ex nihilo," though the question of creation, whether from nothing or not, has yet to be discussed.[35]

Maimonides expounds upon the theme of (the absence of) divine attributes in chapters 47–54 of part 1. God for him has neither accidental nor essential attributes, nothing that would introduce multiplicity into His essence. Hence, not only does God not have "external" senses that would enable Him to see or hear mankind, He also is devoid of "internal" senses and faculties whereby He would possess (a divine) imagination or intellect.[36] All biblical references to God's thought and comprehension, as to His sight or hearing, are anthropomorphic projections that the prophets resorted to in order to communicate with the people on their terms, in human language.

Similarly, the Bible portrays angels in mostly human terms, and for Maimonides they too, like God, *are* purely intellects and do not *have* intellects, that is, their entire being is an intelligible idea.[37] Paradoxically, though, this idea is conveyed through the imagination, and specifically the imagination of prophets. Prophetic visions are thus in part the products of an inspired imagination, communicating intelligible ideas in fantastic and sensory terms.

In chapter 49, Maimonides observes that people who believe literally in the biblical portrayal of angels do so because they do not subject their belief to rational inquiry, relying solely on what they imagine to be true. Foreshadowing his critique of the tenth premise of the *mutakallimūn* in *Guide* 1.73,[38] Maimonides states that such people—and they form the "majority of those who speculate on these matters"[39]—believe that whatever they can imagine can exist. Maimonides expands his critique of this view in chapter 50, stating that every belief that can be imagined has to be compatible with a rational affirmation of its contents. It is not enough to conceive of some idea, it has to be acknowledged as something that actually exists. A true belief is therefore no different from any other cognitive assertion; it simply announces the speaker's conviction of the accuracy of his statement, having carefully considered it.[40] This is made crystal clear in Maimonides' following remark that "belief is the affirmation [*al-taṣdīq*] that what has been represented [*bi-mā tuṣawwara*] is outside the mind just as it has been represented in the mind."[41]

Maimonides then proceeds to address philosophically an essential issue in the *Guide:* what may be predicated of God, what attributes, if any, *are* proper to use? This is particularly apt here, given the conditions of legitimate belief Maimonides just enunciated. Will it be possible to affirm believe in a being that cannot be represented adequately, one that is beyond our comprehension?

In chapter 51, Maimonides calls the denial of essential attributes to God a "primary intelligible," since an attribute "is not the essence of the thing of which it is predicated, but is a certain mode of the essence and hence an accident."[42] Were the attribute the essence, it would either be a tautology or an explanation of the term, part of its definition. Maimonides accepts this latter type of attribution in general, but not in reference to God, as he explains in the following chapter. First, though, he insists on a strict interpretation of oneness: "For there is no oneness at all except in believing that there is one simple essence in which there is no complexity or multiplication of notions, but one notion only . . . not divided in any way and by any cause into two notions; and you will not find therein any multiplicity either in the thing as it is outside of the mind or as it is in the mind."[43]

As Maimonides makes clear in chapter 52, none of the five types of attributes he describes is predicable of God; He is not subject to definition, in whole or part, and has no essential or nonessential attribute of any sort, neither quality nor quantity, disposition or affect. Maimonides specifically mentions that God is not endowed with a soul that would give him a certain character or "habitus" (*hai'a*) such as clemency, a claim that Maimonides will modify, though not deny, soon after.[44]

God cannot be defined, since that would assume the existence of causes anterior to, and responsible for, His existence, a logical impossibility in Maimonides' emerging description of God. The other types of attribution mentioned are rejected for entailing composition in the divine being. While that charge cannot be brought against the predication of relationships that God may have with others, Maimonides faults this kind of attribution too. Any relation with the world would implicate God in time and space, the necessary concomitants of every object in this world. For the philosophers consider time as an accident attached to motion, and motion, like place, is attached to bodies.[45] God, however, is not a body and therefore has no (direct) relation to physical objects.

Maimonides knows this position will be difficult for many of his readers to accept, so he suggests indulging them in their belief that God is in a relationship with the world, and with mankind in particular.[46] After all, this belief, however wrong, does not necessarily posit multiplicity or change in God's essence.

The fifth kind of affirmative attribution is the only category that Maimonides accepts as valid, namely, when an action is predicated of God. This is acceptable, on the condition that the actions are only (our) expressions of God's essence, not essential qualities of it, and therefore do not infringe on His Oneness. As we shall learn, the effect of these actions occurs at considerable remove from that essence and, as we have seen, is not physically related to them.

Following the literal text of Scripture, people insist upon attributing life, knowledge, power, and will to God. Maimonides acknowledges this in chapter 53, and he has no wish to deny these attributes. He wants them, however, to be understood as terms interchangeable with the divine essence or manifestations of His actions.[47] In chapter 54, Maimonides glosses Exodus 33 and 34 as teaching that Moses was denied knowledge of God's essence, but was vouchsafed knowledge of God's "ways," which are for Maimonides attributes of action.[48] These are the thirteen attributes that later received prominent place in the holiday liturgy, attributes largely emphasizing God's merciful, gracious, and long-suffering character.

One of these thirteen attributes, though (and the one modified in the later liturgy), has God not exempting those guilty of criminal and errant behavior, even "visiting the iniquity of the fathers upon the children" for three and four generations. Recognizing that this action is not compatible with the other attributes, Maimonides does his best to limit it only to persons who commit the sin of idolatry. Maimonides feels this is justified, in that idolatry *necessarily* leads to "great corruption" in society.[49] For Maimonides, then, the entire moral fabric of civilization depends upon the ethical teachings that he believes are implicit in the monotheistic idea. Yet Maimonides is quick to point out that God does not possess these or other moral qualities; rather He is the "agent of actions"[50] like those that in us derive from such moral qualities. We thus project our moral sensibilities and actions upon God.

Maimonides boldly equates knowledge of God with finding grace in His sight, a state not achieved by those who "merely fast and pray."[51] Anyone (not only Jews, presumably) who knows God enjoys His favor and proximity, while those who are ignorant of God's nature suffer His anger and remoteness.

These affective and spatial terms, we need to remember, do not adhere to God, however much they may appear to do so. Nor, for that matter, should the entire dialogue in which God appears to respond to Moses be taken literally, given the restrictive nature of divine attributes that Maimonides has taught. Maimonides works with and accepts the language of the Bible, while subverting its mindset.[52]

Maimonides presents us next with a central teaching of his philosophy, using the statement from Exodus 33:19 as his proof text. God says there to Moses that "I will make all my goodness pass before thee," which "goodness" Maimonides interprets as all of nature, following the Genesis 1:31 declaration that everything God made was "very good." Moses and we are thus led to realize that all of nature manifests God's benign presence and governance, the more manifest the more we understand the interrelationships of natural objects.

Maimonides is not deterred from seeing God's providential regard as evident in every natural occurrence, including floods, earthquakes, and storms, as well as in the genocidal actions of human armies. Though he acknowledges these as calamities, Maimonides believes their victims receive their due;[53] their fate is not capricious. God may be called jealous, avenging, or angry, but that is again a human projection, for He presides over the world as a dispassionate governor.

Maimonides makes much of this image of the deity. Man should emulate God as much as is possible in governing society dispassionately, feigning anger when necessary, but greatly preferring acts of mercy and forgiveness to their opposites.

In Chapter 55, Maimonides claims that the denial of the four kinds of attribution mentioned in the preceding chapters can be clearly demonstrated, following as they do from "universal primary propositions," viz., that all affections entail change, and that were God subject to affect in any way, He would be acted upon and thus changed by a source other than Him. That, in turn, would entail that God had lacked some perfection (all change having to be for the better), and that He had been deprived of that perfection and had it only potentially. Potentiality and privation are concomitant, and both are contrary to God's being, which is pure, unchanging, perfect actuality.

In this chapter and the following, chapter 56, Maimonides claims it necessary to deny any similarity between God and anything else. The reasoning here is implicit, that similarity relativizes the deity, introducing a third term and cause by virtue of which the similarity occurs. This, though, destroys God's totally uncaused, unique nature. The attribution to God of terms such as "knowledge," "power," "will," and "life," as well as of "existence" itself, is purely equivocal for Maimonides; they have nothing in common with the terms as commonly predicated.[54]

Maimonides elaborates, in chapter 57, on the attribute of existence. He asserts that "it is known" that existence is "an accident that accidentally occurs to that which exists" (*'ariḍ 'araḍa li'l-mawjūd*), and therefore is something added to its essence.[55] As an accident, existence cannot be attributed to God, any more than any other attribute that would introduce multiplicity into His oneness. Maimonides feels it is permissible, though, to attribute existence to God once it is identical to His essence. In effect, God does not *have* existence but *is* existence; His existence is as necessary as it is essential. As Maimonides says, "[God] exists, but not through an existence other than His essence; similarly He lives, but not through life," and similarly with divine power and knowledge.[56] Later, in chapter 58, Maimonides says that God's existence, which is the same as His essence, is the source, via emanation, for the existence of other existents.[57]

Maimonides pauses in chapter 57, however, to acknowledge that customary words are inadequate to express the notion of God's unique oneness, and he must do with a certain "looseness of expression"[58] or imprecision that is used in saying that God is one, or that He is eternal, when He is not bound by quantity or time. However, the person "trained to understand notions according to their true reality" can penetrate the "summary fashion"[59] in which words are used to describe the attributes.

In chapter 58, Maimonides attempts to resolve the difficulties involving attributes by adopting an oblique approach to them, that of negating attributes that are themselves privations of affirmative terms.[60] Affirmative propositions are to be understood as the negation of the privation of that which has been affirmed. This is intended to avoid attributing anything to God directly, even negative predications, removing the deity from any relationship whatsoever.

Thus, for example, the affirmation "God exists" should be understood as "God does not not-exist," or as Maimonides says, "His nonexistence is impossible." Similarly, "God lives" is meant to mean that "God is not dead," while "God is powerful, knowing, and willing" equates to "God is not powerless, ignorant, inattentive, or negligent."[61]

Here Maimonides makes a logical leap and—seemingly indifferent to what he has just asserted—assumes something that he has yet to explain in detail, let alone demonstrate. He says that we apprehend that the Necessary Existent grants existence to many (really all) other (possible) existents, in that existence "flows" or emanates from Him to them. This unchanging emanation establishes duration and order for existent beings, signifying a well-designed governance. It is this appearance of an ordered nature that brings us to say that God is powerful, knowing, and willing.

Maimonides would have us say such things of God, but mean them only in the roundabout way of negative predication, in order to prevent ruining our understanding of the deity. He thus closes the chapter with a peroration extolling the God whom we do not and cannot know directly, if at all, and yet who we are convinced is responsible for the world as we know it. It is the concept of a benevolent being from whom existence necessarily emanates in an eternal unchanging way that leads Maimonides to attribute will and purpose to the deity, whatever his reservations about using such terms.

In a similar fashion, Maimonides says in chapter 59 that apprehension of God "consists in the inability" to completely apprehend Him,[62] and Maimonides quotes Psalm 65:2, that "silence is praise to thee." Maimonides says this, however, after arguing at some length, in this chapter and the next, for the validity of negative attribution, each additional negation supposedly bringing the speaker closer to apprehension of the true reality of God. Maimonides is arguing with his compatriots who ascribe many qualities to God. He sees the descriptions employed by poets and preachers as both ridiculous and blaspheming, evidence of their unknowing unbelief, which then leads the people into false beliefs about God.

As an example of the uniqueness of God's knowledge, Maimonides says in chapter 60 that God knows the many and ever-changing things of this world in one (eternally) unchanging act of cognition, knowing a thing both before and after it exists with the same unchanging knowledge.[63]

In chapters 61–63 Maimonides discusses certain combinations of letters that were used in the Bible and Talmud as the names of God, and he identifies the tetragrammaton YHWH as the only name that truly represents Him. This, because God identifies Himself to Moses at Sinai as "I am that I am."[64] Maimonides notes that *Ehyeh,* treated as a noun, derives from the verb *hayah,* which denotes existence (literally, "he was"). The compound name *Ehyeh asher ehyeh* repeats the subject in the predicate, thus equating them and denoting existence only, an existence not dependent on anything else.[65] For Maimonides, that is the Necessary Existent, previously identified as a term "well known" to the philosophers. The Bible thus anticipates the philosophers' realization of God as the Necessary Existent. (It was Avicenna, as we saw,[66] who distinguished essence from existence and introduced the concept of God as the Necessary Existent, contrasting Him with all other "possibly existent" beings, beings whose existence depends upon an external actualizing agent.)

The names of God mentioned in the Talmud are combinations of 12 or 42 letters that to Maimonides represent metaphysical notions in coded form. Maimonides then equates knowledge of metaphysics with apprehension of the "Agent Intellect,"[67] a term he introduces here without elaboration, probably assuming his readers are or should be familiar with it from its appearance in his rabbinic writings, as well as in the philosophical writings of others.

In chapter 65 Maimonides dares to disabuse his readers of the notion that God spoke to Moses in creating the Torah. Maimonides has already informed us that God does not have a voice and that He cannot speak, but inasmuch as this idea goes against the plain text of the Torah, and against popular opinion, Maimonides wishes to reiterate his position. Doubtless, he is also interested in alluding to the fact that the Torah is created, in contrast to the Muslim claim of an eternal Qur'ān. Maimonides does not go further into this question that so engaged the Muslim theologians, the *mutakallimūn*. Had he done so, he would have had to explain that though the "giving" of the Torah was a temporal event, the (essential) content of the Torah had to have been with God forever.

Maimonides disengages God from the words ascribed to Him in the Torah by saying that "the words heard by Moses were created[68] and brought into being by God *just as He has created all the things that He has created and brought into being*" (my italics). In so writing, Maimonides indicates to his attuned readers that just as God acted through intermediaries in all that He brought into being, so the words, or voice, heard by Moses were/was communicated to him through an intermediary, namely, the Agent Intellect, of which we have just heard mention. Maimonides alludes to this by immediately saying that he will speak of prophecy later, a topic in which the Agent Intellect plays a major role.

Maimonides then qualifies his position, saying that when speech is attributed to God it denotes either the divine will or a notion that is understood to have come from God. In the latter case, Maimonides says it is a matter of indifference whether the notion was conveyed by a "created voice" or grasped in a state of prophecy.

Chapter 67 seems to upset the interpretation offered of God always working through intermediaries, for there Maimonides speaks of a "primal will," *mashi'a ūlā,*[69] that brought the tablets of the Ten Commandments into existence, just as it did for the stars in the spheres. However, Maimonides concludes the chapter by saying that this is the consensual view of the people, indicating thereby that this is not necessarily his view, at least not in the literal sense. For him, the writing on the tablets, like the emergence of stars in the heavens, is indeed an expression of the divine will, though not directly produced by God.

Chapter 68 returns to the theme enunciated in the first chapter of the *Guide,* that God is an intellect, i.e., an intelligent being (though not a being that *has* intelligence, in which case the intelligence would be an attribute of God's being).[70] Maimonides acknowledges from the start that the view he is about to expound is one the philosophers commonly accept. Indeed, it is first articulated by Aristotle[71] and endorsed by such of Maimonides' predecessors as Alfarabi, Avicenna, and Ibn Bājja. As Maimonides says, the widespread philosophical view, which he has already endorsed in the *Mishneh Torah* as a foundational principle of the *shari'a* of Judaism, i.e., of its Law, is that God is the subject, object, and act of intellection, all one and the same. God as intellect is an ever actual thought that thinks itself, a self-contained, fully realized active intelligence.[72]

It is the total actualization of the divine intellect that differentiates it from the intellect of human beings, Maimonides says, for we don't always think, or use our intellect. We do, though, have the ability or potentiality to do so, a faculty dubbed by Aristotle a potential intellect.[73] Maimonides follows the post-Aristotelian tradition in calling this potential intellect a material or "hylic" intellect (from the Greek word for matter), and situates it (ambiguously) in man. When a person puts his mind to something, Maimonides says, the potential or material intellect becomes activated and is now an "intellect in act." This active intellect strips the form from the matter of the object it contemplates and cognizes the pure or universal, intelligible form of the object. At that point, and in a fashion similar to God's own activity, the subject, object, and act of the human intellect are united as one.

Maimonides subscribed to the philosophers' cosmological tradition that saw the matter of the heavenly bodies as informed by intellects and souls that together moved them. The matter of the heavenly bodies was thought to be *sui generis* in that it did not undergo generation or corruption, insuring thereby that the movements of the planets were uniformly circular, or should have been.[74] No material obstructions affected the motions of the heavens, guaranteeing thereby a continuous chain of being in the cosmos that culminated in the natural world as we know it on earth.

On earth, however, there is change as well as constancy, and the orderly plan of nature often appears to be stymied. Maimonides briefly alludes to this toward the end of chapter 68, when he says that the Agent Intellect, which is the last of the "separate" (that is, immaterial) intellects of the heavens and as such is responsible for emanating forms upon all the material bodies on earth, resembles human beings in being an active intellect only intermittently. Unlike us, however, the Agent Intellect fails to be as perfect and reliable as its sister heavenly intellects not because of its own limitations but because of an "impediment" (*'āik*) external to it, some accidental occurrence.[75]

As Maimonides did not believe the intelligences of the heavens ever varied in their behavior, the occasional failure of the Agent Intellect to accomplish its mission must be due to the material substrate of the body with which it unites. Unlike its heavenly counterpart, terrestrial matter is changeable and hence often unprepared for its formal accouterment, frustrating the Agent Intellect's action, itself constant.

Maimonides will make much of this issue in his discussions of prophecy and theodicy, but for the moment he wishes, as he says, to concentrate on God's uniqueness as an intellect constantly in act, with neither internal nor external impediments to His apprehension. Everyone's intellect in act, however, has the same trifold unity of subject, intellect, and object as has God's. Moreover, as we shall learn, for Maimonides the fact that there are no impediments to God's intellectual being does not mean that He can completely apprehend absolutely everything.

Analysis

The introduction to the first part of the *Guide* is multilayered, consisting of a brief personal note that Maimonides writes, dedicating the work to his former pupil; a lengthy introduction that states the purposes of the treatise and the difficulty in conveying its teachings, together with mention of his past attempts to do so; and a further, brief introduction that sets out seven kinds of causes for the contradictory or contrary statements that can occur in any philosophical work. The lengthy introduction is made so by an extended instruction in the nature of scriptural parables and the diverse techniques to employ in evaluating them. Parables, Maimonides states, hold the key to understanding prophetic discourse.[76] As soon becomes evident, Maimonides will view much of the Torah's discourse as parabolic, or allegorical.

Commentators and scholars have long since fastened upon the third tier of Maimonides' introductory statements, looking to identify places in the *Guide* that exemplify one or another of the seven kinds of contradictory or contrary statements he enumerates. Maimonides has been seen as inviting the reader to do this, admitting in effect that he has planted misleading and conflicting statements, challenging the reader to find them and in disentangling them get to Maimonides' true beliefs. He is seen as mostly resorting to misleading statements of the fifth (simplistic and illogical) and seventh (revealing only part of the discourse) kinds, for the reasons associated with them. Yet one can also find places in the *Guide* that are illustrative of types 3 (unstated changes) and 4 (claims not made explicit and not in their proper place), and some scholars who detect a shift in Maimonides' views within the *Guide* point to the second type (unstated authorial changes of opinion).

The esoteric interpretation of the *Guide,* taking it to be a work that does not necessarily mean what it says but can be deciphered to get to its true meaning, is thus an approach that Maimonides encourages. Famously, it has led Leo Strauss to explore every word of the text and find subtleties and hidden meanings everywhere. Many scholars have joined in this pursuit, to greater and lesser degrees, and I am in essential agreement with it too. There has been a backlash, however, to what is viewed as Strauss's hermeneutical excesses, and a cottage industry has arisen to evaluate Strauss's interpretation of Maimonides.[77] It is not my purpose here to defend or critique Strauss, and I leave it to the reader to assess my debt to him. I do wish to acknowledge Strauss's attempt to keep Maimonides' teachings secret, accessible only to the highly attuned reader, in accordance with the Master's wishes. I believe this attitude also affected the otherwise magnificent translation of Shlomo Pines, my disagreement with whose readings on crucial terms and sentences will be found in the footnotes.

I am guilty of not following these two great Maimonidean interpreters in honoring Maimonides' wishes to shelter the *Guide* from the general public. Times have changed, and the need to rescue the *Guide* from obfuscation and misunderstanding is great.

A considerable number of chapters in the first part of the *Guide* are devoted to exegetical interpretations of biblical passages that portray God as a corporeal being, with very human emotions and actions. Maimonides ingeniously deconstructs these passages to have them affirm the opposite of what is claimed. The God that emerges is barely recognizable, though readers of Islamic philosophy would have become familiar with the deity to whom Maimonides points. He "points" to God, rather than defines Him, since he cannot have a definitive idea of a being that is unique and beyond comprehension. As such, Maimonides may not be able to believe in God, not having the conviction that his representation of God adequately expresses His reality.

This is Maimonides' criterion of belief, as given in chapter 50 of the *Guide.*[78] For him, belief is not to be disassociated from the normative ways we acquire and express knowledge. A belief cannot represent an idea that is divorced from reality, a reality that is framed by logical principles and empirical observation. Maimonides employs the terms his predecessors regularly used when describing the components of knowledge and meaningful speech, *taṣawwur* and *taṣdīq,* respectively, representation or conceptualization (by the imaginative faculty), and affirmation (due to confirmation by the rational faculty).[79] The belief in question may be false, but it is posited of actual, and not imaginary, impossible subjects.[80] Maimonides' belief in God, to the degree that it is possible for him to assert such a belief, will have to be constructed using logic and the observed facts of the sciences, particularly that of astronomy. He doesn't begin to do this thoroughly until the second part of the *Guide,* where he offers what he considers proofs for God's existence. In what follows, his best "belief" relies on proofs that follow Aristotle's principles of physics, though he is also drawn to the unempirically based logic positing Avicenna's Necessary Existent.

In the chapters before us, Maimonides lays out in detail his idea of what may be said, or predicated, of God, what can be attributed to Him or, simply put, what are His attributes. The whole project is rendered suspect, however, by Maimonides' statement in chapter 57 that he can't speak precisely about this topic, since it falls outside the matrix of scientific language, which is bound to a spatio-temporal reality.[81] Maimonides concedes, however, that the qualified philosopher can get beyond inadequate locutions to understand the topic correctly. He does this by abstracting the essential forms of an object from their material accidents, the standard procedure to establish scientific knowledge.[82]

A main purpose of this first section of the *Guide* is metaphysical, Maimonides being intent on clarifying the idea of God and ridding it of every anthropomorphic expression. That is a goal commonly shared by the philosophers Maimonides read, the ultimate goal of Aristotelian and Neoplatonic thought. Maimonides already made his belief in a nonpersonal deity clear in the opening chapter of his *Mishneh Torah,* where he made it a commandment required of all Jews.[83]

Accordingly, for Maimonides the biblical terms depicting God are to be understood metaphorically, and every kind of attribution but one is inappropriate.[84] Such attributes compromise the absolute oneness of the divine being, bringing it into logically impossible relationships. Maimonides tolerates only the "attributes of action," believing they do not (necessarily) implicate the divine essence.

That essence is conveyed by the tetragrammaton, the four-letter specific name of the God of Israel that Maimonides finds perfectly suited to the universal idea of God.[85] The Hebrew verb from which the noun YHWH is derived denotes existence, and God for Maimonides is essentially that—an existent, or being. His essence is existence, with nothing added to qualify—or quantify—that essence. The attributes of life, wisdom, will, power, and goodness that are believed to "belong" to God do so, for Maimonides, only as expressions—our expressions—of that inscrutable being. Hence, God's being is unique, conveyed by the Avicennian term "Necessary Existent" (*al-wājib al-wujūd*), which denotes a being whose existence is not contingent upon anything else, has no cause, and is therefore eternal and unchanging. God has no agent or faculty that can desire to make changes, He has no "will" with which to act otherwise than He has always acted and will forever act. The "will" of which Maimonides speaks is synonymous with God's wisdom, as well as with His power, life, and goodness. They are all equivocal terms connoting the Necessary Existent as it (traditionally, He) appears to us, through actions in nature that we attribute to Him.

Maimonides has taken the absolute unity of God as a given premise of the idea of a supreme being, and only later will he attempt to prove it. Compromising that unity introduces, even on an immaterial, conceptual level, a multiplicity that Maimonides equates with idolatry. God, for Maimonides, cannot have more than one thing, or, more correctly, He cannot *be* more than one thing, which is being. His essence is existence, necessarily.

Maimonides adopts a version of the negative theology practiced by Muslim philosophers and theologians alike, in both the Sunni and Shīʿī traditions.[86] He believes that understanding a positive attribution as the negation of its privation allows one to retain traditional predications while not formally endorsing them. It is politically imperative, of course, for Maimonides to stay with the traditional set of divine attributes, however much he appears to vitiate their meaning.

It is questionable whether negating the privations of affirmative propositions brings one closer to understanding God's being.[87] The fact that no affirmative attribute can ever succeed in describing God's nature, in that it would form a composite entity out of what must remain strictly one, does not make the negation of the privation of that attribute any the more effective in this attempt.[88] Saying what God is not, however many ways one may phrase it, does not bring a person closer to understanding the unintelligibility of divine being. At best, these negations get rid of false ideas; admittedly, though, this is no small matter.

Moreover, while the approach of negative theology, which negates the privation of an affirmative proposition, does not affirm anything of God, neither does it explicitly deny that which it must not affirm. That is, the given attribute, which of course cannot be affirmed of God, is not negated either; only its privation is negated. The attribute in question is left in limbo, as it were, neither applicable to God nor totally inapplicable. Whereas one knows not to translate the negative predication to a positive one, a person would be inclined to think of it in positive terms, while acknowledging the lack of common meaning to the terms used. This is seductive, and Maimonides would appear to be accommodating the traditional reader in this way.

Accordingly, Maimonides allows people to speak of God in traditional terms, however much he alerts them to the inadequacy of their language. One must "indulge" people in their need to believe in a personal God, Maimonides believes, and he clearly understands the Torah to be doing just that when it "speaks in the language of man." Much of the *Guide* may be seen as an extended act of indulgence by Maimonides toward his community, for he presents God frequently in biblically personal terms as active and responsive. Yet Maimonides has alerted us, with the idea of a pure One, to the logical incoherence of this historic image. This One, however, is not totally uninvolved with the world, though He is not dependent upon it.

Following a Neoplatonic paradigm, Maimonides sees the world as emanating from the One to the many. Unlike Plotinus, though, Maimonides does not have being unfold in stages of greater cosmic complexity and intelligibility: from the unknowable pure One to *nous,* the Universal Mind, in which the many essential forms are unified; on to *psyche,* the Universal Soul, in which the generic essences that together compose the One first make their discrete identifiable appearance; down to the dispersed many of *physis,* Nature, in which specific forms ultimately combine with matter to form individual beings.[89]

Rather than Plotinus, Maimonides' immediate mentor is Avicenna, and Avicenna's God is a Necessary Existent "contending" only with possible existents. They, however, comprise all the beings of the world. In this view, God knows, and has known from all eternity, those beings that are possible existents. The possible is understood as belonging to that genus which requires actual instantiation of at least one of its members. Similarly, something is said to have (had) potentiality once its realization as an actual being has occurred to some member of its genus. Possibility thus requires necessity eventually, even as potentiality is contingent upon actuality of being.

Accordingly, for Avicenna as well as for Maimonides, God cannot know impossible existents, for there is never anything then for Him to know;[90] impossible existents do not exist, and by definition cannot ever exist. God, therefore, does not choose between possible and impossible existents, nor does He choose at some point which possible beings will exist, that is, which essences will comprise the species of our world.[91]

The plenitude of God's perfection requires that all possible beings exist, populating the world as we know it. God, whose essence is existence, has nothing to do with nonexistence. The species that emanate from Him somehow are as eternal as He; originally they are within His being, one with Him. The beings that are possible existents in themselves, *bi-nafsihi* (*per se*), are necessary existents *bi-ghayrihi* (*per aliud*), "by another," and the other is God, in whose Necessary Existence the necessary existence of the possible existents is eternally subsumed.

God is thus the ultimate source of being for everything that exists. All beings are to be found essentially within the indivisible unity of the Necessary Existent, and are known to God as the object of His knowledge. He knows the many as one, a knowledge that is dynamic and expressive of God's will and providence. Avicenna, like Al-Kindī, the "first philosopher of the Arabs," thus identifies Will as the operative aspect of divine providence (though not dissociated from God's wisdom). God brings the potential beings into existence and has always done so, for His name's sake, to endow existence wherever possible, to maximize the good, which is being, and preeminently His being.

Avicenna's concept of the Necessary Existent, which Maimonides adopts, harbors within itself the three hypostases of the Neoplatonists. As the existent whose essence is simply existence, the Necessary Existent is like the unknowable One beyond being of Plotinus and Proclus; as the existent that somehow assimilates all possible beings into the necessity of its being, thus treating the many as one, the Necessary Existent is like the Neoplatonists' universal intellect; and as the ultimate source from which the possible beings originate in their multiplicity, the Necessary Existent is akin to the universal soul of the Neoplatonists.

Avicenna adopts an emanative scheme similar to one employed by Alfarabi before him in an attempt to explain the mechanics of the emergence of the many from the one. The immaterial intelligent being that is the first to emanate from God's unitary being is somehow seen as responsible for the multiplicity of thoughts that result in the formation of a heavenly ensouled body and another intelligence, starting a process that fills the heavens with animated and intelligent spheres and terminates with the appearance of the Agent Intellect and the sublunar sphere.

For Avicenna, as well as for Alfarabi, this emanative process has been going on eternally, since God's being—absolutely perfect as it is—does not brook change. There could be no reason for God to change, no cause to effect change, internal or external to God. God could not have reasoned with Himself to create or destroy the world at any particular time or for any particular reason without introducing particular ideas into His essence and involving Himself in external contingencies. Maimonides, who accepts Avicenna's identification of God as Necessary Existent, had to have understood this, though he resists it.

The caused, contingent existents of the world (i.e., everything in the entire world) are, then, in themselves possible existents. They exist as such in a state of potential existence, their potentiality expressed in the world through their material dimension. God, who is completely immaterial, is not the direct cause of physical beings; He can only know the idea of matter as substratum of form and the principle of change, and know that it is physically realized only in the emanative process.

When a given object moves from potential to actual existence, it is instantiated with a particular form and becomes, by virtue of its cause, a necessary existent. It is God as the unconditioned Necessary Existent who ultimately brings these possible existents into being as necessary beings. He has always done so, since an eternally unrealized possible existence is logically self-contradictory and hence inconceivable. Following Aristotle, Avicenna believes that that which has the possibility of existing must do so at some time for it to qualify as truly possible. The possible existents of this world are thus concomitant with the necessary existents. Avicenna thus maintains with Aristotle that necessity governs the universe, while insisting upon its theoretically contingent nature.

Avicenna further combines opposites in stating that the first existent in the world, the intellect of the outermost sphere, is created from nothing in an atemporal eternal process.[92] He uses the term *ibdā'* to express this coming to be from nothing, and Maimonides, as we have seen, follows suit.[93]

5

Kalām Claims and Counterclaims (*Guide* Part I, Chapters 69–76)

Paraphrase

Maimonides changes gears in chapter 69, opening an attack upon the Muslim theologians, the *mutakallimūn.* He begins his attack in medias res, as it were, assuming the reader has some familiarity with the claims of the *mutakallimūn* and the religious philosophy known as *kalām* that had become dominant in Islamic rational thought.[1] Soon he will describe what he considers to be the main tenets of *kalām,* but in chapter 69 he is intent on debunking what the *mutakallimūn* regard as a fundamental difference between their physics and that of the philosophers.

Maimonides denies the *kalām* claim that designating God as a "maker" (*fā'il,* literally, "agent") carries none of the entailments or obligations of the philosophers' designation of God as a "cause." For the theologians of Islam, while "cause" entails "effect," "maker" has no necessary entailment. Thus, while the philosophers are saddled with a concurrence of cause and effect that allegedly necessitates the doctrine of the eternity of the world, the theologians are not.

Maimonides dismisses this argument, claiming that a maker precedes his creation just as a cause precedes its effect. Both agents are *in potentia* before their action, and the effects of both follow necessarily. As Michael Schwarz has pointed out,[2] Maimonides contradicts himself here in positing that God, whom he has previously insisted is totally in act, could, as Final Cause, have a potential dimension. Moreover, Maimonides deliberately attaches the category of potentiality and actuality to the theologians' "maker," though the basic thrust of their physics, as Maimonides himself will tell us later, is to dismantle the entire physical and causal structure of the philosophers.

Maimonides' opening salvo against the *mutakallimūn* thus has a polemical and unsatisfying ring, foreshadowing a basic difficulty he will face later in contesting their physics. His mention of the philosophers' designation of God as first cause does, however, facilitate his ensuing "summary account" of philosophy's basic doctrine of four causes, viz., material, formal, efficient, and final cause. Full knowledge of how each of these causes functions in a given object was universally thought by philosophers to constitute complete knowledge of it.

Maimonides testifies to his agreement with the philosophers' view that God is the efficient, formal, and final cause of the world, though in each case He is an indirect and remote cause, acting through intermediate causes. Though the ultimate formal principle of the world, responsible for the formal identity of all objects, the God of Maimonides, unlike Aristotle's (and Averroes') God, does not relate directly to the world, or more specifically to the outermost sphere of the universe, and thus He avoids any material entanglement. Maimonides briefly adduces the doctrine of emanation, which he promises to discuss later,[3] as the process whereby God endows the world with its permanent formal characteristics.

Maimonides follows a circuitous route in presenting God as a final cause, likening Him to a king who wishes to be seen as great in order to be feared, and feared in order to be obeyed, obedience then promoting civil behavior that ensures an orderly and long life. God as final cause is thus the architect of a successful life, a desideratum facilitated by God's will and wisdom, which are identical with God's essence. It is God's will that all created objects strive to live and be as perfect as they can be, imitating God's perfection as much as is possible for them.

Maimonides is silent in this chapter as to God's relation to matter. He pointedly does not say that God is the material cause of the world, not even in a remote sense. Indirectly he addresses the issue in general terms in the next chapter, as well as subsuming it somewhat in his discussion of creation.

Thus in chapter 70, Maimonides writes of God's relation to the entire world, approaching the topic exegetically by interpreting various biblical and talmudic passages as in agreement with both the philosophers' view of the heavens as spherical[4] and with his own view of God as the mover—through His power and will—of the highest heaven (i.e., the outermost sphere), "by whose motion everything that is in motion within this heaven is moved." God, though, "is separate from this heaven and not a force subsisting within it."[5] Maimonides thus believes God relates to matter indirectly, more indirectly than to the formal component of being.

Maimonides takes advantage of his talmudic source[6] here to slip in a view that had to be devastating to his traditional readers. Parsing the talmudic quotation, Maimonides finds support for his belief that the only part of an individual soul that survives death is an intellect that has "become actual," i.e., has realized some degree of universal, eternal truth, and that such an intellect, being immaterial as well as universal, has no physical boundaries. In Maimonides' words, "what is separate is . . . one thing only."[7]

It is apparent, moreover, that Maimonides hereby rejects the survival of individual bodies as well as of individual souls and intellects. His defense elsewhere of the idea of resurrection, a theme totally absent from the *Guide*, is based on extraphilosophical sources, as we have seen.[8] Tersely but boldly, Maimonides here subscribes to a doctrine known as "monopsychism," a term historically identified usually with Averroes, referring to the survival after death of but one intellect, conjoined with the universal Agent Intellect.[9]

Maimonides indulges in some questionable historical reconstructions in the beginning of chapter 71, positing an earlier and happier time in which Jews pursued science and philosophy, before external persecution and internal censorship combined to squelch such studies. He feels that a longstanding general resistance to committing oral teachings to writing contributed to the lack of a well-defined body of scientific knowledge among Jews. He believes the Talmud and *midrashim* need to be scoured for nuggets of scientific information; they are overlaid by "many layers of rind," which has led people to believe wrongly that Judaism has no scientific core. In this manner, Maimonides justifies using the Talmud and midrashic literature to support his philosophical claims, offering much the same exegetical approach he adopts in mining the Bible.

Maimonides is aware that in the more recent past (of some two hundred years) some of the leaders of both rabbinic and Karaite Judaism wrote theological treatises, but he dismisses their writing as insignificant. He is correct, however, in identifying the theological treatises of the *mutakallimūn* as the major influence upon the development of this initial attempt at a Jewish theology.

This leads Maimonides to sketch his view of the history of *kalām* and its major divisions, tracing initial *kalām* views to the theological responses to philosophy of educated Greek and Syrian Christians.[10] In the course of time, Maimonides says, Islamic theology developed a unique character, though in common with Christianity and Judaism it retained a belief in the creation of the world, a condition for validating the existence of miracles.[11]

For Maimonides, theologians of all stripes (though he mentions only Christians and Muslims) have the same methodology; they force physical reality to conform to their ideas of what it should be, in order to corroborate their a priori religious beliefs. The *mutakallimūn* go even further, in denying any special validity to the appearance of things, "custom," not necessity, ruling nature, an idea Maimonides will soon examine in greater detail.

Maimonides objects to the *kalām* argument for a Creator God, argued from the premise of a temporally created world. That premise, Maimonides claims, has never been decisively, i.e., demonstrably, proved, however great it would be to do so.[12] As he feels this is impossible, and as the *kalām* premises repudiate the reality of the natural world, Maimonides boldly chooses to establish the existence and oneness of the deity, as well as His incorporeality, upon the premise of the eternity of the world. The conclusion concerning God, Maimonides believes, will remain valid whether the premise is true or false (and he will offer strong objections to its validity before long).

Maimonides claims that both a created world and an eternal world require a single creator, viz., God. The God of an eternal world is described by him as uncaused and permanent, not capable of change. Presumably, He is also a volitional deity, as is the Creator God, but Maimonides, following the philosophers' Aristotelian-based arguments, dispenses with declaring this attribute for the time being.

Maimonides informs the reader that he will not interrogate the premises of the philosophers himself, considering most of them "demonstrated and indubitably correct."[13] He will simply repeat them, and then offer his own adaptation of them. The *Guide,* it is clear, is not meant to be a primer in philosophy. Nevertheless, Maimonides will lay out the premises of the philosophers, as well as those of the *mutakallimūn,* presumably in order to achieve transparency in his own approach. He obviously feels that whatever secrets concerning God's nature that he needs to keep will not be harmed by these arguments.

Accordingly, in chapter 72 Maimonides offers a précis of Aristotelian-based descriptions of the heavens and earth,[14] seen as "one individual," a completely integrated reality. Much as he wrote in the *Mishneh Torah,*[15] he says that the heavens are structured in concentric spheres moving in circular uniform motion with diverse rates of speed and direction. The outermost sphere is the fastest-moving one, having a diurnal motion that moves all the other heavens along with it.[16] Planetary bodies are affixed to the spheres and move with them, not having an independent faculty of motion. The matter of the spheres is unique, a fifth element, unlike the four elements that form the foundation of all other material bodies. This celestial matter is unchanging and apparently transparent in the spheres, allowing us to see the stars and planets that reside in them.[17]

Maimonides considers the number of spheres and the possibility of epicycles—spheres that revolve around other spheres and not around the earth—as unresolved issues, open to speculation. He thus appears to dismiss these questions. The existence of epicycles, however, is part of a larger question concerning the validity of Aristotle's cosmological paradigm, and he will address this problem later.[18]

Now, though, Maimonides proceeds to mention the Aristotelian doctrine of four sublunar elements: earth, water, air, and fire. They are formed by (diverse and partial) mixtures of four "primary forms" that Maimonides does not identify, but by which he must mean the basic qualities of hot, cold, wet, and dry. The elements as well as the qualities or "forms" that precede them constitute a kind of matter different from that of the heavens. Maimonides again does not discuss the nature of this underlying prime matter.[19] Instead, he describes the inanimate nature of the elements, in contrast to the animation of the bodies of the heavens, or spheres; each sphere has a soul.

Maimonides at this point leaves open the question whether the spheres also have intellects that allow them to have mental representations. This is surprising, since the Aristotelian model that Maimonides has adopted and will soon discuss obliges the spheres to move. They do so in response to a desire for perfection that is an expression of a conscious, intelligent being. Moreover, the emanative principle that Maimonides has adopted conceives the spheres to have intellects that transmit the forms that ultimately coalesce in the Agent Intellect to inform all bodies on earth. Finally, Maimonides assumed already in his *Mishneh Torah* that the spheres have intellects.[20]

Maimonides understands the motions of the heavens as forcing the elements on earth to interact with one another and become the various mixtures that compose all animal, plant, and mineral bodies. The bodies and the elements of which they are composed are all subject to generation and corruption, even as the elements are seen as passing away into one another. Maimonides thus assumes transformation of the elements, not their total annihilation. They have a common substratum in prime matter, "for the matter of the all is one."[21]

This matter cannot exist without form of some sort, even as no "natural form," one subject to generation and corruption, can exist without matter. The changing forms of matter have a repetitive pattern similar to the circular movement of the heavens, Maimonides states, understanding nature as constant even as it changes.

Maimonides then embarks upon an extended description of the harmony to be found in nature, the bodies and souls of all things on earth deriving from the motions and souls of the celestial bodies. The whole of being is one individual, Maimonides emphasizes, and this perspective will be "necessary or most useful"[22] later in demonstrating the oneness of God. Viewing the universe as an integrated whole also necessitates a stability, indeed a permanence, in the species of all beings, even as it requires the corruption and passing away of individual members of that species.

Maimonides is prepared to call the force in living bodies that governs and protects their various parts "nature," but he is reluctant to attribute to God the direct management of the universe as a whole, the permanent preservation of its species and temporary protection of individual members of the species. Puzzlingly, he says, "As to this force, there is speculation whether or not it subsists through the intermediary of [the sphere of] heaven."[23]

Maimonides has just told us that all things on earth derive from the heavens, and he is on the way to establishing God as the ultimate cause and creator, in one sense or another, of the world. The question he is not prepared to engage here is whether God acts, or can act, independently of the structures He has established in the cosmos.

As a man of his time, Maimonides is convinced of the teleological aspect of nature. It is part of nature's design that what is generated must pass away, the corruption of the faculties of living bodies as inevitable as the harmful effects of natural disasters. Maimonides understands, however, that God is the being that rules nature as a whole and initiates the process whereby the heavens move and affect the earth. This raises questions of an ethical sort regarding God's responsibility for the tragedies and evils on earth, but Maimonides defers this issue until later.

It is also worth noting that Maimonides refers to God here solely as a principle of physics, a "thing" (*amr*) that is the deity.[24] Maimonides offers a more traditional and supposedly personal image of the deity a few pages later, in saying that the world benefits from God's governance (*tadbīr*) as well as providence (*'ināya*).[25] It remains to be seen, however, how personal this providence is.

Though Maimonides first presents God here in primarily personal terms, he understands the deity as anything but a corporeal being. His nature is best described, however inadequately, as an intellect, and this is what gives human beings a special affinity with Him.[26] Maimonides lists the similarities and differences between humans and God, the most distinctive difference being that the heart and mind of a person are inseparable (for the most part) from the body, whereas God is separate from and unaffected by the world that He influences (by way of emanation).[27]

Notwithstanding their differences, the most distinctive similarity between God and man, Maimonides acknowledges, is in their respective relations qua separate intellects to the world and body. Maimonides speaks here not of the hylic or material, potential intellect in man, but of his acquired intellect, the intellect that has moved from potentiality to actuality and acquired universal truths, separating it from any and all individual and material forms, and thus from the bodies in which these forms appear. As such, the acquired intellect can be identical with (part of) the universal Agent Intellect, in which these eternal truths and forms abide. This identification allows Maimonides to say that the acquired intellect (acting as a surrogate Agent Intellect)[28] emanates its forms upon the body, i.e., upon its rational and imaginative faculties.

Maimonides is aware that he has presented these philosophical matters simply, without proving them, but he is disdainful of anyone who doubts them. He is interested in detailing at some length the *kalām* understanding of the world and proceeds with that in chapter 73. He offers a list of twelve premises that underlie the arguments of the *kalām* treatises that he has studied or heard discussed, a list that is apparently an original compilation and synthesis. It is not representative of the ideas of all the *mutakallimūn,* as scholarship has shown,[29] but is credible, on the whole, both historically and logically. Maimonides gives us a picture of *kalām* that is certainly not a straw man, for all his critique of it.

Kalām is known for its doctrine of atomism, the momentary existence of indivisible particles of being that have no properties whatsoever of their own. They exist together with "accidents," i.e., properties that happen to be attached to them but have no necessary connection that would guarantee continuation of the given body and its activities beyond the instant of their creation. All of nature is dependent on God's will and His "continuous re-creation" of the world. In this view, God graces us with the illusion of a natural order of things, of permanence and causal relations, but these are not inherent in nature; there is no necessity to nature, there is no nature.

Maimonides presents *kalām* thought mainly in this radical posture, though he is aware that some Mu'tazilites (the more "rational" group of *mutakallimūn*) modified this radical occasionalism in the direction of a provisional causality, believing in relations and objects that had some duration and did not depend upon God's constant re-creation of them, while not receiving essential autonomy either.[30]

Maimonides' list of *kalām* premises includes the atomization and fragmentation of time and space, time atomized into momentary "nows" without any necessary or dependable relation between them;[31] the existence of atoms and accidents as self-contained successive (though not related) units of being; the existence of a vacuum; the equally unprivileged status of any state of an object, so that both the presence and the absence of a given "property" are equally possible and unrelated accidents dependent upon an "efficient cause," i.e., God;[32] the impossibility of infinity in any form; and the rejection of sense data as reliable sources of judgment and demonstration.[33]

There is one other premise, the tenth one, that Maimonides considers the "main proposition" of *kalām*. It gets to the heart of his quarrel with the *mutakallimūn*. Maimonides first describes it as premising that "the possibility of a thing should not be considered in establishing a correspondence between that which exists and mental representation."[34] As he later says,[35] this premise asserts that anything that may be imagined is admissible (*jā'iz*) conceptually; that is, a thought does not have to represent anything existing to be existentially possible. Whatever may be imagined may possibly exist, since there are no necessary constraints or rules to nature.

Maimonides uses a dialogical style in presenting the arguments for and against this premise, which hinges on the weight given or denied to the concept of possibility and the philosophical or antiphilosophical framework in which it is posited. Maimonides is aware that his opponents are not logically naïve, they do not consider that logically contradictory propositions may be validated existentially. They limit such propositions to strictly logical impossibilities, however, and view empirically based definitions as having no necessary validity that precludes alternative imaginative possibilities.

This premise repudiates the scientist's assumption of a predictable, defined universe. It gives God the sole responsibility for allowing us to perceive the world as we do, with the illusion of permanence. Maimonides places God at the head of the natural order but believes that there is such an order and that it is necessary to oppose those who would dismiss it. His opposition to this premise does not belie his acknowledgment of its strength,[36] yet the attempt to refute it speaks volumes for his commitment to philosophy and to a natural world order, despite his awareness of the limitations of the philosopher's argument.

Maimonides proceeds in chapter 74 to describe *kalām* proofs for the creation of the world. Particularly interesting and favored by both the *mutakallimūn* and Maimonides[37] is the fifth "method," that of "particularization," *al-takhṣīṣ*. Based upon the tenth premise that allows possible existence to anything that may be imagined, this method regards that which exists as the product of a deliberate selection or particularization that differentiates it from all its possible alternative manifestations. There are no necessary causes that can explain why an object has one set of particular attributes rather than another; everything depends upon God's free choice and will. When Maimonides later adopts this method, he is brought to it from lack of scientific data with which to explain the movements of the spheres. His use of this argument is thus due to lack of data; for him it is not an a priori principle, as is the case with the *mutakallimūn.*

In the seventh method, Maimonides takes to task a particular argument he says the *mutakallimūn* use to bolster their opposition to the concept of infinity. The argument attempts to reject the notion of an eternal universe by positing that in such a world there would have to be an infinite number of simultaneously existing immortal souls. As it is logically contradictory to posit that an infinite number of numerable things can exist simultaneously, the world cannot be eternal, in this view.

Maimonides dismisses this argument first by referring to the "hidden" nature of the topic, the survival of the soul. Then Maimonides gives the opinions of "some of the later philosophers" that immortal souls would not, without bodies, be subject to enumeration in place and position, so that they would not constitute an infinite number. Maimonides essentially confirms his agreement with this view,[38] mentioning that intellects, as separate from matter, are not subject to multiplicity or differentiation except as involves causal relations (having in mind the intellects of the spheres). As for human beings, though, "what remains of Zayd is neither the cause nor the effect of what remains of Umar." All are one in number, Maimonides concludes, concurring with other philosophers, and mentioning Ibn Bājja specifically.[39]

Maimonides thus reiterates a view he touched on before,[40] one that directly denies the individual immortality of the soul, and with it the sense of an enduring personality. The intellect that survives death is joined with others insofar as it adheres to universal truths, these truths part of the one universal Agent Intellect, as we shall see.

In chapter 75, Maimonides outlines some of the proofs that the *mutakallimūn* bring for the unity of God. Like most of the proofs adduced for the creation of the world, these proofs attempt to establish their point by refuting counterarguments. Thus, the "first method" described assumes that two gods would necessarily hinder each other, willing contrary actions. Here, as in the related "fifth method,"[41] Maimonides responds that it is conceivable for a god (the nature of whose oneness has not yet been proved) to have a limited purview that would not conflict with the actions of another deity. It is not a deficiency or weakness in the gods if it is impossible for them to exert influence upon things beyond their sphere of control.[42]

Maimonides further supports this rebuttal with his opinion, which he claims is that of "the community of believers in [God's] unity," that "it is no deficiency in the One that He does not conjoin contraries in one substratum, and His power is not affected by this and by other similar impossibilities."

Other examples of such impossibilities that Maimonides attests as commonly accepted (by Jews) is God's inability to "corporify His essence or to create someone like Him or to create a square whose diagonal is equal to its side."[43] These are not "incapacities" in God, as the propositions affirming such are logical absurdities for Maimonides, given his definition of God and of geometric entities.

Maimonides thus faults the *mutakallimūn* for assuming what they have not proved, viz., God's unity, even as he does just that. While they would have agreed with him that logical absurdities do not bear on divine limitations, they could have challenged him (though being Muslim they would not) on the logical necessity to deny incarnation or the multiplication of deities, as he has not provided argument to that effect. Beyond the polemical thrust of Maimonides' discourse, however, is his apparent acceptance of "limitations" on God's abilities that are based on logical definitions of His nature, limitations that have physical entailments that may follow necessarily from them. This will become clearer in our discussion of Maimonides' view of God's relation to matter and evil.

In chapter 76, Maimonides describes and rebuts *kalām* disproofs of the corporeality of God. While the *kalām* notion of corporeality is based on atoms that problematize God's unity, Maimonides acting as devil's advocate posits a notion of a continuous indivisible body that can withstand such criticism, the notion being logical in itself though totally foreign to atomistic assumptions. The *kalām* definition of body does not exclude the notion of a continuous indivisible body.

Maimonides also argues against the *kalām* proofs for God's uniqueness, it being a major tenet of Islam, as well as Judaism, that it is impossible for anything to resemble God. At first, Maimonides finds that partial resemblances are not logically absurd, but he favors a "more arduous," philosophically established argument that would have any resemblance be considered as posited in a "purely equivocal" sense, *bi-ishtirāq maḥḍ*. Thus God can have a body, though of a kind unique to him, not resembling any other.[44]

Maimonides compares this view to that of "those who have reached true knowledge of reality," who attribute "being" to God in an equivocal manner. Maimonides is one of those who do just that, so his opposition to attributing corporeality to God in an equivocal manner is somewhat puzzling, assuming he accepts "pure" or absolute equivocation. Apparently, his animus against the notion of God's having a body, however equivocally meant, is so great that he cannot entertain the idea at all.

Maimonides' interlocutor now is apparently Jewish, for Maimonides refers to views that attribute unique bodies to the Shekhinah[45] and to the "Pillar of

Cloud" that accompanied the Israelites in their desert wanderings. Though he considers this entire view "sick" (*saqīm*), Maimonides feels it cannot be refuted by *kalām* arguments.

Analysis

In this section of the *Guide,* Maimonides contrasts two visions of reality. One is an essentially Aristotelian natural philosophy, the other a theologically prescribed atomism. Maimonides sides with the philosophical view and offers a brief description of the basic tenets of its physics and metaphysics. He reserves his doubts about the validity of Aristotelian metaphysics for later, being concerned to settle his quarrel with the theological position first.

The theologians of Islam were proficient in *'ilm al-kalām,* "the science of *kalām.*" *Kalām* is a term that literally means "speech" or "language," the paradigm of which was the speech of God in the Qur'ān. The *mutakallimūn* were those men who wished to rationalize that speech, verbalize a worldview that would support their desire to understand God and His relation to the world in logical terms. Their point of departure, based on the Qur'an, was that He is the Creator of the world, an omnipotent, omniscient, and just being whose nature is beyond human comprehension.

The *mutakallimūn* believed that God, in his compassion for humanity, gives us the illusion of perceiving a natural body that has permanent or at least enduring properties. Mostly, they saw Him as recreating the world each instant through momentary combinations of atoms (*jawāhir,* sing. *jawhar*) and "accidents" *(a'rāḍ,* sing. *'araḍ*). Nothing has substantive weight of its own.

In this manner, the *mutakallimūn* gave voice to a deep sensibility in Islam that echoed the Qur'ān's insistence on God's unilateral sovereignty in the world, not to be challenged by any "natural" law or normative physical intermediaries. The *mutakallimūn* saw the scientific tradition to which the philosophers subscribed, even though it came to accommodate traditional religious beliefs in many instances, as positing an autonomous or semi-autonomous natural world. In their animus against philosophy, the *mutakallimūn* developed arguments voiced earlier by John Philoponus and other Christian thinkers against Aristotle's scientific treatises, becoming sophisticated advocates of their position.[46]

The philosophers, on the other hand, viewed the *mutakallimūn* as dogmatic and pseudorational thinkers, threatening the legitimacy of scientific inquiry in Islam. Alfarabi, Avicenna, and Averroes all opposed the *mutakallimūn,* Averroes trying valiantly to rebut Al-Ghazālī's *Incoherence of the Philosophers* in his *Incoherence of the Incoherence.*

Maimonides is thus following a venerable philosophical tradition in challenging the views and methodology of the *mutakallimūn.* Nor is he favorably disposed to earlier Jewish writers like Saadia Gaon who compromised their attempts at philosophizing with *kalām*-style arguments. In the *Guide,* however, Maimonides ignores his Jewish predecessors and attacks the Muslim adherents of *kalām,* though without mentioning any by name. His description of their tenets and arguments is a pastiche drawn from various sources,[47] an attempt to get at what he believes is the heart of their arguments, describe the major schools of *kalām* thought, and persuade the reader of the sophistic nature of their reasoning. Maimonides is engaged in a polemic against *kalām* teachings, and like all polemicists, he may be simplifying and distorting the complex and qualified positions of his adversaries. The picture of *kalām* that emerges is thus not representative of the rich diversity of views held by the *mutakallimūn,* but rather reflects Maimonides' own projection of their key premises, arranged systematically, as is his practice.[48]

The reader of the *Guide* is ostensibly (and in all likelihood was originally) a Jewish intellectual who was attracted to the methodology and entire theological orientation of the *mutakallimūn.* Maimonides was aware that *kalām* could be attractive to a bright and devout person, and that its core arguments for an omnipotent Creator could be adopted by Jews (and Christians) as well as by Muslims. Karaite Jewish authors had already shown an affinity for *kalām* arguments, and Maimonides may have feared its appeal to Rabbanite scholars too.

The Rabbanite tradition lacked a systematic theology that incorporated a scientific worldview, leaving a void that Maimonides tried to fill, in outline form, in his rabbinic writings. Now, in the *Guide,* he is explicit in attempting to construct a theology based on classical philosophical sources. He felt it his duty to refute *kalām* arguments and the principles on which they were based, convinced that the path to God's presence lay solely through study of science and philosophy.

Maimonides feels most challenged by what he calls the tenth premise of the *mutakallimūn,* calling it "the main proposition of the science of *kalām.*"[49] It is the affirmation that whatever may be imagined may possibly occur, short of logically absurd (because self-contradictory) statements. Future events are not limited to the range of previous experience and the categorization of it in generic, universal terms. The intellect must accept as "admissible" (almost) whatever possibilities the imagination places before it.[50]

Maimonides presents the view of a *mutakallim* on this issue as best he can, but pauses to issue a "call" to the reader's attention, a summons (*tanbīh*)[51] or reminder of what for him are the epistemological facts of life. He offers what is in effect a paean to the human intellect. It is the faculty that distinguishes man from other animals (and relates him to God). It takes the individual impressions of objects that the imaginative faculty presents it with and abstracts from them to determine the essence and attributes predicated of its subject and to understand the matrix of causes with which the object is involved and which help define it.[52] It is the intellect and not the imagination that constructs the universal terms by which we define objects and delimit their possibilities.

Maimonides brings "demonstrated proofs" from the mathematical sciences as evidence of the superiority of the intellectual faculty to that of the imagination, in assessing what is "admissible" to imagine as truly possible. Of course, the postulates of mathematics assume the existence of the world as we know it, an assumption that the *mutakallimūn* reject. Maimonides knows this and delineates the difference between the philosopher and the *mutakallim* in just this manner: the *faylasūf* accepts "that which exists" as the basis for distinguishing between the necessary, the possible, and the impossible; and the *mutakallim* rejects the objective facticity of "that which exists," seeing it as a product of divine will with no necessary entailments. The proofs that mathematics and other sciences bring do not compel the *mutakallim* to deny their nonnecessary and hence noncertain nature, as they are all contingent upon the will of God and could be imagined differently in different existential scenarios.

Maimonides is thus aware of the fundamental and unbridgeable difference between the basic existential premises of the philosophers and the *mutakallimūn*. He believes the latter do not accept the necessary validity of sense perceptions any more than the proofs that the intellect offers; their atomistic physics is a self-contained alternative reality.

Maimonides' quarrel with *kalām* is testimony, therefore, to his firm belief in the enduring existence of that world which presents itself to our senses and serves legitimately as the arbiter of that which may be possible, based on that which is and has been actual. This is the world that the Aristotelian philosophical tradition has largely described, recognizing the intellect's role in discerning essential and accidental properties of a thing, and establishing categories of thought and speech that identify an individual object in relation to other objects with which it shares common properties.

For Maimonides, then, the imagination is, or ought to be, controlled by the intellect. The imagination cannot function properly without depending on the concepts that the intellect provides, as a result of past experience. The atomistic theory of the *mutakallimūn* recognizes no necessary connection between past and present moments, and for Maimonides would be exploiting a discredited past in using terms that have no essential definitions. Each existential moment for the *mutakallimūn* is its own reality, created by God from nothing.

The *kalām* world for many of its adherents is thus a world of continuous *creatio ex nihilo,* supported by an elaborate atomistic physical theory. Maimonides will proceed to punch holes in the *kalām*'s proofs for creation, but as we shall see, he is not immune to the lure of positing creation from nothing on grounds not entirely unlike those posited by the *mutakallimūn.*

6

Philosophy Affirmed and Qualified; Creation (*Guide* Part II, Introduction and Chapters 1–31)

Paraphrase

Maimonides introduces the second part of the *Guide* by presenting the premises that the philosophers use to demonstrate the existence and oneness of God, as well as the impossibility of His being a body, including provisionally their premise that the world is eternal. Aristotle's *Physics* and *Metaphysics* are his primary sources, which he refers to by name, though the Stagirite's teachings reached Maimonides through the writings of Alexander of Aphrodisias, Avicenna, Alfarabi, and possibly Averroes as well.[1] The premises include notions of infinity, potentiality, and actuality; magnitude, change, and motion; essence and accident, time and body, matter and form; and causation in its various aspects.

As he does with the proofs of the *mutakallimūn,* Maimonides extracts a certain number of premises—in this case twenty-six—from his sources that he believes are required to demonstrate the existence, unity, and incorporeality of God. Twenty-five of these premises have already been demonstrated as indubitably true, he says (at first), concurring with this judgment and not feeling it necessary to prove them himself. The twenty-sixth premise, asserting the eternity of the world, does not, he feels, enjoy the status of certain truth, and he will interrogate it in due course.

The twenty-five premises begin with the concept of infinity and the assertion that it is impossible for there to be an infinite magnitude, or an infinite number of magnitudes, or an infinite number of causes and effects of an incorporeal nature, i.e., of intellects. Maimonides' first concern, therefore, is to establish the necessity for a first cause within a closed if eternal system, and to avoid an infinite regress of causes.

The eternity of the system is based upon the belief in the continuous, uninterrupted circular movement of celestial spheres, circular motion alone being regarded by Maimonides and the philosophers as guaranteeing continuity.[2] This movement occurs an infinite number of times, though at any one time it is a finite body that is traversing a finite distance. As Maimonides points out at the end of this part's introduction,[3] this infinity is one of succession, not simultaneity, the future movements and the time in which they occur being potential. This acceptance of the notion of potential infinity separates the philosophers from the *mutakallimūn* (and their Christian theological predecessors), Maimonides declares.

Maimonides lists the four kinds of change that Aristotle identified: that of generation and corruption, quantity, quality, and locomotion or change of place.[4] Maimonides introduces the key Aristotelian concepts of potentiality and actuality in the fifth premise, pointing out that every kind of motion is a change from potentiality to actuality, produced in the potential body by something actual external to it.[5] Bodies themselves are compounds of form and matter, the form not always divisible with the body, as is the case with the soul and the intellect of a body. Separate intellects (as in the heavens), being neither a body nor a force in a body, can be thought of as multiple only when they function as causes and effects.[6]

In the nineteenth and twentieth premises, Maimonides introduces the Avicennian concepts of possible and necessary existence, the former possible "in respect to its own essence" (*bi-i'tibār dhātihi*), being dependent on its component parts (form and matter) and on an external cause to become actual and, once actual, necessary. A thing that is necessarily existent "in respect to its own essence," on the other hand, has no cause at all for its existence; it is self-sustaining and immaterial. This will be God, of course.

In the twenty-third and twenty-fourth premises, Maimonides says that possible existents that are "*in potentia*" may not exist in actuality at a certain time, and that whatever is in potentiality (when it is latently present in something else) is necessarily endowed with matter, "for possibility is always in matter" (*li-anna al-imkān huwa fi al-māddah abadān*).[7] Matter is thus the locus for change, the site for the possible actualization of that which is potential. Of course, matter is but the substratum of form, and it is the form that exists potentially in a given matter that is realized.

Maimonides concludes his discussion of the twenty-five premises as he began it, with the statement that all of them have received (by others) demonstrative proofs that are indubitable.[8] He then proceeds to sketch out the twenty-sixth premise, that of the eternity of the world, eternal in both its time and its movement. Given the finite magnitude of the world, the continuous movement of the spheres is again attributed to their circular motion, as stated before in the thirteenth premise. This premise, Maimonides adds, also asserts that "that which is infinite must necessarily exist as a succession and not simultaneously."[9]

The *mutakallimūn* deny this notion of a temporal succession of an infinite number of things, Maimonides says. They find the notion unintelligible; it violates a "first intelligible," that is, a basic premise, of their system (by which Maimonides is probably referring to their denial of essential duration in an object). Aristotle's successors, on the other hand, believed this principle to be necessary.

Maimonides then declares he considers the premise possible, neither necessary nor impossible, and defers further discussion of it. It appears that he is referring to the thirteenth premise, but that raises a problem, in that he has stated repeatedly that all twenty-five premises, including the thirteenth, had been demonstrated and were indubitably certain. It is only the twenty-sixth premise that Maimonides identifies as undemonstrated, claiming Aristotle himself believed it correct simply as "the most adequate and fitting" of assertions on the topic.[10]

Hence, it is this twenty-sixth premise that Maimonides must be referring to when he says, "This is the premise that Aristotle constantly wishes to establish as true."[11] The thirteenth premise is central to the belief in the continuous motion of the spheres and thus bears upon the argument for eternal motion that is given as the twenty-sixth premise, but we must wait until chapter 15 to learn Maimonides' reason for thinking that the latter premise, and the former, indeed all of Aristotle's premises are merely possible, neither necessary nor impossible.[12]

Maimonides begins chapter 1 of the second part of the *Guide* with arguments based on the premises just outlined to demonstrate the necessity for believing in a single noncorporeal existent that is the ultimate cause of movement in the world, and specifically of the movement of the spheres. The activity of forms and matter on earth is derived from the movement of the heavenly bodies and the forces they generate.[13] Following his Aristotelian model, Maimonides concentrates here on the physics and interrelations of bodies and leaves the formal dimension of intelligible and universal ideas aside, for the time being. His explication of the philosophers' reasoning is concise and logically rigorous, following the style he set in detailing and critiquing *kalām* teachings, but without the polemical or dialogical dimension that he resorted to there.

The first argument Maimonides presents on behalf of the philosophers establishes the need for a mover of the first (or outermost) sphere, the motion of which is deemed the cause of all subsequent movements.[14] Through a process of elimination, Maimonides shows that the mover of the sphere cannot be another body or a force within the sphere. The latter hypothesis would render the force a component of the body of the sphere and hence an "accident" requiring a cause for its combining with the matter of the sphere. As every accidental motion in a body comes to rest eventually, and the body of the first sphere (and the other spheres) is thought to be in perpetual motion, the mover of the spheres must be outside it.

Maimonides thus argues in the name of the philosophers that the first mover of the world, i.e., the mover of the body of the first sphere, has to be a cause that is outside the world as a whole, being separate from the sphere and from anything material. "The mover of this sphere would have no movement, either according to essence or to accident, and would not be subject to division or to change . . . Now this is the deity [*al-Ilāh*], may his name be sublime."[15]

This first argument thus posits a deity that is an unmoved mover. Separate from body, this divine being has no principle of quantification, therefore cannot be multiplied, and must be a single unique entity. Not in motion, it has no relation to time (which measures the movement of bodies) and is therefore unchangeable.

Another argument that Maimonides brings on behalf of the philosophers argues for the necessary existence of some being that is not subject to generation and corruption.[16] Without such an eternal being, all other possibly existent beings would be candidates for annihilation. Their possible corruption would have to be realized at some time, as a possibility that is never realized is not a true possibility.[17] The necessarily existent being, moreover, must be such in respect of its own essence, uncaused. As such, it cannot have components, i.e., be composed of multiple notions that would require a cause; and therefore it cannot be a body or a force in a body. There cannot be more than one such being either, for that would introduce a species of necessarily existent beings that would compromise the essential simplicity of the Necessary Existent. This being represents to Maimonides "absolute simplicity and absolute perfection," and again he says, "It is He who is the deity, may His name be sublime."[18]

In another, similar proof, Maimonides conflates potentiality and possibility, arguing that whatever has potentiality requires an actual agent to bring it forth, and that in turn needs its agent, being potential previously. This chain of potential cause and effect cannot go on to infinity, given the existence of actual beings now. Thus, there must be a first cause that is purely actual and has no potentiality or possibility of nonexistence, and no material aspect, being separate from matter.

Maimonides mentions in this proof that one of the reasons a cause might not have its intended effect can be that a hindrance prevents it, and this reason will come to play a significant role in explaining what are often held to be examples of divine injustice.[19]

Maimonides adduces additional but related arguments to prove that there can only be one god, lest the self-sufficient simplicity and character of the deity as "necessary of existence" in respect of its own essence be compromised. Maimonides finds it absurd to assume that two (or more) deities could relate to the world at separate times, as this would involve them in the world temporally and hence spatially. This would entail that "each one of them, at the time of his action, would have to pass from potentiality to actuality," which potentiality would also introduce possibility into their essence.[20]

In chapter 2, Maimonides starts to present a short version, or "epitome" (*talkhīṣ*) as he calls it, of "our" method, by which he means his own, and that which other Jews should adopt, for demonstrating the existence, unity, and incorporeality of God. He feels the Aristotelian/philosophers' arguments for the existence of such a deity that he has described are valid should the world be eternal, i.e., if the fifth body (which contains the heavenly spheres) is not subject to generation and corruption; while if the fifth body along with the ensuing world is not eternal but created, then it is in need of a creator who has brought it into existence from nonexistence.

Maimonides is not focusing here on the question of the nature of such a transition; he will deal with alternative scenarios of creation later. More important, he is not troubled by identifying the Creator God with a deity who has been identified as necessarily existing in respect of its essence. That is, Maimonides believes that the philosophers' proofs of God's existence and nature remain valid whether the physics of the universe are coeternal with God or are subsequent to His creation. Maimonides' confidence in the nature and de facto permanence of the natural world order is unassailable. His conceptualization of God follows naturally from his physics and sense of logical imperatives and is unimaginable apart from the world (however separate and ultimately unimaginable He purportedly is).

Perhaps Maimonides' daring equation of the philosophers' god with the God of Israel causes him to pause in this chapter. Before proceeding to discuss the philosophers' proofs regarding the existence of separate celestial intellects and their identification with the angels of religious tradition, another bold assertion that many of his readers would have found offensive, Maimonides feels obliged to write a small preface that he says should be borne in mind throughout his work. In it he reiterates his introductory remarks that his purpose in the *Guide* is not to compose a philosophical treatise on physics or metaphysics, but rather to show that the subjects of these disciplines can be brought to bear upon difficult areas in the religious tradition, particularly as regards prophecy and knowledge of God and His law.

It is the secrets in the traditionally named Account of the Beginning and the Account of the Chariot that Maimonides wishes to disclose (to those prepared to understand his esoteric language), but it becomes clear that it is Aristotelian-based physics and metaphysics, respectively, that give Maimonides access to this (alleged) tradition and allow him to refashion it. He is interpreting the faith along borrowed philosophical lines,[21] giving it a rational interpretation that he believes it needs in order to be acceptable.

Maimonides concludes his preface by remarking that he will now return to explaining the nature of the separate intellects of the spheres. He hesitates to do so, however, without first saying, in chapter 3, that Aristotle's views on this topic have not been demonstrated as true, and that they are simply the views on this theme least subject to doubt and the most coherent.[22] They also harmonize well with biblical and midrashic teachings, elucidating which is his principal goal in writing the *Guide,* as he has just stated. Thus, while Maimonides would like to believe that philosophy has demonstrated the nature of the deity, he knows that philosophy has not proved its theses about the mechanisms whereby God relates to the world, which is the subtext of the metaphysical issues he is about to address.

In chapter 4, Maimonides gives the reason Aristotle and his followers posited that each sphere in the heavens is endowed with a soul that has an intellectual aspect.[23] It was in order to explain the unique movements of the spheres, conceived as circular and unending. The soul functions as what we may call the efficient or mechanical cause of the sphere's movement, its intellect as its formal cause, the intellect conceiving of an object that attracts the soul, the soul then moving the sphere in which they reside. While inanimate bodies move by compulsion, and return to their "place" when the external cause of their movement subsides, the continuous, uninterrupted motion of the spheres—a feature unique to circular motion—indicates that they are not compelled to move in ways contrary to their nature. The immediate cause of their movement, their intelligent soul, is thus internal to the spheres.

The intellect is necessary in order, as it were, to set the compass of the sphere's movement, which it does through a "certain mental representation" (*taṣawwur mā*) of perfection that it has. This representation is "a notion that is most exceedingly simple, in which there is no change and no coming-about of a new state, and from which good always emanates."[24] As Maimonides says, this "notion" is of the Deity.

The intellect of the (first) sphere responds to this idea of God with a desire to emulate Him by having the sphere be as perfect as it can be. This can be expressed only by simple and perpetual circular motion, devoid of any change in its essence or in its emanation of "good effects" (*al-khayarāt*). The "final cause" of the movements of the spheres is thus the deity, in imitation of whom the spheres strive for perfection.

God, however, is a remote final cause for all but the first intellect of the highest, or outermost, sphere. Each of the other spheres' intellects relates to the "separate," i.e., immaterial, intellect of the sphere above it that serves as the proximate final cause for the next lower sphere's motion. Though Maimonides insists that God or, as he chooses to call Him here, the "Necessary of Existence" (i.e., the Necessary Existent) is not the intellect that moves the outermost sphere either, it is difficult to remove Him from that role in the scheme that Maimonides has adopted. He wants to preserve God's singularity or simplicity by excluding Him from the category of separate intellects. However, without God as the direct object of its intellection, the separate intellect of the outermost sphere would lack a reason or cause for its action.[25]

The animated intellects of other spheres—and Maimonides counts ten such, as do other post-Aristotelian philosophers—thus may be said to have two final causes of motion: God as the remote cause, and the separate intellect of the preceding sphere as the proximate cause. In a downward spiral of effects, the motions of the heavenly bodies—and particularly of the sun and moon—determine the material composition of our earth, even as the tenth or last of the separate intellects, the intellect that presides over the sublunar body that is earth, is its final as well as formal cause.

As Maimonides has mentioned elsewhere, the matter on earth is different from that of the heavenly bodies, and is characterized by inconstancy and change, taking on a myriad of forms. All these forms are seen as deriving from the Agent (or Active) Intellect (*al-ʿaql al-faʿāl*) by the same process of emanation that pervades the universe, an overflowing of "good effects."[26] As do the intellects of the spheres, so the intellects of human beings respond to the conception they have of their final causes, both the deity and the Agent Intellect; they desire to emulate them, as much as is possible, by achieving intellectual perfection through knowledge of them.

Maimonides uses chapter 5 to assert the agreement of the Bible and midrashic literature with the philosophical notion of the spheres as "living [and] rational" (*ḥayyah nāṭiqah*), i.e., animated and intelligent beings. He also believes that the philosophers' description of the spheres' movements entitles him to claim it expresses the heavens' obedience to the Lord and praise of Him, as Scripture asserts. Both the Bible and the philosophers agree too, Maimonides says, that the spheres "apprehend and know that which they govern,"[27] the governance (*tadbīr*) achieved by the spheres' emanation of forms and matter on earth.

As intelligent beings, the spheres are aware of their movement and its effects. However, all this is contained in the one mental conceptualization that each intellect has, expressed by its uniform motion and unchanging emanative power. Thus the spheres know the world here and "govern" it insofar as they know themselves. Maimonides hints at this at the close of the chapter, mentioning the "true reality of governance" that he will discuss at length elsewhere. It will bear directly upon his notion of God's governance of the world.

In chapter 6, Maimonides daringly expands the term "angels" beyond his already bold identification of them with the intellects of the spheres, to denote every natural force through which God shapes the world. As Maimonides says, "all forces are angels."[28] He finds midrashic support for the view that God acts only through these "angelic" intermediaries, whose presence Maimonides detects in the miracles and prophetic visions recorded in the Bible. Consequently, he also identifies the imaginative faculty in man, critically important in prophecy, as an angel, though deferring further discussion of this and the entire subject of prophecy to a later chapter.

At one point, Maimonides draws attention to the similarity between a midrashic gloss that takes God's statement "Let us make man in our image" (Genesis 11:17) as implying the presence (and for Maimonides the participation) of angels at creation and Plato's statement that God created the world after looking "at the world of the intellects," that is, at the eternal ideas.[29] This may indicate that Maimonides has a certain sympathy for the Platonic notion of creation, a sympathy that Maimonides will evince later as well.

At the end of this chapter, however, it is only Aristotle with whom Maimonides is concerned. He reiterates his view that Aristotle's view of the role the heavens play in forming the earth agrees with that of the Jewish tradition, or "the Law" (*al-shari'a*), as Maimonides calls it, except for one critical issue. Whereas in Aristotle the system is eternal and all proceeds necessarily, "we ourselves believe," says Maimonides, that God created the separate intellects, the spheres, and their governing forces.

In chapter 7, Maimonides distinguishes the "angelic" action of the separate intellects and their spheres from that of inanimate forces of nature. Only the former apprehend, choose, and govern their actions.[30] Maimonides immediately qualifies his remarks, claiming that the choice and governance the spheres and their intellects have are different from ours. Where we must contend with actions (and governance) that are at times inadequate and always preceded by inactivity or, as Maimonides says, "privation," the intellects and spheres "always do that which is good, and only that which is good is with them." As Maimonides says, he will explain this several chapters later, but he concludes with the additional remark, "all that they [the separate intellects and spheres] have exists always in perfection and *in actu* since they have come into existence."

Maimonides embarks upon a discussion of astronomical issues in chapters 8–11, reporting on the advances made in the field since Aristotle's day, and its problematic current status. Maimonides shows considerable familiarity with the subject and states that he studied texts with a pupil of one of the leading Muslim astronomers of Andalusia.

Maimonides' first concern is to declare his belief in the existence of four astral spheres, or "globes": the sphere of "fixed" or stationary stars; the sphere that encompasses the five planets;[31] the sphere of the sun; and that of the moon. Maimonides finds the number four "wondrous" (*'ajîb*),[32] as evidenced in midrash as well as in an arrangement in the universe that he finds quite possible. Thus, he points out that the number of forces proceeding from the four astral spheres onto earth is four, the elements here are four, and there are four causes of the spheres' movements.[33]

Again, Maimonides insists that the motion of the spheres has to be circular in order for it to be continuous and always return to the same place. He sees this as entailing the existence in the body of the sphere of an intellect and a soul that, respectively, conceive and desire that which is conceived. Maimonides also reiterates the position he mentioned in *Guide* 1.72 that the four general forces that proceed from the motion of the spheres account for the generation of minerals and the vegetative, animal, and rational soul.[34] Maimonides clearly is taken with what he perceives to be order and harmony in the universe, revealed through the recurrence of a fourfold programmatic scheme. He closes the chapter with unmasked contempt for those who fail to see this, though by his own admission he has offered only a possible interpretation of the workings of the cosmos.

In chapter 11, however, Maimonides casts doubt on the accuracy of his astronomic model, saying in effect that it is more demonstrable mathematically than it is empirically. Based on observation, the astronomers cannot prove whether the sphere of the sun's motion is eccentric or epicyclic,[35] so they cling to the view of circular uniform movement because of the coherence of that view with their assumptions. Maimonides says he sides with Ptolemy in assuming the sun has an eccentric motion, not immediately spelling out the problem this view poses to the uniformly circular harmony of his scheme.

Maimonides can skirt the issue he raises here because his purpose, he says, is "to count all the forces that we have apprehended in a general way in that which exists without troubling to give a precise account of the true reality of the intellects and the spheres."[36] His real purpose, he contends, is to emphasize the division of all existent being into three kinds: separate intellects, spherical bodies, and bodies subject to generation and corruption with a common (prime) matter.

Moreover, Maimonides says, his purpose in describing the heavens is to show that there is an emanation of "governance" from God that passes from the separate intellects of the spheres to the bodies of the spheres and on to earthly matter. Each level of being receives "good things" (*khayarāt*)[37] as an expression of this governance, the good being that which fulfills its nature.

Emanation from the deity of a dynamic and intelligent form of being is, then, the medium through which the first of the separate intellects comes into existence (*îjâd*), and through which ultimately each empowered intellect brings the next into being, until the Agent Intellect is reached. Additionally, the separate intellects have the emanative ability to bring the matter of the spheres into being, followed by the spheres' emanating effect upon sublunar bodies.

Maimonides takes care to point out that emanation is a process that follows from God's nature and is not intended (primarily) for the benefit of the recipients. One could say accordingly that God's governance of the world is not specifically intentional. Perhaps it is owing to this realization that Maimonides next feels it incumbent to explain the "true reality" (*ḥaqīqa*) of emanation, in chapter 12.

Emanation, Maimonides stresses, is a process whereby a form is transmitted from an immaterial agent to an object when its matter is prepared to receive it.[38] The giver of the form, being a separate intellect, is in a state of constant actuality and not in a necessary relation with the receiver. As the matter of the heavenly bodies is unchanging, it is always receptive of the forms that are emanated upon it. The changeable nature of matter on earth, however, causes emanation to affect each being here diversely, individuating their forms.

While admitting the inadequacy of the comparison and terminology, Maimonides remarks that "it has been said" that God, as the incorporeal "efficient cause" of the universe, is the source for this emanative process: "He has emanated upon [the world] everything in it that comes into being [*kullu mā yuḥdathu fīhu*]."[39] It has also "been said," Maimonides adds, that "He caused his Knowledge to emanate upon the prophets," bringing prophecy within an explanatory theory of a "natural" and impersonal kind, implicitly disassociating God from a direct relation with any one thing or person.

Maimonides proceeds to indict the imaginative faculty as incapable of representing incorporeal objects and relations, leading "some of the mass of people" (*baʿḍ al-jumhūr*) to imagine all sorts of things he finds radically wrong.[40] This includes representing God as commanding the angels, the angels as having direct contact with people, and God as communicating through speech similar to human speech.

Maimonides stops himself here, saying in effect that he has digressed from the object of the chapter, which is to understand emanation as regards God and the separate intellects/angels. He adds that emanation may also be used to explain the effect of the spheres' actions, though they proceed from the body of the sphere. Apparently he regards the forces communicated by the spheres as akin to the forms that the intellects emanate, in that the forces exercise their power also at a distance from their objects. This is true although the body of the sphere affects bodies on earth, and its physical power is affected by the distance between them, whereas the force of the separate intellects, being separated from physical properties, is not so affected and is restricted to the formal properties of bodies.[41]

In closing, Maimonides quotes from Psalm 36:10, "In thy light do we see light," interpreting it to mean, "through the intellect that has emanated from you we use our intellect, are guided correctly, derive proofs, and apprehend the [Agent] Intellect." Succinctly then, Maimonides is saying that emanation is the key to his cosmogony and epistemology, using "emanation" in both the classical sense of an overflow of formal causes and as a more general term for a celestial outpouring of material effects.

Maimonides changes the topic in chapter 13 to discuss an issue central to his task of offering a rapprochement between philosophy and Jewish belief, namely, whether the world is eternal or created, assuming in either case that a deity exists. He describes three views held: that of "all who believe in the Law [*shariʿa*] of Moses our Master"; that of Plato; and that of Aristotle.[42]

The Jewish view as Maimonides presents it is that God brought the world into existence from nonexistence, or more literally, "after pure and absolute privation" *baʿda al-ʿadam al-maḥḍ al-muṭlaq*. Initially, God existed alone, and "then" (*thumma*) He brought everything, including time, into existence "not from a thing," *lā min shay*.'[43] God acted, in this view, solely "through His will and volition,"[44] which in Maimonides' opinion should equal each other, and both be equal to God's (unchanging) simple essence.

Maimonides informs the reader not to take the (apparently) temporal dimension of God's action literally, since time is a function or "accident" of motion, as Aristotle has said, and was therefore created with it, in this (non-Aristotelian) construal. The world and time are not eternal, they both begin with God's bringing them into existence in a moment that has no antecedence. This view of a created world, Maimonides says, is a basic belief of the law of Moses, second only to belief in God's Oneness, and no other view should be entertained.

The second view Maimonides describes is essentially that of Plato, though Maimonides attributes it in addition to all other philosophers besides Aristotle.[45] In this view the matter of the world is eternal, since it is impossible for God to generate it out of pure ontic nothingness, or "privation." Creating something *from* absolutely nothing is a logical and hence empirical impossibility; it is self-contradictory, and its impossibility does not imply a deficiency on God's part. Even He cannot overturn the "firmly established nature" of what is inherently, logically, impossible.

Though the matter of the world is co-eternal with the deity in this view, it is not co-equal in rank, for He is the willing cause of the particular forms matter assumes. Both heaven and earth are created in this way, and may pass away in due time as well, though not into nothingness, which logically would be impossible also. A thing cannot change into nothing; absolute privation or nothingness does not exist as a meaningful possibility for that which exists.

Aristotle's opinion in this matter, according to Maimonides, is like Plato's, but goes beyond it in extending the world's eternity to its material as well as formal dimensions. Thus, not only are the heavens not subject to generation and corruption, but the species on earth are also not so subject. Indeed, "this whole higher and lower order cannot be corrupted and abolished."[46] Individuals may perish (though their matter does not, absolutely), but the species and order of things are permanent.

Maimonides' Aristotle is modified with post-Aristotelian contributions, as is clear by Maimonides' contention that Aristotle believed that the deity has a will through which He brought the universe into existence. That is, the world is co-eternal with God but yet caused by a divine will that cannot change, any more than can the simple unitary image of God as the unmoved mover. Of course, that oneness of the divine being leaves no room for the divine will as a separate attribute of God. Therefore, the divine will is both unchanging and undifferentiated from any other attribute one might assign to God, e.g., divine wisdom, and is solely germane to the relation of God to the world as its cause. It is, though, a necessary volition, and Maimonides will challenge Aristotle on this point.

Maimonides closes the chapter with the statement that it is "useless" to debate the second, Platonic, position, for it is essentially the same as Aristotle's, even if they differ on whether the heavens (and earth) are subject to generation and corruption.

Following his declared intention, Maimonides begins chapter 14 with a synopsis of Aristotelian and post-Aristotelian arguments for an eternal universe.[47] The first argument asserts that motion itself, and the time that is attached to it, are not subject to generation and corruption, for everything that moves (or everything that changes) is preceded by something that is also in motion, effecting the change. To avoid an infinite regress of causes, a first motion, necessarily eternal, must be posited.

The second argument Maimonides brings concerns the necessarily eternal nature of first or prime matter. Were it a generated substance, it would need a formal principle to generate it, whereas by definition prime matter is without form, being a substrate for forms. Not being generated, prime matter, the material basis of all physical objects, must be eternal.

A third argument is based on the circular motion of the heavenly bodies. As such motion has no contrary to impede its uniform and constant motion, it is not subject to passing away. That which is eternal in one direction is (by definition) equally eternal in the other, so the matter of the heavens is eternal.

A fourth argument gives in effect the philosophical response to the *kalām* notion of possibility. As everything produced in time had the possibility before that of being realized, the world, before it was created, would have had that as a possibility. Yet a world created from absolutely nothing would lack a substratum, or underlying matter, which is the necessary condition for this possibility. As Maimonides says, "there indubitably must be an existent thing that is the substratum of this possibility and in virtue of which it is said of the thing that it is possible."[48]

Maimonides supplements these Aristotelian arguments with a number of arguments for an eternal universe derived from Aristotle's teachings by Proclus and others. One concerns the need to posit God as a potential agent before He acted as an actual agent in creating the world, were He to have done so. Potentiality implies possibility, which requires a cause to realize it, and God is understood to be uncaused and unchanging.

Another argument assumes that God would have no reason to act at any particular time, since there are no circumstances that require Him to change. His will is never impeded; it is always active, and has always been so. Thus at no time would God have created the world; He could not without contradicting His nature.

A third, similar argument contends that God is the very acme of perfection, and the world is governed with wisdom, nature acting "in the most perfect possible way."[49] As God's wisdom, which equals His essence, is eternal, so is the product of that wisdom, the world. The notion of God's unchanging perfection underlies a related, anti-Platonic argument that Maimonides mentions, for it sees the deity as having no more reason to create past multiple worlds than to have created a single one yesterday, both being impossible by (Aristotle's) definition of God.

In Chapter 15, Maimonides begins his critique of the Aristotelian position by claiming that Aristotle did not himself believe he had demonstrated that the world is eternal, though his followers thought he did.[50] Maimonides interprets certain rhetorical statements Aristotle makes as proof that he lacked more stringent proofs.[51] He does believe Aristotle's opinion is more correct than other opinions, "in so far as inferences are made from the nature of what exists,"[52] but Maimonides does not want to grant his arguments certain truth.

In chapter 16, Maimonides claims that neither the arguments for an eternal nor those for a created world are logically demonstrable,[53] and that all the philosophical proofs for eternity have a "certain point [*wajh*] through which they may be invalidated."[54] He is alluding here to his later critique of the legitimacy of arguing from the physics that we recognize, "the nature of what exists," to a situation prior to it.

Given the logical stalemate on this issue, Maimonides believes it more reasonable to maintain the creationist position, particularly since it is supportable without proof by prophecy, even though the philosophers who believe in the eternity of the world also accept prophecy. Of course, Maimonides is aware that the philosophers' understanding of prophecy differs from the traditional reading of biblical prophecy. He will attempt to bridge the differences, though not over the issue of creation. His claim here of philosophical support for creation rendered by the philosophers' belief in prophecy is thus a red herring.

Maimonides' main critique of Aristotle's physics begins in chapter 17. He creates an elaborate analogy between the state of a being *in utero* and in maturity, and the state of the world before and after its creation, arguing that the conditions of the latter state do not permit one to infer the nature of the former. Maimonides chooses to illustrate this point with an extended parable that depicts the ignorance of developmental physiology of a man brought up on a desert island who had never seen a woman;[55] he would be unable to believe in the changes that nature brings about. Even less are we able to fathom the changes wrought in the physics of the world upon its creation by God.

Aristotle's arguments, Maimonides asserts, assume an eternally stable and perfect nature. Maimonides rejects the eternal aspect but agrees that nature acquired a stable and perfect state after its initial creation. The laws of physics that Aristotle enunciated obtain then, and "one cannot imagine" motion as a whole, and the circular motion of the heavenly bodies, having a beginning or end.

Maimonides' point, he reiterates, is "that a being's state of perfection and completion furnishes no indication of the state of that being preceding its perfection."[56] This notion is a "great wall" that Maimonides says he has constructed to protect the Law against those who attack it. He admits he has not proven his creation thesis; all he wishes to do is establish the possibility of such a deed.

After refuting the basic premise of Aristotle's arguments for an eternal universe based on his physics, Maimonides in chapter 18 attacks the metaphysical arguments for an eternal universe based on the nature of the deity, as advanced by Aristotle's followers.[57]

Firstly, Maimonides denies that God in creating the world would have had to pass from potentiality to actuality, since such a change requires a material substrate (where potentiality and thus possibility are located), as well as a cause responsible for the transition. God, however, has no material component; nothing exists in Him in potentiality (and He is uncaused). He therefore has no possibility of changing and is always *in actu,* the same essentially. Thus, Maimonides concludes, a being separate from matter like God can act at (what is for us) one time and not another without its being considered change or a transition from potentiality to actuality. While this argument absolves God from being subject to the material entailments of change, Maimonides does not explain how different acts can be that of the same unchanging being.

Maimonides finds a parallel to God's behavior in the (seemingly) inconstant actions of the immaterial Agent Intellect; these actions also do not warrant the assumption that the Agent Intellect undergoes change or passes from potentiality to actuality.[58] There is a reason why the Agent Intellect acts (and doesn't act) as it does, Maimonides acknowledges, but he cautions that it is irrelevant to his thesis, since he is not searching for a cause of God's actions. Nevertheless, Maimonides offers the reason for the Agent Intellect's apparently changing actions: they are due to the state of preparation in which the matter that is to receive the intellect's emanations finds itself, and not due to change in the Agent Intellect itself. "Its action is perpetual with regard to all things properly disposed."[59] Though Maimonides rejects any explanation of God's actions here, the reasons offered for the actions of the Agent Intellect will serve to explain Maimonides' understanding of divine providence too.[60]

Maimonides' second argument against the notion that the world is necessarily eternal tackles the contention that God would have no reason or "incentive" (*dāʿiya*) to change His (eternal) will, and there exist no accidents or impediments to thwart it. Maimonides' first response is that God's will is unlike any other, not defined by external desires, impediments, or accidents. His will is totally uncaused, self-willed, free of any external motivation.

Nor, Maimonides says, does a will that expresses itself at one time and not another imply a change of will, since "the true reality [*ḥaqīqa*] and essence [*māhiyah*] of will is to will and not to will."[61] A being separate from matter has an autonomous will the diverse expressions of which do not constitute, for Maimonides, a change in its essence. Accordingly, Maimonides concludes this argument by saying that he uses the term "will" equivocally when referring to human beings and to a being separate from matter, there being actually "no likeness between the two wills."[62]

Maimonides briefly dispatches a third argument for the eternity of the world, that which assumes that God's actions must follow immediately upon His wisdom and be as eternal as it is. Maimonides agrees that God's wisdom ordering the universe is "perpetual [*dā'imah*] and immutable [*ghayr mutaghayyirah*]," but he argues that we are ignorant of the way in which that wisdom is expressed. Maimonides thus is not bothered by the picture of a deity who defers creation while thinking it eternally. For Maimonides, the God before creation is no less perfect or good than the postcreation deity, the presence of a created world not being superior to its absence. Yet Maimonides has conceded that God's wisdom, His knowledge, is eternal and immutable, a thesis that will complicate Maimonides' later argument for creation from absolutely nothing.

Maimonides also chooses to remark in this context that even as the universe follows God's wisdom, so does God's will. This would seem to give wisdom the upper hand over will, though Maimonides adds that the will and wisdom of God are the same, God not having any attributes. Still, it is hard to escape the impression of a wise deity whose will is an expression of His wisdom. At any rate, Maimonides promises to develop this subject later in his discussion of providence.

In chapter 19, Maimonides mounts a prolonged attack upon the empirical foundations of Aristotle's metaphysics and astronomy. He wishes to argue, in a manner that "comes close to being a demonstration," that the structure of the heavens cannot be explained by Aristotelian principles and requires assuming a divine agency that particularized the spheres and their motions idiosyncratically. Maimonides contrasts the necessity that characterizes the actions of Aristotle's deity with the (presumably) free choice that God had before willing the world into being.[63] This God has a purpose (*qaṣd*) that Aristotle's god supposedly lacks, or a purpose that would have stood in contradiction to the presence of eternal beings.[64]

Maimonides acknowledges the essential similarity of his argument from particularization (*al-takhṣīṣ*) to that of the *mutakallimūn,* but insists that he argues within the context of Aristotelian physics, whereas the *kalām* position is based on an a priori rejection of the natural world and the adoption of atomism.[65] Still, Maimonides' arguments posit particularization as a response to Aristotle's inadequate cosmology, and do not offer anything near to a "demonstration" of its truth.

To make his case, Maimonides runs through a brief synopsis of basic Aristotelian teachings in physics and astronomy, starting with prime matter, the four elements—air, earth, fire, and water—that can inform it, and two of the four qualities of heat, cold, wet, and dry that in different combinations constitute each of the four elements.[66] The uniqueness of an object's matter is explained by the diverse proportions of the qualities that constitute the elements, as well as by the particular compound formed by the mixture of the elements.

Aristotle viewed both the initial emergence of the four elements and their subsequent mixture into compound material objects on earth as caused by celestial motion and the location of diverse spheres in the cosmos. While prime matter, being void of form in itself, is able to receive any form, Aristotle limits its domain to the earth, positing another, unchanging matter in the heavens, evidenced by the (supposed) fact that the bodies of the spheres move in circular directions, while the terrestrial elements (allegedly) possess rectilinear motion.

Maimonides agrees with this description of the formation and constitution of the elements and compound bodies on earth, but finds fault with Aristotle's cosmology. Aristotle regards the fifth element that constitutes the matter of the heavens as common to all celestial bodies; it is their prime matter and remains untouched by any other material element. Why, then, Maimonides asks, do the spheres not act uniformly, why do they vary irregularly in speed and direction? What is the individuating or particularizing principle in their actions?

Maimonides dismisses Aristotle's view that the separate intellects of the spheres serve this purpose,[67] claiming that as the intellects are not bodies, they cannot affect the particular velocity or direction a given sphere takes. Presumably, Maimonides also dismisses the souls of the spheres as the real efficient cause of their motions, not even mentioning them here. Though not separate from the matter of a sphere, the soul, being its animating principle, has no physical component that could account for the sphere's specific trajectory.

Thus, though he retains the scaffolding of Aristotle's heavens,[68] the planets, the stars, and the spheres in which they move, as well as the intellects, souls, and separate intellects that serve respectively as their formal, efficient, and final causes, Maimonides reduces the immaterial set to the status of live automatons. It is God who is responsible for the specific actions of the spheres and the irregular, particular constellations of the heavens; the intellects and souls of the spheres still explain *what* happens, but not *why*.

Maimonides returns, in chapter 20, to the distinction he just made between actions that result necessarily from their causal antecedents, and actions that are the result of purpose and will. Maimonides now contends that Aristotle's first cause "wills what is necessarily derived from it and rejoices and takes pleasure in it,"[69] but insists that this cannot be called "purpose," since that term should apply only to willed acts that are not necessary, in which the purposed act may or may not occur, so that the will exercises a decisive function. For Maimonides, one doesn't purpose to do something that is inevitable, and in his opinion positing that something can exist both by virtue of necessity and through a purpose and will "comes near to being a combination of two contraries" (*al-jamʿu bayn al-ḍaddayn*).[70]

In chapter 21, Maimonides reiterates his insistence that Aristotle's causal theory as applied to his belief in the eternity of the world leaves no room for a meaningful sense of purpose, indeed, renders that term absurd. Maimonides makes this claim, though admitting that some "latter-day philosophers" do in fact assert just this, combining a necessary nexus of causal relations with divine choice, purpose, and particularization.[71]

Maimonides may realize he is at a linguistic as well as philosophical impasse, so in order to support his position he begins in chapter 22 to identify what he perceives as critical failures in Aristotle's explanation of the movements of the heavenly spheres. Assuming universally accepted philosophical premises that affirm necessary causal relations and the impossibility that a single simple thing can produce anything other than another simple thing, Maimonides challenges what he regards as the Aristotelian notion that composition and multiplicity can come from the one.

Maimonides is referring to the view that the first intellect (Aristotle's god) is the cause of the second (separate intellect), the second of the third, and so on.[72] Maimonides is prepared to yield and accept composition (of notions) within each intellect, but draws the line at the emergence of matter (the spheres) from the intellect. Celestial matter itself poses a big problem for Maimonides, since there is no reason for it to remain tied to a particular sphere, being common supposedly to all spheres. What though is the principle of individuation that differentiates the motions and luminosity of the spheres and stars respectively? And if the matter of the spheres is unique to each sphere and its stars, what would explain the common properties they share, to the degree they do?

Maimonides' answer to these questions is relatively simple: God in His wisdom and will, which we cannot understand, particularized the heavens as

He purposed. While asserting that all of Aristotle's explanations of matters on earth are "indubitably correct," Maimonides finds Aristotle's account of heavenly matters largely conjectural, and particularly his view of the order of the intellects and "some" of his opinions regarding God.

Maimonides knows that he has not conclusively established his anti-Aristotelian position, and he believes both the eternity and the creation hypotheses are not demonstrable. He adopts the approach suggested by Alexander of Aphrodisias,[73] to see which view poses fewer "doubts" (*al-shukūk*), i.e., logical and philosophical inconsistencies. In contrast to the conclusion of all others (i.e., all the other philosophers whom he admires), Maimonides says, he opts for the creation thesis because it is less problematic, and only secondarily, as it were, because the belief in eternity "is more harmful for the belief that ought to be held with regard to the deity," as well as being the opinion of "Abraham our Father and our prophet Moses."[74]

Maimonides, then, chooses to argue against Aristotle primarily on philosophical grounds, though it will entail asserting that a position that relies on unknown mechanisms, a divine will and purpose beyond our understanding, has fewer philosophical problems than a scientific explanation, however flawed.

In chapter 23, Maimonides pauses in critiquing Aristotle's metaphysics to deliver a lecture on the character needed to pursue the truth without bias. One must not let one's past upbringing or hope for future advantage figure in this quest; one must have a good mind and sound disposition, be well trained in mathematics, logic, and the natural sciences, and be morally self-controlled. A person of this type will not succumb to doubts concerning the creation of the world, doubts that lead to the "destruction of the foundation of the Law" and are an affront (*iftiyāt*) to God. Accept the authority of Abraham and Moses for believing in creation, Maimonides urges, unless a demonstrative proof is shown, which he is sure does not exist "in nature."

Maimonides thus presents something of a mixed message to his reader.[75] On the one hand, be scrupulously objective in your investigations, while on the other, incline toward the opinion of the religious leaders of your faith. This approach may well reflect the diverse readership Maimonides' book was sure to acquire, and be intended to facilitate broad acceptance of his views. He may be somewhat embarrassed by the rhetorical appeal to authority that he uses, for he acknowledges and excuses it on the (alleged) grounds that Aristotle employed a similar technique in arguing on behalf of an eternal world.

Chapter 24 contains the heart of Maimonides' critique of Aristotle's cosmology, building on Ptolemy's *Almagest* and the later work of Muslim astronomers.[76] The gist of it is that empirical observation of the movement of the planets, confirmed by mathematical models, has disproved Aristotle's claim that the spheres revolve around the earth in perfectly concentric circles. Instead, the spheres appear to move eccentrically or to have attached epicyclical movements that do not revolve around the center of the sphere or of the earth. In either case, the motion described by the spheres is not aligned as Aristotle would have it; the epicycles have no fixed position, and the centers of the eccentric spheres' motion vary considerably in relation to their adjacent spheres. Moreover, even when two spheres are intimately connected, with a smaller one inside the larger, they seem to move independently of each other.

No explanation for these apparently anomalous movements exists, in Maimonides' opinion, even where the existence of epicycles has been proved, as Ptolemy has for the epicyclical motion of the moon. This lack of explanations challenges the scientific understanding of astronomy, and that is "the true perplexity," *al-ḥayrah bi'l-ḥaqīqa*.[77] This leads Maimonides to reiterate his belief in the limits of man's knowledge to "what is beneath the heavens," God alone having full knowledge of the heavens. The distance in space and stature between the heavens and mankind is too great to be bridged, Maimonides says; from our inadequate knowledge of celestial matters one cannot even conclude that God exists!

In chapter 25, Maimonides wishes to assure the reader that his opting for a created rather than an eternal world is not due to a literal acceptance of the text of the Torah. He says he could have interpreted the texts figuratively, as he did with the even more numerous texts that depict the deity in corporeal terms. God's incorporeality has been demonstrated, however, and the eternity of the world has not, and thus there is no necessity to allegorize creation.

Maimonides' second reason for preferring creation to eternity is more fundamental to his beliefs. Whereas the belief in an incorporeal deity does not in his opinion destroy the "foundations of the Law" (*qawā'id al-shari'a*) or invalidate the claim (*da'wā*) of any prophet, the belief in eternity, in the necessitarian way that Aristotle understands it, with nature brooking no change, does fundamentally destroy the Law and invalidates every miracle. The eternity thesis, moreover, strips away (*ta'ṭīl*) the hopes and threats that the Law conveys; i.e., it fatally weakens the political clout of the Law, its ability to command obedience through promises and threats.

Yet Maimonides concludes his tirade against the Aristotelian view by vacillating over the invalidating effect it has on miracles. He says that belief in miracles could be maintained even in an eternal universe, if they were interpreted figuratively. Apparently, Maimonides is thinking that the truths that miracles are meant to convey are universal and do not depend on belief in the particular circumstances in which they allegedly occur.

Maimonides sees Plato's doctrine of a created yet everlasting world as more accommodating to the foundations of the Law and to acceptance of the possibility of miracles (since a demiurge hovers over the world he has created out of eternal elements). The texts of the Torah could also be interpreted figuratively to agree with this position, Maimonides declares. Lacking demonstrative proof of the correctness of Plato's view, however, Maimonides finds an esoteric approach unnecessary. "The Law," he says, "has given us knowledge of a matter the grasp of which is not within our power, and the miracle attests to the correctness of our claims."[78]

This testament of faith is followed by the claim that belief in creation validates the possibility of all the miracles and particularly (the revelation of) the Law, and obviates the need to explain the particularities of all the revelations. They are all expressions of God's inscrutable will and wisdom. Aristotle's doctrine is to be opposed, then, for its damaging effect upon belief in the Law.[79]

In chapter 26, Maimonides turns to a midrashic source to support the philosophical contention that the matter of the heavens is other than that of the earth. He has to navigate carefully around the statement he chooses to expound, since it portrays God as creating the heavens and earth from parts of his attire.[80] Maimonides is interested in this passage also for the insight it may contain concerning early rabbinic views on both "ends" of eternity: eternity *a parte ante,* an eternal period before the creation of the world, and eternity *a parte post,* after creation. While Maimonides regards the biblical and midrashic sources for believing in an eternal *a parte ante* universe as slight and equivocal, they are unequivocal, in his judgment, in affirming eternity *a parte post.*

This belief in the everlasting or "sempiternal" nature of the world after creation is the message Maimonides derives from biblical sources, in chapters 27 and 28 as well. He believes the philosophical objection to predicating eternity of something that has been generated, and that therefore has to pass away, is overcome by the extraordinary nature, the unnatural nature, of the world's genesis. Of course, God could will the end of the universe's existence, as He willed its beginning, but the Bible assures us He will not.

Accordingly, Maimonides quotes Scripture in chapter 28 to impress upon the reader that Solomon, David, and Jeremiah have uttered their conviction that God reigns over the earth forever, His statutes unchanging. God's law cannot change, Maimonides explains, since all the works of the Lord are perfect, with nothing excessive or deficient in them. Consequently, the statutes have no need, and no possibility, of change. This leads Maimonides to foreshadow a conviction he will expand upon later, namely, that the perfection that characterizes all of God's work extends to His creatures,[81] who have neither deficiencies nor excesses, and whose lives are enveloped in absolute justice (*'adl maḥḍ*) and that which wisdom requires.

In chapter 29, Maimonides defends his assertions of a perfect, unchanging, and sempiternal world, challenged by the many prophecies of doom and destruction that the prophets, and particularly Isaiah, pronounce. As Maimonides explains, one must understand the linguistic style of the prophets, their use of rhetoric, of parable and metaphor, and not take their words literally. There will be no new heaven or earth; all the sages of the Mishnah and Talmud agree with Solomon: "there is nothing new under the sun."[82]

In taking this position, Maimonides does not dismiss the reality of the vicissitudes and defeats that the prophets foretold; rather, he removes the cosmic significance they give them. For Maimonides, it would seem, the history of Israel in biblical times, as no doubt later too, is all part of a divine plan that is unchanging, just, and exemplary.

This brings Maimonides to qualify his notion of miracles, given that the nature God established on earth is perfect and not in need of change. Maimonides first points out that the miracles mentioned in the Bible did not cause permanent changes in nature. Quoting a text found in two midrashic sources, he then mentions the view that miracles were created by God when He created the world and simply programmed to occur later, so that God would not have changed His will by creating something new.[83] Maimonides appears to reject this position, though he appreciates the attempt to preserve God's unchanging nature. Without elaborating, Maimonides apparently finds that accepting the occasional miracle does not contradict his thesis of an unchanging, God-given nature.

Maimonides concludes the chapter with two preambles to his next topic, which is what the rabbis call the "Account of the Beginning" and what the philosophers know as physics or natural science. In the first preamble, Maimonides cautions against taking the Torah's account of this topic literally. Still, one must honor the rabbinic tradition that wished to keep the subject secret, to be transmitted only to those prepared intellectually for it. A person who has attained some perfection in the subject is obliged, however, by "divine commandment" (*al-amr al-ilāhī*), to communicate what he knows of the subject, however discreetly.

The second preamble briefly goes over the main teaching of the first preamble, emphasizing now the equivocal nature of prophetic terms, and giving some examples. In these preambles, Maimonides repeats what he said in the introduction to the *Guide* on this matter, preparing the reader for subtle and esoteric discourse in what is to follow.

Accordingly, in chapter 30 Maimonides embarks on a detailed exegetical exercise to show that the account of creation in Genesis conforms, with the exception of creation from nothing, to (a version of) Aristotle's *Meteorology*.[84] Maimonides labors mightily to remove the temporal framework in which the Bible apparently presents the creation story, since that would imply a time period, presumably eternal, that preceded the completion of creation. Maimonides quotes certain midrashic texts that support just this view and urges the reader to discount them, again insisting that "the foundation of the whole Law" is the belief in creation from nothing or, literally, not from anything, *lā min shay*.'[85] Maimonides forces the text to his purposes and adduces support from rabbinic speculations regarding creation.

Chapter 31 is brief, extolling the Sabbath as a day to commemorate both creation of the world and redemption from slavery. Maimonides probably added this chapter to round out the account of creation given in the previous chapter. He may well have thought that the tone of this chapter allowed it to stand alone, without exegesis or midrashic support.

Analysis

The chapters of this section of the *Guide* attest to Maimonides' struggle to reconcile the perplexities with which philosophy challenged his faith. Having confronted the challenge of *kalām* resoundingly, if not entirely successfully, Maimonides now takes on "the master of those who know," the person whom he greatly admired, Aristotle. It should be remembered that this was in many ways a post-Aristotelian Aristotle, an Aristotle as commented upon and modified by a host of late Greek and Muslim philosophers, yet discernibly Aristotle in the naturalistic orientation of many of the views held.

The issue that attracts Maimonides' attention first is a continuation of the debate begun with the *mutakallimūn* over the proofs for the existence, unity, and incorporeality of God. Maimonides is very sympathetic initially to the premises of the philosophers, premises that he feels have been well demonstrated, for the most part. He believes that even the premise of an eternal world, with which he takes issue, can be used to secure his main thesis, viz., that there is but one God.

Maimonides' reservations about "Aristotle's" cosmology center on empirical questions concerning the noncircular movement of the heavenly bodies and the alleged failure of the supernal intelligences and souls of the spheres to adequately explain the spheres' movements. Moreover, beyond specific scientific conundrums there lay, Maimonides suspected, a general epistemological impasse that confounded any metaphysical claims.

Only some of Maimonides' proofs for God's existence, unity, and incorporeality are based on physical arguments that assume the discredited circular motion of the spheres; other proofs, while empirically grounded, are more self-contained logically and rely on the impossibility of an infinite regress of causes and the assumption of a necessary first existent cause. For all his doubts about the state of astronomical knowledge, Maimonides feels the heavens exhibit an order and beauty captured to a large extent by Aristotle's description. Moreover, Maimonides believes that Aristotle's views match well with those presented in the Bible and Jewish tradition, a sign of philosophy's legitimacy. For Maimonides, then, Aristotelian proofs for God's existence, unity, and incorporeality are acceptable, whereas Aristotle's cosmology is not.

The distinction between the two issues is not as clear-cut as Maimonides may have wanted, however. The perfection of Aristotle's universe and the divine providence that it manifests depend in no small measure on accepting the thirteenth premise, that which affirms the circular movement of the heavenly spheres. Aristotle deemed circularity a condition of the continuous actual existence of the spheres, distinguishing supernal from sublunar being, assuring continuity in the emanation of forms on earth. This premise is critical, therefore, for Maimonides' acceptance of Aristotle's metaphysics; yet Maimonides chooses to ignore, at first, the entailments of the doubt he has about it.

While the contradictory statements Maimonides makes as to the demonstrative nature of all these premises may be taken as deliberate, in keeping with Maimonides' own declared intentions to put off those who are unprepared for his teachings, it may as well indicate Maimonides' determination to use as many demonstrative arguments as he can on behalf of proving God's nature and His relation to the world, despite his ambivalence toward their validity. It would seem to have made little sense for Maimonides to lay out a systematic, detailed cosmology that he felt was largely accurate if he intended to upend belief in its essential teachings subsequently. Nor should Maimonides have labored to find parallels in the Bible and Jewish tradition for a philosophy whose validity he would eventually reject.

Maimonides' arguments for the existence, unity, and incorporeality of God are based on principles of Aristotelian physics and metaphysics that require an unmoved mover as the first cause for the initial movement of the heavens. While Aristotle had already posited that the unmoved mover had to be separate from and unaffected by anything material, calling it a "god," Maimonides was attracted to Avicenna's alternative formulation of this god as the "Necessary of Existence," *wājib al-wujūd*.[86] This formulation, Maimonides may have felt, further distanced God from everything else in the universe,[87] the existence of which was in itself only possible, contingent on causes outside themselves. The *wājib al-wujūd*'s existence was necessary, being uncaused, and required for the actualization of all other beings' existence.

Maimonides' adoption of Avicenna's conceptualization of God is not free of difficulties that Avicenna also faced and did not fully resolve. As the being whose essence is solely existence, the Necessary Existent has in theory only existence to offer the world. Yet in the originally Plotinian emanative scheme that Avicenna adopted, and that Maimonides followed, this unique being, the God of Necessary Existence, is also portrayed as the Giver of Forms, *wāhib al-ṣuwar*, known to the Latins as *Donor Formarum*.[88] Avicenna's God, therefore, while less analogous to other beings than was Aristotle's unmoved mover, was closer to them as the source of their essences, as well as the cause of their existence. To consider the Necessary Existent as solely endowing essences with existence, as its name indicates, one would have to posit a realm of essences or forms that have some measure of being before they receive God's gift of existence, the "possible existents" being originally and theoretically independent of God's necessitating effect upon their being.

Avicenna does not entertain this idea, and neither does Maimonides.[89] For Avicenna, the world is eternal, so that there never was a time in which the possible existents were deprived of their existence. The Necessary Existent has always granted existence to them, as part of the plenitude of its being, converting them from (theoretically) possible to necessary existents, as caused.

Maimonides, however, cannot adopt this view, if he believes that the world is created and that the Necessary Existent antedated possible existents. He might, however, have felt that before creation all that existed was the Necessary Existent (though the term is oddly anachronistic, absent possible existents), and that the moment God created the possible existents, He created them as theoretically contingent, but actually necessary existents, being caused by the existence He granted them. While this view may save the Necessary Existent as a meaningful concept in a creationist scenario, the term is less adapted to that purpose than to establish the relation of God to possible existents in a postcreation universe.

Maimonides' use of Avicenna's description of God as Necessary Existent cannot be limited, then, to the literal meaning of the term. It has to be conflated with the ultimately Plotinian notion of a being that emanates both essence and existence, together, in stages of increasing specificity. Avicenna's nomenclature of the divine is helpful to establish the contingent nature of all beings but does not in itself explain their origin.

As Avicenna describes it, the origin of the universe is compounded of seemingly contradictory theses. It is both eternal and created from absolute nothing by God, a product of will and necessity. Avicenna may have taken the latter pair of contrary modalities from the widely disseminated Neoplatonic literature that passed as Aristotelian[90] and that, in adding will to necessity, made emanationism more acceptable to medieval religious communities. Then, too, the assertion of a creation from absolute nothing had an imposing religious imprimatur,[91] though Avicenna could not quite explain it in itself and surely not in conjunction with the belief in an eternal universe.

Medieval philosophers believed, as did their classical predecessors, that the heavens were animated and hence alive; each sphere was endowed with a soul that was able to conceive and strive to move toward the objects of its desire, viz., the separate unmoving intellect in the next higher sphere, and God, the intelligent progenitor of all being. There is in this theory a decided emotive aspect to the apprehension that the soul's intellect was believed to experience. It takes "delight" (or longing, *ishtiyāq*)[92] in approaching and emulating its object, an emotion that accompanies every living being that has a true cognition. True knowledge attracts and moves the stars, even as it does people on earth.

Maimonides brings this out dramatically toward the end of the *Guide*,[93] where the ultimate experience of truly knowing God transmutes into passionate love. Intellection is not a sterile detached mental exercise; it captures one's feelings and passions, creating a sense of joyous communion with the divine.

This emotion that the (intellects of the) spheres experience is not diminished by the single-mindedness and necessity of their intellections, which cause each sphere to move continually in its own orbit. Maimonides wants to see this motion as deliberately chosen, the spheres being for him animate creatures that apprehend and govern, as well as exercise choice for their actions. Yet, as Maimonides says in chapter 7, these terms when said of the spheres denote something quite different than when predicated of human behavior. Conceived as having no impediments to realizing their nature, which is to move in perfect circular motion, the spheres always act as they should, doing what is good (for them and the world) in realizing their being.

Maimonides conceives the supernal intellects and their spheres just as Aristotle did, with the exception of seeing them as created and possessed of will and choice. They have no reason to vary that choice, however, being in an active state of perpetual perfection. They "always do that which is good," which is the constant actualization of their nature. They have no potentiality for bad choices, for "only that which is good is with them." So understood, not only is the "choice" Maimonides accords the intellects and spheres equivocal but it is unintelligible. If the intellects of the spheres have no potentiality for making bad choices, it is impossible for them to do so, since Maimonides understands possibility, with Aristotle, as a meaningful concept only when it can be realized.

Maimonides' attributing choice and will to the separate intellects of the spheres[94] and his insistence on the equivocal nature of the terms foreshadow his discussion of God's actions in creating the world. The heavens follow God in being voluntaristic, even as they are utterly predictable. Their predictability, one could say, is willed, however determined.

Maimonides is not deterred from believing in emanation as the key factor in explaining God's ordering and "governing" the world by his knowledge that Aristotle's picture of the circular motions of the heavenly spheres is inaccurate, and all that entails, or should entail, for the stability and continuity of the emanative process. Maimonides knows he has not given a "precise account of the true reality of the intellects and the spheres,"[95] yet he is sure that the general division of existent beings into separate intellects, animated and intelligent spherical bodies, and sublunar informed bodies is accurate, and that an emanative force originating with God connects them.

In keeping with his reluctance to posit any predicate of God, Maimonides attributes emanation to Him obliquely and is upset by those who interpret this in popular terms, having God speak to angels and humans. For Maimonides, emanation, though willed by God, functions rather mechanically, though without the pejorative associations of such a term. Maimonides does not want to dwell on this view, which he knows must be repugnant to many of his readers, so he proceeds to another topic, one that on the face of it would recapture the allegiance of those who may have begun to doubt his belief in a traditional God of creation.

Beginning with chapter 13, Maimonides lays out in succinct form the case for a created world, which he claims is that supported by all who believe in the law of Moses, and the case for an eternal world, as understood by Plato and Aristotle.[96] The Jewish view, as initially presented and as later defended, assumes the legitimacy of terms for which there is no philosophical support other than the general thesis Maimonides offered in his prior debate with a *mutakallim*.[97] Maimonides now speaks of a creation "after pure and absolute non-being" (*'adam*, literally, "privation"), claiming that for the philosophers this is "absurd," i.e., a self-contradictory proposition.[98] Later, Maimonides will defend concepts of choice and will that are likewise taken out of their philosophical contexts.

Maimonides justifies his irregular use of terms by the unique status of God and the unique event of creation, which displace the normative meaning of terms that are applicable to postcreation reality only. Maimonides knows he cannot prove his assertions and strives just to persuade the reader of the possible truth of them. Yet even here, he is stretching the philosophical meaning of possible truth, since there is no prior material basis, or condition, for that possibility.

Maimonides is adamant here that the act of creation is the generation of being from absolute nothingness, pure privation.[99] This is not the relative privation that assumes the existence of some being that is now in a potential state yet has the ability to be potential because of an actual existent that will bring it into actuality. That is the privation that Plato's demiurge encountered in forming the world out of preexistent eternal matter, and that Maimonides probably thought Avicenna and Alfarabi really meant, in affirming creation in an eternal universe. Eternity seemed to Maimonides to chain God to necessity and rob Him of a meaningful will, or so Maimonides claims, despite Avicenna's protestations to the contrary.

What, though, can Maimonides be thinking of in asserting creation from absolute nonexistence? He knows, as the philosophers say, that God cannot bring the world into existence "from" or "after" nonbeing without there having been such a state from or after which He created the world. This reduces privation to a relative status, which Maimonides strongly resists. Yet Maimonides could not have believed that God created an evanescent state of absolute nonbeing at the moment He drew being from it, as this would entail sudden movement and change in the deity.

Still, Maimonides has to have something in mind in thinking of creation as he does; he wants to affirm it as the unilateral action of the God whom he has insisted is incorporeal, eternal, and unchanging. Maimonides should have (must have?) realized that such a deity would have had the idea of creating the world *ex nihilo* from all eternity, that the world in its entirety had always existed in the divine mind, and that He had always intended it to be realized existentially at some (nonexistent) "time."[100] Similarly, it may be said that God always had to have had in mind the thought of first matter, that is, its ideal or formal reality,[101] which, paradoxically, is the absence of form. Thus, whether God created the world directly or indirectly, it was for Maimonides a creation only relatively after "absolute nonexistence."

Maimonides, however, does not address the possibility of situating the form of the world—all its forms, including the form of matter—in an eternal Mind, the many transformed there in the unity of God's being. Whatever Maimonides may have understood by the "absolute nonexistence" that preceded the creation of matter and the world, he was determined to emphasize God's agency in creating the world.

Maimonides is left, as are his philosophical predecessors, with a God that acts out of necessity, even one that is willed; the unique act of creation from absolute nothing, even if accepted, does not change that. Maimonides' position is, then, an amalgam of Plato's and Aristotle's views. With Plato he shares a creator god (though the "mechanism" of creation is Plotinian); with Aristotle a stable (postcreation) and enduring universe. For the sake of creation, Maimonides takes the necessity that enveloped Aristotle's God as the Unmoved Mover in an eternal universe and internalizes it into the very being of the deity, where it is subordinated, as it were, to the divine will.

Maimonides presents the Platonic and Aristotelian positions rather fairly, minimizing the difference between them, in that they both hold it necessary to posit a universe that is eternal in one sense or another. Maimonides thus collapses Plato's creative deity with Aristotle's unchanging first mover, and concentrates his critique against Aristotle. Maimonides is emphatic: "Every follower of the Law of Moses and Abraham our Father" should believe that nothing exists co-eternally with God, and that it is an obligation, not an impossibility, for Him to bring something into existence from nonexistence.[102]

This ringing declaration is striking, in part because its view of the Platonic challenge to monotheism is questionably extreme, and in part because Maimonides later qualifies it. There is considerable difference between the Platonic and the Aristotelian positions. The Platonic view proposes a deliberate and designed creation in which eternal matter does not pose a challenge to God's authority. This view could easily be accommodated to the biblical depiction of creation, so Maimonides may here be deliberately minimizing the attractiveness of this position.

Maimonides' standard presentation of the arguments for an eternal universe that Aristotle and his followers offered is stylistically and philosophically compelling. He can cast doubt on their veracity only by the supposed doubts that Aristotle himself had as to whether the arguments had been demonstrated, and, more important, by his own supposition of an alternative precreation scenario. Maimonides appeals to the testimony of the prophets to tilt the scales between the mutually undemonstrated arguments for both creation and eternity, an appeal to authority that is begging the question philosophically. Nor is the prophetic—and rabbinic—testimony unanimous as to creation, and certainly not regarding the eternity *a parte post* of the world, which Maimonides oddly (or perhaps not so oddly) finds necessary to affirm.[103]

The post-Aristotelian arguments for an eternal universe derive from the impossibilities that an act of creation would impose on God. Maimonides reframes the deity's relation to these impossible, since illogical, actions, declaring their impossibility void. Thus, Maimonides claims that God can transition from not acting to acting without passing from potentiality to actuality, as these terms do not apply to an immaterial being and are not a sign of change.

Maimonides also believes that the separate intellects of the spheres, being separate from the bodies of the spheres, do not pass from potentiality to actuality. That is because they do not change, accounting for the permanent nature of the movement of the spheres. Maimonides realizes, however, that his attempt to draw an analogy between God's action and the Agent Intellect's apparently changing effects on earth is flawed, as that intellect never changes its behavior. In that, it is similar to God, apparent change being due to the nature of the material objects that receive the emanations issuing from God (remotely) or the Agent Intellect (proximately). Maimonides would like us to believe, moreover, that there is no similarity between God's unique act of seeming change and the uniform action of other unchanging beings, viz., the intellects of the spheres.

Similarly, God's will is unique, for Maimonides, not responsive to any affect or impediment, free to express itself in what appears to be different modes, again without implying change in its essence. This will is equal to divine wisdom, since there are no separate attributes in God, all seeming attributes being simply expressions of the single divine essence. God's wisdom, consequently, is as eternal and unchanging as He is.

Maimonides concedes that he is speaking equivocally of will in relation to God, and could as well make the same claim for wisdom. He is sure of the immutability of that wisdom, however, since his image of God requires, he believes, a being whose essential unity precludes innovation and change.

This premise of Maimonides' thought underlies the distinction he draws in chapter 19 between Aristotle's god and his God. Whereas Aristotle's deity acts by necessity, the world having to be eternal, Maimonides' God acts purposively, "choosing" to create the world. Though Maimonides uses the Arabic term for "choice," *ikhtiyār,* it is hardly a "free" choice, given that his God had to know from all eternity that He would create the world as and "when" He did, and nothing could change His (necessarily unchanging) mind. Thus, though the true reality of a divine will is, as Maimonides says, "to will and not to will," the divine will, as governed by the divine unchanging wisdom, is not free at all.

It is perhaps surprising that Maimonides strips Aristotle's god of purpose, for purpose, as the end or final cause of an action, is integral to a full Aristotelian scientific explanation, and certainly fits Aristotle's understanding of the unmoved mover. Nor does the god that the medieval philosophers thought was Aristotle's lack will, choice, or even a particularizing aspect, as Maimonides acknowledges in chapter 21. The philosophers' deity simply (though fatally) lacks the kind of freedom that we normally associate with these terms, and that Maimonides wants us to associate with his God.

While Maimonides had to know that his assertions of the feasibility of positing a creator God who does not change lacked philosophical rigor and while he admitted that they were nondemonstrable, he probably considered his critique of Aristotle's cosmology scientifically grounded. The common and simple matter of the heavens, and the intellects and souls of the spheres, could not account, Maimonides believed, for the nonuniform motions of the spheres. Their irregularity requires an extrascientific cause, viz., God's will.

This position is problematic, however. Maimonides has no problem with the composition of the heavens as originally charted by Aristotle, and with the action of celestial intellects and souls upon the bodies of the spheres that accounts for the uniform motion of their orbits. The lack of evidence for perfectly circular motion of the spheres would seem, however, to threaten the entire Aristotelian argument for continuous, eternal motion. Maimonides is right, therefore, to doubt its validity. Yet he does not doubt the continuous motion of the spheres. Apparently, he considers that the same efficient and formal causes of soul and intellect, respectively, are present in irregular motion, accounting for epicycles and eccentric movements, rather than for circular motion. These "irregular" motions are thus the result of consistent and reliable patterns, rather than the results of "chance." They are subject to laws of physics and are theoretically explicable, as Maimonides admits. Neither he nor others of his time can scientifically explain their motions, however. His move to a theory of divine particularization substitutes for his ignorance of the science required, as he knows, and is taken from the *kalām* vocabulary and mind-set, which Maimonides also knows.

Maimonides brings additional challenges to the philosophers' understanding of the dynamics of heavenly motion in chapter 22.[104] He feels there is no adequate explanation for the emergence of multiplicity in the heavens, or for the relation of the forms of the spheres to the bodies of the spheres. It is really the latter issue that Maimonides believes cannot be explained, since he is willing to accept the view that the intellects of the spheres have multiple cognitions, though each one emanates from a single cause (the prior intellect). One of these cognitions causes the formation of the body of the sphere, and Maimonides finds it implausible that the body of a sphere could come from a separate, i.e., immaterial, intellect. The complexity of the spheres, with their attendant stars, also calls for more than the one intellect acting upon them.

Maimonides has here picked a quarrel with Aristotle that is more relevant to post-Aristotelian philosophers than to the Greek sage himself. For Aristotle did not assume a hierarchic causal order from which one thing was generated out of another, multiplicity emerging out of unity. His universe was an eternally complex amalgam of form and matter, their relationships existing in dynamic symbiosis with a first cause *primus inter pares* in the heavens. Maimonides can critique the relation of intellects to spheres, but it is futile to look for ontic origins in Aristotle's account of an eternal universe.

Maimonides' challenge rather is to the metaphysical scheme adopted by most medieval philosophers, principally Avicenna and Alfarabi, influenced ultimately by Plotinus and Proclus. Here the heavens emerge from God in seemingly diachronic order, albeit eternally, one following the other. Maimonides is right to question the adequacy of the explanation that grants a single separate intellect causal responsibility for the body of its sphere, with its material component.

However, the scheme that Maimonides is questioning, the appearance of multiplicity and diversity within supposedly simple entities, is one that he accepts, implicitly, when theorizing about God. The emergence of the many from the One, a tenet of Neoplatonism, underlies Maimonides' notion of God's responsibility for the world, certainly as its creator. Yet Maimonides objects to the view that entities perform multiple functions when posited as simple beings. Later, he will admit that someone may come along with scientific explanations that will satisfy his questions, but for the moment he chooses to affirm a theological alternative, God acting in a hands-on particularizing manner, to explain the anomalies of the heavens.

This image of God conflicts with that of an unaffected deity that is only indirectly related to the world, so it may be to deflect attention from this seeming inconsistency that Maimonides next pours scorn upon Aristotle's necessarily perfect deity. He could not change anything in his world, neither lengthen a fly's wing nor shorten a worm's foot.[105] Though Maimonides acknowledges that Aristotle would not see this as a deficiency in his god, Maimonides has undoubtedly scored polemical points with (many of) his readers in making this comment.

Maimonides will continue to polemicize and offer rhetorical arguments for creation in chapter 23, but he "sums up" his position cogently toward the end of chapter 22. He accepts without doubt the veracity of Aristotle's sublunar physics, but regards most of his supralunar physics, or metaphysical assertions, as conjectures, "analogous to guessing." The latter beliefs, including some concerning the divine, actually "propagate evil," Maimonides states,[106] an extreme statement that testifies to the presumed effects upon society that Maimonides believes philosophy can have.

Maimonides' statement that some of Aristotle's opinions about God are merely conjectures foreshadows his more extreme remark in chapter 24 that the data the heavens provide are too distant to be reliable, so that proofs of God's existence cannot be inferred from them. A great deal has been made of this last statement of Maimonides, which seems to reject much of his own attempts to argue for God's existence from the evidence of the intelligible order of the heavens, an order he has now rejected. Is Maimonides casting doubt on his own assurance that God exists and that His existence can be known by the intellect?

Maimonides' statement in chapter 24 is ambiguous, however, both grammatically and substantively, and some scholars have provided alternate readings that have Maimonides doubting all knowledge concerning the heavens *except* that they indicate the existence of God.[107] Even assuming, though, that Maimonides does express his reservations here about the validity of proofs of God's existence based on faulty cosmological data, we need not take it as Maimonides' last word on the subject. As we have seen and shall see, Maimonides vacillates on the utility of such metaphysical proofs; he certainly spent a great deal of time and energy in the introduction and opening chapters of part 2 affirming the validity of metaphysics. He may well be struggling with this question, a struggle that is reflected in other areas as well.

Maimonides' assertion of the inaccessibility of celestial data, leading him to what some see as a skeptical approach to metaphysical questions, is undercut, however, by his concluding remark in this chapter. It opens the door he has just shut, claiming that "it is possible that someone else may find a demonstration by means of which the true reality of what is obscure for me will become clear to him."[108] Thus, metaphysical knowledge is not in principle beyond man's grasp, and the heavens may someday be understood as scientifically as is the earth. Rather than closing the door on further speculation, Maimonides appears to want to leave it open.[109]

In chapter 25, Maimonides employs rhetorical arguments to support his assertion of belief in a created world. As though oblivious to his reservations over the proofs for the existence of God that he expressed in the previous chapter, Maimonides now states that God's incorporeality "has been demonstrated."[110] This remark is said apropos of comparing biblical passages that treat God anthropomorphically with passages that speak of creation in time, and is the reason why Maimonides feels permitted, even obliged, to treat anthropomorphic statements figuratively, an approach he cannot endorse in creation passages. They should not be allegorized, since the arguments on behalf of an eternal world have not been demonstrated.

Maimonides is here touching a sensitive nerve in the confrontation between philosophers and their conservative critics, best exemplified in the charges of unnecessary allegorization of sacred Scripture that Al-Ghazālī brought against the philosophers. Averroes defended the philosophers' use of allegory, though limiting it to passages where it is philosophically impossible to maintain the literal meaning of the text.[111]

Maimonides has justified his more literal treatment of the creation story on just these grounds, feeling it not philosophically compelling to do otherwise. This may well be the reason for his condemnation of the allegorical practices of the esotericist Ismāʿīlīs, which were widely considered excessive. Maimonides calls them "ravings," referring to their figurative treatment of miracles, which also in Maimonides' opinion undermines traditional belief.[112]

Maimonides may be overdoing his criticism of the Ismāʿīlīs here. While they were radical allegorists of the Qur'ān, they believed in a created universe and did not devalue miracles. Their esoteric approach to Scripture is very close to Maimonides' heart, though he does not share their theosophic assumptions, or, naturally, their particular readings of the Qur'ān. Nevertheless, his slandering them here is gratuitous and misleading. Maimonides may well be preempting critics who could have drawn attention to similarities in his esoteric approach with that of the Ismāʿīlīs.

Maimonides says the belief in eternity destroys the law. Yet he concedes that (postcreation) miracles could be accommodated in a causally determined scheme. The real opponent of creation that Maimonides sees in Aristotle's scheme is not eternity itself, but the necessity and lack of any change in nature; together, these circumscribe God's actions and will. It is not the miracle per se, then, that renders it a foundation of the Law, but the nature of the source to which it points.

One would assume that a foundational principle of Judaism is the existence not just of a deity responsible for the cosmos, but of a personal God, who has uttered and communicated to the prophets the commandments that inspire hope and fear. Yet Maimonides has gone out of his way to deny any personal affect to God, placing the peoples' destiny in an unknown and impersonal deity. It would appear the charge he brings against Aristotle of threatening belief in the law may in good part be turned against himself.

Maimonides' rejection of Plato's position is qualified: Plato's position could be adopted to the biblical text and made compatible with the belief in miracles, if it were shown to be conclusively argued. Maimonides prefers what he claims is the biblical position on creation not because it offers God greater freedom than a Judaized Platonic demiurge would have, and not because the creation in time argument is any the more demonstrable. He prefers it because of his reservations about Plato's (as well as Aristotle's) notion of an eternal matter, a threat to God's unilateral sovereignty. Given an apparent philosophical stalemate, Maimonides opts for tradition, his people's theological tradition.

Maimonides abruptly changes gears in chapter 26 and the following few chapters, dismissing those statements of the prophets that call for an end time, preferring midrashic and biblical statements that he interprets as attesting to an eternal (postcreation) universe. In so doing, he disregards the widely held belief among his co-religionists, based on Scripture, in an apocalyptic end to the world. Tied as that doctrine was to belief in a messianic advent, and to the belief in resurrection—which he himself treated in his *Commentary on the Mishnah* as a fundamental principle of Judaism—Maimonides' affirmation of a universe that is eternal *a parte post* is iconoclastic. He is not afraid here to confront popular opinion, and implicitly to repudiate what he has said is a principle of the faith.[113]

Maimonides is driven to this position apparently by his belief in God's absolute perfection, which is reflected in every aspect of His creation, obviating the need for any radical change ever. This perfection extends to the human condition, as concerns both individuals and society. The counterfactual nature of this last statement is striking, as is the claim that God's law, being perfect, will never be changed, ignoring the many post-biblical innovations of rabbinic law.

Coming after Maimonides' argument for a created world that introduces innovation in the world, with God's will trumping what would seem otherwise to be change, Maimonides' insistence that God would never have reason to change His law, however perfect, seems inconsistent and arbitrary. Nevertheless, Maimonides contends that after creation, God does not change the "laws" of nature (with the exception of the rare miracle), His creation being perfect as it is. The revealed law is part of that perfect creation, and perhaps Maimonides regards the world as eternal *a parte post* for the sake of the Torah's unchanging law, to guarantee its abiding validity. Here Maimonides' predilection for agreeing with a tenet of Aristotelian philosophy (even if he is only half agreeing, on the issue of eternity) is joined to his pleasure in affirming a Jewish belief in the superiority and unsurpassed validity of its law.

Maimonides goes to some length in chapter 29 to rein in what he regards as the hyperbolic liberties that the prophets take with nature, rejecting their prophecies of unnatural and miraculous events. Nature for him follows its predictable (and causally necessitated) course, with the exception of the occasional miracle recorded in the Bible. Maimonides can accept predictability and unpredictability as an expression of God's will, "the true reality and essence [of which] is to will and not to will," as he has said.[114] Not having any external constraints, the divine will can appear to change its mind and have a new volition, manifested in what we would regard as a miracle. It is not a change of mind, however, since the essence of God's will is just that: change, or the ability to change, to will and not to will. God's will is unchanging in its (theoretical) changeability.

That is logically true in speaking of the divine will alone, unfettered. As Maimonides believes, however, the divine will is never alone; it is always related to and an expression of divine wisdom, a wisdom that is both unchanging and eternal, brooking no novel ideas.[115] There is no multiplicity or change in the divine essence, Maimonides continually insists, so that any act of the divine will has to have been known eternally to God, its "novelty" foreknown. As such, the view of miracles as preprogrammed events that Maimonides recounts from midrashic sources[116] is not that different from his own position. However novel and "unnatural," the miracles that Maimonides may accept, like creation itself, are not new or exceptional to God.

Maimonides' profound admiration for Aristotle's physics is evident in his elaborate attempt in chapter 30 to square the Genesis account of creation with Aristotle's *Meteorology.* Maimonides' reading of Scripture in this chapter will strike the average reader as bizarre, the work of a man with an *idée fixe* who had to square his scientific convictions with his Bible. The very strained nature of his exegesis is testimony to Maimonides' conviction that there is but one truth, though there are many ways to express it.

7

Prophecy (*Guide* Part II, Chapters 32–48)

Paraphrase

In chapter 32, Maimonides lays out three views of prophecy, which, he says, are like the three opinions people have concerning the issue of eternity versus creation in time. This has been seen through the ages as an invitation to match the two sets of opinions, and deduce which is Maimonides' own view. On the surface, however, it would seem that the correspondence is straightforward, though the matchups are asymmetrical.

The first opinion Maimonides presents is one that he concedes is held by most believers in prophecy, both Jew and Gentile.[1] It is that God grants prophecy to whomever He wishes to receive it. Prior education is not a necessary condition for eligibility, though a moral and good character is. Maimonides presents the second opinion as that of the philosophers, for it requires a "certain perfection" (*kamāl mā*) in man that can be reached only after a period of training that strengthens his rational, moral, and imaginative faculties. Barring temperamental or external hindrances, a properly endowed and prepared person must necessarily become a prophet, in this view.

Maimonides identifies the third opinion as that of "our Law and the foundation of our doctrine" (*rāyy sharīʿatinā wa qāʿidah madhhabinā*), and declares it identical to the philosophic view, with one exception. Whereas necessity brooks no exception in the philosophic opinion, in this view God can intervene in nature and assert His will, preventing a person who is qualified in every apparent aspect from becoming a prophet. God generally allows nature to take its course but does interfere rarely, a view Maimonides supports with (not immediately apposite) biblical proof texts.

As Maimonides restricts prophecy to an elite few, he is obliged to treat the public revelation at Sinai as a subprophetic event for the entire nation. In chapter 33, Maimonides limits the people's experience of receiving the Decalogue to that of hearing a voice, or sound, *al-ṣawt,* created by God but mostly unintelligible. The people comprehend the sound of only the first two commandments, but that is because God's existence and unity are "knowable by human speculation alone."[2] Revelation here simply must be the occasion for voicing a universal truth accessible to human reason, and Moses is not necessary to mediate the meaning of these commandments.

Moses is absolutely indispensable for conveying the remaining commandments, however, as only he understands the sounds uttered as discreet words; he turns the voice heard into language. Maimonides finds ample support in the text for seeing Moses as having a privileged dialogical relation with God, but Maimonides believes he must disabuse the reader of the impression that God speaks, or has a voice. As with all other attributes predicated of God, so too must voice be denied Him, in a literal sense. Maimonides thus understands the divine voice as a metaphor expressing God's will,[3] an intention that Moses intuits and "translates" correctly, i.e., in language the masses can understand

In chapter 34, Maimonides asserts, based on Scripture, that all prophets other than Moses received their revelations through an angel. This establishes both the unique, direct relation Moses had with God, and the legitimacy of the private relations with angels that the other prophets experienced. With some exceptions that Maimonides minimizes in the next chapter, most prophets are reputed not to have encountered angels or worked their miracles in public, so that Maimonides feels obliged to articulate the institution of biblical prophecy.

In chapter 35, Maimonides begins to explain philosophically that which he has just defended on scriptural grounds, specifically distinguishing the prophecy of Moses from that of all other prophets. Maimonides feels justified in doing that, having already, in both his *Commentary on the Mishnah* and his *Mishneh Torah,*[4] identified four differences between Moses' prophecy and that of other prophets. For Maimonides, the only thing Moses and other prophets have in common is the name "prophet," and that only in a nonessential sense.[5]

In a similar fashion, the miracles associated with Moses are different from all other miracles worked by other prophets, Maimonides claims, though his exegeses here of the biblical sources are particularly forced. His main point is the uniqueness of Mosaic revelation, Moses' apprehension (*idrāk*) of God's wishes being different from and superior to that of all other biblical prophets, and all the more from the apprehensions of non-Jews.

Maimonides thus denies the supersessionist claims concerning prophecy made by both Islam and Christianity, basing himself solely on the biblical text that he recognized, the Hebrew Bible. He does not offer a historical or biological rationale for the superiority of Mosaic revelation, as did Judah Halevi, but rather justifies Mosaic law on rational grounds, later.[6]

In chapter 36, Maimonides offers the philosophical explanation of prophecy that was normative among the Muslim as well as the few Jewish philosophers who preceded him. It is a theory largely adapted in Hellenistic times from Aristotle's *De anima* (*On the Soul*).[7] Its key theme is that of intelligible concepts that emanate from God[8] and reach people through the intermediary of the Agent Intellect, the last of the separate intellects of the spheres. This intellect is the immediate source of forms on earth, as well as the source that presents these forms and the ideas formed from them in a way that our intellects and imaginations can comprehend.

Maimonides does not discuss the process of emanation, whether or how one all-inclusive form evolves into many; presumably one all-inclusive form could not have been known to God as many separate forms, for that would introduce multiplicity into His being. That which emanates from God is thus an outpouring of formal being that He does not know in its discrete states of multiplicity, for all that He is their author.

The Agent Intellect transmits its intelligible content to its intellectual counterpart in persons, located in the rational faculty, and through the intellect of the prophet to his imaginative faculty as well. For the distinctive mark of a prophet—that which places him in the highest rank of the human species—is his extraordinary imagination as well as intellect. It is the prophet's gift to be able to receive the universal truths of intelligible ideas in specific imaginative terms.[9]

The prophet, for Maimonides, needs to have as perfect a nature as is possible, intellectually, morally, and physically. One not endowed with a balanced temperament cannot expect to reach the standard required of a prophet. Perhaps reflecting his medical training, Maimonides may well be echoing here the Greek and later Roman standard of *mens sana in corpore sano.*

Maimonides treats the presence and roles of the rational and imaginative faculties of the soul as well known to his readers, since he views these faculties in the way considered standard in Greek and medieval psychology and assumes the intended audience of the *Guide* to be familiar with this topic. "You know," he tells his reader, that the imaginative faculty retains sensory impressions and combines and imitates them. Though Maimonides does not mention it here, this is the function of imagination in all healthy individuals, the stage preliminary to the rational faculty's abstraction of these images in order to consider their universal dimension.

The imaginative faculty has another function, however, one that Maimonides calls its "greatest and noblest action," and that is when the senses are not functioning, being asleep or at rest. This is when the emanation from the Agent Intellect is able to reach a properly disposed imagination, causing "veridical dreams" (*al-manāmāt al-ṣādiqa*), i.e., dreams that accurately portray future events. Everyone can have dreams of this kind; the dreams of a prophet are simply greater in kind, with philosophical import.

Maimonides thus allows the Agent Intellect to transmit specific, particular images as well as universal propositions. This emanation of images, the contents of prophetic revelations, was a view accepted by Alfarabi and Avicenna, as we have seen,[10] though they considered the souls of the spheres to be the source of such emanations. The dreams and visions a prophet has are thus given him by celestial powers, ultimately deriving from God. For Maimonides, this compels belief in the legitimacy of prophetic revelation in its exoteric (as well as esoteric) sense. The prophet's creativity is completely attuned to the ideas and images emanated upon him. The Torah is the product of divine inspiration, received from the Agent Intellect in either universal or particular form.

It could appear that the emanation sequence in dreams can do away with prior sensory input altogether, but Maimonides says that "it is known" that something that engages a person while awake, when his senses function, is that which preoccupies his imagination while asleep. The same process also may be said to underlie the vision that the prophet has while his senses are nominally at rest. Maimonides, it is clear, has attempted to naturalize prophetic dreams and visions considerably, even while accommodating a popular belief in the literal emanation of images.

Maimonides considers the emergence of a prophet as the end result of a natural process, beginning with a brain that is "extremely well proportioned" and that possesses a temperament that is not hindered by other parts of the body. Initially, then, the prophet is insulated against the excesses of one kind or another to which most people succumb. He naturally gravitates toward perfecting his intellectual as well as moral character. While achieving that, the prophet is drawn toward "the secrets of what exists," i.e., the mother of all sciences, metaphysics, which is ultimately, for Maimonides, knowledge of God and His actions.

At this point, Maimonides believes that the aspiring prophet will have left his bestial desires behind him, viz., the pleasures of eating, drinking, sexual intercourse, and whatever pleasures the sense of touch offers. Maimonides quotes Aristotle in disapproving of this sense.[11]

Maimonides finds the ideal person—and that is the prophet—to be detached as well from desiring to dominate others and from seeking their acclaim and obedience in "spurious kinds of rulership." For Maimonides, the "perfect man, the solitary" (*al-kāmil al-mutawaḥḥid*)[12] views people as either domestic animals or beasts of prey, to be avoided if possible so as not to be harmed, or to be handled in such a way as to gain advantage over them, if necessary.

The prophet-elect so secluded is then able to apprehend divine matters, "see" God and His angels, and acquire true opinions and directives that promote interpersonal relations. Maimonides thus balances his negative opinion of most people with a desire to improve their political condition; the prophet or perfect person should not stay in seclusion.[13] This sentiment will be echoed at the conclusion of the *Guide* as well.

Maimonides ends the chapter with the observation that the prophet is prevented from functioning when his imaginative faculty is weakened or troubled. He finds scriptural and rabbinic support for this view, citing a change in the nature of Moses' revelations in the extended period of wandering in the desert, due to his suffering over the reaction of the people to the spies' report of the challenge awaiting them were they to attempt to conquer Canaan (Numbers 14).

Moses experienced this adverse effect even though his prophetic state should not have involved his imaginative faculty, as the Agent Intellect emanated solely upon his intellect, in Maimonides' view. For him, this is Moses' unique kind of prophecy, which does not have recourse to imaginative parables. Yet even Moses, Maimonides apparently assumes, could not isolate his intellect from the emotions that affected his imagination and entire being. The Agent Intellect is indifferent to the psychic state of the recipient of its emanations, but the recipient's intellect cannot be similarly unaffected.

Maimonides here contradicts his earlier remark that he will not discuss Moses' prophecy at all. Maimonides also leaves us wondering how Moses' prophecy could be received without the linguistic medium, the words, sentences, and pictorial constructs that the imaginative faculty provides.

In chapter 37, Maimonides expands upon the diverse effects that the "divine emanation" (*al-fayḍ al-ilāhī*) of the Agent Intellect has upon people other than prophets. Scientists (and philosophers) are people (like Moses) who receive the emanation only in their rational faculty, while rulers and legislators, prognosticators and even dreamers of veridical dreams access the Agent Intellect in their imaginative faculty. The Agent Intellect thus can affect the rational and imaginative faculties separately, its emanations producing either intelligible abstractions or particular symbolic images. A person's proficiency in one or the other faculty, and corresponding deficiency, determine the manner in which the Agent Intellect finds expression.

Prophets, however, absorb this emanation in both their rational and their imaginative faculties, both highly developed. Prophets are then distinguished by the degree to which they feel compelled to go public with their revelation, to "address a call to the people, teach them, and let [their] own perfection emanate upon them."[14]

Actually, each class of persons has some individuals who respond to the emanations received in a private manner, in varying degrees, while others share their insights, through teaching and writing. Knowledge of the sciences depends on this shared wisdom, transmitted (and augmented) by one recipient of emanations to another. Ultimately, Maimonides claims, an individual appears who is the recipient of the entire contents of the Agent Intellect, i.e., a person who knows all of theoretical science. Such a person feels it necessary "to address a call to people" (*yadʿū an-nāṣ*), whatever the personal consequences may be, even injury or death.

In chapter 38, Maimonides completes the picture he draws of the prophet. In addition to being courageous and having perfected the temperament of his natural disposition, the prophet has a highly developed intuitive sense that allows him to jump from premises to conclusions in the shortest of intervals. While persons other than prophets may also have this gift, the prophet alone can apprehend what amounts to conclusions of arguments, i.e., assertions about the true nature of things, without having apprehended their premises. In Maimonides' construal, then, the prophet receives an emanation that allows him to dispense with the normal processes of reasoning, presenting truths in dogmatic terms that others must reconstruct syllogistically.[15] This understanding of prophecy underlies Maimonides' whole approach to the prophets' pronouncements.

In chapter 39, Maimonides emphasizes the uniquely legal character of Moses' prophecy. None of the prophets before or after Moses issued commands in God's name to follow a corpus of laws, a *shariʿa*. Even Abraham, who received and fulfilled the commandment of circumcision, did so without resorting to commands, leading, in Maimonides' account, by means of persuasive speech and rational argument.

Mosaic law is unique and will never be surpassed, according to Maimonides, because it is perfect. Its perfection is evidenced in its wisdom and moderation, or "equibalance" (*iʿtidāl*), a theme Maimonides will attempt to justify in the third part of the *Guide* when he suggests reasons for the commandments.[16] Whoever does not recognize the exemplary and beneficial character of Mosaic law is "wicked, vile [and] morally corrupt," Maimonides insists. The Law of Moses is the only "divine *shariʿa*"; all other "political regimes" (*al-tadbīrāt al-madanīya*) are the creations of men who were not prophets.[17]

Maimonides begins chapter 40 with the (unacknowledged) statement of

Aristotle that "man is political by nature" (*al-insān madanī bi'l-ṭib'*) and that it is in his nature to live in society.[18] At the same time, Maimonides acknowledges that great moral differences exist between individuals. He attributes this to their physical compositions, to the material substratum that affects their psyches. For Maimonides, only a strong and wise ruler can resolve these differences, by establishing a standard of practices and moral norms that, by abjuring extremes, will create a unified and well-ordered society.

This means to Maimonides that the institution of law is quasi-natural, or, as he puts it, "the Law, although it is not natural, enters into what is natural."[19] Fully natural, however, is the ability to rule found in some individuals, a fact that leads Maimonides into a comparison of types of rulers and their regimens. First and foremost is the prophet or lawgiver,[20] followed by a ruler who accepts the prophet's law, either in full or in part. This may well be a false prophet, eager to claim the law as his own creation.

Maimonides recognizes that there are both secular and religious legal systems, i.e., regimens established either by human initiatives or by allegedly prophetic revelations. The former is concerned with establishing a just and happy society, but it ignores theoretical issues and makes no attempt to perfect the rational faculty of its citizens. The legal system where the law is prophetically based, on the other hand, is concerned with issues that affect both the body and the soul, with "correct opinions" regarding God, angels, and all that exists.

For Maimonides, the prevailing model of law was that which claimed divine authorship, the major contenders being the *shari'a* of Moses and that of Muhammad. The character of the prophet was the determining factor, Maimonides claims, in distinguishing between a true and false prophet, and hence between an authentic divine law and a plagiarized one. For Maimonides, the true prophet is one who renounces physical pleasures, particularly those brought about by the sense of touch, and most particularly by "the foulness of copulation."

While Maimonides adduces biblical examples to support his claim, it is obvious that he is alluding negatively to the reputed behavior of the Prophet of Islam,[21] as well as to the ascetic reputation that Moses acquired among Jews. Besides the polemical feature of Maimonides' remarks here, it is important to note that he considers it an axiom of faith that only a person of fine moral character can produce a good political system, whether secular or religious. It is also worth remarking on Maimonides' trust in the superiority of a legal system that educates toward a monolithic set of ideas and religious observance. This is also indicative of the medieval, indeed entire premodern, mind-set he inhabited. Yet it is probably not only his confidence in the divine source of this system that can justify this belief. Like Alfarabi, Maimonides is aware of the religious sanction that must be evoked in order to secure allegiance to a given political system.

Chapter 41 shows Maimonides at his most daring, challenging self. In straightforward fashion, he considers prophetic visions and dreams as expressions of the prophet's imagination. As Maimonides has said before,[22] the imaginative faculty represents in its way true statements that it has received from the rational faculty, the intellect being the initial recipient of the Agent Intellect's emanating force.

Whether explicitly stated in Scripture or not, Maimonides insists that all non-Mosaic revelations, including those ascribed to God, actually are mediated through an angel. The angel, of course, is the form whereby the prophet's imaginative faculty presents the truths that the prophet needs to communicate. Angels do not exist, for Maimonides, independent of the ideas emanated upon the prophet's intellect and then transformed by his imagination.[23]

Maimonides insists that all revelations, however they are presented, occur to the prophets either in a dream or in a vision. Using biblical examples, Maimonides is constrained to point out that nonprophets may also have veridical dreams, all in fulfillment of a divine plan. In chapter 42, Maimonides reiterates his position that angels are encountered only in visions or dreams, whether specifically mentioned or not. Maimonides does not hesitate to cite as prophetic visions, i.e., events imagined by the patriarchs, such critical moments in Israel's history as Abraham's encounter with the three angels in Genesis 18, or Jacob's wrestling with an angel in Genesis 32. Given the ubiquity of angels in the Bible, and the transposition of all prophetic revelations to dreams and visions, it could well be thought that Maimonides regards biblical history as essentially an imaginative representation. That does not make it false, but it does not make it literally true either.[24]

Maimonides' theme in chapter 43 is an analysis of the parables (*amthāl*) employed in prophecy, an early example of literary criticism of the Bible. He classifies parables according to their transparency, some understood immediately by the prophet, others requiring him to seek out their meaning. He also classifies them according to their terminology: some words have denotative meanings, others connotative; some are clearly equivocal, others coded with puns.

From Maimonides' viewpoint, the prophet's skill at creating parables (couched as dreams or visions) does not reflect essentially on their poetic gifts; rather it attests to their creative ability to transmit God's will, as expressed in universal truths, in effectively concrete imaginative terms. Thus, while Maimonides critiques parables from a literary viewpoint, he does not wish us to view them as works of art, or see the prophets as poets. Though he has naturalized prophecy a great deal, he does not even think of secularizing it.

Maimonides continues in chapter 44 to insist upon his view that all (non-Mosaic) prophetic revelations occur only in a vision or dream, whatever the prophet has to say about seeing or hearing God directly while awake. The chapter serves as a transition to chapter 45, where Maimonides sets out to distinguish eleven degrees of prophecy, first mentioning that the degrees or kinds of prophecy a given prophet receives in his lifetime can vary.

Maimonides considers the first two degrees cited preprophetic stages, though it may be better to consider them quasi-prophetic. The first occurs when an inspiration attributed to the "Holy Spirit" (*ru'aḥ ha-qodesh,* also known as the "spirit of the Lord") moves an individual to some momentous virtuous action. This is a case of special providential assistance, characterized by the presence of a divine emissary technically other than an angel. The "Spirit of the Lord" or "Holy Spirit"[25] serves Maimonides here as an instantiation of the emanative force that issues from the Agent Intellect and mostly takes up residence in the imagination of an individual who is well endowed in that faculty but ignorant of the theoretical entailments of the action he then pursues.[26] Though Maimonides claims this divine spirit remained with Moses from the time he reached maturity in Egypt, before and after he became a prophet, most of the persons he cites as inspired by the "Spirit of the Lord," viz., the judges and kings of Israel, including King David, are not prophets. They are primarily men of action, not of contemplative thought.

The "Spirit of the Lord" is instrumental also in the second "preprophetic" degree of prophecy, in which an individual feels as though something has possessed him,[27] allowing him to speak wisely on a broad range of matters. The recipient of this form of inspiration differs from the prophet not only in being fully alert and awake when he has his spiritual encounter, but also in feeling compelled to say what he says. Thus David in the Psalms, Solomon in Proverbs, Ecclesiastes, and Song of Songs, Daniel, Job, and the authors of all the books assembled in that third portion of the Hebrew Bible known as the "writings" (*ketuvim*) are seen as conduits of the Holy Spirit. This, however, is not to deny the contributions made in each case by the imaginative faculty of the author of a given statement or book.

The third degree of prophecy represents those prophets who understand the parable of their dream already in the dream, while the fourth degree consists of those prophets who hear clear speech in their dream, without seeing the speaker. This contrasts with the fifth through seventh degrees of prophecy, in which the prophet (dreams he) sees a man, an angel, and God Himself, respectively. The eighth to eleventh degrees of prophecy concern visions in which the prophet sees parables and encounters speech, man and angel, respectively.

Maimonides considers the eleventh degree of prophecy, in which an angel addresses the prophet in a vision, as the highest form prophecy takes, again excluding Moses' unique form of prophecy. God cannot speak to the prophet in a vision as He can in a dream, Maimonides contends, because the imaginative faculty of (even) a prophet cannot conceive it. Maimonides bases this opinion on a verse in Numbers 12:6 that he interprets as assigning speech to dreams and conjunction with the Agent Intellect, i.e., cognition of scientific matters, to visions.

Maimonides ranks prophetic visions above dreams, then, for their allegedly superior cognitive status, similar, he says, to that of the knowledge obtained through theoretical reasoning.[28] Of course, every stage and occurrence of prophecy is meant to convey some rational idea or truth, and the imagination is the dominant faculty in both dreams and visions. Nevertheless, Maimonides distinguishes between visions and dreams in terms of the relative strength of the imaginative and rational faculties engaged.

Maimonides devotes chapter 46 to driving home the point that the visions prophets have are imaginative parables, however detailed and seemingly long in duration, and not to be taken as actions or events that actually happened. This is obvious with the visions of some of the prophets, less so with the Patriarchs, but for Maimonides it is all one and the same. God and His angels relate to human beings (Moses excluded) through their imagination. The imaginative faculty of prophets is attuned to perfection to present these visions as accurately as it can, but they remain imaginative representations, and as such approximations of the essential, universal truths that are sought.

In chapter 47, Maimonides expands his discussion of prophecy by moving from parables to single terms, figures of speech that are not meant to be taken literally: figurative terms, hyperboles, and similes. Maimonides concedes that people mostly understand when the prophets use language of this sort, but he is concerned that certain key terms are still taken literally, viz., the attributes and affects of God, usually expressed in corporeal terms. Maimonides thinks mistaken beliefs of this sort can lead to a faulty idea of God and to loss of faith. Proper understanding of biblical language is thus the key to a correct notion of the deity.[29]

In chapter 48, Maimonides concludes his discussion of prophecy and part 2 of the *Guide* on a strong naturalistic note. As God is "the First Cause of all things," Maimonides says,[30] the prophets regularly ascribe to Him events that actually have intermediate and more proximate causes, as the prophets fully know. The prophets thus give the impression that God is the immediate cause of all that occurs. This is a tenet of *kalām,* as we have seen.[31] Maimonides has vigorously opposed this view, sure that it was not the view of the prophets, as it is not that of rabbinic Judaism.

Maimonides identifies four kinds of proximate and temporal causes that the prophets attribute to God *fī ʿibārātihim,* "according to their manner of expressing themselves," i.e., for Maimonides, rhetorically. This rhetoric takes the form of having God "command, say, speak, send and call" for action that really has natural causes.

Bringing examples from Scripture, Maimonides shows that the prophets and Scripture in general portray God as directly responsible for natural events, voluntary acts of both humans and animals, and chance, accidental events as well. He commands the snow to melt (Psalms 147:18), sends a king to free Joseph (Psalms 105:20), and speaks to the big fish (Jonah 2:11). In treating these statements as rhetorical, Maimonides effectively distances God from nature and assumes the existence of free will and chance in human affairs.[32]

Analysis

Belief in prophecy was a central tenet both of medieval philosophy and of theology (in all three monotheistic traditions), and Maimonides struggled to accommodate both perspectives within the *Guide.* Philosophically, he borrowed freely from the conclusions of Avicenna and Alfarabi in particular, without detailing systematically the epistemological and political foundations of the doctrine as expressed by those two great *falāsifa.*[33] Maimonides' teachings on the epistemological foundations of prophecy, which offered a philosophical rationale of the phenomenon, have to be gleaned from disparate remarks he makes throughout the *Guide,* particularly at 1:68.[34]

There, Maimonides describes the process of intellection, i.e., the activity of ʿ*aql,* the intellect. As was customary, he considers this activity as culminating in a complete identification of a person's intellect with its intelligible object; the intellect having first abstracted this form from the matter with which it appears (via the sense and imagination).[35] Maimonides dwells upon the fact that the intellect, in cognizing the intelligible form or "intention" (from the Latin *intentio,* translating the Arabic *maʿnâ*), is completely identified with it: "For in the case of every intellect, its act is identical with its essence," *li-anna kulla ʿaqlin, fiʿluhu huwa dhātuhu.*[36]

There is, Maimonides thus insists, no other being for the "intellect *in actu*" (as it is often termed) besides its activity; in it we may say being and becoming are merged. This is certainly true for the intellect *in actu* in its final stage of activity, once it has stripped the form of its matter, as Maimonides puts it. In the initial stage of cognition, however, the intellect must relate to the material representation of the form, before and in order to abstract its essence from it. Calling this initial stage of the rational faculty the *hylic* or "material" intellect does more than signify its potential status, matter being the principle of potentiality; it also establishes the connection of this faculty to the body from which it derives its sensations and images. Therefore, when an intellect begins to act, when it starts to think, we should assume it is not immediately the form that it thinks; rather, it retains an identity and an intellectual self-consciousness separate from those acts of intellectual cognition through which it loses its individuality upon full conjunction with its intelligible object.

Maimonides does not identify by name this intermediate aspect of one's intellect; he may simply assume its presence, subsuming it under the rubric of the intellect *in actu* mentioned in *Guide* 1.68. He also does not speak of the intellect *in habitu, al-ʿaql biʾl-malakah,* which some of the Muslim philosophers, following Alexander of Aphrodisias, designated as a person's accumulated but latent knowledge that could be tapped into at will.[37] In *Guide* 3.51, Maimonides alludes to this stage of cognition, using the classic example of a skilled scribe who is not presently writing. Such a person is analogous to one who is in a state of potential apprehension, "close to" actuality. He or she clearly has a habituated or experienced intellect that is not being used at that moment. When it is again employed, it will link up with the universal object of its concern quickly. Thus, individuality in Maimonides' conceptualization of the intellect can be located in an activated material intellect, i.e., in the intellect *in actu,* and presumably in an intellect *in habitu.*

A fourth stage of an individual's intellect was often posited as well, one that could be seen as an advanced and activated stage of the intellect *in habitu,* viz., the "acquired intellect," *al-ʿaql al-mustafād.* This intellect had been identified by Alfarabi as denoting the stage at which the person's intellect has acquired knowledge of all or nearly all that it is possible for a human being to know.[38] At this point the individual may be said to have his or her own perfected intellect, following which conjunction with the Agent Intellect is possible. The assumption here is that the amassed knowledge in the acquired intellect puts it on the same ontological plane with the Agent Intellect, permitting the conjunction of like entities.

Maimonides, however, does not speak of the acquired intellect in these terms. He actually speaks of it very seldom, mentioning it by name just twice, in *Guide* 1.72 (p. 193). He emphasizes that it is not intrinsically part of the human intellect: "this intellect is not a faculty in the body but is truly separate from the organic body and overflows towards it." This sentence bears a strong resemblance to *Guide* 2.4 (p. 250), in which Maimonides says that our intellect in act comes from an emanation of the Agent Intellect, *al-ʿaql al-faʿāl,* and it is through this emanation that we apprehend the Agent Intellect.

Mention of the Agent Intellect obliges us to modify our impression of intellection as a function of the individual person's activity only, as Aristotle had conceived it. After Alexander of Aphrodisias's emendations, though, philosophers concurred that the individual was assisted in the act of comprehension, indeed enabled to act, by the presence of the hypostatized Agent Intellect, the bestower, in one sense or another, of all terrestrial forms.

As we have observed, Maimonides speaks of the Agent Intellect and the acquired intellect in nearly identical terms. On his understanding of intellection, the Agent Intellect becomes the acquired intellect when it devolves (i.e., emanates) upon a person whose intellect is disposed—and eager—to receive it. In the act of intellection, the subject and object meet and join. The Agent Intellect then becomes or functions as the acquired intellect in relation to us.

It is worth emphasizing that for Maimonides, as for others in this tradition, conjunction is possible only when the intelligible that is being thought is real, or, to put it differently, only when the notion thought is a real intelligible, part of the essential nature of the world's being. The imagination may be deceived in this, but not the intellect, certainly not the trained intellect. The person who has reached a high level of intellectual perfection may be said to think only of universal truths, in the most comprehensive of judgments. Whereas initially, each cognitive act had to abstract the universal from the particular, the practiced and perfected intellect is now able to think its thoughts in more immediately abstract form, making ever more abstract inferences, moving to greater and greater degrees of fundamental universal truth. While it may well be the case that this person must still think in representational, imagistic terms, the thoughts are of the essential meanings of the terms, as always. This is the condition of conjunction, in which Maimonides clearly believes.[39] Such a person may be said to think of the Agent Intellect itself, directly, i.e., to be in conjunction with it.

Maimonides is reticent in discussing the ultimate stage of prophetic knowledge, that which coincides with mastery of all science. Yet it is this very "conjunction" (or union, *ittiṣāl* in Arabic, *devequt* in Hebrew) that occurs between the individual intellect and the universal Agent Intellect that is the conduit for the particular expression of God's will. The Agent Intellect, the celestial principle that endows forms on earth and gives humans the ability to conceptualize universal truth, is treated as an angel, allowing for a synthesis of the philosophical and the religious traditions. Maimonides courageously returns the angel to philosophy in seeing it as able to impress itself both upon the rational intellect of a person and, in dreams, directly upon his imagination.

Maimonides' comparison of three understandings of prophecy with three views on the question whether and how the world was created has challenged his medieval and modern commentators and fairly tied them in knots searching for correspondences in the two positions. Strong arguments have been presented for viewing Maimonides as an Aristotelian, Platonist, or Jewish traditionalist. This last view would have God grant prophecy to whomever He chooses. While seemingly innocuous, the problem with this construal of prophecy is that Maimonides rejects it, seeing it as a view of the *jumhūr* or mass of philosophically naïve, common people.

It appears that the first view Maimonides offers of a creation from nothing by the will of God would best fit the third view of prophecy, in which God interrupts the natural order at will. The third, eternity opinion, that of Aristotle, may then match with the second prophecy view that affirms a necessary occurrence of prophecy when deserved; while the Platonic position on creation, positing a primal matter upon which God works His will as He wishes, is akin to the first, popular but ignorant view of prophecy as essentially granted in accordance with God's wishes. In terms of numerical equivalents, with the first number the eternity or creation opinion, the second number the prophecy opinion, we than have an ordering of 1:3, 3:2, and 2:1.[40]

This matching of views does not in and of itself prove which pair Maimonides favors, though unless conclusive arguments can be brought to show he is deliberately lying about his preferences, Maimonides should be taken at his declared word and seen as endorsing views 1 and 3, creation from nothing and willful interference with the granting of prophecy.

Taking Maimonides at his word does not mean his word is transparent, however. We have seen in the previous chapter that Maimonides can endorse creation from nothing without abandoning (all) philosophical assumptions. Similarly, he can here accept a view of God's presence in human affairs that does not necessarily contradict his stated position on God's unchanging and impersonal nature. The key is to be found in Maimonides' understanding of the divine will. As he mentions a number of times, it is not to be seen as a separate aspect of the deity, different from God's wisdom. God has no attributes, and those that we regard as essential in describing His being are all used equivocally, out of compassion for our need to relate to Him.[41] The essence of God is strictly one, which we divide into wisdom, will, power, or goodness, depending on the circumstances that affect us.

Thus, the fact that a person who deserves to be a prophet, according to the philosophical criteria that Maimonides accepts, but who does not succeed in becoming one, may be said to have been prevented from achieving that status by the "will" of God. We can understand that more easily by substituting "wisdom" for "will," and by subsuming both within the (non)relation of God to the world, or rather, within a nondirect relation. For we must remember that Maimonides has tempered his Aristotelianism with Neoplatonic emanationist theory. Therefore, Maimonides' God is not Aristotle's unmoved mover absorbed in self-contemplation only; He is also the One from whom all being derives, and who has a providential regard for His creation.

Thus, everything that happens in this world is the result of God's wisdom and His will, i.e., the result of the effulgence of His being. We attribute good and bad occurrences to the wisdom and/or will of God, depending on the circumstances, reluctant to accept the fact that it is all part of the divine plan for the universe. That plan is fixed in its universal lines, even as God does not change,[42] and the failures and unfair events that may befall people are inescapably part of it. These "failures" are not the primary intention of God's design of the universe, and they are certainly not designed on an ad hoc basis, with a particular person or group in mind.

As one whose goodness is identical with His being, God cannot intend to see that goodness qualified. That is why whatever happens must be seen ultimately as an expression of His (mysterious) benevolence, as willed by Him. The immediate cause for the failure of a qualified person to become a prophet must be located elsewhere, however, and it is the same cause that is responsible for all the natural catastrophes and political and ethical failures of mankind. It is the material element in creation that is the guilty party, the one element that is volatile, changing, and unresponsive at times to the form that is imposed upon it.

God is and is not responsible for the effects of matter on the universe.

Ultimately, He is the remote cause of all that exists, and matter, as the substrate of form, is a necessary condition for the changes that substances undergo on earth, part of the divine plan. Still, as the principle of change and becoming on earth, matter is as remote as possible from the unchanging reality that is God. It is as this antithesis of the One, though not as an autonomous opponent, that matter is considered evil. Its evil is the absence of good, a privation of the being that is unchanging.

Here Maimonides shows his Neoplatonic colors, in regarding matter as residing on the lowest rung of reality, so much so that it can be considered nonbeing, or the privation of being (*'adam*). It is the (benevolent) wisdom of God that accedes to a universe (of His making) in which privations of the good can (and must, as the price of change) occur. When they do, we say it is God's will, as it is, in a sense.

Of course, it is also (and especially) God's will for the obviously good to be manifested, so that it is also His will for a qualified prophet to be recognized as such. That process, however, has been sufficiently well explained by Aristotle, and Maimonides expends much effort to reconcile the biblical text with his teachings.

Why, then, does Maimonides distance himself from what he regards as the Aristotelian view of prophecy? Again, the answer lies in the concept of divine will, which Maimonides feels Aristotle does not sufficiently appreciate. He presents Aristotle in an overly naturalistic light, considering that Maimonides received him with the Neoplatonic coloration given him by Muslim philosophers that added divine providence to the solipsistic concentration of Aristotle's own god. Reacting, then, to what he portrays as and perhaps believes is a doctrine of unyielding causal determinism, Maimonides proffers what seems to be a view of a personal, hands-on God, a deity foreign to his own teachings, or so it would seem.

If forced to choose, Maimonides' readers would prefer Plato's positions on creation and prophecy to those of Aristotle. Plato's god is more akin to Maimonides,' in that the demiurge works his will upon creation. However, Maimonides would have had difficulty in accepting Plato's acceptance of a primordial eternal matter. The prophetic "twin" to this view is the opinion that allows God to work His will in placing the mantle of prophecy upon any and everyone. There are no natural restraints on God's actions here, as there are none on the demiurge when he adapts matter to whatever form He chooses, and for howsoever long, in Plato's view on creation.

Maimonides is more outwardly sympathetic to Plato's creationist view than to Aristotle's cosmogony, though Maimonides understands that both stand for a universe that is eternal; that is, both assume the universe has an eternal material element. Hence, Maimonides rejects Plato's position as not significantly different from Aristotle's. It is quite different, however, in not having the natural restraints that characterize Aristotle's (and Maimonides') position. Moreover, the prophetic analogue to Plato's creationist position, the view that would have God act arbitrarily to create prophets, is considered crude by Maimonides, probably because of the lack of any set of requirements that a potential prophet need have.

Beginning at chapter 33, Maimonides deconstructs the phenomenon of prophecy and of apparitions of other kinds, conveyed in visions and dreams that were commonly considered miracles. He begins with the most important event in the history of the people Israel, that which rendered them a people, namely, the revelation at Sinai.

Maimonides thinks belief in the historical authenticity of this event, and in its miraculous nature, is as important to affirm as belief in the miraculous creation of the world from nothing. Indeed, the belief in one is tied to that in the other, in that validation of the miracle of creation permits belief in a miraculous theophany, and it is the revelation at Sinai and the Torah taught there that confirms God's creative powers. That is, belief in creation is supported by the Torah's account of it, and believing in the miracle of revelation at Sinai is justified by the miraculous precedent of creation. It would be surprising if Maimonides did not recognize the circular nature of this reasoning, and his presentation of it should be seen as part of the rhetorical posture he frequently adopts in the *Guide*.[43] His beliefs in creation and revelation are not, however, dependent philosophically on exegetical exposition, and not understood by him in the literal terms of Scripture.

It is accordingly not entirely surprising that Maimonides sets out to delimit the sphere of the supernatural in describing what transpired at Sinai. He does not directly deny the encounter with God that the people had there, but he goes to great lengths to circumscribe the people's role. Thus Maimonides reports, based on rabbinic readings of Scripture, that either the voice of God was totally unintelligible to the people, or they could make out the sounds of just the first word or words of the first and second commandments. This, though, supposedly allowed everyone present to reason out the truth of the existence and unity of God, these propositions being demonstrable logically (as Maimonides has shown).

The people, however, are totally dependent on Moses for comprehending the remaining eight commandments, though these are less philosophically challenging, belonging, as Maimonides says, to the class of opinions and traditional propositions, and thus not amenable to the certainty of demonstrable proof.[44] These commandments, and the entire body of laws that Moses later proclaims, receive their validation not from their unique character, for they are strictly conventional, but from the unique circumstance of their transmission. They are conveyed by a mysterious sound, issuing forth amidst fire and lightening, causing the people to tremble and be afraid. Moses alone remains calm and rational, articulating in speech the incomprehensible voice of God.

Maimonides, though, is uncomfortable with the notion of a divine voice, which is contrary to his belief in the impermissibility of attributing anything to God. He therefore adopts the notion advanced before him by Saadia Gaon (tenth century) and others of a "created voice," some sort of reified sound, other than God Himself.[45] Such a creation is akin to others that Maimonides allows (with reservations), such as the Holy Spirit and the entire panoply of angels.

All these apparitions are imaginary for Maimonides, that is, they are the product of imaginations inspired by emanations from the Agent Intellect received by the people as visual and aural sensations. To the prophet's intellect, however, the intelligible source of these imagined sensations transmits a universally true proposition. The prophet's imagination then converts it to a specific image that captures its essential meaning symbolically. These images often take the form of parables; indeed, Maimonides concludes the discussion of prophecy with the claim that the "greater part" of the prophets' prophecies are parables.[46] He cautions the reader not to take them literally, to allow for hyperbole and figurative expression.

Nevertheless, Maimonides in chapter 34 relies on scriptural passages to insist that God (through the Agent Intellect) forbade disobeying "that angel whose words the prophet would transmit to us."[47] The words of a true prophet are sacred to Maimonides; the Torah and Hebrew Bible are immeasurably more to him than mere poetry or elegantly crafted prose, their creative spark being divinely inspired. Moses' prophetic mission is unique; he is the conduit for the law that binds Israel to its God.

In his earlier rabbinic compositions, Maimonides differentiated Moses' prophecy from all others, as he says in chapter 35. Thus, he described Moses as receiving prophecy while awake, not in a dream or visionary state; as being in direct, "face to face" relation with God, not having an angelic intermediary; calm and not terrified by the experience; and, unlike other prophets, as being perpetually prepared and able to receive prophecy, which required him to live in a state of ritual purity apart from his wife.

Maimonides later concedes that Moses went through difficult times when he was not in touch with his prophetic persona. Yet Maimonides remains insistent that all of Moses' prophecies are unique in not being the product of an angelic intermediary, and therefore not the products of his imagination, however inspired. The Agent Intellect endowed Moses' rational faculty, which understood it completely without the need for imaginative representation. In this, Moses is the extreme example of the type of person Maimonides calls a scientist;[48] he is also therefore the perfect man.

Maimonides does not explain how Moses could have written the Torah, given that its language is not that of the theoretical scientist, or does not appear to be so. The text seems rather similar to the work of an imaginative writer, replete with symbols, parables, and allegories, which Maimonides is constantly interpreting "back" to their theoretical foundations.

Perhaps to forestall such questions, Maimonides had dogmatically insisted, in the eighth of the thirteen principles of faith that he enunciated in his *Commentary on the Mishnah,* that the Torah "was received in its entirety from the 'mouth of God' . . . in a way that is figuratively called speech [*kalām*]," and that Moses' role was strictly that of a scribe, a secretary taking down dictation.[49]

Maimonides would thus have the reader of the *Commentary on the Mishnah* believe that God entered into an intimate relation with a human being, and that He communicated with Moses using the very words that Moses transcribed. Maimonides is thereby as much as saying that it is not the Torah that speaks in human terms, it is God Himself. In saying all this, however, Maimonides contradicts his entire image of a deity who has no direct relation with other beings, and of a God whose thoughts are not ours. Maimonides obviously allowed himself such statements when speaking as a nonphilosopher to a largely (philosophically) unsophisticated readership, but he avoids repeating them in the *Guide.* Now he does not contradict himself, however much he remains determined to claim a special and unique status for Moses as a prophet. Moses' uniqueness lies in the purely intellectual nature of his prophetic utterances, appearances to the contrary notwithstanding.

Maimonides' description of Moses' uniqueness built on what was portrayed in the biblical text, i.e., on Moses' own account of his experience, as well as on what tradition had added to that account. Moses long since had been glorified and sanctified in rabbinic thought, as well as in Muslim theology.[50] In the previous generation, Maimonides' father, Maimun ben Joseph, had described Moses, building on common tropes, as possessed of the utmost strength and beauty, surpassing that of angels, among whom he witnessed the light of God.[51] Maimun also endorsed a talmudic view that Moses did not die but remained immortal in heaven, interceding there with God on Israel's behalf.[52]

Maimonides quotes the same talmudic statement in the introduction to his *Commentary on the Mishnah*,[53] and he refers to the angelic status of Moses again in the introduction to his commentary on chapter 10 of Sanhedrin (*Ḥeleq*), when discussing the seventh principle of the faith, Moses' unique prophetic status.

Maimonides actually vacillates in his rabbinic writings when portraying Moses, reining in the popular tendency to treat him in supernatural terms.[54] The *Guide* reflects this more rational approach, where Moses, for all his unique qualities, remains a mortal.

Thus the dilemma remains, how Maimonides' Moses could receive emanations in purely abstract, universal terms, and yet transmit them in human idiomatic language, composing what could well pass as an imaginative work of art. This is, after all, what all authentic prophets do, except Moses, for Maimonides. We would seem to have two persons inhabiting the one body of Moses, or two images of Moses colliding, the divine or semidivine Moses and the human Moses.[55]

This combination in one person of the supernatural and the natural was a well-known belief in Ismāʿīlī Shīʿī circles, and Maimonides would have been familiar with it.[56] Each one of the six great prophets of the Ismāʿīlī tradition (Adam, Noah, Abraham, Moses, Jesus, and Muhammad) was believed to have led a dual life, comprehending the essential and nondescribable unity of being on the one hand, and particularizing it in the specific language of his community on the other. The initial revelations were believed to contain universal teachings. They were expressed, and disguised, in popular, exoteric language that needed to be interpreted by a trusted associate.[57] Each prophet was called an "Enunciator" (*nāṭiq*), the associate a "legatee" (*waṣiy*). Moses, for example, had Aaron as his *waṣiy*, Jesus had Simon Peter, and Muhammad had ʿAli.

For Maimonides, Moses could well exemplify the *nāṭiq* image of a supreme prophet, divorced from the Shīʿī pattern of ongoing revelations and from the presence of an accompanying *waṣiy*. Maimonides appears further to break with the Shīʿī model in regarding Moses' transmission of his prophetic encounters as recorded in the Torah as a subprophetic experience, in that it is immersed in imaginative discourse, employing that faculty which Maimonides excludes from Moses' prophecy. The Torah as we have it is thus the product of Moses' imagination, conveying the philosophical truths he received in prophecy, but not the prophetic revelation itself.[58]

The Torah, rather, is an exoteric popularization of emanated esoteric truths, a coded, seemingly conventional narrative that requires intellectual deconstruction. For Maimonides, these esoteric, philosophical teachings in the Torah had gone without explication for too long. In Maimonides' mind, consciously or not, he and not Aaron was Moses' legatee, his *waṣiy*, revealing to the initiated the secrets of Scripture.

Thus, the Ismāʿīlī model of prophecy afforded Maimonides an explanation that allowed the Torah to be treated as a cogent exemplification of an ultimately inexpressible intellectual revelation. Moses did not need to be divinized, in Maimonides' partial adoption of this model, a model that was tied to philosophical as well as theosophical sources.

The Ismāʿīlī theologians of the ninth and tenth centuries, who were the theoreticians of the Fatimid empire still in the twelfth century when Maimonides arrived in Egypt, had combined Neoplatonic metaphysics with their own set of divinized prophets and semidivinized imams. Their chain culminates in a seventh imam, Muḥammad b. Ismāʿil, who is waiting in heaven to return to earth as the *mahdi* or messiah.

It is this messianic motif in Ismāʿīlī thought that contributed greatly to political unrest in Yemen and elsewhere in the Islamic world in Maimonides' day, with repercussions in the Jewish community. Without disavowing the messianic tenet of Jewish faith, Maimonides strenuously attempted to defer its political immediacy, as shown in his *Epistle to Yemen,*[59] written shortly after he completed his *Commentary on the Mishnah.*

In the *Guide* itself, the notion of an imminent messianic advent is completely absent, and Moses is not portrayed with messianic features. The salvation he offers is to be found in the proper understanding and observance of the Law, which is never to be repealed by a sudden messianic epiphany. Moses is a (supreme) lawgiver, not the Messiah; his legacy is political and philosophical.

As indicated in chapter 36, Maimonides is ambivalent in his attitude toward society. He has a poor opinion of most people, considering them either passive or aggressive, and considers the perfect person to be a *mutawaḥḥid,* a hermit who is "alone" with all but God.[60] Yet that same person, in the perfection of his knowledge, will come to understand the general principles of governing society for the common good. He will then have to decide whether or not to leave his self-imposed isolation (and tranquility) and engage with those whom he mostly disdains.

Prophets, like philosophers,[61] vary in response to this question, but

Maimonides clearly feels that the very best of both classes of men have the courage and moral integrity to enter the public sphere and give witness to their revelations. While the prophet Jeremiah is Maimonides' example of this sort of courageous person, it can well be that Maimonides is thinking of himself as well. He believes he has a *da'wa,* a mission, to accomplish,[62] is convinced that he is in possession of the highest truths a person can obtain, and feels obliged to share them. The *Guide* embodies the philosophical (and theological) expression of his perceived social obligation, even as his *Mishneh Torah* represents his halachic response. Notwithstanding his elitist views, or perhaps because of them, Maimonides spent his entire life in engagement with and service to his people.

For Maimonides, Moses' *da'wa,* his mission, is prophetically unique in that it alone presents a body of law. This law is perfect, and as such can never be improved upon or altered. It is divine in origin, so that denying it is wicked, tantamount to denying belief in God. Maimonides makes these claims dogmatically, as part of his polemic with Islam primarily, but also with Christianity. Later, in part 3, Maimonides will attempt to illustrate his thesis, but in chapter 40 he is interested in segueing into a discussion of political regimes and the various kinds of law that underlie them.

Though Maimonides' statement that "man is political by nature" was widely known to be originally uttered by Aristotle, Maimonides' principal mentor in political philosophy, as in prophetology, logic, and ethics, was Alfarabi.[63] In eloquently subtle treatises, that tenth-century philosopher dissected different types of political regimes and showed the vital role that religion and prophetic leaders played in society. Alfarabi's understanding of the prophet's faculties of imagination and intellection and their relation to the Agent Intellect is generally adopted by Maimonides. He followed Alfarabi (and Avicenna as well) in believing that the Agent Intellect imparted universal intelligible notions to the rational faculty, as well as particular impressions, in dreams, to the imaginative faculty.[64] Maimonides does not, however, follow his two mentors in ascribing effects upon the imaginative faculty to emanations from the souls of the celestial spheres. That must have seemed to Maimonides to be philosophically unnecessary.

Alfarabi emphasized that religious teachings employ dialectical and rhetorical arguments, and thus have only a probabilistic truth-value at best. They are nevertheless of crucial importance in supporting popular beliefs, thereby strengthening the social fabric of the society and affording personal happiness.[65] Alfarabi affirmed that religious assertions, when properly interpreted, can yield theoretical truths, offering certainty, as well as practical insights. A final or best religion will contain both.[66]

Alfarabi is remarkably nonpartisan in accounting for the rise and position of religion in the state, though he must be thinking of Islam as the final religion, and apparently inclines toward the Shīʿī branch of the faith. Yet he remains objective and avoids giving examples from the Muslim experience. Avicenna is more parochial, and at the end of his *Al-Shifā' Metaphysics* he offers what may well be an apologia for having written an objective discourse on metaphysical issues. There he offers examples matching Islamic teachings and practices to philosophical truths. Yet even he avoids bringing the Prophet of Islam directly into what is essentially an academic discourse.[67]

For his part, Maimonides has no problem in asserting the superiority of Jewish law to all other legal and religious regimes. He is presenting not a general exposition of political philosophy but rather what is essentially an apology, a defense of Mosaic prophecy and a detailed rationalization of Jewish law. His remarks may be seen as an illustration of Farabian teachings on the role of religion in society and the role of its spokesmen.

Maimonides' treatment of the presence of angels in the Bible, and of God Himself, shows how well he absorbed the lessons in statecraft Alfarabi taught. Maimonides is quite explicit in chapter 41 that such appearances are imagined, though their origin is in the Agent Intellect (and thus ultimately in God). The Agent Intellect takes the form of an angel in a person's imagination. Even when God Himself is "unqualifiedly" said to speak,[68] Maimonides insists that the words are those of an angel, i.e., the words, and entire vision, are imagined.

Maimonides takes each biblical encounter with angels, and the appearance and pronouncements of God Himself, with the utmost seriousness, often without qualification. He ingeniously interprets and finds a category for each kind of divine encounter, retaining its sacred aura even while naturalizing the supernatural. He can do this convincingly, given his belief in the varieties of expression that emanate from the Agent Intellect, i.e., both particular images and universal propositions. Through these manifestations of the divine will, Maimonides has a heartfelt conviction that God is present in the biblical narrative, and in the world, however mythically He and His emissaries are depicted.

Maimonides' distinction between prophetic visions and dreams[69] relies on the type of emanation that the prophet receives. Visions are communicated by the Agent Intellect first to the rational faculty and passed on, to be transformed, to the imaginative faculty. Dreams, on the other hand, are received by the prophet's imagination directly from the Agent Intellect, in narrative and imagistic form.

Maimonides' belief in a God without affect does not leave Maimonides unaffected. He finds that the emanations that issue ultimately from God structure the world in a providential manner, and this divine providence, through the Agent Intellect primarily, inspires people to behave as the Bible depicts. Moses tells what appears to be a very human story for Maimonides, but he believes it conveys essential truths in symbols and parables. These truths are both metaphysical and political, concerning God and Israel. The Bible is the constitution of the people, its laws not to be changed. In fact, Maimonides takes much greater liberty with the traditional God of Israel than he does with the Law. Yet however radical his image of the deity, Maimonides responds to it as to a personal God, in awe and love. This emerges most clearly in the *Guide* at the end of the book, as we shall see.

Maimonides concludes part 2 of the *Guide* in chapter 48 in a way that persuaded two of the last century's greatest interpreters of his thought to believe that he secretly denied free will and affirmed divine determinism of all events.[70] Whereas the summary of the chapter presented above[71] emphasized the prophets' ascription of all events to God as a rhetorical device that did not contravene natural causality and did not preempt free will and chance from affecting events, Shlomo Pines and Alexander Altmann understood Maimonides here as subsuming these factors within a causal chain that was completely determined by God.

It is true that Maimonides commences this chapter affirming by God as the first cause of all things, all intermediate causes following in strict causal relations that can be traced to God's will and choice. In a key sentence, Maimonides writes, "For inasmuch as the deity is, as has been established, He who arouses a particular volition [*tilqa al-irāda*] in the irrational animal and who has necessitated this particular free choice [*awjaba dhāliqa al-ikhtiyār*] in the rational animal and who has made the natural things pursue their course . . . it follows necessarily [*lazima*] from all this that it may be said with regard to what proceeds necessarily from these causes that God has commanded that something should be done in such and such a way or that He has said: Let this be thus."[72]

Maimonides then provides biblical examples of God's immediate causal responsibility for human and natural occurrences, worded in the rhetoric of prophetic discourse. The essential truth of these passages for Maimonides, according to Pines and Altmann, is that God is the determining cause of everything, leaving man without free will.

This position goes against every statement on the subject that Maimonides made in his *Commentary on the Mishnah* and his *Mishneh To-*

rah, as well as the statements he was to make in his *Letter on Astrology;* and it goes against the *Guide*'s own image of a remote and unaffected first cause. As Maimonides knows and has acknowledged, a view of God as absolutely omniscient, possessed of detailed foreknowledge, renders the entire system of law, the *halakha,* otiose; man has no choice or free will and should not be punished or rewarded for acts he was compelled to do. Maimonides rejects the Ash'arite *kalām* position that espouses this view and cannot adopt it as his own without trashing much of what the *Guide* is about.

Yet there remains the presumably careful wording of this chapter as quoted above, attributing whatever happens directly to God. He it is who arouses a "particular" volition (*tilqa 'al-irādah*) in the irrational animal, and He it is who has necessitated "this particular" free choice (*awjaba dhāliqa 'al-ikhtiyār*) in the rational animal. While this translation is acceptable, it should be noted that *tilqa* and *dhāliqa* technically should be rendered as "that" and not "a particular" or "this particular." Maimonides may well be saying that while God is the ultimate cause of all that happens, He does not know things in their very particularity. He knows "that" volition and "that" choice, *whatever they happen to be,* knowing as He does the full range of possibilities.[73] Maimonides does not here speak to the problem of foreknowledge as precluding free choice, so we shall leave that topic for chapter 9.[74]

8

The Metaphysics of the Chariot (*Guide* Part III, Introduction and Chapters 1–7)

Paraphrase

In the introduction to part 3 of the *Guide,* Maimonides reminds the reader that the main purpose of the work is to explain "what can be explained" of the "Account of the Beginning" and the "Account of the Chariot," rabbinic terms adopted for the sciences of physics and metaphysics. He also reminds the reader that these subjects are considered by the rabbis to be mysteries of the Torah, not to be taught in public, and, as for metaphysics, not to be communicated to more than one (qualified) person at a time, and then conveyed only in cryptic fashion, as "chapter headings."

These strictures and the exclusively oral nature of the teachings led in time to complete ignorance of metaphysics among Jews, Maimonides declares, though he has managed on his own to gain clear and perhaps indubitable knowledge of the subject.[1] He accepts the possibility that matters may be different from what he thinks, having come to his knowledge by means of intuition and conjecture (*ḥads wa-takhmīn*).[2] Yet he is certain he is right; both Scripture and philosophical premises support his views.

Maimonides feels bound to honor the prohibition against publicizing his knowledge,[3] though he also feels it cowardly to deprive others, like his addressee Joseph, of information that would alleviate their perplexities, information that otherwise, he is sure, would perish with his own demise. He tells the reader that he has resolved the dilemma with divine assistance, by interpreting Ezekiel's account of the chariot in such a way that the unprepared reader will think it a mere paraphrase, while the prepared reader, who has read all the preceding chapters of the *Guide,* will uncover the true teachings Maimonides wishes to convey. The subject is central to all else, Maimonides concludes.

In this manner, Maimonides again, as in the opening introduction to the

Guide, announces he will write esoterically. He offers a historic rationale for accepting metaphysics as a Jewish subject, and for treating it with great discretion. He is convinced of the need to accommodate Jewish intellectuals in their search for a scientifically plausible and rational faith, and of the need, at the same time, to keep the community intact. Whether he consciously fabricates history is another matter.

Accordingly, Maimonides devotes chapters 1–7 of this third part of the *Guide* to a coded retelling of Ezekiel's "vision of the chariot," the source of much of the mystical tradition in Judaism. Maimonides' exegesis is likely intended as much to rescue Judaism from the clutches of mysticism as to appropriate Ezekiel for the rational tradition. Jonathan ben Uzziel, a second-century (CE) rabbi known to Maimonides from talmudic and midrashic sources, gives him the legitimacy he seeks in explicating, however obliquely, a subject that is not supposed to be written about or taught publicly. Of course, Maimonides takes Jonathan out of context as much as he takes Ezekiel, but that is standard for all his exegetical moves, as it is for the rabbinic commentary tradition in general.

Commentators through the ages, from Maimonides' contemporary and Hebrew translator Samuel ibn Tibbon on down, have offered interpretations that seek to harmonize Maimonides' treatment of Ezekiel with his earlier explicit discussion of cosmology in the *Guide*.[4] Thus, Maimonides' consideration of Ezekiel's vision of four "living creatures,"[5] each with four faces, resembling a man, ox, lion, and eagle, is taken by many commentators as symbolizing four areas of the heavens, viz., the sphere (or "globe") of fixed stars; the (five-member) planetary realm; and the spheres/globes of the sun and the moon.[6] The creatures' four faces are taken as symbolic of the four causes of the spheres' motion, the material, formal, efficient, and final cause. The body of the sphere, its intellect, soul, and the separate intellect that it desires to emulate are taken to represent these causes, respectively.

Maimonides explicitly interprets only the *ru'aḥ* (literally, "wind") that guides each distinctively circular motion of the living creatures, as mentioned in Ezekiel 1:12. Maimonides believes it connotes "air" and regards it as an expression of divine purpose and will.[7] Maimonides also takes pains to demonize the "living creatures" and to show that they must be understood metaphorically. He follows Ezekiel's lead in first identifying the "living creatures" with human beings,[8] and then with cherubs, a species of angels.[9] As such, they are for Maimonides creatures of the prophet's imagination (derived from the Agent Intellect), the locus of angelic visions.

Maimonides scarcely elaborates on Ezekiel's vision of a wheel on the earth attached to each living creature, with wheels within each wheel, all rimmed with eyes.[10] The wheels move with the creatures and have the creatures' spirit within them. For Maimonides, this means that the motion of the wheels is not essential to them, but is caused by the living creatures, to which they are attached.[11] Many commentators take this to mean that Maimonides identifies the body of the wheel with prime matter, and the wheels within wheels with the four elements (air, earth, fire, and water) that together give prime matter its distinctive shape. The natural motion of the elements (like the elements themselves) derives from the spheres, and in that sense is caused and "nonessential."[12]

The last part of Ezekiel's vision is of "something like" a crystal dome that is over the heads of the creatures. "Something like" a sapphire throne is situated over the dome, and seated upon it is "something like" a human form, ablaze in splendor, which Ezekiel identifies as the "likeness of the glory of the Lord."[13] While the commentators tend to see the figure on the throne as representative of the uppermost and hence first celestial separate intellect,[14] Maimonides simply concentrates on distinguishing "the likeness of the glory of the Lord" from God Himself. The "glory of the Lord" is the chariot, not the rider, Maimonides says, as God is beyond parabolic representation.[15]

Maimonides' conviction that God cannot be seen (or fully known) by humans also guides his interpretation of Isaiah's vision of the Lord in Isaiah 6:1–2.[16] Maimonides follows the talmudic teaching that equates Ezekiel's apprehension with Isaiah's.[17] For Maimonides, this means neither prophet actually saw God, notwithstanding their declarations to that effect.

Maimonides has gone to great lengths to hint at profound truths contained in Ezekiel's vision, and the commentators have drawn inferences accordingly. Maimonides presumably finds in Ezekiel confirmation of his previously outlined cosmic scheme in which God inspires the intellects/angels of the spheres to have perpetual revolutions; the spheres, affected by their intellects, move with them. Beings on earth are affected by both the intellects of the spheres and the motion of the spheres themselves, and knowledge of the first separate intellect is the highest apprehension possible for (exceptional) humans.[18] Maimonides points out that Ezekiel's vision apprehends three scientific realms,[19] which the commentators take to be those of mathematics/astronomy, physics, and metaphysics. All this is represented by the heavenly creatures, wheels, and the figure on the throne, respectively.[20] Metaphysical knowledge must follow the other two kinds of knowledge, Maimonides says, repeating a view he enunciated in his opening introduction to the *Guide*.

Maimonides concludes this section with the conviction that he has enabled the attentive reader to grasp certain fundamental principles of metaphysics, however elliptically stated by "chapter headings" (*ro'shei peraqim*) alone.[21] Maimonides is convinced that by combining this material with what has preceded it the reader should have complete, or nearly complete, knowledge of the scientific corpus of knowledge Maimonides wished to convey in writing the *Guide.* He informs the reader that he will not discuss the subject again, having said everything possible to say, and will move to a new subject.

Analysis

Maimonides' addressee has awaited these chapters, which establish the congruity between the biblical Account of the Chariot and metaphysical doctrines, since the beginning of the book. There, in the introduction to the first part of the *Guide,*[22] Maimonides wrote of the importance of the subject, and of the need to write guardedly and cryptically about it. He is writing for a person who knows philosophy and science,[23] to assure that person that Ezekiel at least was equally cognizant of these disciplines and expressed them in his own unique way. Maimonides' subtext is that Judaism has nothing to fear from science, not even the science that describes the mechanics of the heavens.

Maimonides was aware, however, that his embrace of the philosophers' metaphysics, even with all his pronounced reservations, was not shared by most of his public. He probably realized that his earlier *Mishneh Torah* philosophical depiction of the Account of the Chariot had not been sufficiently persuasive to his readers.[24] Their disapproval of his philosophizing could endanger his leadership of the community. Hence his elaborate excuses for secrecy and coded associations, meant to ward off the uninitiated. Yet his extensive exegesis of Ezekiel's vision represents Maimonides' determination to marry his faith with his reason. If he doubted the essential validity or possibility of metaphysical knowledge, and was not convinced of the necessity of conveying it, this entire exercise would be pointless and cruelly misleading.

The modern reader may look at Maimonides' treatment of Ezekiel's vision with a combination of fascination and exasperation, being both amazed at Maimonides' ingenuity and put off by the (seeming) arbitrariness of his identifications. As with all of Maimonides' exegeses, he assigns physical and metaphysical meanings to biblical terms without argument. The critical feature Maimonides seeks in each term is coherence with others, forming a whole that corresponds with a scientific view that he considers true, albeit without demonstrative certainty. His exegesis of Ezekiel's utterances may be seen as the litmus test of Maimonides' commitment to the biblical text, his desire to have it say what he believes it must say to make sense philosophically, and to justify his allegiance to it. There is, however, a surprise, and disappointment, awaiting the reader who is expecting Maimonides now to reveal the most intimate secrets of metaphysics. Instead, a lesson in celestial physics and cosmogony will be taught.

As Gad Freudenthal has shown, Maimonides' interpretation of Ezekiel's vision is based on Maimonides' innovative understanding of the structure of the heavens, mentioned in *Guide* 2.9 and 2.10.[25] There Maimonides placed the five supralunar planets within one sphere, or "globe," as Freudenthal prefers, and proceeded to conceive of the heavens as composed of four such globes: the fixed stars, the five planets, the sun, and the moon. Each globe was then assigned responsibility for the emanation of one of the four sublunar elements. The motion of the elements was conceived as the result of the circular motion of the four heavenly globes; terrestrial physics was viewed as a product of celestial physics.

Now, in Guide 3.2, Maimonides identifies his four-globed heaven with Ezekiel's four "living creatures" (*ḥayyot*) and their dependent four *ofanim,* the "wheels" that represent the sublunar elements. Ezekiel is thus shown to testify to the correctness of Maimonides' cosmology and reinforces his view that the governance of the sublunar world is dependent on physical celestial forces.

For Freudenthal, Maimonides has, in explicating Ezekiel's vision, completely altered his understanding of what metaphysics comprises.[26] No longer does it deal with the great secrets of God's being or of the separate intellects; it now is concerned solely with the architecture of the heavens and the relation of heaven to earth. The angels and separate intellects are now to be viewed in physical terms, as corresponding to material substances.

Freudenthal regards Maimonides' changed position on the nature of metaphysics as highly significant, amounting in effect to a repudiation of the expectation, cultivated by Maimonides over many years, that great secrets were contained in Ezekiel's vision. For Freudenthal, Maimonides' treatment of this subject may well express his skepticism about metaphysics as traditionally understood.[27] However, this interpretation of Ezekiel is not necessarily Maimonides' final word on the scope of metaphysics. Though in explicating Ezekiel's text, Maimonides scants the intellects and angels of the spheres, and the cosmological significance they represent, they remain formidable building blocks in the metaphysical scheme that Maimonides relies upon to explain emanation.[28]

As Maimonides predicted, only the person already familiar with philosophy can benefit from this section on metaphysics, since it is entirely referential, identifying Ezekiel's and Isaiah's prophecies with the cosmic structures described previously by Aristotle and Ptolemy. Maimonides may well be offering a revised view of the structure of the heavens, but he knows that it is conjectural. He feels he has said all there is to say on the subject, here and in preceding chapters. He knows he has broken new ground mainly in associating the biblical text with the scientific corpus outside the Jewish tradition, not in proving the validity of that corpus. With one exception,[29] he largely accepts the popular astronomical tradition, whatever the reservations he expresses elsewhere in the *Guide.*

Ezekiel's Account of the Chariot was a central text for Jewish mystics, so Maimonides' philosophical approach to it may be seen as a riposte to what he deplored in Judaism. Certain elements of Maimonides' own creed are not dissimilar to mystical beliefs, but for Maimonides they were part of an essentially rational program.[30] His personal God (as opposed to the god he occasionally fashions for his public) remains impersonal, never to be united with another being.

We have observed Maimonides attempt to naturalize miracles and prophecy, and have seen him disparage charismatic behavior. Here he takes the "living creatures" of Ezekiel and interprets them ultimately as expressions of the prophet's imagination. The wheels within wheels become metaphors for physical principles. Nevertheless, there is an unmistakably mystical element in Maimonides' belief that, like Ezekiel and Isaiah, one may have visions that bring a person closer to God, based on knowledge, however uncertain, of the workings of the heavens.

9

Providence and (Apparent) Evil (*Guide* Part III, Chapters 8–25)

Paraphrase

In chapter 8, Maimonides begins a lengthy discourse on the physical element that is matter, which he views as the root of evil. The consequences of indulging in material and physical pursuits send Maimonides off on an ethical tangent from the "purpose of the treatise," as he admits at the end of the chapter, but his strong feelings on the subject do not let him pass over the issue in silence. The purpose he alludes to has to do more with the scientific nature of matter than with its ethical entailments, with matter's relation to form, and ultimately to God. Maimonides is extremely reticent about the last mentioned relationship, and what he does say is problematic.

Matter, Maimonides affirms in the opening sentence of the chapter, is the sole cause of the corruption (and death) of everything subject to generation and corruption. The essential form of an object, which is equivalent to the species to which the individual belongs, is incorruptible and permanent (as species, being purely form, have no principle of change). The form of a given object may indeed perish with its material substrate, but this, Maimonides says, is "only by accident" (*wa-inamā . . . bi'l-'araḍ*), owing to its attachment to matter.[1]

Maimonides attributes the inability of matter to remain attached to any one form to its essential attachment to "privation," a term denoting absence, and as such used by Maimonides also to connote "nonbeing."[2] What is absent from matter, and what it lacks, is the only thing that qualifies as true being for Maimonides, and that is form. Its attachment to form gives matter a temporary substantiality, what may be seen as a quasi-ontic instantiation, but matter's existentially corrupt and unstable nature forces it to dissolve its connection with one form and take on another.

Maimonides depicts matter in this fashion, rather than in the more neutral Aristotelian terms whereby matter is simply a principle of change as well as of generation and corruption, closer ontically to form. Maimonides, however, likens matter to a married harlot,[3] always in search of another man, and finds it solely responsible for all physical deficiencies and moral vices, as well as, of course, for illness and death.

As stated, Maimonides embarks upon an extended moral, passionate diatribe in this chapter, condemning indulgence in physical pursuits in general, and particularly those involved with the sense of touch, like eating, drinking, and copulation, activities that in his estimation should be reduced to a minimum. Conversely, he praises those who strive for intellectual cognition, for grasping the true nature of everything, and for "conjoining with the divine intellect, which emanates upon them that through which that form exists."[4]

The proper end of man qua man, for Maimonides, is solely, and as much as is possible, to conceive of the "intelligibles," universal ideas, the noblest of which is God, but which also include the angels and "the rest of His works" (*wa-ṣā'ir af'ālihi,* viz., the world He has created).[5] Individuals who attain this state are "permanently with God," Maimonides declares, again invoking God's name, though intending His emissary, the Agent Intellect (as God is beyond having relationships).

Twice in this chapter Maimonides tests, as it were, his own condemnation of physically based activities and his denigration of matter as joined to privation. "Divine wisdom" (*al-ḥikma al-ilāhīya*) has stipulated, Maimonides acknowledges, that it is impossible for matter to exist without form, and for forms (of sublunar existents) to exist without matter. The form of man, created in the image of God, thus finds itself bound to "earthy, turbid and dark matter," which it must dominate.[6]

The second possible snag in Maimonides' denigration of matter—and women—comes in his explanation of King Solomon's praise in Proverbs 31:10 of a "woman of virtue." "When it might happen" that the matter of a man (his feminine element) is excellent, neither dominant nor corrupt, then Maimonides allows that matter to be a "divine gift," *mawhaba ilāhīya.*[7] Suitable matter, Maimonides says, is easy to control both by exhortation and by law.

Maimonides continues his indictment of matter in chapter 9, though changing his depiction of it. Though previously he described matter as essentially nonbeing and hence evil, he now calls it a "strong veil" (*ḥijāb 'aẓīm*) that prevents "the apprehension as it is of that which is separate [from matter]," i.e., apprehension of the essential form of an object. Even the "noblest and most pure" matter there is, which for Maimonides is the matter of the heavenly spheres, is affected with this opacity, which is much more pronounced in the "dark and turbid matter that is ours."[8]

Maimonides takes this opportunity to explain that the clouds and darkness that the Psalmist recounts as circling the deity, and in which God appears at Sinai,[9] are parables indicative of the limitations of human beings. As we may say today, the parables are expressive of the existential state of the subject, not of the object, of the vision. God is to be associated with perpetual, dazzling light, not darkness, light that illuminates via emanation "all that is dark."

Maimonides begins chapter 10 with a critique of *kalām* physics, specifically the kalamic assertion that the privation or absence of a particular trait or "habitus" (*malaka*) has the same ontic status as its presence. In this view, sight and blindness, life and death are merely contrary states of being, one is not the privation of the other, and God is the agent of both. This follows from the *kalām* rejection of the concept that there are natural states of being, with the privileging of actual and present states over the corresponding privative and potential states. The only nonbeing or privation recognized by the *mutakallimūn,* Maimonides asserts, is that of absolute nonbeing.

Maimonides follows Aristotle in seeing privation as the secondary, side effect of an action,[10] and compares it to Isaiah's statement that God "forms the light and creates darkness, makes peace and creates evil."[11] Maimonides here interprets darkness and evil as the privations of light and peace, and not as substantive states of being directly created in themselves. The privation "from" or "after" which the world is created,[12] according to Maimonides, is thus not a state of being, whatever it is. Maimonides is quite insistent that, "according to every opinion, the act of an agent can in no way be connected with a privation; the agent can only be said to have produced the privation by accident."[13]

Maimonides makes the point that evils are always privations: privations of being and form in the case of death; privations of *habitus,* i.e., a (desirable) state of realized being, in the case of illness, poverty, and ignorance. It is demonstrable knowledge, Maimonides says,[14] that the production of an essentially evil act (*sharran bi'l-dhāt*) cannot be predicated of God; His primary purpose cannot be to do evil. Rather, all God's acts are (expressions of) absolute good (*khayr maḥḍ*), for God acts only to produce being (*wujūd*), and all being is good.[15]

Maimonides' position, then, is that while God does not intend to do evil, and cannot by definition do evil, evil nevertheless occurs, in the form of privations of the good that ensue from His actions. Evil thus is an accidental but inevitable by-product of the good, given the changing and corrupt nature of matter. Maimonides acknowledges this in saying that "God has brought matter into existence according to the nature it has—namely, a nature that consists in matter always being associated with privation[16] . . . the cause of all passing-away and of all evil."

Chapter 11 testifies to Maimonides' confidence in the ability of reason and rationality to abolish the hatred and enmity humans have toward one another. The evils inflicted are due to ignorance, the privation or absence of knowledge. Ultimately, it is knowledge of the "true reality of the deity" (*ḥaqīqa al-ʿilāh*) that will bring the desired amity, Maimonides says, quoting Isaiah 11:6–9. He does not here add the caveat that this knowledge requires mastery of science and true knowledge of God's world.

In chapter 12, Maimonides presents his theodicy, a detailed defense of God's benevolence in the world (a direct consequence of the goodness synonymous with His being). Maimonides first insists, against the "ignorant masses" that look about them and believe there is more evil than good in the world, that they are mistaken, being totally self-centered. They should realize that what happens to an individual person is of "no value" (*lā qadr lahu bi-wajh*)[17] in relation to the whole of existence, and that the human species as a whole is inferior to the spheres and stars. Man is "merely the most noble" of the sublunar species, those subject to generation (and corruption). His very existence (despite his lowly cosmic status) is a "great good," benefited and perfected by God with the singular properties he has. Men, Maimonides says, are themselves mostly responsible for the evils they choose to do,[18] though they blame God for the suffering that follows.

The first species of evil that Maimonides discerns is due to the physical frailty of the human species, in that people fall ill or react negatively to climatic upheavals. Yet the passing of an individual is a necessary occurrence in a species divine wisdom has determined is marked by generation and corruption. Moreover, the continuing coming-to-be of individuals in a species testifies to the outpouring of the good, which is being, in the world. Furthermore, it is the matter in a person that receives impressions (through the senses, engendering both physical and intellectual reactions), thereby creating individuals, so matter is also in a sense good.

Maimonides finds in Galen[19] endorsement of the proposition that it is the matter in all beings that prevents them from achieving the perfection with which they are generated. Nevertheless, human beings, defined as living, rational, and mortal, represent the most perfect species to emerge from the blood and sperm of their origins. Thus the evil that matter represents exists of necessity.

Taking the long view of things of this sort, Maimonides concludes that (at least some of) the evils in this category occur seldom, having in mind natural disasters and impaired births. Nature on the whole functions well and is an expression of the good from which it emanates, even death testifying to that.

The second kind of evil Maimonides identifies is in essence political, the domination of some men over others. Though more numerous than evils of the first kind, this expression of evil is also deemed to be rare and not a dominant feature of city life, in times of peace. In times of great wars, on the other hand, Maimonides concedes that this evil affects many people, though he believes such conflicts do not occur most of the time.

Maimonides identifies the third kind of evil as self-inflicted and due to uncontrolled passions, and this evil he regards as common and more numerous than evils of the second kind. It is the rare individual who is blameless in this regard. Maimonides targets the vices of excessive eating, drinking, and copulation, the excesses that create physical and psychic illness and lead men to their ruin. "Men of excellence [and of] knowledge" (*al-fuḍalāʾ al-ʿulamāʾ*),[20] on the other hand, understand what is necessary for maintaining a healthy body, and live in accordance with what nature requires, understanding the wisdom exhibited in it. They seek the true end of man, apprehension of the nature of being and of God, insofar as is possible.

The necessities of life—air, water, and food—are generally available and accessible to all men, Maimonides says, taking it as a sign of divine beneficence and generosity (*ifḍāl wa jawd*). So too is the natural equality that exists at birth in all members of a species, their physical differences due to the diverse proportions of their corporeal components. Economic differences, Maimonides proclaims, do not indicate injustice or inequity in the scheme of things, for riches are illusions or superficial amusements. God brings into existence what is necessary; His great goodness toward human beings is shown in bringing them into existence, and His mercy is revealed in the creation of the governing (i.e., rational) faculty in them.

In chapter 13, Maimonides follows up on the theme he broached in the beginning of the preceding chapter, locating man's place in the universe. He does this by asking about the final end of existence, a question that he says can be asked only of created beings, as they were created supposedly with some purpose in mind. An uncreated being such as the Necessary Existent, on the other hand, does not have an agent, and therefore cannot have a final end.

Maimonides first explains Aristotle's position on this issue. Believing as he does that "nature does nothing in vain,"[21] Aristotle construes the species of all natural existents, however eternal, as having a final end, or cause, which is integral to the formulation of the identity of the species. Aristotle, Maimonides notes, treats the final cause of natural things as one, or interchangeable, with their efficient and formal cause.[22] Beyond this final cause as embedded in the natural or physical world, Aristotle and later philosophers posit an "intellectual or divine principle" that makes one thing for the sake of another.[23] This is a reference either to the Agent Intellect for our sublunar world, or to the Unmoved Mover for the entire cosmos.

Maimonides finds this teleological perspective supports proof (*burhān*) for the production of the world in time, since purpose indicates a being that possesses purpose. While believing that most philosophers, like himself, find knowledge of the ultimate purpose for the existence of specific species, and a fortiori for existence as a whole, a "very difficult matter,"[24] Maimonides reports that for Aristotle the ultimate purpose of species in the natural world is to maintain perpetually the generation and corruption of their individual members. This insures the generation of being in a species of which the individual members cannot endure, as they are generated out of a material, and hence corruptible, substrate.

Beyond preserving the very existence of species, Aristotle conceives the final end of generated beings is their attainment of perfection in that which is generated, according to Maimonides. While every species has its model of perfect being for that species, *homo sapiens* is regarded as the ultimate embodiment (theoretically) of perfection for all generated beings. Though Maimonides does not say so here, this privileged position is due to the unique rational faculty man possesses, in Aristotle's opinion. There is no further purpose or perfection that Aristotle would propose for man other than the exercise of his rational faculty. The person who does that has achieved the final end and purpose of his life.

While for Maimonides the eternal nature of Aristotle's species makes it impossible to look for an ultimate purpose for being as a whole, the opinion that the world comes to be in time after privation,[25] which view Maimonides calls "our view" (*rāyyinā*), is "sometimes" thought to require such a quest. Accordingly, people believe everything exists for the sake of man, to enable him to worship God.

As this is a theologically based argument, Maimonides responds to it in kind. God would not need other species to serve man if He wished simply to create and perfect human beings, the existence and perfection of other species being then superfluous. Furthermore, Maimonides says, the notion that man's perfection consists in worship of God is problematic, since it does not serve the purpose of adding to God's perfection, any more than the absence of every thing that exists would detract from His perfection.[26]

Maimonides realizes that the final perfection aimed at in the worship of God is the perfection of the worshiper, and no reason can be given why worship is required other than that God willed it, or that His wisdom required it.[27] (As elsewhere, Maimonides treats the will and wisdom of God as equivalent terms.) The other species thus do not exist for the sake of man, but each has its own final end.

Maimonides draws on many biblical passages to buttress his point, adducing the creation story in Genesis to show that every thing created was seen to be good in itself. Man may be the most perfect and noble thing generated from matter, but compared with the spheres and separate intelligences of the heavens he is "very very contemptible" (*ḥaqīran jiddan jiddan*).[28] Nevertheless, Maimonides concludes, a person who knows his own soul unerringly, and understands every being as it is, can become tranquil and forsake looking for a final end beyond the mere existence of a thing, since its existence is the product of divine will and/or divine wisdom.

In chapter 14, Maimonides brings astronomical data to bear to buttress his view of man's highly circumscribed position in the universe, and to oppose the anthropocentric image that believers feel religion endorses. Maimonides cites the enormous and astonishing (*mudhish*)[29] distances the science of his day established between the center of the earth and the highest part of the sphere of Saturn, and extrapolates from that to the greater distance that exists between the center of the earth and the concavity of the sphere of the fixed stars and beyond. The dimensions of the sphere of the fixed stars (like those of other spheres) dwarf those of the earth, Maimonides rightly claims, asking how one could think the spheres exist for the sake of human beings.

Introducing the separate intellects of the spheres into the equation further sharpens the question, for Maimonides. The spheres and their separate intellects were commonly thought to govern human beings on earth, and in that sense to serve them. The disparity between these spheres and individual persons being immense, some philosophers found this conceivable only on a generic level, so that the spheres relate to the human species only and not to the individual man. Maimonides, however, claims that this view is not philosophically tenable, for even on the generic level the more noble substance, the eternal heavenly spheres, would have as its final end the perfection of an inferior substance, a species whose individuals are associated with corruptible matter.

This issue, Maimonides claims, helps advance belief in the production of the world in time, though it is not immediately apparent how it does that. Presumably, Maimonides' opinion is that astronomy and logic do not support an anthropocentric view, and yet man is served by the heavenly spheres and their intelligences; they facilitate human perfection. For Maimonides, the only way to explain this is to attribute it to the will and/or wisdom of God.

In chapter 15, Maimonides returns to an issue he first discussed in connection with the *kalām* challenge to Aristotelian physics over what determines the possibility or impossibility of a proposed assertion.[30] Again he says that certain propositions, those that are clearly self-contradictory, are deemed impossible (i.e., absurd) by both theologians and philosophers. This impossibility is "stable," i.e., intrinsic to the proposition and God has no power over it, and therefore it is not a deficiency or inability in His power.

Disagreement arises where the definitions of the terms in a proposition are disputed, so that some persons do not consider the proposition self-contradictory, whereas others do. Such is the case among the *mutakallimūn*, some of whom believe an accident could exist without a corresponding atomic substance, should God so wish, while others consider this impossible, given their definition of atom and accident. Another disagreement concerns the philosophers' denial and Maimonides' acceptance of the possibility of bringing a corporeal being into existence "from no matter whatsoever" (*min lā madda aṣlan*).

As before, Maimonides agonizes over the criterion to adopt in delimiting the range of possible and impossible assertions. Though posed mostly as whether the criterion should be the intellect or the imagination, the real question is whether or not to restrict the realm of possibility to that which is consonant with the scientific description of the natural world and can be inferred from it without logical contradiction. Imagined possibilities, on the other hand, cannot be self-contradictory, but are free of empirical constraints.

Maimonides' reason for going over the issues he discussed earlier may be gleaned from his closing paragraph in this chapter, which emphasizes the opinion that God is not to be associated with actions (expressed by propositions) that are universally considered to be impossible. God has the power neither to create them, nor to change them; they are not the product of an agent, they are necessarily as they are (which they aren't, not existing). The importance of this statement will emerge in Maimonides' discussion of divine providence, to which he next turns.

Maimonides begins chapter 16 inveighing against an opinion he attributes to philosophers concerning God's knowledge of the world that he finds "terribly offensive."[31] It is the opinion, based on what "at first sight" appears to be the frequent plight of the righteous and success of the wicked, that God must be ignorant of human affairs. The philosophers are led to this conclusion by eliminating other possibilities that Maimonides skillfully recounts. The conclusion follows from the belief that God cannot be conceived either as having no power to affect that which He knows, or as not caring to ordain matters for the best. In order to avoid becoming complicit with evil, He must, it is thought, be ignorant of human affairs, for the world does not exhibit the excellent order He designed for it.

Maimonides sees the philosophers as compounding their error: to save God from being unjust, they deprive Him of omniscience. For Maimonides, the basic premise of the philosophers is false. According to him, the world is well ordered in its entirety, including whatever befalls human beings; it is viewing matters from the human perspective as the philosophers do that can create a false impression. As Maimonides has made clear, though, and as the philosophers know, the evils people experience are often self-induced, as well as due to the necessity of their corporeal nature.

Maimonides then cites other arguments the philosophers brought on behalf of the view that God's knowledge of the world is limited: His knowledge is had by intellection and is of universal truths, whereas knowledge of individuals is particular and requires apprehension by the senses. As there are an infinite number of particular things,[32] there can never be universal knowledge of all of them, the sort that God's knowledge requires; and knowledge of temporal events, which are particular, would entail change in God, to keep up with the events as they happen.

Maimonides says the philosophers accuse religious people who believe in God's omniscience, in the sense of His awareness of an event before as well as after it occurs, of holding that there can be knowledge of pure privation, and of considering the potential and actual states of being of an object as one and the same.

The philosophers are not all agreed as to their view of divine knowledge, Maimonides adds. Some limit it to species and not individuals; others to self-knowledge only, denying any multiplicity in God's cognitions; and yet others expand it to knowledge of everything. Maimonides identifies explicitly with this last position, calling it "our belief" (*'itiqādunā*), though he has yet to respond to the philosophers' criticisms and fully to articulate his position.

In chapter 17, Maimonides surveys five different views of providence, a theme related to that of God's knowledge, which Maimonides discussed in a preliminary way in the preceding chapter. The first opinion, which Maimonides ascribes to Epicurus, is that there is no providence, and all that happens is due to chance. Maimonides appeals to Aristotle's authority to refute this opinion, claiming that Aristotle demonstrated that there is an ordering and governing agent[33] in the world.

Maimonides next amplifies his report of Aristotle's view, aided by Alexander of Aphrodisias's summary of it, saying that basically Aristotle believes that "providence corresponds to the nature of what exists."[34] Thus, as the spheres are eternal and unchanging (except in their locomotion), providence may simply be said to reflect their state of being. Likewise, as the spheres have an emanating influence upon the species of beings on earth, species that are eternal also, this emanation may be deemed providential. Individual members of species, though mortal, are also affected by this emanative force, so that providence may be seen as responsible for the faculties that encourage growth and survival. Finally, human beings can be considered as providentially provided with an intellect that assists their survival as individuals and as members of a species.

Aristotle does not extend providence further, seeing that chance obtains frequently in nature and in human affairs when the orderly course of things (symptomatic of providence) is disrupted. It is impossible for providence to affect chance, given the eternal necessity that that which exists is as it is, i.e., that chance does occur.

Maimonides concludes his resumé of Aristotle's position by saying that those Jews who follow this view have adopted Ezekiel's remark that "the Lord has forsaken the earth."[35] For Maimonides, Aristotle's providential deity does not determine matters, only confirms them, as it were. (Maimonides conflates Aristotle with Plotinus, in positing a providential emanation, but one without an overriding will.)

The third opinion that Maimonides summarizes is that which Maimonides associates with the views of the Ash'ariyya sect of the *mutakallimūn.* It is that nothing happens by chance, and that God knows and determines every thing. This is the view of God as completely omniscient and omnipotent, as well as just and good. This renders every thing that happens necessary, being foreknown and decreed by God, eliminating possibility and free choice.

Maimonides points to the conflicts this view poses to the apparent position taken in the Qur'ān regarding personal responsibility for actions, with attendant rewards or punishments, all assuming free choice. The Ash'arites, he knows, see this as limiting God's knowledge; they read the Qur'ān differently, and leave it to God to determine what is just and deserving.

Maimonides takes the Mu'tazila, a more rational sect of *mutakallimūn,* as representing a fourth understanding of providence, one that insists upon (a transparent) justice as decisive in God's being. As a consequence, human beings have freedom of choice, by which they are then judged. At the same time, God is omniscient as well as good; the Mu'tazila leave the conflict between free will and foreknowledge to God and appeal to an afterworld in which God rewards those denied justice in this world.

Maimonides introduces the fifth opinion regarding providence as that of "our law," *shari'atunā,* which is that man "has an absolute ability to act . . . in virtue of his nature, his choice and his will." Animals too move "in virtue of their own will," God having eternally willed it so for both man and all the species of animals.[36] This willful granting of autonomous will to God's creatures is an indication that He is not unjust. The good and the bad that human beings encounter are the deserved consequences of their actions, with no injustice involved.

The standard Jewish view on providence, according to Maimonides, is that a just deity dispenses rewards and punishments as deserved to all people. Maimonides does not take exception here to this formulation of providence, however much it attributes a hands-on approach to God. Maimonides is upset, however, with some rabbinic sages' concept of "sufferings of love" (*yiṣurīn shel ahavah*),[37] according to which undeserved misfortunes befall a person to test him, a greater reward supposedly awaiting in heaven if he passes the test. Maimonides cannot accept this, as his God does not ever act unjustly, nor is justice His arbitrary, private determination.

Maimonides then proffers his own belief as concerns providence, a belief that he considers more rational and "less disgraceful" than the other views and closer to the intention of Scripture. As Maimonides words it at first, divine providence in the sublunar world involves[38] only individuals belonging to the human species, and whatever happens to them is deserved. In all other matters, both above and below the moon (though Maimonides refers only to the sublunar sphere), Maimonides says he agrees with Aristotle. Though this would have God's providence present to a degree in all existent beings, as Maimonides has said, he emphasizes the element of chance that Aristotle saw as prevalent in nature. Maimonides thereby excludes particular providence, i.e., God's knowledge and direct involvement, from much of what happens in the natural world.

Maimonides then says that his considered opinion is that "divine providence follows the divine emanation," where "follows" (*tābi'*)[39] means "corresponds to." This is the same position Maimonides gave before as Aristotle's, though Maimonides focuses on the effect of emanation on the human species, and particularly on its endowing man with an intellect through which he can discover truths. Providence is a function of the effect this intellectual emanation has on man. Maimonides understands that the consequences of a person's response to this endowment are considered[40] as rewards or punishments from God.

Among the examples Maimonides brings to illustrate his point that the tragedies that occur to people are deserved, and not the accidental results of chance, as Aristotle has it, is that of the sinking of a ship and the drowning of its passengers.[41] This is a particularly chilling example, given that Maimonides' brother David, whom he loved and whose death depressed him greatly, suffered this end. Yet Maimonides stoically attributes this and other such "deserved" calamities to the inscrutable divine will, i.e., providence.

Maimonides insists that providence affects only individuals who are human beings, agreeing with Aristotle as to the effect of providence/emanation on the species only of animals (as well as plants), and not directly on individual animals. As always, Maimonides also finds scriptural support for his position, dismissing those verses that appear to contradict it.

Maimonides concludes this chapter with an explicit statement that providence, as stemming from a source of supreme intellectual perfection, affects people in proportion to their own intellectual achievement, since thereby they (partially) conjoin with the intellect emanating upon them. Maimonides does not mention that this is the Agent Intellect with which man's intellect conjoins. It serves as God's agent vis-à-vis the sublunar world, and man in particular. Maimonides has not, in fact, discussed the Agent Intellect or the entire subject of conjunction philosophically as yet.

Maimonides reiterates in chapter 18 the main teaching of the previous chapter: providence follows upon, or corresponds to, the intellectual achievements of an individual. It is an individual or group of individuals who benefit from providence, not their species. "No species exists outside the mind," Maimonides says, it and all other universals being solely "mental notions," or constructs.[42]

Maimonides' disavowal of the substantive reality of universals such as species (and genera) follows Aristotle's consideration of them as "secondary substances."[43] As such, though, they play a critical role in categorizing individuals with similar features, an indispensible tool for defining and pursuing scientific knowledge. As Maimonides reported Aristotle's position in chapter 17—a position with which he said he agreed—providence affects the species of animals other than man (and also plants) to some extent, giving them the faculties with which to survive and flourish. This is a species-wide providence, though it appears necessarily only in individuals. Maimonides' statement regarding the presence of providence only in human beings must then be qualified; he is apparently thinking only of the special providence that confers intellect upon people.

Though emanation befalls every person equally, people respond differently to it, depending on their material disposition and training, or education. Hence, Maimonides says, providence "will of necessity" affect them differently and unequally. Maimonides ranks the prophets, excellent (*al-fuḍalā'*) and righteous (*al-ṣāliḥūn*) men, as recipients of the greatest degree of providence, while ignorant and disobedient persons are no more than animals, who may as such be killed (after due process of law, no doubt).[44]

Maimonides' elitist view here is striking, even allowing for the rhetorical dimension of the remark, and ought to be balanced by his regard, expressed in his halakhic works, for the sanctity of life. His feelings about this issue appear to have carried him away. He brings both scriptural passages and a passage from Alfarabi, quoting Plato, to confirm his view that providence benefits those who perfect their souls through moral and intellectual efforts.

In chapter 19, Maimonides begins to discuss diverse views on God's knowledge, beginning with the view of those Maimonides deems ignorant. It is the position mentioned and rejected previously, that God lacks omniscience. This flies in the face of what Maimonides regards as a theological axiom, that God, in whom all good things must exist, cannot be deficient (in anything that is good), and that as ignorance of any thing[45] is a deficiency, God cannot be culpable of such ignorance.

It is the lack of order and the presence of evil in the world that lead people to this view, abetted by a misreading of scriptural passages, in Maimonides' opinion. These people do not appreciate the order that does exist in nature, and the fact that, having free will,[46] they are largely responsible for the disorder they see.

Maimonides makes the analogy between a produced instrument pointing to the existence of a knowledgeable maker and the world as an ordered artifact pointing to the existence of a knowing and purposeful God. As presented, these arguments are more rhetorical than substantive, affirming positions he has previously discussed.[47]

In chapter 20, Maimonides assumes a more philosophical stance, weighing in on topics regarding God's knowledge that were central to the divide between philosophers and theologians, apparently siding with the latter. The first issue concerns the extent of God's knowledge and whether He acquires new knowledge. That would entail change in God (His knowledge being synonymous with His being), as well as implying that He acquired something He lacked (where He is known not to lack anything). It is probably for these reasons that Maimonides begins the chapter by saying that there is a "general consensus" (*amr majmu*ʿ), i.e., among philosophers and theologians alike, that no new knowledge occurs to God. Relatedly, Maimonides correctly declares, it is also widely held that God does not have a "multiplicity of cognitions" (*ʿulūm kathīra mutaʿaddada*). As Maimonides explains, God "knows with one single knowledge the many and numerous things,"[48] so different objects of knowledge do not cause Him to have multiple cognitions.

These theses follow from the belief in God's simplicity of being, a Oneness that does not admit of multiplicity of any sort, combined with the belief in

God's omniscience. Maimonides therefore adds that God has foreknowledge, eternally knowing all things that are produced in time before they occur. God may thus be said to know things that do not now exist, knowing that they will exist and that He is able to bring about their existence. On the other hand, that which will never exist, instancing absolute privation of being,[49] is never known to God (and thus is not a deficiency in His knowledge).

Maimonides next takes up the thorny issue of God's knowledge of the infinite, which for the philosophers is as impossible as His knowledge of non-existent things. Though Maimonides does not give their reasons here, the philosophers believe that the unstable, ever-expanding infinite number of data requires constantly new cognitions that can never, by definition, fully capture its totality. God, however, has no new cognitions. His knowledge is of that which is permanent and immutable; hence He cannot know the infinite.

Maimonides mentions a doubt some philosophers had of the validity of attributing knowledge of even permanent things to God, since that too would imply a multiplicity of cognitions in His essence. Hence, the logic of God's unity of being should require Him to have but the one object of knowledge, and that is His own essence (with which His knowledge is equivalent).

Maimonides does not respond specifically to the philosophers' view of the limitations of God's knowledge. Instead, he faults the philosophers for treating human and divine knowledge analogously, especially since it is they who demonstrated that there is no multiplicity in His essence and no attributes beyond His essence, His knowledge and essence being the same. Moreover, it is the philosophers who have demonstrated that our intellects cannot truly apprehend God's essence. God's knowledge, Maimonides stresses, is totally different from ours, having nothing in common with it beyond the equivocality of the word. Therefore God can know things that are impossible for us to know or comprehend.

To illustrate his point, Maimonides says that God's knowledge that some possibility[50] will come into existence does not change its status as a possibility (despite it having to come into existence in the future, and in that sense being necessary, as we would think). For Maimonides, it is a fundamental principle of the law of Moses, a basis for religious legislation and commandments, that possibilities are real, that God has not determined human actions (though He knows them before they are committed), and that man is free to choose between real possibilities.

We cannot understand these things, not being able to comprehend God's essence. Yet, Maimonides maintains, we do know that God's existence is the most perfect of existences, not having any deficiency, change, or affect, always cognizant. Just as the word "knowledge" is equivocal when said of God and human beings, so are the words "purpose" and "providence." The chapter closes on this note of epistemological equivocation.

In chapter 21, Maimonides continues to insist upon the disparity between God's knowledge and our own. He appeals to the difference between the knowledge the maker of something has, and the knowledge of one who views it as a finished product. The former person has causal and total knowledge of the object, the latter person gleans cumulative knowledge from the effect created. The one's knowledge is deductive, the other's inductive (though Maimonides does not use these terms here).

God's position vis-à-vis the world[51] is that of the artisan whose knowledge of the things he created preceded them, and who need not have any additional or new knowledge of them. God, moreover, knows "the totality of what necessarily derives from all His acts" in knowing His own immutable essence.[52] This is of course totally beyond our apprehension, and we must accept this as so. It is, however, Maimonides admits, an opinion that has no demonstrative proof, no more than the opinions of the philosophers. We need, therefore, as regards the question of God's knowledge, to follow the method Maimonides has adopted in all such cases that lack decisive argument, though Maimonides does not say here what that method is. He assumes his readers will understand where his sympathies lie when there is no certain argument against traditional belief.

In chapter 22, Maimonides begins to offer an extended interpretation of the Book of Job, treating it as a parable designed to teach the various opinions people have of divine providence. His treatment of the biblical text is selective, following the method announced in the introduction to the *Guide*.[53] It is, nevertheless, quite comprehensive, a tour de force of exegesis, the elegance of which a brief summary cannot capture.

The first point Maimonides makes, which is central to his understanding of providence, is that Satan is not on the same level as the "sons of God" who present themselves before the Lord.[54] For Maimonides, Satan is not the direct object of God's attention; he simply appears with the other heavenly creatures. Whereas the others are subject to the divine order and will, Satan is not. He roams over the earth[55] and is excluded from the upper world, where the sons of God enjoy permanent and lasting existence. Satan has a "certain portion" of existence too, but it is less than that of the others.[56]

Maimonides reports that Job and his friends mistakenly assume that God is directly responsible for what befalls Job, ignoring Satan's intermediary role. Satan has power over everything on earth except man's soul,[57] which Maimonides equates with intellect, that which remains after death.

In closing, Maimonides follows a talmudic saying that identifies Satan with the "evil inclination" and the angel of death.[58] Culling scriptural and rabbinic passages, Maimonides contrasts the evil inclination, present at birth, with the "good inclination" that requires training and intellectual perfection. By now it should be clear that Satan represents the material dimension of being on earth, evil in its absence of permanent being.

In chapter 23, Maimonides identifies Job and his four friends with five positions on providence that attempt to defend what is assumed to be God's action. All concerned agree that God is responsible for what befalls man and that He cannot be unjust. They seek to find a reason why a righteous person is visited with suffering, indeed, why Job, the most perfect and righteous of persons, is given over to the greatest of misfortunes.

Maimonides equates each position he discerns in the Book of Job with a school of either philosophical or theological thought known to him. Job's initial view is that the inequitable circumstances of the righteous and wicked are alike to God (i.e., He is indifferent to what happens to individuals), and that there is no afterworld to make amends for injustice suffered here. This is subsequently identified[59] with Aristotle's position on providence.

Maimonides presents the view of Eliphaz as compatible with that of "our law," *shariʿatunā,* by which he refers more to the (nebulous) theology of the faithful than to the *halakha* or legal corpus of Judaism. In this view, Job is punished for sins that he unknowingly performed; everything he gets is deserved.

Bildad the Shuhite emphasizes the compensation that Job will ultimately receive, if he is innocent, and this corresponds to the doctrine of the Muʿtazila and their insistence on the primacy of divine justice. In contrast to that, the view of Zophar the Naamathite asserts the primacy of the unknowable divine will, not questioning the moral dimension of God's actions in any way, and assuming that the will is guided by, if not equal to, divine wisdom. This view is identified with that of the Ashʿariyya, the rivals of the Muʿtazila.

The last opinion given is that of Elihu, which Maimonides praises and with which he clearly—though implicitly—identifies. He believes Elihu's unique contribution is that of representing providence parabolically, as an angelic intercession,[60] and seeing it manifested in various types of prophetic encounters as well as in natural phenomena. That is, Elihu represents providence as a function of wisdom; he describes the mechanisms for acquiring it through angelic and prophetic encounters, as well as through confrontations with the phenomena of nature.

The prophetic revelation Job finally receives, which rectifies his view of providence, is entirely devoted to the wondrous workings of nature, beyond man's capacity to grasp fully.[61] For Maimonides, man can only accept that God's governance of the world, His purpose in ordering things, and the providence that that shows, is unique. Misfortunes should not lead to questioning or doubting God's providence; rather they should spur the believer to increase his love of the deity.

In chapter 24, Maimonides offers his interpretation of the six "trials" (*niṣyanot*) that God is said, in the Torah, to impose upon people afflicted with undeserved misfortune, in order to reward them for keeping the faith. Maimonides cannot accept the "widespread" opinion, as he calls it,[62] that God is causing unmerited punishment in order to increase subsequent reward, since that conflicts with the Torah's description of a just deity, "a God of faithfulness and without iniquity."[63] Nor can Maimonides accept the plain meaning of the Torah's text, that the trials are meant as tests of faith and obedience, set by a deity who does not know the outcome in advance.

Instead, Maimonides explains that the trials are meant to educate people to correct beliefs and deeds; the actions requested serve as paradigms of proper conduct. For example, the binding of Isaac, which was Abraham's trial, was meant to teach the extent of love and fear of God incumbent on everyone.

Abraham's trial conveys a second message, Maimonides says, and that is the validity—to the prophets (and us)—of prophetic revelation as transmitted in dreams and visions through the imaginative faculty. Abraham would never have been prepared to sacrifice Isaac had he doubted the veracity of the command he received, according to Maimonides, in a dream or vision.

In chapter 25, Maimonides stresses that all of God's actions are good and excellent, as determined by His will. None of His actions are futile, frivolous, or in vain. Human beings do act in such ignoble fashion, though they are also capable of good and excellent actions, when pursuing a noble end or purpose (*ghaya*).

For Maimonides, all that God does for His creatures is necessary and useful for their existence, a teleological view of nature similar to that held by the philosophers. He faults those who believe that God's actions are inscrutable, His will alone being the determining factor in all His actions.[64] For Maimonides, that divine will is synchronized with and ultimately equated with the divine wisdom, which dictates actions the purpose of which is transparently clear.

Maimonides makes two statements that seem similar but that pose a problem to be discussed in the analysis of this section. First he says that the entire purpose of God's actions in nature is to bring into existence everything the existence of which is possible, as dictated by His wisdom.[65] Then, after citing biblical verses that appear to grant God unlimited power to act, Maimonides comments that indeed God can achieve anything He wants, but that He wills only that which is possible, "and not everything that is possible," but (as stated before) that which His wisdom dictates.[66]

In speaking of the intentionality of God's actions, which brook no interference, Maimonides cites the instantaneous creation of the world when God in His wisdom desired it, just as that "selfsame immutable wisdom necessitated privation before the world came into existence."[67] Maimonides is saying that God's wisdom or knowledge does not change, though the actions that emanate from Him differ. As far as possible existents go, they were always either really possible or not, only the real being those that have the potentiality for coming to be.

Analysis

Maimonides begins this section discussing the nature of sublunar matter, seeming to have forgotten his pledge at the conclusion of chapter 7 that he had nothing further to say on scientific matters. He has already outlined the division of matter into primary or first matter and the subsequent four basic elements of air, earth, fire, and water that in varying combinations compose the material substrates of all substances on earth. Now, beginning with chapter 8, he "digresses" to speak of what he conceives to be the ethical dimension of matter, giving nature moral value that is rooted in what he believes is its place in a hierarchical scale of being.[68] God is at the top of that scale, though He is formally off it, not having anything in common with the beings of this world. In his formulation of the deity as the Necessary Existent, however, Maimonides understands that the entire world of contingent or possible existents is dependent upon, and thus subservient to, Him.

Seen as the source of emanation, the being of the One is identified by Maimonides with goodness; He is the absolute good, as He is the absolute truth. These terms are then synonyms for that being which is eternal and unchanging, and all beings are good and true to the degree that they are such. In this evaluation of beings, matter, which embodies the principle of change, must come last; in itself, without form, matter is devoid of being, and hence devoid of what constitutes goodness.

In accordance with this perspective, Maimonides portrays the relation of form to matter in a given object as "accidental," that is, nonessential to the nature of form. Of course, the relation of form to matter is not "accidental" existentially; rather, for there to be corporeal bodies of any kind, it is necessary. "Hylomorphism," the combination of matter (*hyle*) and form (*morphē*), is one of the pillars of Aristotelian-based physics (to which Maimonides subscribes). A consequence of this form-matter, or "hylomorphic," union, though, is that the form of the particular object "happens to" disappear with the body. This disappearance is only "accidental," in the sense that the given form disintegrates with its material substrate; however, the species represented by that form, which is its essence, endures.

This would seem to be contradicted by Aristotle's stated view, with which Maimonides allegedly concurs, that species (and genera) are logical categories and do not exist apart from the material instantiations of their forms. Yet the epistemological theory endorsed by many medieval philosophers, Maimonides included, that accepts the existence of an Agent Intellect is predicated on the existence in it of pure forms that emanate onto earth and there unite with matter when it is ready for them. Considering the existence of these species (or specific forms) in the Agent Intellect as their permanent, "essential" state, as opposed to their earthly "accidental" appearance, reflects the values placed on heavenly and earthly domains, respectively, and the inferior status of the particular, individual object versus its universal manifestation.

Maimonides' view of matter is Platonic essentially, rather than Aristotelian, and is particularly indebted to Plotinus, who shares a negative view of matter with Gnostic thought. Maimonides' animus against the material dimension of life is more than academically derived, however; it must also well up from the core of his psyche. However much he endorsed rabbinic affirmations of married life, his own inclinations were to sexual abstinence, which he projected upon Moses and the prophets. More though than the disparagement of sex, particularly in the female, Maimonides had a dim view of the physical, and thus material, dimension of life in general. Life's redeeming character lay for him in the possibility for an individual to transcend the physical and access the world of intelligible, permanent being.

Maimonides' attitude toward matter is complex; he is obliged to acknowledge its importance in the divine scheme of things as the necessary concomitant of form, the substrate of being.[69] Moreover, matter can be trained to assist form, and not oppose it, being a party to virtuous behavior. Still, the brunt of Maimonides' message is that matter is usually intractable and that most people do not control its urgings. The "divine gift" of mastering one's physical desires that some people are fortunate to have is an exception to the rule, attributable to God as is everything that occurs in nature. The view of matter as a divine gift is also forced upon

Maimonides by Solomon's tribute to a "woman of virtue." Yet Solomon's praise of matter, as Maimonides interprets it, does not change his basically negative attitude toward all things physical, and does not change his judgment of the unstable and unreliable, privative nature of matter.[70]

Maimonides' view of the adversarial character of matter is evident in two other chapters of this section.[71] In chapter 9, matter, pictured as a "strong veil," emerges as a double-barreled barrier to a true apprehension of an object. It is not only the material aspect of the *object* of our perception that blocks apprehension of its essential form, but equally if not more the materiality of the *subject's* own organs of sensation. One's intellect cannot conceive of God or the separate, purely formal intellects of the heavens (or of any universal form) because of the "veil" of the subject's own materiality.

If taken literally, Maimonides' "strong veil," which is a veil of unknowing, would foil any attempt to achieve true, scientific knowledge.[72] He follows this image with biblical quotes that refer to the cloud and darkness that accompanied the theophany at Sinai, giving these impediments a subjective, metaphorical meaning and making it impossible to have a true apprehension of God there.

These statements are similar to others that Maimonides makes in the *Guide* that limit, or deny, the possibility of attaining truth. Yet Maimonides concludes the chapter on a Neoplatonic note present in Avicenna and other Muslim thinkers: God is surrounded not by darkness but by light, a brilliant light from which issues the emanations that illuminate the world, i.e., that bring it into being. Maimonides appears confident in his ability to say this of the God who, therefore, is not entirely unknowable. Our senses are not completely beclouded, our intellects not entirely inadequate.

Accordingly, Maimonides in chapter 10 is quite sure that the *mutakallimūn* are wrong in considering the presence and absence of attributes as equally valid states of being. Maimonides introduces the *kalām* denial of the concept of privation because of the role it requires God to play as the direct cause of all that happens on earth, including those physical states that are commonly deemed deficient or defective, like blindness or deafness, and of course death. Maimonides rejects this view of the deity's agency, and though he could have nature alone take full responsibility for all the privations that occur in beings, he prefers to find some explanation for the presence of evil in the world that will reflect on, while not impugning, the goodness of the Creator of the universe.

Maimonides' solution, as we have seen, is to regard matter and all the negativity it represents as a necessary concomitant of form, not a direct effect of God's actions.[73] For Maimonides, assuming he held to some doctrine of *creatio ex nihilo,* God created the world from privation not in the sense that He turned the (nonexistent) state of nonbeing into being, but rather in the sense that He turned the absence of forms into forms. That is, the forms (as we know them) did not exist before they were created, but at the moment of their creation (which is the beginning of time as well as space), the forms appeared with their attendant "privations," the matter that necessitates change.

The absolute privation of being that Maimonides posits as obtaining "before" God created the world may be absolutely devoid of expression in the world, but Maimonides would have to agree that God had, in his unchanging being, full knowledge of that which He would create. As such, God always had to be aware of the problems that matter posed to His goodness. Maimonides thus is obliged to accommodate (what we would regard as) evil within the general benevolence of the deity, however forced his attempts to distance God from matter may seem.

Thus, it does little good to pretend that matter is autonomous, as could be taken to be Maimonides' intention in saying that "God has brought matter into existence provided with the nature it has . . . the cause of all passing-away and of all evil."[74] (It is another matter entirely, if God has to contend with an eternal matter, but Maimonides seems determined not to have recourse to that view, at least not in the sense of an eternal physical matter.)

Whatever he may think, Maimonides' statement does not absolve God of responsibility for evil in the universe, or for any of the privations that matter forces upon form, if God is the ultimate creator of matter. For it is an essential and not accidental aspect of matter that it is the principle of change and that privation is the state that a potential form takes in matter. Moreover, the evils associated with matter, even if not God's primary intention in creating material beings, had to be known to Him to some degree.

It is thus not surprising that Maimonides concludes chapter 10 by endorsing the statement in Genesis 1:31 that all of God's creation is to be seen as "very good," including the privations of "death and all evils" induced by matter. These individual impairments or terminations of being are to be subsumed within the ongoing being of the species.

In taking this long view, Maimonides would appear to have come to terms with the animus he has shown toward matter and all things physical. He has had to resolve the conflict between his head and his heart, his rational self forced to include matter, with all its evils, in the category of good beings, though his heart detested the defects and deficiencies that matter caused.

Starting with chapter 12, Maimonides argues in support of this "long view" of God's manifested goodness in the world. People are mistaken to take an anthropocentric, let alone an egocentric, view of the world, blaming God for their own failings. Looking toward the heavens, observing the cosmos in all its grandeur, should give one a proper perspective of the place of human beings in the total scheme of things. It is a great gift that God has given us the intelligence to comprehend, as much as we are able, the order and beauty of nature, a gift that allows us as well to accept with equanimity the unfortunate occurrences of life such as illness and death.

Maimonides invokes the authority of Galen[75] to identify matter as the cause of human failings, giving a medical endorsement to an argument formerly conducted along metaphysical and theological lines. Maimonides adds his own quantitative estimation that the actual number of personal and collective tragedies, all originating in one way or another in the material component of human beings, is relatively small, historically.

Maimonides specifically includes, in minimizing the occurrence of evil, the conflict that attends the struggle for power in cities. Though they are not uncommon, and leave the victims of tyranny with no recourse, Maimonides finds such conflicts localized and not affecting the majority of a city's inhabitants. He concedes this is not the case with "great wars," i.e., wars between cities or between countries, but for him such events are not, on the whole, i.e., taking a global view at any one time, all that common.

Maimonides relativization of political evil, of the amount of evil caused by civic and national conflicts, is fairly stunning, coming from a man who was exiled from his birthplace and knew of the particular precariousness of existence for Jews in the Yemen and elsewhere in his day, due to political upheavals. Moreover, he knew that Jewish history, and certainly its historiography, is often seen as one long tale of persecution,[76] a tale embedded in the liturgy and rituals of Judaism.

Yet Maimonides writes here as if he is unaware of all this. His philosophy has enabled him—or so it seems—to transcend misfortune and tragedy and to minimize the significance of history. In doing this, Maimonides severs ties with one strand of Jewish identity, and that a critical strand. He parts company *as a philosopher* with the collective memory of his people.[77]

Judaism remains for him the primary religion that teaches its believers how best to fashion a society and how to achieve happiness. That latter goal is best attained, however, by recognizing the universal dimension in the texts and rituals of the faith; and for Maimonides, that universal dimension puts the Jewish historical experience in perspective, a perspective that diminishes its existential significance. The individual's quest for scientific understanding and consequent happiness is of paramount importance for Maimonides here, and it is an understanding that will draw the person ever closer to God. Jewish history, like all history, does not essentially alter the unchanging course of nature, which, however divinely well ordered, is indifferent to human affairs; nature is testament, rather, to God's unchanging sovereignty and goodness.

The contrast between Maimonides' view in the *Guide* of the significance of Jewish history, and of history in general, and that of his illustrious predecessor, Judah Halevi, could not be more striking. Halevi's whole philosophy can be seen as an affirmation of the centrality of Jewish history in testifying to the uniqueness and superiority of Judaism.[78] For Halevi, historical vindication will be had one day in a restored Zion, and he offered up his life in physically identifying with its land.

As a philosopher, Maimonides had no such attachment to an earthly Zion, its place in his rabbinic writings and prayers notwithstanding. Beyond prayer, however, lay the yearnings of Jews for a reconstructed, redeemed world. Maimonides, it would appear, did not as a philosopher indulge that dream, at least not in its traditional terms.[79] His messianism was more of a realistic kind, holding that the world was slowly moving toward belief in the one God and acceptance of His dictates.[80] The Torah, as Maimonides understood it, showed the way toward this goal. Man's perverse behavior did not essentially affect the sense of happiness and contentment that this Torah offered the person sensitized to appreciate its teachings.

Accordingly, Maimonides largely accepts the world as it is, with its haves and have-nots, rich and poor, well and infirm. As a doctor, he tried to help the sick, and as a conscientious rabbi he tried to guide his community toward beneficial social regulations and appropriate religious behavior. As an ethicist, he adopted Aristotle's golden-mean approach, preaching moderation in one's actions as the norm. Maimonides thus did not turn his back on his fellow man or fellow Jews. Yet he was not a revolutionary and did not aspire to change the world. Nor did he believe God would (or could) change the order He had instituted. It was God's world, designed by Him gradually to bring all of mankind to acceptance of His dominion.

In chapter 13, Maimonides contrasts Aristotle's and his own view of final causality, the end or purpose of a thing's existence. While ubiquitous in nature and extending to the heavens and ultimately to the first cause or God, the final cause for Aristotle cannot be said to act purposefully, being eternal and necessary at every level of being. Yet Aristotle also considers nature teleologically ordered, with certain species existing for the sake of others. However, this does not amount to real purposive action for Maimonides, since for him only a cause that is not bound to eternal necessity, viz., the God of creation, can be said to act purposefully.

Though it is in order to ask after the purpose of creation for Maimonides, he claims that he has no answer other than that God so willed it.[81] The deity benefits neither from His deed, nor from man's worship of Him. Worship serves to perfect the worshiper, not God, in a universe in which every species strives for perfection of its being. Maimonides brings many biblical citations in support of his position that the world was not created for the sake of man and that humans share with every other organism the same dynamic of being.

Despite all his textual proofs, Maimonides' position is the same as Aristotle's, except that Maimonides believes that his view reframes the concept of the ultimate final cause, or God, giving Him a will and purpose that Aristotle's unmoved mover lacks. However, as Maimonides' God has always known what He will do, His unswerving will is essentially constrained by His wisdom.

Yet the opposite is also true: God's wisdom for Maimonides is bound to His will. As both attributes are synonyms for the unity of being in the divine, God's wisdom is willed to be what it is, what it has to be to be itself, viz., an agency for the good, which is the creation and preservation of being. Though this is a necessary definition of God's being, it also comports with Maimonides' desire to consider the providence that ensues from God's action as willed.

In chapters 15 through 25 of the *Guide,* Maimonides hammers home his view of divine providence and knowledge, circling the issues repeatedly in a compelling literary style that both clarifies and obscures his position.[82] Beginning with chapter 16, Maimonides tackles the issue of God's omniscience, which is seen by some as challenged by the evil in the world that a good and all-knowing God would not tolerate.

Maimonides first, in chapter 15, rehearses—inconclusively—the quarrel he supposedly debated earlier with a representative *mutakallim,* over the limiting factor, imagination or logic, in establishing what is a valid possibility, and whether God is bound by the same logical rules as we are, whether He can do things we judge by definition to be impossible. Not surprisingly, Maimonides sides with what he considers the universal opinion of philosophers that God cannot do that which is logically impossible, since such an assertion is a self-contradictory and hence meaningless proposition. Having touched upon the issue in passing[83] in chapter 20, Maimonides returns in chapter 25 to the question of the limits of God's power, in relation to determining what is possible for Him to do.

In chapter 25, Maimonides views bringing into existence whatever is possible to exist as "the entire purpose" of God's actions. God's wisdom determines what is possible, but that wisdom, as His will, is synonymous with God's essence, which is that of a being whose "nature" is to emanate being as much as is possible. This is a sign of God's omnipotence, a necessary aspect of His nature. In a sense, God's wisdom establishes His course of action, and His will accomplishes it.

Maimonides then says that God, following His wisdom, wills only a portion of that which is possible, giving the impression that Maimonides believes God chooses some possibilities and rejects others.[84] This statement appears to posit a category of possible existents that God does not deem suitable for our world, which would imply that He considered and rejected them. This conclusion, though, entails admitting the possibility of change in God's knowledge and thus in His being, a conclusion Maimonides would not condone.

Nor is it likely that Maimonides would have held that God had always known of possible existents that He did not consider worth actualizing and rendering necessary, since the litmus test of a genuine possibility for Maimonides is that it must become actual and necessary at some time.[85] Accordingly, Maimonides cannot be taken to believe that there may be possible beings or events that will never be actual. God's wisdom and being, as Maimonides says toward the end of the chapter, is to bring into being "everything whose existence is possible, existence being indubitably a good."[86] If the existence of a being is truly possible, it will be realized in due course, as part of the effulgence of being that derives from God. His wisdom does not choose one possible existent over another, but has always known and brought into being the one appropriate expression of being in each species. Maimonides' seeming acceptance of God's consideration of unrealized possibilities is thus misleading, and probably deliberately so.[87]

Maimonides devotes a number of chapters in this section to affirming God's omniscience. In chapter 16, and again in chapter 19, Maimonides insists that the evil in the world is not a sign of God's ignorance, impotence to affect change, or indifference to human misbehavior. Evil, when properly understood, is a necessary part of a benevolent divine scheme, known as such to a God who knows everything. For Maimonides, God does not sanction evil, He accepts it within a perspective that transforms it.

Maimonides does not at first fully explain this, and does not offer responses to the philosophers' arguments in chapter 16 for the impossibility of God's omniscience, of His having discrete, multiple, even an infinite number of cognitions, all presumably entailing multiplicity and change in the deity's knowledge and thus being. When Maimonides repeats these charges in chapter 20, he appears to accept them, joining in the philosophical "consensus" that God has no new or multiple cognitions. It follows, for Maimonides, that God has foreknowledge, knowing from all eternity that which will happen on earth.

This foreknowledge, Maimonides claims, does not alter what we would call the modal status of a given action, i.e., the possibility of its occurrence versus the necessity of it. Unrealized possibilities remain in themselves indeterminate logically, though God knows which possibility will eventually be realized. God's knowledge does not, Maimonides wants to insist, prevent the exercise of a free will for man, however inconceivable asserting both positions is to us.

Alfarabi discussed the issue of God's foreknowledge of possible events and the problem it poses for believing in man's free will and in divine justice in his commentary on chapter 9 of Aristotle's *De interpretatione*. Following Aristotle's lead on the indeterminate status of possible existents, Alfarabi writes, "it is in the nature of possibilities to be unknown . . . because of their incomplete existence."[88] This view conflicts, however, with the theological assertion of God's knowledge of the determination of future contingent possibilities, so Alfarabi searches for a solution "which does not entail anything objectionable according to what exists, is commonly accepted, or [is believed by] religious communities."[89]

Among the views Alfarabi mentions is that which Maimonides appears to adopt, that God's definite knowledge of the future existence of a possible existent does not eliminate its modal status as a possibility. Without endorsing this view, Alfarabi concludes wryly, "this opinion [*ra'y*] is more helpful than others, in religious communities."[90]

Alfarabi, then, sees this position as preferable for its political correctness and does not attempt to resolve it philosophically.[91] Maimonides may be adopting this strategy as well, having the highest opinion of Alfarabi's logical acumen. As a philosopher, though, Maimonides would have been uncomfortable leaving the issue unresolved, with the implications for divine justice left hanging. Yet Maimonides knows that the theses of divine foreknowledge and man's free will are fundamental to Jewish law and faith.

Maimonides is fully aware that the *mutakallimūn* grappled with this issue, and that the Ash'arites concluded that as God has foreknowledge of human actions, man is not free to act as he wishes. Nevertheless, the Ash'ari *'ulamā'* ruled that man is not absolved of responsibility for actions he "acquires," thereby justifying the imposition of rewards and punishments consequent upon the rule of law.[92]

This Ash'arite response to the problem of foreknowledge and free will is unacceptable to Maimonides. Earlier, in his *Commentary on the Mishnah,* he endorsed the rabbinic statement *ha-kol ẓafui ve-ha-reshut netunah,* "all is foreseen, yet [literally "and"] authorization [for free choice] is granted."[93] Maimonides appears to take refuge in the logical incomprehensibility of this statement; otherwise his assertion of God's total omniscience would lead to a covert acceptance of determinism.

Maimonides' position, as we have seen, is to consider God's knowledge as unique, not to be compared to that of human beings. God sees the many as one, and in that sense knows everything. This goes beyond knowing the individual only as a member of a genus; it collapses all the genera of being into one, which is the being of God. In this way, in knowing Himself, God knows the world.[94]

Maimonides knows that his position, viewing God's behavior as *sui generis,* lacks demonstrative proof, but so, he believes, do the philosophers' assertions. In asserting God's knowledge of everything, and His foreknowledge of the actions people undertake, Maimonides has offered a view more theological than philosophical in substance, more in conformity to popular beliefs. He leaves unresolved the dilemma of asserting both that man has the ability to choose between contrary possibilities, and that God has foreknowledge of which possibility will be chosen. Maimonides, however, may well have resolved the issue philosophically for himself, though choosing to keep his solution to himself for fear of the insight it would give his readers into the profound distance between his view of the deity and the popular Jewish conception of God.

While admitting that he has no logical demonstration for his position on divine providence, Maimonides claims it is more cogent logically (*aqrabu min al-qiyāṣ al-'aqlī*) than other views.[95] As his view on providence follows his professed belief in divine omniscience, Maimonides, one should assume, had a rational reason for believing in an all-knowing

God too. In what way, then, could he have held that God's foreknowledge of a possible event does not make it a necessary one?

For Maimonides, God would know this in that His knowledge is total and perfect. That is to say, God knows (and has always known) all the causes that would affect any possibility to render it necessary, so that whenever a given possibility occurs, He may be said to have known it. His knowledge of possible as well as future events is shaped by their correspondence to real, i.e., formal being. However, the material, individualizing component of an existent being is removed from God's direct knowledge. Being corporeal, it is alien to His being.

The particular occurrence of an object or an event is known to God as the result of the collision of its matter with form. God knows the myriad ways form responds to matter and shapes it, and the recalcitrance of matter to the imposition of form. Whatever the result of a particular hylomorphic union, and the choice of a possible action that a person makes, God knows the pattern of causal events that can bring about such a choice and constitutes such a union.

God may be said to know what happens in a person's life, then, in that He knows the universal patterns of that life, as applicable to that person. He does not know the person as such, or the event as such, in its material, corporeal individuality. That lesson Maimonides teaches with restrained poignancy in speaking of a person (like his brother) who goes to his death at sea, a death that is "deserved" by the laws of a providential deity that decree such an end to persons who do not act circumspectly when facing danger.

Maimonides is careful here to word the relation God has to individuals in an impersonal manner, something that is not obvious in the Pines translation,[96] and that Maimonides probably meant to obscure from his average reader. "Some" individual, rather than a "certain" individual, is known to God, whose knowledge encompasses every possible action that individual takes, once he takes it. Before—and after—the action, God simply knows that "some" person will have actualized one of the possibilities that God has established as real. They are real possibilities because God knows they will be realized.

In the century after Maimonides, Gersonides (1288–1344) constructed his great work *Milḥamot Hashem, Wars of the Lord,* largely in response to the philosophical views of Maimonides and Averroes. Despite earlier criticism of what he thought was Maimonides' acceptance of the contradiction involved in maintaining both God's foreknowledge of possible existents and man's freedom of will, he concludes his book 3 discussion of divine knowledge by citing Maimonides' remark in *Guide* 3.20 that "any believer in a revealed religion who is guided by the necessity of reason" will say that "God's knowledge refers to the species and in another sense [*be'inyan aḥer*] encompasses all members of the species."[97]

This is Gersonides' own position, that God does not know individuals as such, directly, and he feels that Maimonides' statement as quoted above belies his protestations to the contrary. Gersonides makes explicit that which I have given as Maimonides' esoteric view: that God knows particulars "in the sense in which they are ordered and determined [*meṣuddarim u-mugbalim*]," i.e., to the degree they conform to universal formal patterns, patterns that coalesce into the one "intelligible order in His mind."[98]

In chapters 22 and 23, Maimonides turns to the Book of Job to impart through exegesis his core understanding of divine providence.[99] Following the Bible, in chapter 22 Maimonides first introduces us to Satan, who is presented in *Guide* 2.30, as Sammael.[100] Maimonides offers *midrashim* that link Satan to the snake that tempted Eve. Commentators elsewhere have suggested that Satan represents in that context either the imaginative or the appetitive faculties.[101] Here, though, it becomes increasingly clear that Satan symbolizes the element of earthly matter. As such, he is depicted in the parable as other than all the other heavenly creatures or angels, who symbolize totally immaterial, purely formal beings. The other angels are under God's command and do His bidding, not Satan. He roams free and wreaks havoc on Job, who mistakenly blames God for his misfortunes.

As matter, Satan represents for Maimonides the privation or absence of form, and thus the privation of being. Matter is kept from being pure privation or absolute nonbeing solely by its attachment to form. Though an "accidental" attachment, it is sufficient to accord matter a portion of being. Maimonides must concede, if he is not to consider matter as totally outside God's realm, that matter is part of His creation. However evil its machinations may be, matter is necessary for the good to prevail in this world, as it does, in Maimonides' view.

Maimonides has here presented as a parable the Neoplatonic doctrine of emanation, according to which earthly matter is the last thing to be realized, its otherness with respect to form technically rendering it nonbeing. Adapting this theory to his perspective of an omniscient God, Maimonides cannot leave matter totally outside His purview. Thus, he has God know everything in His own way, though absolving Him of responsibility for man's deeds, which are the result of yielding to his material physical nature.

Maimonides has here expressed his innermost thoughts concerning matter. Matter is that part of creation that is quasi-independent of God's control on earth, being inherently unstable. The most God may know is the idea of matter, that it is the substratum of form, though what happens to that form when it conjoins with matter in a given object is not predetermined, matter being unpredictable. God knows all the possibilities that may occur, so that when one does, God may be said to have known it beforehand; but He does not know, before or after the event, exactly which of the possibilities is the one realized. His knowledge is theoretical, concerning the universal intelligible aspect of the world, with all its possible interactions with matter. God does not track the particular event or action as such, owing to His alienation from matter and the corporealization it would introduce into His being.[102]

This is not a limitation on God's knowledge, since the realization of any possibility is in part contingent upon matter, which is foreign to God's being and hence to His knowledge. It is thus impossible for God to act contrary to His being, to be intimately cognizant of and thus related to material being.

Put another way, Maimonides may well have believed that God could not know evil in itself, since His being is pure good. He has so designed the world, though, that matter never appears by itself but always with form, and it is as such, through its formal dimension, that God knows the world. Ultimately, Maimonides must accept God as the cause of all that exists, even of that relative privation of being that is matter; but that privation is sufficient to insulate matter from God's direct regard.

In chapter 23, Maimonides repeats much of what he already said in chapter 17, bringing now "proof texts" from the Book of Job to help convince his readers of the legitimacy of his position on providence. Maimonides first presents Job's indictment of a God who appears indifferent to injustice, an attitude that Maimonides identifies with Aristotle's. The identification is correct, though Maimonides portrays Aristotle negatively here. God for Aristotle is impersonal, so that his indifference to the human condition is not due to contempt for the human species or abandonment of it, as Maimonides' Job claims; nor does Aristotle's god laugh at the "calamity of the innocent."

Elihu and finally Job represent Maimonides' position on providence, one we have come to know. The Book of Job for Maimonides reinforces his view that empirical evidence of the harmony in nature, when understood in the proper perspective and with the enlightenment gained through education, entirely reframes the issue of providence. No longer is it a matter of rationalizing skewed rewards and punishments, or of looking at the world through anthropocentric lenses. Providence now is acknowledgment of the awesome and beautiful mystery of existence and of its Creator. While God is unknown to us, His creation elicits our love and obedience.

This ignorance of God is an informed ignorance for Maimonides, not total ignorance. Earlier in the chapter, when speaking of Job's final confession of error, Maimonides writes that "when he knew God with a certain knowledge, he admitted that true happiness, which is the knowledge of the deity, is guaranteed to all who know Him and that a human being cannot be troubled in it by any of all the misfortunes in question."[103] For Maimonides, then, one may have a limited but true knowledge of the God who cannot be known, and that knowledge will grant such happiness that the injustices and cruelties of life will not disturb the person's equanimity. This is neither skepticism nor agnosticism; it is the faith of the true believer, abetted by circumstantial knowledge. Using the tools of the philosopher, it reaches the pinnacle of absorption in God's presence that the piously devout person craves.

In chapter 24, Maimonides offers his perspective on the biblical tests, or "trials," that God supposedly sets for good people, waiting to see their response and rewarding (or punishing) them accordingly. This, Maimonides knew, was a popular belief, an attempt to exonerate God from committing an apparent injustice. Yet Maimonides will have none of it. Having just formulated a view of providence that removes God from personally administering rewards and punishments, Maimonides feels obliged to respond to the notion that God does just that, in testing a person's loyalty.

In responding to this notion, Maimonides adopts its terms, that of a personal God. His remarks must therefore be read with caution, treated as metaphors. This is Maimonides' standard operating procedure in explicating his views through the biblical text. The God of the Bible is very active and personal, and Maimonides treats Him as such, though he has plainly said not to believe this literally. Thus, though Maimonides cannot accept the notion that God tests Abraham's faith, he is prepared to assert that God put him and Isaac to an ordeal meant to convey lofty spiritual beliefs.

Maimonides does say, however, that Abraham was commanded, in a dream or vision, to kill Isaac, which Genesis 22:1 does not say. For Maimonides, though, it is a given that Abraham's imaginative faculty, either awake or asleep, imparted God's will, that all prophecy is an interpretation, set to a particular circumstance, of a universal moral imperative. Hence, Maimonides is both endorsing the biblical story and reshaping it. God is the source of all that is good, and Maimonides understands that the Bible conveys that message in popular, if at times misleading, parables.

10

Rationalizing the Law (*Guide* Part III, Chapters 26–50)

Paraphrase

In chapter 26, Maimonides adapts the belief in God's action as always purposeful to the political sphere, as exemplified in the revealed religious law. He takes issue with those who explain everything as solely due to the will of God and do not look for reasons or causes for a particular commandment. The overwhelming belief of the people, to which he subscribes, is that every commandment and prohibition is rational and purposive, though not always transparently so.

Maimonides adopts the rabbinic distinction between commandments mentioned in the Torah as *ḥuqqim,* "statutes," and those called *mishpaṭim,* "judgments." Though the usefulness of judgments is clear to all, and the usefulness of statutes is not, Maimonides is determined to propose a rationale for the latter too. He distinguishes between the generalities of the statutes' commandments, whose utility is obvious, and the particular *halakhic* details of the *ḥoq,* which are (or may appear to be) arbitrary. The Torah's injunctions concerning dietary and clothing restrictions, as well as the commandments concerning the scapegoat on Yom Kippur, are examples of such *ḥuqqim.*

It is necessary that there be such statutes, Maimonides says, though one may challenge the necessity of whichever set of details are chosen. (The rationale of having these seemingly arbitrary details lies in the necessity of embodying a general principle of recognized utility in a specific stipulated praxis.)[1]

Maimonides then announces his intention to classify the 613 commandments of Jewish law in terms of their causes and utility, after first clarifying the premises underlying this classification.[2]

Accordingly, Maimonides in chapter 27 lays out the fundamental premise of "the Law as a whole," *jumlah al-shari'a.*[3] He is apparently referring by this term to any *shari'a* or body of law perceived as revealed, which for Maimonides would include Islam as well as Judaism. Later he refers to the Torah as "the true Law," *al-shari'a al-ḥāqqa;*[4] though he claims it is unique, it yet falls within the recognizable category of a *shari'a.*

The fundamental premise of any *shar'īa,* for Maimonides, is to promote the welfare of the soul and the welfare of the body.[5] (This, in contrast to the solely material aims allegedly pursued by a *nomos,* i.e., the law of a secular society.) Though it is the soul and body of an individual that the law addresses, that individual's physical welfare depends on the way people live with one another, i.e., on the political well-being of society. The law must therefore promote altruistic actions and not permit some people to hurt others through unbridled exercise of their will and power. The welfare of the body also requires, for Maimonides, that people acquire (presumably through education) civic virtues that will assist them in managing their city.[6]

The welfare of the body is, then, a political matter; the individual is unable to satisfy his basic material needs other than in society. "It is already known," Maimonides says, referring to Aristotle's statement without mentioning his name, "that man is political by nature."[7] The successful governance of a city, for Maimonides, is a condition for achieving individual perfection of the body, and this, he says, must precede the perfection of the soul.

This second perfection is a private matter, each individual striving to his utmost for (theoretical) knowledge of all that exists. The ultimate perfection here is to have one's intellect be in a state of such actualization that one essentially becomes a being "rational *in actu,*"[8] i.e., an actualized rational being. The second perfection needs the first, but it is only the knowledge gained through theoretical speculation that can cause "permanent preservation,"[9] i.e., immortality.

In chapter 28, Maimonides identifies the correct views that lead to the ultimate perfection sought (which is conjunction with the eternal Agent Intellect). These are belief in God's existence, unity, knowledge, power, will, and eternal being. They are communicated by the Law only in a general way,[10] Maimonides says, one that highlights their end or purpose (*ghaya*). Knowledge of each of these beliefs requires prior familiarity with the many propositions[11] that lead to these assertions, Maimonides claims, acknowledging implicitly that it is not the Law's responsibility to provide such arguments. The *Guide* is his attempt to offer substantive, if not demonstrative, philosophical reasons for these tenets of the faith.

There is another set of beliefs that the Law calls for, Maimonides then says, those that are necessary to maintain an equitable society.[12] (These beliefs are necessary to achieve the first perfection, the "welfare of the body" discussed in the preceding chapter.) The belief that God is furious with those who disobey Him, and that it is necessary to fear Him, is given as an example of this category of politically motivated beliefs. Another example, given at the end of the chapter, is the belief in God's immediate response to the prayer of one who was oppressed or deceived.

Maimonides rationalizes the fear of God as a political necessity, contributing to the first perfection the Law aims at. The love of God, which Maimonides next addresses briefly, belongs to the second perfection. It is expressed through cognitive apprehension of all that exists, and of the (divine) wisdom evinced in it.

Maimonides repeats the assertion made in chapter 26 that the commandments that trouble people are those not obviously useful for either the first or the second perfections the Law addresses, and he will attempt to integrate such commandments with these two perfections. He will show all the commandments as either advancing a correct belief (the second perfection) or assisting in abolishing reciprocal oppression and acquiring moral qualities (the first perfection).

In chapter 29, Maimonides lays the groundwork for justifying many of the commandments whose purposes are not clear. He does this by describing at length the religion of the Sabians, pagans he mentioned before, in part 1, chapter 63. Maimonides was familiar with Sabian practices and beliefs from Arabic literature, particularly a book called *The Nabatean Agriculture,* which he mentions by name. The Sabians appear in the Qur'ān as monotheists[13] and are described by later writers as a syncretistic sect with a version of early biblical stories, star worship, and theosophies derived from Hellenism.[14] Maimonides locates them in the time of Abraham and sees the first patriarch as their opponent, even as he regards the laws and practices of Judaism in part as responses to everything Sabianism stood for.[15]

Maimonides comments on the Sabians' belief in the eternity of the world; on their erection of statues for worshiping the planets and their belief that the statues communicated with them; on their sacrifices of seven each of beetles, mice, and bats to the sun; and on their belief that talismans cause demons to appear. Maimonides summarizes tales told in *The Nabatean Agriculture* that refer to a cult of a pagan prophet named Tammuz and to pagan versions of Adam in the Garden of Eden.[16]

Thus Maimonides treats the Sabian faith, with its temples, statues, altars, sacrifices, festivals, prayers, and other rituals, as the existential reality against which the laws of Judaism find their rationalization. The foundation of the "whole of our Law," Maimonides says, "consists in the effacement of these

[Sabian/pagan] opinions from the minds and of [their] monuments from existence."[17]

In chapter 30, Maimonides gives what may be seen as a prime example of pagan false belief, the popular conviction that the sun and stars must be worshiped for agriculture to succeed and that the spirits of these planets punish with drought those who do not do so. Maimonides quotes a passage in *The Nabatean Agriculture* that commands playing musical instruments before the statues during festivals to please the gods and to receive rewards from them of long and healthy life and good crops.

In order to eradicate this false belief and, Maimonides believes, spare people the exhaustion of tiring and useless practices, Moses proclaimed the very opposite of these beliefs (as an indication of divine mercy), namely, that worship of the stars and planets would bring about an agricultural and personal disaster. Worship of God would, however, bring all the benefits previously promised.

Maimonides reprises in chapter 31 his belief that every commandment serves a purpose and is useful to human beings, indicative of a wise and understanding deity. The commandments address opinions, moral qualities, and political civic actions, commending and condemning right and wrong views in each area.

In chapter 32, Maimonides elaborates on his historical approach to the commandments and laws of the Torah, seeing them as an extension of God's actions toward the world in its entirety. All His acts are done with wisdom and a "gracious subtlety"[18] that makes for both physical and political perfection. This is evident in the human body, the parts of which are designed to create a healthy organism.[19]

Maimonides cites, as an example of the "wily and gracious arrangement" God has designed for mammals, the mother's ability to suckle her newborn, who is unable to feed on dry food. Analogously, Maimonides announces, "many things in our law" are so designed, it being impossible for people suddenly to abandon that to which they are accustomed, their nature being incapable of radical change.

Sacrifices are a case in point. It would have been no more possible then to have proscribed sacrifices, Maimonides says, than for a prophet now to prohibit prayer, fasting, and supplicating God's assistance and substitute solely meditation (*fikra*). The original insistence upon sacrifices and the Temple cult was all a "divine ruse,"[20] Maimonides says, one, however, that succeeded in eradicating the "memory of idolatry" and of establishing belief in the existence and oneness of God.

Maimonides anticipates the (average) reader's rejection of what we may call his historicist and utilitarian approach to the Law, not to mention his view of God as benevolently manipulative. To the assumed question of his critics why God could not have altered human nature to have the Israelites immediately accept practices expressing the true nature of the Creator, Maimonides responds disarmingly that God does not change human nature, not that He cannot, but that He does not, never has and never will.[21] The entire legal stratum of the Torah, with its concomitant notion of physical rewards and punishments, and the institution of prophecy itself, are predicated upon the independent, free—and frail—will of human beings.

Having compared the forms of religious devotion in his day to the practices of ancient times, both considered as substitutions for true worship, Maimonides retracts a bit. He now justifies prayer and observance of the Sabbath and of the civil laws the Torah prescribes as necessary for achieving the "first intention" of the laws, which is to have a true (if limited) apprehension of God. In contrast, the ancient practice of sacrifices represents a "second intention," viz., to gradually wean the people away from false beliefs; as such it is more removed from achieving the Torah's goal of knowing God.

Though Maimonides defends the laws of sacrifices as historically necessary, his aversion to the institution is such that at the end of the chapter he finds scriptural and midrashic support for the view that the first laws given after the Exodus were of a theoretical and civil kind, having nothing to do with sacrifices. This is particularly striking, given that in his *Mishneh Torah* Maimonides pays full attention and respect to the laws of the Temple cult with its sacrifices, not historicizing or relativizing them at all. But then that is part of the striking difference between the Code and the *Guide,* and between Maimonides the legist and Maimonides the philosopher.[22]

In chapter 33, Maimonides declares that the first purpose of Jewish law, which he calls the "perfect law" (*al-shari'a al-kāmila*), is to restrain desire and curb the appetite for physical and sexual licentiousness.[23] Indulgence in one's passions has a destructive effect upon one's body and the body politic, as well as upon one's soul, or intellect. The laws are a "gracious ruse" to counter these desires, forbidding "everything that leads to lusts and to mere pleasure."[24]

Maimonides stresses that the Law aims at cultivating the traits of gentleness and docility, obedience and responsiveness. It also aims at purity and sanctity, which Maimonides identifies primarily with the renunciation and maximal (though not complete) avoidance of sexual intercourse. Maimonides has very strong feelings about this issue that he will elaborate later, in chapter 49.

In chapter 34 Maimonides expresses a fundamental principle of law: it is addressed "only toward the things that occur in the majority of cases"[25] and is indifferent to the rare or exceptional situation. The Law (meaning Jewish law) is a "divine thing" (*amr ilāhīy*), Maimonides says, and like the laws of the natural world, can damage certain individuals while benefiting the many. It is therefore not surprising that the Law does not benefit everyone, even as the natural form of a given species is not fully realized in every individual of the species. Both the laws of nature and the laws of the Torah derive from the same divine source and cannot be constructed otherwise, in order to favor the exception. Maimonides goes so far as to say that this would be a logical impossibility, and as such is unalterable.

In chapter 35 Maimonides introduces his division of the laws or commandments (*miẓvot*) of the Torah into fourteen classes, to be explained in detail in the following chapters. His categorization builds upon the arrangement of the laws that he produced in the *Mishneh Torah,* to which he refers. He views three and a half of the classes as dealing with the relation between man and his fellow man, while the remaining ten and a half classes deal essentially with the relation between man and God. This indicates that for Maimonides the primary emphasis of the Jewish faith, the "first intention" of its law, is to achieve a close and private sense of intimacy with and proximity to God.

In chapter 36 Maimonides touches upon the first class of commandments, which he called the "Foundations of the Torah" in his Code, the *Mishneh Torah.* He assumes the reader is familiar with his earlier work, so that he does not enumerate these commandments.[26] He has, moreover, gone over the metaphysical and physical doctrines that underlie the commandments in this class earlier in the *Guide,* doctrines that constitute the reason for the commandment to believe in, love, and fear the one God and creator of the world.

In addition to the commandments listed in the first chapter of the *Mishneh Torah* that constitute this class, Maimonides here mentions commandments regarding oaths, appeals to God—to be made in times of distress—and actions that express repentance.

In this chapter, Maimonides warns against interpreting events as due to chance and not to God's governance. God, Maimonides says, apprehends our personal situation, and our welfare or ruin is in his hands; He responds to our belief or disbelief with reward or punishment. Believing otherwise leads a person astray.

Maimonides claims that the belief in chance necessarily leads to further "corrupt opinions" as well as "unrighteous actions." It is these consequences of the belief in chance that alarm Maimonides and allow him to invoke the popular image of a God dispensing rewards and punishments forthwith. For Maimonides, the social order as well as one's personal happiness and well-being is disrupted by the belief in chance.

In chapter 37, Maimonides refers to his second class of commandments, those that he listed in the "Laws concerning Idolatry" in the *Mishneh Torah.*[27] He believes these commandments are a reaction to the various practices of magicians, sorcerers, and the like found among the Sabians and other pagan peoples. Maimonides divides these practices into three kinds: those dealing with a single object; those that emphasize the time of the practice; and those that require actions of a charismatic sort.

These practices may be combined in one magical action, Maimonides says, offering examples that he was familiar with either personally or from his extensive reading in occult literature. As before, the Sabian book called *The Nabatean Agriculture* is Maimonides' main source for the pagan practices, to which the Bible's agricultural commandments and others related to them are, in his view, a riposte.

Maimonides describes a number of bizarre practices, many of a sexual nature calling for women performers, intended to solicit the assistance of the stars and planets. This renders the practice idolatry, and Maimonides has no compunction in following the biblical commandment and urging that all those who engage in magic be killed.[28]

Maimonides views the biblical animus against idolatry as extending to the (presumed) appearance and apparel of pagan priests. Thus, unlike their pagan counterparts, Jewish males are not to shave the corners of their beards, and no one should wear clothing of mixed strains of cloth or cross-dress, the latter practice prohibited also, Maimonides believes, for its potential to arouse desire and "necessarily" cause debauchery.

Maimonides likewise considers various agricultural commandments as reactions to pagan antecedents. Such are the laws regulating the harvesting of fruit and prohibiting mixed-species grafting of trees and sowing a vineyard with diverse seeds.

In chapter 38, Maimonides briefly mentions the commandments of the third class, those he discussed in the section of the *Mishneh Torah* devoted to "Laws concerning Character Traits."[29] His treatment there is sufficient, he believes, the purpose—acquisition of noble moral qualities—sufficiently obvious to allow him to pass over the topic here. He promises to discuss separately commandments that have a hidden moral dimension, as they appear in different contexts. No commandment is without a purpose.

In chapter 39, Maimonides discusses the fourth class of commandments, those culled from the "Book of Seeds"[30] and other sections of his *Mishneh*

Torah that dictate acts of charity and benevolence. Maimonides views the commandments requiring tithing and gifting to the poor and the priesthood as expressions of humility and devotion to God. The commandments concerning the Sabbatical and Jubilee years benefit the poor and slaves, as well as redistribute land ownership, avoiding permanent disenfranchisement of the poor. Maimonides finds the commandments concerning lending and borrowing, as well as those dealing with slavery, "imbued with benevolence, pity and kindness for the weak."[31] These sentiments should not be extended to the wrongdoer, even if he is a member of one's group, as protecting an evil man is misplaced pity and tantamount to cruelty to others.

In chapter 40, Maimonides discusses his fifth class of commandments, those contained in the "Book of Torts" section of the *Mishneh Torah*.[32] These are laws meant to counter injustice and wrongdoing, to prevent personal or property damage. The benefit of these laws being obvious, Maimonides dilates only upon the care shown in not overreaching in the pursuit of justice, thereby perpetuating injustice.

In chapter 41 Maimonides discusses the commandments of his sixth class, those concerning punishments, treated before in the *Mishneh Torah's* "Book of Judges."[33] The benefit to society of these laws is also obvious, Maimonides says, and it would be misplaced mercy not to punish offenders. Maimonides here offers rationales just for those laws he deems "peculiar" (*gharība*),[34] beginning with the *lex talionis* of Leviticus 24:20, the law stipulating retaliation in exact measure for the crime committed (i.e., an eye for an eye). The rabbis mitigated the severity of the biblical law, but Maimonides pointedly refuses to discuss their action. He says he has an opinion about it that he can mention orally only, a most unusual response for him.

Maimonides first classifies the level of penalties prescribed according to four criteria: the magnitude of the harm caused; the frequency of the crime committed; the strength of the incitement, for only the fear of punishment will deter someone drawn strongly to a wrong action; and the ease with which a crime can be committed secretly.

Secondly, Maimonides describes what he sees as the Torah's fourfold classification of punishments: a court-ordered death; excommunication (*karet*), which the rabbis altered to whipping; whipping for lesser crimes; and verbal prohibitions for transgressions in which no overt action was committed.

Maimonides' list of transgressions warranting a court-ordered death penalty includes actions that have both religious and sociopolitical significance, such as idolatry, adultery, incest, profanation of the Sabbath, and rebellious behavior by both elders and children.[35] Maimonides acknowledges that in practice the courts do not administer the death penalty in absolute fashion, and that there must be judges "in every town" to administer fair decisions, based on the testimony of witnesses. He also emphasizes the importance of a ruler whom the people rightly fear, to back up the judges.

Maimonides then explains his formal rejection of changes in the Law, as previously stated in chapter 34; he sees such changes as the action of a "rebellious elder." He says that God forbade changes[36] in order to prevent corruption of the Law and loss of public trust in its divine authority, though He knew that the Law would have to be modified when circumstances require it. Therefore, Maimonides states, God permitted members of the High Court, and only they, to make ad hoc temporary modifications of the Law, in order to preserve its original format ultimately.

Maimonides distinguishes transgressions according to the intentionality of the perpetrator and finds that anyone who issues a legal decision or acts on it on his own authority, not being in the High Court or a High Priest, is to be considered a "deliberate transgressor" (*al-mezid*) and put to death as a "rebellious elder" (*zaqen mamre'*). Similarly, one who transgresses "in a high-handed manner" (*'oseh be-yad ramah*), acting deliberately, is to be killed also. He has flouted the law, which is equivalent to reviling God, and this in turn is espousing idolatry.

Maimonides then declares that all deliberate acts contrary to the law deserve the death penalty, for both individuals and entire communities, considered as infidels. Cultic acts are thus tied to fundamental issues of allegiance to God, Maimonides having no qualms about condemning people to death in principle for disobeying the Law.

Maimonides concludes the chapter by mentioning those laws in his "Book of Judges" that concern both private and public hygiene, as well as the consideration that should be shown a captive woman. The Law can be severe, but also wise and compassionate, Maimonides is saying; all are attempts to forge and maintain a sanctified people, devoted to God.

In chapter 42, Maimonides mentions the seventh class of laws, those concerning property, formerly discussed in his *Mishneh Torah*'s "Book of Acquisition and Judgments."[37] The reason for these laws is obvious, to establish justice in commercial relations and fairness to all concerned. Maimonides is particularly interested in seeing that family inheritance procedures be strictly followed, without succumbing to favoritism. Relatives should be duly remembered in one's will, even if the relative has done one an injustice.

In chapter 43, Maimonides touches on the commandments he discussed in his *Mishneh Torah*'s "Book of Seasons" (*Sefer Zemanim*),[38] viz., laws of the Sabbath and festivals. The reasons for these occasions are mostly given in the Bible, and Maimonides emphasizes their beneficial effect upon the people.

The Sabbath is a day of rest from labor as well as a commemoration of creation; Rosh Hashanah and Yom Kippur are days of repentance; and the three pilgrim holidays are opportunities for commemorating history and, through pleasurable gatherings, fostering the feelings of friendship that are necessary for living in political society.

In chapter 44, Maimonides tersely mentions the ninth class of commandments, those he listed in his *Mishneh Torah*'s "Book of Love" (*Sefer Ahavah*).[39] They deal with prayer and blessings that are to be recited at various times, such as when eating, putting on phylacteries, or reciting the Shemaʿ. The purpose of these commandments is to ensure that we constantly remember,[40] love, and fear God, and to instill observance of the commandments in general and acceptance of whatever beliefs in Him are necessary. These activities "bring about useful opinions," Maimonides concludes, their obvious merit making further discourse unnecessary.

Maimonides compensates for the brevity of chapter 44 by going into greater detail in chapter 45 when discussing the tenth class of commandments, those concerned with the Temple worship. Maimonides had written of this in portions of his *Mishneh Torah*'s "Book of Divine Worship"[41] as well as earlier in *Guide* 3.32, but he felt a further exploration of the reasons for everything concerned with the sanctuary was in order. His point of departure and recurring motif is that this class of laws is preeminently a response to the idolatrous practices of paganism (even as it appropriates them).

Thus, he explains the erection of two (formerly pagan) cherubs in the Holy of Holies as an antidote to the belief in foreign gods. The cherubs are there, Maimonides contends, to remind us of the angels who carry out God's commands and are the vehicle through which prophecy and the Law are conveyed. For prophecy, Maimonides reminds us, is received only through the mediation of an angel.[42]

In chapter 46, Maimonides discusses commandments of the eleventh class, those concerned with sacrifices, taken also from his *Mishneh Torah*'s "Book of Divine Worship," as well as from its "Book of Sacrifices."[43] Once again Maimonides finds that many particularities of sacrifices were meant as antidotes to pagan practices. Thus he believes that the choice of particular animals to be sacrificed was determined by the Egyptian reverence for them, and the prohibitions against eating blood followed upon the Sabians' incorporation of blood in their homage to *jinns*. Maimonides cannot find a rationale, however, for the biblical commandments concerning the ritual offerings of wine, which apparently for him do not differ significantly from the rituals of idolaters.[44]

Having accepted the necessity of sacrifices in biblical times, Maimonides offers esthetic and moral reasons for the various peculiarities of sacrificial rituals. Thus, sacrificial animals must be in perfect physical condition as a token of the worshiper's esteem for God, and frankincense was employed for the good odor it gave to the proceedings.

In chapter 47, Maimonides discusses the commandments of the twelfth class, which he enumerated in the *Mishneh Torah*'s "Book of Cleanness" (or "Purification," *Sefer Ṭaharah*).[45] These laws stipulate the physical conditions that render a person eligible or ineligible to enter sacred space or to participate in a community chosen to be a "holy people." The numerous prescriptions and proscriptions concerning ritual states of cleanliness in the Temple were intended, Maimonides states, to augment the awe and fear with which one was to approach it.

Again, Maimonides contrasts Jewish law with Sabian analogues, claiming that Jewish law is more lenient and life affirming. A menstruating Jewish woman, for example, is not isolated in her home and treated as an outcast, but is free to do all the work she normally does for her husband, without, however, touching him.[46] (Maimonides is writing, need one say, within the sensibilities of his time.)

Toward the end of the chapter, Maimonides offers the talmudic explanation of leprosy as a punishment for slander, the disease spreading as long as the person remains unrepentant. Maimonides says "the utility of this belief is manifest,"[47] indicating that he does not agree with the explanation on a factual level but finds great benefit in it as, presumably, a deterrent to uttering slander.

In chapter 48, Maimonides discusses the commandments of the thirteenth class, those concerning forbidden foods and the slaughtering of animals that he considered in the "Book of Holiness" and those concerning vows and nazaritism that he considered in the "Book of Asseverations" (*Sefer Hafla'ah*) of the *Mishneh Torah*.[48] As he commented in chapter 35, Maimonides sees the common purpose of these laws as to deter people from lusting after what they perceive as the greatest pleasure, and for taking the desire for food and drink as an end in itself.

Maimonides singles out pork as abhorrent due to the unhygienic conditions in which pigs live and feed. He also considers prohibitions against the ingesting of intestinal fat and blood as due to concerns for healthy digestion. Such passages attest to the influence of Maimonides' medical experience upon him.

Maimonides regards other prohibitions in this category as motivated by the desire to curb cruelty and encourage compassion. As examples, he mentions the prohibition against eating a limb torn off a living animal; slaughtering an animal and her young on the same day; and taking a bird's eggs from the nest in its mother's presence.

Uncharacteristically, Maimonides is not sure of the reason for the prohibition of boiling a kid in its mother's milk,[49] the basis for the rabbis' injunction against eating milk and meat together. He assumes it was a reaction to idolatrous practices, though he admits not having found such a practice in the Sabian books he consulted.

In chapter 49, Maimonides engages in a lengthy discussion of the commandments of the fourteenth class, those he enumerated in various sections of his *Mishneh Torah:* the laws on prohibited sexual relations in the "Book of Women" and the "Book of Holiness"; the laws concerning the interbreeding of beasts in the "Book of Seeds"; and the commandment of circumcision in the "Book of Love."[50] As he stated in chapter 35, the common purpose of these laws is to diminish the desire for sexual intercourse and decrease its frequency, so that it will not be pursued as an end in itself.

In this chapter, Maimonides begins by referring to Aristotle's praise of friendship, as expressed in book 8 of his *Nicomachean Ethics.*[51] Maimonides seconds Aristotle's observation of the benefits friendly relations provide, and of the fraternal feelings that naturally occur among family members. The "greatest purpose of the Law," Maimonides claims, is to promote mutual help and love among people, a goal he feels is best attained when they have a common ancestor and constitute a "single tribe" (*qabīla wāḥida*).

Harlots are prohibited, therefore, in Maimonides' opinion, because of the threat they pose to the values of family and tribal harmony and amity. The laws against adultery and the sexual exploitation of women, intended to prevent licentious, immoral behavior, also have the welfare of the society as a whole in mind.

Maimonides finds that prohibitions against illicit unions are intended to decrease the frequency of sexual intercourse and to make such behavior abhorrent. As Maimonides believes that even the "natural" form of sexual intercourse between man and woman should be engaged in as little as possible and only as necessary, for procreation, so he considers it even more appropriate that the Law bans the "deviant" actions of homosexuality and bestiality, which are performed solely for pleasure.

Maimonides traces the prohibitions against intercourse with members of one's family to the natural feeling of shame that it elicits. The law attempts to steer one's thoughts away from sex and toward study of the Torah. Maimonides again finds support in Aristotle, seeing him, in both the *Nicomachean Ethics* and his *Rhetoric,* denigrate those who are sexually intemperate and who indulge their appetite for food.[52]

One of the reasons for the commandment of circumcision, Maimonides believes, is to weaken the penis and decrease its lustfulness and sexual activity. Maimonides believes this effect of circumcision is an "indubitable fact" (*amrun lā shaqqan fīhu*), intended not as a corrective to nature but to enhance morality.

Another reason for circumcision, perhaps greater than the first mentioned, according to Maimonides, is to signal membership in the people so marked. This enhances the love and assistance extended within the group, establishing a covenant with one's (circumcised) fellow as well as with God.

Maimonides offers various reasons why circumcision must take place on the eighth day after the infant's birth, one being that the parents, and particularly the father (who should perform the operation), are not as attached at that point to the child as they are when he is older. The commandment would not be followed were it delayed a few years, Maimonides avers.

Maimonides concludes the chapter and this entire section of the *Guide* by reaffirming the centrality of combating idolatry as the main incentive for the commandments, including the particular aspects of some that he cannot explain. Idolatry has to be opposed for its false beliefs as well as for the uselessness of its practices, its subjugation of people to an unnecessary and burdensome way of life. Maimonides' implacable opposition to idolatry thus has social as well as "religious" motivations; it is for him a competing political ideology.

In chapter 50, Maimonides summarily treats an issue that he says belongs to the "mysteries of the Torah," *ṣitrei torah.* Maimonides, however, has no trouble unraveling mysteries of this kind; they do not contain secrets that require coded explanations. What has mystified many people and caused them to fall by the way, he says, is the inclusion in the Torah of what seem to be pointless stories, such as the genealogies of other peoples, lists of their kings, and the detailed itinerary of the Israelites' forty years of wandering in the desert.

Maimonides adopts the same attitude toward these narrative tales that he took toward the legal stratum of the Torah. Everything in it is there for a reason. There is a purpose to each story, either to support a legal opinion, or to rectify hostile behavior between men.

With these goals in mind, Maimonides proceeds to explain the genealogies in Genesis from Adam on as intended to make the explanation for the proliferation of peoples and languages credible. Similarly, the enumeration of the many places in the desert at which the Israelites stayed during their years of wandering is to strengthen belief in the miracle of the manna.

In this way, Maimonides stays loyal to the rabbinic dictum that there is no word, or even letter, in the Torah that is superfluous. It is a sacred text in its every detail; nothing in it is written in vain; one hand and one mind guides everything in it.

Analysis

In this section, Maimonides attempts to offer a comprehensive defense of the rationality of biblical law, the foundation upon which the rabbis codified what they deemed the oral law in the Mishnah and Talmud. Maimonides is not interested here in the development of that law in postbiblical times; he dealt with that subject in his *Commentary on the Mishnah* and his code of law, the *Mishneh Torah.* Now Maimonides reverts to the 613 biblical commandments that he outlined in his earlier *Sefer ha-Miẓvot,* "Book of the Commandments,"[53] to say not what they are but why they are exactly as they are.

This unit of the *Guide* is apologetic at the core, defending with rhetorical skill what Maimonides regards as the best system of law ever devised, and ever to be devised, because it caters in an exemplary manner to both the body and the soul of a person and a society. Biblical law has to be exemplary, for it is presented as commanded by God and is thus sacrosanct. Maimonides even claims that Jewish law is unique,[54] though he knows that the *shari'a* of Islam has a parallel structure, offering a parallel rationale.

These chapters accordingly are obliquely polemical, meant to assure the faithful of the sense and superiority of a Judaism that is rooted in the Bible, a text never to be superseded. Maimonides knows, of course, that the written law of the Bible was modified, and even changed, by the oral law, primarily owing to historical necessity. However, Maimonides (elsewhere) presents these deviations from the written word of God as conditionally applied, temporary accommodations to an exilic life that will be reversed in messianic times.

Maimonides does not discuss the Messiah in the *Guide,* however, any more than he mentions the historical development of postbiblical *halakha,* Jewish law. His object is to explain and extol the commandments of the Torah as valid and beneficial, even salvific. They are part of a document deriving via Moses from God, and Maimonides considers his exegesis as helping to substantiate that claim.

While Maimonides is not interested in history as it affected biblical law after the completion of the Bible, he is very interested in the alleged history of peoples that preceded Israelite history, particularly those known as Sabians.[55] Maimonides claims to have read all that was extant in Arabic literature about the Sabians and their religious practices, and he quotes from books attributed to them. He believes in the antiquity of the Sabians, as reported by Muslim historians, and identifies the more puzzling laws of the Bible as responses to Sabian beliefs and rites.[56]

The claim that biblical law is indebted to the pagan books that Maimonides cites is wildly anachronistic, but Maimonides is undoubtedly right in seeing apparently anomalous commandments in the Bible as reflecting pagan practices encountered by the Israelites. The Bible itself constantly warns the Israelites not to follow pagan practices, and Maimonides shows both how pervasive such practices were, and how adroitly the Torah appropriated and transformed them into worship of the God of Israel.

Maimonides has us understand that God (through Moses) allowed the people to retain their cherished images and symbols of divinity, while changing the object of their worship from the many to the one God. For Maimonides, God in this manner accommodated Himself (as it were) to human nature and people's attachment to the familiar, permitting and even commanding actions that are otherwise of dubious if not negative value.[57] God's actions thus exhibit for Maimonides the "wily graciousness" (or "gracious subtlety," both suitable translations of *talaṭṭuf*)[58] in law and ritual that He showed in history, working with and not against human nature, slowly transforming His people into a holy nation.

God's "wily graciousness" is also rendered sometimes as a "gracious ruse," and as such it has an expanded usage. Sometimes it entails concession to human failings and clever manipulation of their needs; at other times the term implies only that the purpose of the law is not explicitly stated. The laws are given dogmatically, with attendant physical rewards and punishments, as though that is their purpose. This is the ruse God employs in order to bring the people into a position where they can begin to appreciate the true purpose of the Law, that of character and intellectual formation. Maimonides sees his task as bringing out the intentions of the Law, rationalizing it along ethical and political lines.

Accordingly, Maimonides sees the genesis of Mosaic law in a historical perspective, even as he dogmatically insists upon the uniqueness of that law, taken as a whole. It perfectly meets the personal and communal requirements of its practitioners, satisfying both their physical and their spiritual needs. It continues to do so, Maimonides intimates, patiently accommodating itself to errant though tenaciously held popular beliefs, such as in the efficacy of prayer or fasting and pleading for divine intercession.[59]

In referring, in chapter 32, to these misguided practices, and opposing them to the silent meditation that he considers the true path to communion with God, Maimonides is signaling that the religious expressions of devotion to God in his day (as still in ours) have no greater validity than the Temple service of former days; they are all imbued with a false and originally pagan idea of God's nature and of the ways to approach Him. Still, for all their undesirable origins and ongoing misperceptions, these practices have a certain positive value and may lead the observer to true belief when properly understood. Hallowed by tradition as they are, the rituals of Jewish life also play a critical role in maintaining group loyalty.

For Maimonides, then, the commandments of the law assume a human nature that is what it is, stubborn and resistant to change, even for the better. Maimonides must know that this perspective only begs the question why God chose to allow man such freedom, which obliges God to act stealthily, even if on man's behalf. Maimonides does not, however, offer any reason for God's decision to let human nature take its course. He could have commended here God's benevolence in creating man a free person rather than an automaton (though that may be a modern perspective on human behavior alien to Maimonides, who prized obedience to the law, even when not understood). His silence here raises the suspicion that Maimonides believed—or wanted to believe—that this was not a choice God really had, that His wisdom dictated that it be so. Maimonides was convinced there was something in the constitution of human beings—and of course it is their corporeal nature—that constrained God's relation to them, but that He willed it so. Otherwise, the matter in human beings, as in nature as a whole, would have an essential autonomy with which God would have to contend.

Maimonides portrays God as a supreme and benevolent tactician, not demanding ritual actions different from those the people of any one age consider appropriate, however wrong they are. Even misguided forms of worship may lead a person to proper beliefs, inasmuch as the one true approach—that of "meditation without any way of action at all" (*fiqratun duna 'amalin aṣlan*)—is beyond the abilities of most people. That, however, will not stop Maimonides from endorsing meditation at the end of the *Guide*.[60]

In the chapters of this section, however, Maimonides is interested in the means rather than in the end of religious practices, the "second intention" of the Law, to wean people away from idolatry and false beliefs, more than the "first intention," to inculcate true beliefs. He would like to find a convincing explanation for every *ḥoq*, each statute of the law, offering proof of its validity and of the wisdom of its author.

That author is ultimately God, for Maimonides, and he presents the commandments as issuing from Him. Yet Maimonides has informed us repeatedly that God does not speak to or enter into any relation with humans; our impression that He does is a projection upon Him of our devising. It is Moses who has articulated God's will in commandments that express it in human terms. Maimonides chooses, however, to present the commandments as the Bible does, attributing them directly and literally to God. In so doing, Maimonides is adopting that "gracious subtlety" or cunning that he claims is God's technique. Moreover, Maimonides' absorption in and defense of the particularities of arcane statutes of the Law would certainly go a long way to appeasing those of his readers who would have been put off by his politically infused theology.

In chapter 27, Maimonides stresses the importance of constructing a viable society, a *medina* (city or state), some political entity that will ensure the welfare of all its members. This takes precedence over the individual's quest for a personal fulfillment divorced from society. In so speaking, Maimonides reflects the views of Alfarabi, the philosopher he regarded as second only to Aristotle.[61]

Maimonides understands the Torah explicitly to speak of the two perfections, communal and personal, and finds that it alludes to an immortality that attends the second one. However, it is the first perfection with which the body of law mostly deals, and Maimonides is convinced of the necessity of observing the minutiae of the Law in order to ensure the health and safety necessary for intellectual pursuits. The Torah's legislation aims at preserving public order so that each individual may acquire the first perfection, which also inculcates the sound beliefs and correct opinions that lead to the ultimate perfection. Necessarily, however, the first perfection inculcates false beliefs also, those required to induce obedience to the Law.[62] These are the beliefs in an angry and vengeful God, one who hears and responds to injustice, beliefs that the people readily endorse. Maimonides is as open as he can be here in acknowledging his belief in an impersonal God.

For Maimonides, the observance of the commandments perfects one's body and soul as a condition for a state of informed consciousness that is essentially intellectual, though suffused with feeling. The theoretical knowledge acquired here is a transformative experience, its universal dimension transcending the practical actions and moral qualities that contribute toward personal and physical welfare.

Maimonides is speaking of the ideal aims of the Torah and has nothing here to say of the political instability that characterized the actual history of post-Sinai Israel. He would have agreed with the prophets that the people did not observe the Law given them, and therefore from his perspective did not give the Law a chance to prove its political sagacity, let alone superiority. Yet here in the *Guide* he does not feel obliged to defend Israelite history, or to blame the people for disobedience to their laws. His political philosophy is decidedly ahistorical, despite its historical genesis.[63]

Maimonides shows his understanding of political realities in stating, in chapter 34, that any law, including that of the Torah, must legislate for the majority and can hurt those outside it. He draws an analogy to the "laws" of nature, which do not benefit every individual in a given species. Maimonides considers the Law not an organic part of nature but an artifact that often approximates nature in its design and purpose. He is encouraged by the general thrust of the Law, unconcerned as it is with exceptional individuals, to claim that it is also impossible for the Law to be dependent upon changing circumstances, of the individual or of the times. The laws, he believes, must be absolute and universal (*muṭlaqa ʿāmma*),[64] not contingent on time and place.

While it is logically impossible to construct general laws tailored just to an individual, it is not a logical impossibility for laws to change with changing circumstances. Maimonides' principled insistence to the contrary is an imperative driven by his theological and not logical commitments.[65] He will later acknowledge that the rabbis effectively modified various commandments, but he claims these are temporary rulings, not to be perpetuated.[66] He believes that in principle Jewish law should not change, but he cannot defend the proposition that it is impossible for it to change.

Even assuming, as we should, that Maimonides believed in an unchanging deity, he could have accepted the notion of a God who planned from all eternity to modify the law to meet changing circumstances. Insisting that Mosaic law is absolute and universal (for Jews) has therefore a polemical thrust addressed to both Muslims and those intellectuals like himself who may feel the Law is not attentive to their own idiosyncratic needs.

In chapter 36, Maimonides argues for the commandment to call upon God when in distress, strengthening thereby the belief in personal providence and the rewards or punishments that ensue from that. This flies in the face of Maimonides' stated belief in an impersonal deity. Moreover, Maimonides just said in chapter 34 that the Law does not benefit all individuals equally, even as not all persons benefit equally in the natural world. Some people would thus appear to be the random or chance victims of laws or events (though in the larger scale of things even that should be seen as necessary).

Maimonides would have people accept this, without attributing their fate to chance, should they be among those who are not beneficiaries of the laws of God or nature. Believing otherwise would have harmful results. Maimonides therefore endorses the "gracious ruse" that he believes the Bible employs. That is, he adapts pagan beliefs in reward and punishment to the laws of the Torah.

Chapters 35–49 are at the heart of Maimonides' attempt to classify and justify the 613 commandments of the Law. They also serve to impress upon the reader Maimonides' deep absorption in the Law, his conviction in the necessity of observing it and his belief in its utility. He is instructing the would-be philosopher addressee of the *Guide* that the path to intellectual perfection entails appreciation and observance of the Law.

In chapter 37, listing the laws relating to idolatry, he offers an extensive summary of pagan magical practices, astrological rituals designed to persuade the supposed spirits and deities that reside in stars and planets to grant the petitioners' requests. Maimonides approaches the subject as an anthropologist, classifying his material and describing it in succinct detail. He notes that women often serve as the erotically charged priestesses and sorceresses of what is for him the equivalent of black magic.[67] In his (premodern) opinion, they and all practitioners of this flagrant form of idolatry deserve to die, since the practices involved lead to moral and political corruption.

Maimonides finds expressions of idolatrous practices in both the appearance and attire of pagan priests and the agricultural activities of lay farmers. He believes a number of the puzzling commandments in the Bible that regulate both classes' behavior should be seen as reactions against such practices, not as accommodations to them. He draws the line, however, at the institution of sacrifices itself, and the temple ritual and priesthood that surround it, despite its pagan origins. As the Bible has divorced this area of religious performance from analogous pagan practices, Maimonides can no more than allude to its idolatrous origins. The rituals associated with sacrifices are not condemnable since they are now directed toward worshiping the one God, but they remain idolatrous in maintaining false belief in their spiritual utility.

The prophets already intimated this, in saying that God did not want sacrifices; but the people—and priesthood—insisted upon the centrality of sacrifices and on the Temple as God's house. In Maimonides' day (as in ours) the Sabbath and Holy Day liturgy included an entire additional section—the *musaf*—commemorating the sacrifices of the day and prayers for the restoration of the Temple service. Maimonides cannot fight this; indeed in his Code he treats all aspects of this institution fully and without reservation, whatever his personal reservations may have been at that time. Here he finds justification for every aspect of the Temple ritual, including the presence of (originally pagan) cherubic icons in the Holy of Holies.

Maimonides identifies the cherubs with angels,[68] understanding angels here as beings that, like God, are separate from matter, their nature a product of emanation. Maimonides does not now mention his identification elsewhere of angels with the separate intelligences of the spheres or with man's imaginative faculty. His reification of angels here is possibly due to his straining to rationalize the cherubs' presence in the heart of what should be an aniconic sanctuary.

To Maimonides, many of the Torah's commandments do not require historical rationalization; they appear to him as self-evidently and eminently rational on moral grounds. He simply refers the reader, in chapter 38, to the relevant section of his *Mishneh Torah* discussion of moral qualities, and elsewhere understands that the laws embody the ethical teachings that both the prophets and Aristotle advocated. Thus, at the end of chapter 41, Maimonides eloquently expresses the sympathy and kindness toward a captured Gentile woman that he finds that the Law commands. In chapter 42, Maimonides urges people to obey the laws of inheritance, honoring family members as called for, without prejudice. As expressed also in chapter 49, Maimonides knows that trusted family relationships form the basis of a strong society. Equally, he recognizes that the ethical dimension of the Law is also its social aspect and forms the basis of a politically successful community.

Maimonides sees charity not only as an altruistic act but as one that helps ensure a stable society. Such a society requires upholding laws that mandate impartial justice, and Maimonides concludes chapter 39 praising biblical law for just that, contrasting it with the partisan behavior of pagan societies in pre-Islamic times.[69] He is careful not to draw comparisons with Islamic law here, or in chapter 49 concerning circumcision.[70] Maimonides there writes of the wisdom in performing that act on the eighth day of an infant's life, aware that Muslims practice circumcision when a child approaches puberty. Whatever his thoughts on this, Maimonides eschews all comparison with Islamic law, no doubt because it was too politically sensitive a topic to dwell on. His readers can draw their own conclusions on this as on other issues familiar to them in their contacts with Muslim society.

Though endorsing the noble motives of the Bible's Jubilee year as a way to redress the effects of slavery and poverty,[71] Maimonides does not advocate radical economic change in the world of his day, or of any day, prior to the coming of the Messiah. The Bible's commandments regulating society are perfectly suited to that task.

Accordingly, in chapters 40 and 42, Maimonides confirms the Torah's laws that protect an individual's property. In chapter 41, Maimonides upholds the punishments the Bible accords to those who break the law, believing that waiving or changing the law does neither the criminal nor society as a whole any good. Apparently, Maimonides even has reservations about the rabbis' conversion of the *lex talionis,* the law requiring an eye for an eye, to monetary remuneration. He declines, however, to commit his thoughts on this to writing.[72]

Maimonides has a somewhat convoluted rationalization of the commandment not to add to or subtract from the revealed law, as prescribed in Deuteronomy 13:1.[73] He says that just because God knew that changing circumstances would require such changes, He forbade them, supposedly as a way to impress upon people the divine authorship of the laws and ensure their obedience to them. A high court, however—presumably the Sanhedrin—could make the necessary modifications in the law, Maimonides says, understanding them not to be permanent changes. In taking this position, Maimonides sides with Rabbanite Jewry, upholding the theoretical inviolability of the Law's specific details, even while permitting (controlled) change.

Maimonides' strong stand against those who challenge the authority of the Law should be seen in the perspective of his time, when the Rabbanite community that he led was being challenged by the Karaites, as well as by would-be apostates to Islam. Moreover, his advocacy of the death penalty for infidelity to the Law did not translate immediately into action, for the Jewish community did not have the authority to unilaterally condemn a person to death. Muslim rulers recognized both the Rabbanite and the Karaite communities equally and welcomed converts, rendering Maimonides' rulings in this area moot. His remarks have theoretical rather than practical significance, showing *inter alia* the orthodoxy of his practice of the faith, his orthopraxis. He may well have believed in the necessity of a draconian interpretation of the law, given that he saw the survival of the people as dependent upon strict observance of its legal corpus.

Maimonides sees the Law as complementing nature. Writing of the seven days of Passover in chapter 43, Maimonides mentions that the Law "always tends to assimilate itself [*tatashabbahu*] to nature,"[74] perfecting it in some way. Though Maimonides admits that this observation is a digression, it shows his conviction that Jewish law enhances one's relation to the natural world both outside and within one's body. The various rituals of the holidays are meant to increase one's pleasure in the day, Maimonides says, as well as to convey moral teachings.

In a further acknowledged digression, while mentioning the four species of plants that constitute the *lulav* used on the holiday of Tabernacles, Maimonides writes of the conflicting views of the homiletical genre of *midrash,* some viewing it as a proper explanatory device for a biblical text, while others deride its utility. Neither group understands the true status of *midrashim,* Maimonides says, which is that of "poetical conceits" (*al-nawādir al-shiʿrīya*),[75] imaginative tales carrying a moral message. Maimonides is prone to use *midrash;* his inserting a defense of it here out of context may indicate that he is sensitive to criticism of it.

Maimonides has avoided midrashic explanations of the Law for the most part; his view of the role pagan history played in the Bible's adoption of many commandments gives his accounts a plausibly rational basis. He has tried to account for many of the 613 laws of the Torah, some more fully than others. For example, he is reticent, in chapter 44, to elaborate on the love of God that many of the commandments are said to promote. Maimonides may feel that these commandments are self-evident, but it is surprising that he is so brief here, as love, both the love of God and God's loving kindness, is the culminating affect that he will mention at the end of the *Guide.*

Maimonides professes to having attained but limited success in his quest for making the reasons of the commandments transparent,[76] and professes ignorance of some commandments that would seem to pose no exegetical or logical problem. Thus, he cannot find in the Torah's sanctioning of wine in rituals any improvement upon the use made of the grape in pagan rites.[77] Nor can Maimonides confidently explain, on the basis of his research, the reason why the Torah forbids boiling a kid in its mother's milk.[78] Ironically, Maimonides' reservations about explaining the reasons for this important commandment, which is the basis for much of the law of *kashrut,* lend credence to his anthropological perspective on many of these laws.

Maimonides' explanations, his "reasons for the commandments" (*ṭa'amei ha-miẓvot*), have varying degrees of plausibility, some very convincing and probably, though not necessarily, true. Maimonides knew this, of course; he was engaged in what was essentially a polemical and apologetic exercise, but one necessary for giving specific commandments an aura of rationality. For him, divine law, like nature, did nothing in vain. He knew he could not prove this demonstrably, and knew too that his effort was fraught with the danger of historicizing and relativizing the Law. His choice of not confronting astrology more frontally here may well be due to his knowledge that Sabianism expressed the relation between the heavenly spheres and earth in emanative terms also, and that he had no conclusive way to prefer his own emanationist scenario.[79]

11

True Knowledge and Perfection (*Guide* Part III, Chapters 51–54)

Paraphrase

Maimonides calls chapter 51 "a kind of conclusion,"[1] in which he describes the ideal form of worship that should be practiced by one who has attained true understanding of God's nature, "what [sort of] thing He is" (*ayyu shay' huwa*), and the path to be taken to reach this ultimate stage of worship, which is the final goal of life. This chapter also informs the reader how providence works, in this world and the next.

Maimonides begins by constructing a parable both simple and daring in its pronouncements. A ruler is in his palace within a city, his subjects situated in varying distances from him, some outside the walls of the town, others inside the walls, but not all within the walls of the palace. Those within are in turn some further and some closer to the king's chamber, until finally some manage with extra effort to be in the ruler's presence.

Those outside the city are people lacking all religious doctrine, whether based on speculation or on traditional authority. This renders them savages in Maimonides' eyes, irrational animals, and thus less than human.

Those within the city but walking away from the ruler's palace are those who have wrong ideas about God. They may on occasion have to be killed, to prevent the spread of false beliefs.[2]

The ones who wish to enter the ruler's palace but never find it are the masses that observe the Law. Maimonides labels them—in Hebrew!—"ignoramuses who practice the commandments" (*'amei ha-'areẓ ha-'oṣqim be-miẓvot*).

Then there are those who have found the palace but walk around it without entering. They are the jurists, the legal scholars who follow true opinions based on the authority of tradition and adjudicate the ritual practices but do not theorize at all over the fundamental principles of religion or attempt to validate faith.

Those who do so engage have entered the inner chambers of the palace. The person who has achieved demonstrative proof of whatever may be demonstrated in these matters, and has come as close as is possible to certainty in them, has come into the ruler's presence.

In a further continuation of this parable, Maimonides identifies those studying mathematics and logic as the fourth class of person, those walking around outside the palace. Those who have mastered physics, on the other hand, have entered the palace's chambers, while the one who has as much knowledge as is possible of both physics and metaphysics is in the inner chamber with the ruler or, as Maimonides literally says, is "with Him in one habitation," *wa ḥaṣalta ma'ahu fī dār wāḥidah.*[3]

Yet there are differences Maimonides detects even among this last class of men. All follow their mastery of metaphysics and the sciences that precede it with complete absorption in God and renunciation of everything else, interested in the beings of the world only insofar as proofs may be inferred from them regarding God. There is, however, one person who surpasses all others, both in the greatness of his apprehension of God and in the renunciation of everything else, enabling him to speak with God, as Maimonides says, "asking and being answered, speaking and being spoken to," *yaṣalu wa-yujāwabu wa-yatakallimu wa-yukallam.*[4]

Obviously, Maimonides is alluding to Moses here, even as he deems the prophets to be the other paragons of intellectual perfection. He regards Moses not only as dispensing with food and drink, owing to the great joy that accompanied his apprehension of God,[5] but as doing without the sense of touch (with which sexual activity is associated) entirely. The other prophets "see" God at varying distances, as discussed before.[6]

Maimonides does not want his readers to feel that this intellectual perfection is necessarily limited to the prophets; all men should strive to achieve knowledge of God and then to think only of Him, their worship increasing the more they do so. This worship is in fact conditional upon intellectual activity, which both precedes it and is concomitant with it. Ultimately, worship *is* the total absorption in the act of apprehending God intellectually.

Quoting Deuteronomy 11:13, Maimonides says that the love of God, which is proportionate to apprehension of Him, precedes a last stage of worship, which is worship of the heart, *'avodah shebalev.*[7] Yet again this ultimate worship is thinking of the "first intelligible" (*al-ma'qūl al-'awwal*) exclusively, as much as one is able. Maimonides is indeed conflating love and intellection, an impression received also by his saying that after the (penultimate) apprehension of God is reached, the aim is to love God passionately through exclusively intellectual concentration upon Him.[8] This leaves no room for anyone else between man and God,[9] and Maimonides indeed recommends solitude and isolation for the individual who arrives at this stage of communion with God.

Maimonides then reminds the reader, in a special "call to attention" (*tanbīh*), that our connection (*al-wuṣlah*) to God is due to the intellect that emanates from Him to us.[10] The choice of whether or not to maintain that connection is up to us, depending on the intensity with which we put our mind to loving thoughts of God. The purpose of observing such practices as reading the Torah and prayer (i.e., laws that are between man and God), Maimonides says, is to train one to concentrate on God and His commandments, rather than on worldly matters.

The first step in this training, Maimonides says, is to recite the *Shema*ʿ prayer (testifying to God's oneness) by "emptying the mind" of every thought, an act of mental abnegation that can take years of practice. Then one can become totally focused on the lessons to be learned from reading the Torah or listening to it, followed after some time by similar devotion to the discourses of the prophets.

Maimonides' pragmatism shows itself, however, in recommending that the person who is in this exclusive relation with God may yet attend to necessary worldly matters while eating, drinking, or bathing, or while in conversation with family members or others.

According to Maimonides, Moses and the patriarchs mastered the technique of talking with people and attending to their physical needs while being totally involved intellectually with God. Their apprehension and love of God, which Maimonides calls their "union" (*ittiḥād*) with Him, resulted in a lasting covenant and beneficent providence.[11] The end result of their actions was to create a people that would know and worship God, and (through them) to spread the doctrine of God's unity, guiding people to love Him.

Maimonides concedes that he cannot aspire to such an achievement, having to be content with the next lower rank. Speaking of divine providence has, however, triggered in Maimonides' mind a "most extraordinary speculation" (*naẓr gharīb jiddan*), one that removes doubts and reveals divine secrets. It is not only that providence occurs proportionately to an individual's intellectual attainments, for that was already explained.[12] It is that the occurrence of evil can be explained as due to the withdrawal of providence, which follows upon the cessation of that intellectual communion with God. This explains, Maimonides believes, why prophets and other "excellent and perfect men" suffer evils: their attention to God was distracted, for one reason or another, and the link to Him was severed. If, though, a person avoids this distraction, apprehends God correctly, and rejoices in this apprehension, then, Maimonides claims, he will never suffer evil of any kind. "For he is with God and God is with him."[13]

Maimonides cites many scriptural passages attesting to God's protecting those who believe in Him, in support of his statement. This indifference to the body's faculties is impossible to attain in youth, Maimonides notes, and is abetted by the quenching of the "fires of desire." So it is that when a "perfect man" becomes old and approaches death, he passes away in a state of increasing intellectual happiness and love of God, the object of his apprehension. This has been called a kiss of death by the sages, bestowed on Moses, Aaron, and Miriam.

For Maimonides, all prophets and those who attain to the intellectual perfection described will arrive in death at a stage of "enduring permanence" (*al-baqā' al-dā'im*), their intellect and its accompanying "intense pleasure" (*al-ladhdha al-'athīma*) intact and unchanging.[14]

In chapter 52, Maimonides reinforces the point he made in his "call to attention" in the previous chapter, that an emanating intellect is the connection between man and God.[15] Through it we apprehend Him, and He us, and by virtue of this intellect God is with us constantly, observing and supervising us. Recognition of this humbles "perfect men" (*al-kāmilūn*) and leads them to fear God and to be in awe of Him.

This is the purpose of the actions prescribed in the commandments, Maimonides states, to create this affect[16] of fear and awe, whereas the love of God is inculcated by the opinions the Torah teaches, principally the apprehension of His being "as it really is" (*'alā mā huwa ta'ālā 'alayhi*).

In chapter 53, Maimonides analyzes three terms that further detail God's relation to the world and serve to introduce the final chapter of the book. The terms are *ḥesed, mishpaṭ,* and *ẓedaqah,* translated traditionally as "loving-kindness," "judgment," and "righteousness."

Maimonides refers to his earlier *Commentary on the Mishnah* explanation that *ḥesed* denotes an excess,[17] mostly applied to meritorious or beneficial acts, and finds that the prophets usually treat God as extending *ḥesed* to people undeserving of it. Bringing the world as a whole into existence is a prime example of God's *ḥesed,* His loving-kindness.

Maimonides next determines that *ẓedaqah,* righteousness (derived from *ẓedeq*), denotes justice, '*adl.* The prophets use the term, Maimonides declares, in connection with distinctly moral virtues rather than with simply equitable action. The justice accomplished when committing a particularly moral act affects the agent's own "rational soul" (*nafṣuka al-nāṭiqa*), i.e., his intellect.

Maimonides is thereby saying that virtuous acts done out of a sense of morality facilitate the intellect's apprehension of God.

Mishpaṭ, judgment, whether it benefits or punishes the person judged, has for Maimonides (following tradition) but one meaning, one standard, unlike the other two terms.

Maimonides shows that the Torah applies all three terms to God, which for Maimonides qualifies them as attributes of action.[18] He again evinces the act of bringing the world into existence as testimony of God's loving-kindness; His righteousness is shown in allowing living beings the faculties for self-governance, which is an act of mercy toward weak creatures; and His role as judge is attested to by the fact that "relatively good" things as well as "relatively great misfortunes"[19] occur in the world, all rendered necessary by a judgment that follows divine wisdom.

We thus arrive at chapter 54, the closing chapter of the *Guide.* In it Maimonides analyzes one last term and concludes in a flourish that may be one last ruse. The term Maimonides feels he needs to clarify is central to his philosophy. It is the Hebrew word *ḥokhmah,* which usually is generic for "wisdom" but was used by the philosophers in the sense of "science" too. (The Muslim philosophers used the Arabic *ḥikma* similarly.)

There are four contexts in which the term "wisdom" is used, Maimonides states.[20] It may refer to the apprehension of the true nature of things, leading to the apprehension of God; to acquiring knowledge of the practical arts; to acquiring moral virtues; and to learning ruses and cunning tactics.[21] This last form of wisdom may be used for good (as by God), in order to promote virtues or the practical arts, or for evil.

A wise person for Maimonides is one who knows both the rational virtues of the Law and the moral ones. Maimonides was aware that traditionally a semantic distinction was made to denote the kind of knowledge contained in the Bible and the Talmud and the kind obtained from other sources. The term "wisdom" in an unqualified sense is used in the latter sense, Maimonides acknowledges, but it is this *ḥokhmah,* in the sense now of philosophy, that offers proof of the rational wisdom of the Torah. This is necessary because the Law itself was received traditionally, i.e., on the basis of an authority traditionally accepted as reliable.

Maimonides accepts the validity of assertions based on tradition[22] but believes Scripture and the sages approve of demonstrative reasoning as well. He recognizes a rabbinic statement that he believes prescribes accepting the wisdom of the Torah first on the basis of tradition, and then verifying its opinions philosophically.[23] While he acknowledges that the rabbis believe there is a difference in kind between the science of the Torah and philosophy (*'ilm al-torah . . . wa al-ḥikma*), he insists that the latter wisdom is necessary for understanding the former.

Maimonides next offers what he considers to be a philosophical consensus concerning the various kinds of perfection found in man. The first and most popular perfection, for all its inferior and destructive nature, is that which Maimonides labels "possession" (*al-qunya*), i.e., the acquisition of money, property, and power, even that held by a "great king." The possessions attained give one an imaginary sense of pleasure, Maimonides claims, being independent of one's essential self and in a transient relation to it. Even if a person's possessions stayed with him his whole life, they would not give him that perfection of the self (*dhāt*) that is the ideal sought.

The second kind of perfection is more closely related to the essence of an individual, being the perfection of the body in all its physiological and physical aspects. Yet this perfection is not unique to man, Maimonides says; it is a corporeal perfection that he shares with other species of animals, and in which he is inferior to some of them. Moreover, man's soul does not benefit from this perfection (at least not directly).

The third kind of perfection is closer still to an individual's essence, for it is perfection of the moral virtues. Most of the commandments aim at accomplishing this kind of perfection to produce a moral being. However, Maimonides declares, as moral acts entail interaction with another person they are not an end in themselves for the self. Alone, a person has no need for this perfection.

The fourth kind of perfection is for the self alone, and it is for Maimonides the true human perfection, that through which "man is man." It is (as we might expect) attaining the rational virtues, i.e., conceptualizing the intelligible thoughts that teach true metaphysical ideas.[24] This type of cogitation is the ultimate end in that, unlike the other perfections, it belongs to the person's essence exclusively and gives him "permanent perdurance," *al-baqā' al-dā'im*,[25] i.e., immortality.

Maimonides is so taken with this last perfection, which alone "remains" for the person, *al-bāqī laka* (or rather, which is that part of the person that alone remains, or is immortal), that he exhorts the reader to desire this perfection exclusively. You should "not weary and trouble yourself for the sake of others," neglecting your own soul.

Maimonides quotes Jeremiah[26] to show that the prophets are in agreement with the philosophers that knowledge of God (which Maimonides equates with the science of metaphysics) is the perfection man should seek over the others. Maimonides interprets Jeremiah as saying that all the actions that the Law commands, both devotional and ethical, i.e., the commandments between man and God as well as between man and man, are not equal to this last and ultimate perfection. They are instrumental, serving but to prepare the person for the intellectual perfection that is his goal; the moral habits the commandments advocate are (merely) useful to people in their dealings with one another.

Maimonides then observes that in the passage quoted, God identifies Himself to Jeremiah through the attributes of *ḥesed, mishpaṭ,* and *ẓedaqah,* loving-kindness, judgment, and righteousness. Jeremiah says "righteousness on [literally, 'in'] the earth," which for Maimonides is a critical acknowledgment that God's providence extends throughout the world, over heaven and earth, a providence corresponding to their natures (*bi ḥaṣbiha*). Furthermore, God says to Jeremiah that He "delights" in these actions, which Maimonides interprets, in line with his understanding of the attributes of action, as a prescription for man to attempt to imitate or resemble (*tashabbah*)[27] these divine attributes, to the best of his ability.

Maimonides concludes the chapter, and the book, on this note, that "it is clear" (now) that the perfection in which a man should glory is an apprehension of God, as much as is in the person's capacity, an apprehension that understands His providence in bringing His creatures into existence and in governing them. Following this apprehension, and imitating God's actions, the man who has achieved perfection should aim throughout his life to perform acts of loving-kindness, righteousness, and judgment.

Analysis

There are fifty-four chapters in this third part of the *Guide,* but chapter 51 may be seen as the penultimate chapter of the book. Though Maimonides says at the start that there is nothing new in the chapter, that it serves as a kind of conclusion to the book, he takes the opportunity to reiterate his core beliefs in language that alternates between extremes of transparency and of concealment. He wants to imprint upon the reader the nature of true worship, and to convince one who apprehends this that divine providence will protect that person from all evil and ensure immortality.

Maimonides' views concerning providence and immortality are not conventional, however. He says that this chapter will inform the person who has truly apprehended God's nature "how providence will be with him," *kayfa takun al-ʿināya bihi.*[28] Providence, as designed by God, will reward that person. Yet this providence is not custom tailored to the individual by God; He does not "watch over" a person as an individual. God's knowledge is of universals, of the species at best, and of them only as subsumed within His one being. The appearance of personal providence, however, is given by the emanations that individuals receive, emanations suited to their particular circumstances. Maimonides is careful linguistically not to personalize providence, though many of his readers have not, and do not, or do not choose to, accept this.

Maimonides is also deliberatively ambiguous in his description of immortality, called here euphemistically in Hebrew *ẓeror ha-ḥayyim,* which is traditionally taken to stand for eternal life. He will make other references to immortality in this chapter and the following ones, without being more specific. This has given rise to speculation that Maimonides believed in the afterlife of the individual soul, though his previous references to immortality rejected individual perdurance.[29]

Maimonides adopts a style in this chapter that is unusual for him, creating a parable that allows him to express his thoughts directly and not through exegesis of the biblical text. The freedom this gives apparently encourages him to be ruthlessly frank and dismissive of the beliefs and practices of most of his fellow Jews. He is severe and intolerant in his judgments, condoning killing those with false beliefs "when necessary," and denigrating the practices of the "ignorant" masses and the traditional practical orientation of their learned teachers.

While rooted in the Bible and rabbinic law, Maimonides' draconian attitude toward those with false beliefs may well have been reinforced by the law and religious zeal of the Almohads, which Maimonides had personally witnessed.[30] Furthermore, not having the authority to enforce his beliefs, Maimonides was free to be as forceful as he wished, or as he wished to appear. Clearly, he is impatient with those who do not appreciate the great bliss awaiting those who truly apprehend God's nature and act in accordance with it.

The apprehension of God requires knowing mathematics and logic for starters, and as much physics and metaphysics, the "divine science," as is possible. Maimonides speaks of achieving "perfection in the natural things," i.e., physics, and presumably also metaphysics, but he has just qualified the degree of knowledge as being "to the extent that is possible." He has also previously insisted on the limits of human knowledge in matters metaphysical, on being incapable of comprehending the essence of the deity and of the separate, immaterial celestial intellects.[31] Yet he has balanced that assertion of ignorance on these matters with statements that affirm the existence and actions of these very unknowable subjects. However limited that knowledge is, Maimonides believes it to be true, and as such he must concede that his intellect has conjoined to some degree with the objects of his cognition, i.e., with God and the separate intellects. Accordingly, Maimonides believes, or should believe, that one may achieve a degree of communion with God without having absolutely full and perfect scientific knowledge.

This parable and the following chapters thus refute those who think Maimonides denies the possibility of intellectually bonding, to some extent, with God. It also lowers the bar required for reaching that state, from perfect, complete knowledge to that which is possible to attain, given human limitations. This lesser level is still dauntingly high, but not beyond the reach of "men of science."[32] In so stipulating, Maimonides parts company with the common philosophical attitude that posits perfect knowledge as a condition for joining in one way or another with the divine.[33]

Maimonides knows that there are different degrees of perfection even among scientists and (unsurprisingly) identifies the Hebrew prophets as inhabiting the top tier of intellectuals. He places Moses at the very pinnacle of human achievement, bordering on the superhuman. This situates Maimonides' parable as clearly Jewish and heavily polemical. Yet there is much in this parable that is true universally, for Maimonides.

True, Maimonides sees Judaism as the ideal religion, best suited to bringing people to appreciate and apprehend scientific truth. Yet he would not assume that Muslims, being strict monotheists too, were necessarily precluded from these attainments.[34] Indeed, Maimonides' path toward communion with the divine through mastery of the sciences is one charted for him by the Muslim philosophers. He has mapped it onto the Bible and other Jewish sources, but in essence it transcends the tenets and dogmas of particular faiths, even his own. Moreover, Aristotle, Plato, Plotinus, and Alexander of Aphrodisias were not conventionally religious, yet asserted belief in an ultimate divine being.

Maimonides devotes much effort in the *Guide* to dissociating himself from Aristotle and those like him whose theism, as it may be called, is impersonal. He is unsuccessful in that attempt philosophically, but certainly earnest in the attempt to distinguish the religious philosophy of Judaism from what he regarded as the irreligious philosophy of Athens.

Maimonides has attempted to show that the biblical commandments and the *praxis* of Judaism are ideally suitable for disposing and habituating a person toward philosophical investigations. This does not rule out the likelihood that another monotheistic religion, Islam for example, could have similar ordinances, which it does, and could produce scientists of the first rank, which it did. Maimonides is thus left with the need both to extol Moses and to distinguish him from the prophet of Islam, which he has done obliquely before as well.[35] Maimonides' insinuation that Moses qua prophet abstained from having sex may be in part a reference to the opposite reputation given the Prophet of Islam by his fellow Muslims.[36]

Maimonides' interest in these closing chapters goes, however, beyond polemics and parochially Jewish apologetics. He uses Jewish sources here to advocate universally attainable ideals.[37] The ultimate worship he advocates is a single-minded intellectual act, seen as an expression of love. Maimonides appears to create a two-tier final stage of ultimate cognition, though the two tiers seem alike. However, in the last stage mentioned Maimonides substitutes *'ishq*, an Arabic term best translated as "passion," for the "love" formerly expressed by the Arabic *maḥabbah* and the Hebrew *ahavah.*[38] *'Ishq* figures prominently in two treatises of Avicenna that might well have influenced Maimonides' adoption of the term.[39] For Maimonides it denotes a passionate love of God so intense that it can obliterate all thoughts of anything but the divine One.[40]

Maimonides is aiming at this state of being for his ideal person, a state that approximates the Sufi experience of *fanā'*, the annihilation of the self in identification with the divine.[41] Maimonides introduces an early intimation of this attitude in the very beginning of the training for which reciting the Shema' is an instrument, when he advocates emptying the mind of every thought other than of God. Yet for Maimonides the person at the beginning of his spiritual *cum* intellectual journey clears his mind only to be able to concentrate fully on what he then hears or reads, being always completely focused on the knowledge he thereby gains.[42]

Though Maimonides believes that solitude and isolation assist the individual in pursuing this goal (another step in the Sufi ladder of ascension to God), he does not insist upon them. He cannot, given the demands of marriage and procreation in Judaism, as well as the whole matrix of laws that require participation in the community. Maimonides was, moreover, fully engaged in the affairs of his people and saw himself as their leader. Yet, if he could not or did not want to advocate an external form of social detachment and withdrawal, he did urge an internal move of that sort. He believes it possible to engage with family members and others while essentially being disengaged from them.[43]

Maimonides views the lives of Moses and the patriarchs as offering proof of the feasibility of this approach; their external activities with other people, however intimate or intense, never affected their inner selves.

Their psyches or souls remained untouched by what happened around them and to them.

Yet this Stoic type of attitude on the part of Moses and the patriarchs did not entail, for Maimonides, indifference to the situations in which they found themselves.[44] As depicted in the Bible, they often initiated change, or, as Maimonides says, "they were occupied with governing people, increasing their fortune, and endeavoring to acquire property."[45] All this, without being fully or essentially focused on their actions or interactions with others!

Maimonides in this manner goes beyond the rabbinic transformation of the patriarchs into paragons of piety, and the midrashic treatment of Moses as nearly superhuman, to offer a model of compartmentalized behavior that has roots in mysticism and philosophy.[46] For Maimonides it is a model, an ideal to which to aspire, which he knows neither he nor anyone can maintain continually.

At a certain point in chapter 51, Maimonides appears to have an idea he has not entertained before,[47] a theory that not only resolves doubts one may have concerning divine providence but actually discloses its secret teachings. It is that a person who is in total intellectual communion with God will never suffer evil, whereas evil of every sort can befall a person when he is not thinking of God, when his mind is not joined to His.

Notwithstanding the many biblical statements that Maimonides brings to support this view, it nevertheless appears quite counterfactual. Maimonides asserts it because he believes that the person who is totally immersed intellectually and psychically with the idea of God assumes another identity, essentially. His intellect has joined with the divine intelligence known as the Agent Intellect and become part of that greater being, closer to God through it. The psychic state that person has entered into is one of essential immateriality, a spiritual intelligibility akin to God's. That person is indifferent to whatever accidents may happen to his body or to his life; they are not significant to him in comparison with the eternal life and being that he has had a taste of now.

In this way, Maimonides confronts and vanquishes the sufferings and cruelties that life visits on the innocent and defends the image of a God whose full benevolence is available to those who avail themselves of it. This amounts in practice to a very small percentage of the human race, those who are scientists and philosophers. The mass of mankind must be content with understanding that all things are ordered for the general good, which outweighs but does not eliminate the evils and injustices that afflict them.

Maimonides writes as though he has not thought of this view before, which is possible. It is, however, prefigured in his remarks concerning the reason why persons otherwise qualified to be prophets did not prophesy.[48] There, Maimonides put it that God had removed His providence from the individual. The truth, however—as Maimonides intimated before—is that the individual had broken the connection to God, for one reason or another. Now Maimonides returns to this idea, with greater force, offering everyone, not just prophets, a way to establish communion with God and avoid every evil, including that of (total) death.

Maimonides promises those who attain intellectual perfection (a condition of which is moral perfection) that they can become immortal; that is, their soul's intellectual faculty can achieve this status. Though this faculty, as its name implies, is cerebral and its activity supposedly without emotional affect, Maimonides claims this intellect will also experience great pleasure in its conjunction with the divine.

Maimonides may here be influenced by Avicenna's theory of immortality, according to which an individual soul retains its memory, imagination, and intellect, as well as the ability to conceive of pleasure and pain and to imagine those sensations after death,[49] in proportion to the degree of conjunction with the Agent Intellect that the person's intellect achieved in life. Avicenna's soul is, then, an individualized immaterial being, the sort of entity most Jews of Maimonides' time (and later) imagine awaited them upon their demise.

Maimonides has, however, offered no such comforting theory, other than the few places in this chapter and elsewhere where he might be taken to be alluding to such a doctrine. However, at the end of this chapter Maimonides emphasizes the fact that the intellect that has succeeded after death in achieving immortality, its "impediment" (*al-'ā'iq*) of physical matter removed, remains "in one and the same state."[50] It is a state of intense pleasure, Maimonides assures the reader, though not a physical pleasure. Elsewhere, Maimonides has said in effect that the soul—specifically and only the intellect of the soul—that has achieved conjunction with the Agent Intellect becomes one with it and all other such souls, all subsumed within the one universal truth or set of universal truths that constitute the Agent Intellect.[51]

Accordingly, in Maimonides' opinion, there is no individual immortality; the self does not enjoy its state of bliss or mourn its absence from eternity after death. What Maimonides can and does teach is that the "perfect man" (*al-kāmil*) and those like him who strive to attain perfection can experience the great pleasure to be had in approaching God intellectually, in knowing that they are and will be part of eternal being. Knowing that, in this life, should give one the courage and strength to accept death and even welcome it as one would a beloved's last kiss. Maimonides has joined knowledge of God to love of Him, and seen His providence as an expression of that love.

One of the best-kept secrets of the theory of conjunction, a secret that Maimonides does not give away fully, is that conjunction does not require perfect or complete mastery of the sciences, and particularly of the divine science, i.e., of metaphysics; for even one proposition fully known reflects a formal structure that is eternally present in the Agent Intellect. The person—i.e., his intellect—knowing that proposition at death shares somewhat in eternal being. Immortality in varying degrees is thus vouchsafed a much greater number of persons than is commonly thought.

Nevertheless, Maimonides, like Averroes and others, makes it seem that conjunction is the province of the intellectual elite only. That small band of perfect or nearly perfect individuals may enjoy the full sense of bliss and happiness that comes with a maximal experience of conjunction; but anyone who knows any universal truth, even a single one, should have something of that sensation. Maimonides possibly kept this knowledge to himself since he may have thought that acknowledging it would be trivializing the theory of conjunction and the effort to reach it.

As Maimonides makes clear in chapter 52, conjunction is really not between man (or woman) and God, at least not directly between them. However much knowledge of and proximity to God is the object of the person's quest, the philosophers all believed, Maimonides included, that the closest one's intellect could come to the divine realm was through conjunction with the Agent Intellect.[52] It was uniformly believed to be the last of the celestial forms emanating from God, directly responsible for the formal stratum of all beings on earth.[53] Our intellects derive from the Agent Intellect, and return to it when perfected, when we share in one or more of the universal truths that stem from it. As a being that is eternal (*a parte post* at least, after creation), the Agent Intellect is part of the divine realm and represents God's will on earth, apportioning forms to matter in accord with God's design. As such, Maimonides often refers to it as though it were God; or rather, he appears to put God in contact with humans when it is really the Agent Intellect that has that relation, God Himself being above all relationships. Accordingly, Maimonides frequently makes use of the "gracious ruse" that he finds in the Bible. He believes it is called for by the people's need for assurance of God's presence in this critical area of religious concern.

In this chapter, Maimonides also allays whatever residual anxiety his traditional reader may feel over his emphasis on the paramount religious importance of intellectual activity. That activity, Maimonides cautions, is preceded by and accompanies observance of the commandments. This observance and the knowledge of God that it elicits will instill love and fear of God: love as a result of knowledge earned, particularly ideas concerning God's being, "as He is in truth";[54] and fear of punishment for disobeying the commandments.

Of course, Maimonides does not believe in direct divine punishments, but he does believe in the efficacy of laws that threaten such. For him, the fear of God that the average person has and is taught to have is to be replaced by the awe that the enlightened person experiences when realizing the magnitude and wonder of God's creation. The Hebrew *yir'ah* has both meanings, and Maimonides would have his educated readers experience the latter, their fear being only that they might not achieve the conjunction that grants eternal happiness.

The terms that represent loving-kindness, justice, and righteousness, *ḥesed, mishpaṭ,* and *ẓedaqah,* open and close both chapters 53 and 54, concluding the *Guide.* Maimonides chooses these terms as emblematic of the actions that we attribute to God and that we ought to emulate in our dealings with others. Maimonides interprets *ḥesed,* loving-kindness, as a beneficent act that goes beyond what is strictly required (as witness the providential way God created the world), whereas he views *mishpaṭ,* justice, as hewing uncompromisingly to the Law.

Maimonides does not deny that terrible things occur in the world, and that they occur necessarily, as part of God's just governance. When they happen, though, it is part of a grand and wise scheme, putting the misfortunes, however great, in qualifying perspective. Likewise, the good things and deeds that occur in the world should be seen in proper perspective, relative to the truly good and virtuous action that Maimonides extols.

That action is mental, or intellectual, the act of acquiring scientific wisdom, true knowledge of being and of its source in God. The term *ḥokhmah,* wisdom, denotes that action, as well as being used in other contexts. This word is problematic for Maimonides because he recognizes its diverse connotations and knows that traditionally the rabbis distinguished knowledge acquired from the Torah from wisdom obtained elsewhere; i.e., they differentiated between faith and reason. Maimonides wrote the *Guide* to refute that assumption, and by returning to press his point at the end of the book, he shows how deeply entrenched he believed that error to be among the people. It may indicate as well a certain anxiety on Maimonides' part that he has not succeeded in presenting his views as convincingly as he had hoped.

Maimonides has not broken any new ground in this discussion; if anything he has shown a measure of sympathy for those who maintain a distinction between the wisdom of Torah and that of science. This is in marked contrast to his former attitude toward those who accept the Torah uncritically, on the basis of tradition.[55] Is he holding out an olive branch to his critics now, at the end of the book?

This possibility is strengthened by Maimonides' returning, in his concluding remarks, to the theme of the three cardinal virtues that a person should adopt in imitating God's actions, namely, loving-kindness, justice, and righteousness, *ḥesed, mishpaṭ,* and *ẓedaqah.* A person should pursue acts that express these virtues throughout his life, Maimonides says, after having apprehended, to the best of his ability, God's nature.

This last statement, the culmination of Maimonides' remarks in the last few chapters, has been taken by a number of scholars as indicating that Maimonides' final word in the *Guide* not only endorses ethical behavior, which it does, but moves the center of gravity of his teaching from the metaphysical to the political plane.[56] In this view, knowledge of God leads to social action. This interpretation of Maimonides is supported by his frequent admissions of the limitations of man's knowledge of God (due to the limitations of metaphysical knowledge), so that ethical acts alone remain viable as ways to approach Him.[57]

It is important, however, to realize that Maimonides' closing remarks follow his unambiguous endorsement of the fourth perfection, that which is decidedly apolitical and even antisocial. A person seeking active involvement in good causes would be sacrificing a chance at true happiness and spiritual fulfillment, if he were capable of scaling the intellectual heights that lead to apprehension of God and did not devote himself to this, and to this alone. His involvement with others, family, friends, and society, must be limited to whatever is demanded of him, whatever is necessary to survive, and not more. The ideal is personified by Moses and the patriarchs, who interacted with others without being deeply or spiritually engaged with them. Psychically all their energies were directed toward God.

To contend that this goal is unattainable intellectually reduces Maimonides' fourth perfection to a chimera and strips the parable of the ruler in his palace, in chapter 51, of its meaning. For there nothing further than mastery of the sciences, and particularly of metaphysics, is asked of the person closest to God. Nor must that person have complete mastery of the subject, but only to the extent that it is possible.

Thus, the closing recommendation to follow God's actions through engaging in social and politically virtuous actions should be seen as Maimonides' endorsement of a way of life for the very many who cannot attain intellectual perfection. Of course, those few with outstanding intellects will also observe the practical virtues, will in fact be the very models of ethical behavior. They will not, however, dedicate their lives to it; their essential selves relate only to God.

Maimonides' teaching is clearly elitist, but then he says at the beginning of the book that he is writing for a select few, fellow intellectuals and would-be philosophers. He knew, however, that many of his readers would not qualify for such a description and would not be able to absorb or appreciate his teaching. Entire sections of the *Guide* are meant to accommodate these readers. If in his introduction Maimonides attempts to distance himself from this more popular audience, in his conclusion Maimonides attempts to accommodate them.

Conclusion

In the preface of this book I spoke of Maimonides as torn in his loyalties between philosophy and theology, however unsystematically the latter term was conceived in his day apart from the work of the *mutakallimūn* that he opposed. Judaism had a core set of beliefs, however, which Maimonides enunciated in his *Commentary on the Mishnah.*[1] While his statement of them there starts with universal principles that reveal philosophical influence, most of the principles are particular to the Jewish religion, and are based on a biblical text that affirms a personal deity in close, historic association with a chosen people. Maimonides could not disavow this belief, having affirmed and represented it to and on behalf of his community throughout his life. At the same time, he believed his faith could be transposed to a universal philosophical plane, and the *Guide* is his attempt to do so.

The tension between these two approaches to Judaism is evident throughout the *Guide,* as it veers from the universal to the particular; from an impersonal to a personal God; from treating the Bible literally to viewing it allegorically; from valorizing the study of metaphysics to doubting its veracity; and from treating observance of the Law as instrumental to viewing it as essential to achieving perfection.

This book is not a psychological portrait of a great thinker, but it views the *Guide* as Maimonides' attempt to resolve problems that were deeply troubling to him. Something drove Maimonides to write the *Guide* other than the desire to give a pedagogic lesson to a prize pupil. I think it highly likely that the accidental death of his younger brother, and Maimonides' prolonged depression afterward, prompted him to try to resolve a conflict between faith and reason that had been festering in his soul for some time. A key theme of the *Guide* is divine providence, and in one place Maimonides tries to make sense of the very fate that his brother suffered.[2] In a way, then, the book is a theodicy, justifying God's ways to mankind, and to Maimonides himself.

The *Guide* may thus be seen as a spiritual biography in which Maimonides lays out his beliefs and his disbeliefs, his doubts and his certainties, all subject to qualification. It is more than a "spiritual exercise," but it is also that, taking its place in a history of such philosophical journeys that goes back to Plato.[3] This does not mean that the *Guide* reveals the "true" Maimonides, but it does presume to identify the philosopher he sought to be, an identification essential to any full evaluation of his beliefs.

Maimonides could have rationalized his behavior as that of a political figure, i.e., a rabbi of considerable influence, but whether his philosophical self dominated his conscience and rabbinic judgments or stood in unresolved opposition to them is another matter, which this book does not address. It is misleading to pin a (single) label on Maimonides' "philosophical self," as he was indebted to many philosophical schools of thought, and was inconsistent in his attachments to each one. His disagreements with Aristotle (and even more with Plato) are less severe than they appear, but he may well have believed otherwise because of his theological commitments.

Maimonides' difficulties as a philosopher and as a theologian begin and end with his concept of God. Well before embarking on writing the *Guide*, Maimonides became convinced, despite his demurrals, that through their physical and metaphysical proofs the philosophers had offered valid descriptions of God, whether as a first cause or as a Necessary Existent. Though Maimonides understood the two terms as arriving through deductive reasoning at the same destination, they carried two different sets of entailments, the one following Aristotle, the other Plotinus.

Maimonides received both traditions in a conflated fashion from the Muslim philosophers who were his mentors, notably Alfarabi and Avicenna. He argues for God as the first cause, Aristotle's unmoved mover, and Avicenna's Necessary Existent,[4] while assuming, with little explanation, the reality of the One as posited by Plotinus.[5] That One, beyond being, is considered by Plotinus and his Neoplatonic successors as the source of being, which emerges in distinct stages of increasing complexity from the One to the many, and from the totally immaterial realm of form to the physical appearance of matter. That final stage is one of compromised reality, however; the constantly changing nature of matter relegates it to the status of nonbeing in comparison with the true being and reality of unchanging form.

Maimonides is an (unacknowledged) heir to this originally Neoplatonic tradition, and accepts it both rationally and emotionally. He denigrates preoccupation with material and physical acts beyond those required for survival and procreation, while exulting over the bliss of approaching God intellectually. All this is in keeping with late Greek thought, conducive as it was to mystical and ascetic strains in medieval Islam and Judaism. The premises in this tradition are not drawn from empirical observation, and the immaterial substances posited are not given to demonstrative proof. Ironically, this inoculates Maimonides' belief in the emanationist core of Neoplatonism against the discredited Aristotelian-based cosmogonies of his day, and the arguments for God's existence based upon them.

Maimonides' struggle to offer a philosophical rationale for the biblical text, to accommodate doctrines of creation and revelation philosophically, is offset by qualifying statements he offers throughout the *Guide* of the limits of our knowledge in such matters. He particularly is skeptical of the validity of the cosmological designs that seemed to compel belief in the structure and movements of the heavenly spheres and in the existence of the first cause.[6] The challenges that the astronomers posed to the Aristotelian model of the universe led Maimonides to conclude that the logical proofs that depended upon Aristotle were invalid. The proofs employed did not supply demonstrative certainty; the premises of the argument were not grounded in necessity. The proofs, such as they were, were of a dialectical sort, offering persuasive but not definitive arguments, given the suspect nature of their premises. This level of proof, it was widely believed, could not support the claim to true science, which only demonstrative argument provided.

Maimonides concurred with this judgment, finding many of the arguments for the existence and nature of God to be not truly demonstrated. He came to believe that the knowledge of the heavens that astronomy required was beyond man's grasp, at least in his day, and that the material dimension of the heavens obscured full comprehension of their essential being. Moreover, beyond the substantive issues that the science of his day, notably astronomy, had not resolved, Maimonides was inclined to conclude that the human intellect was in principle unable to conceive of and give voice to central issues in metaphysics, particularly those concerning God and the separate intellects. Our very thoughts and the language used to articulate them were hopelessly restricted to the materially constructed imaginative faculty, unable to comprehend purely immaterial substances.

And yet, for all his reservations about metaphysics, on both the ontological and the epistemological planes, Maimonides repeatedly in the *Guide* affirms and assumes belief in its basic constituents: God, the separate intellects and souls of the spheres, and the heavenly bodies that they propel. These are the instruments through which an emanative process was believed to unfold, and notwithstanding his denial of their intelligibility to human beings, Maimonides obviously feels he has sufficient knowledge of them to affirm emanation, the causal link between God and the world.

Indeed, Maimonides understands prophecy and the entire governance of the world through this process, interpreted as manifestations of the divine will. Thus, Maimonides was prepared to forge ahead with claims that lacked certain truth, and with substances barely comprehended; he had to believe that the little he knew was sufficient to describe the metaphysical realm, and to affirm its congruence with the basic tenets of religion, as he understood them. The appeal philosophy held for him, the satisfaction and soul-fulfilling happiness it offered, were too compelling to be retracted by the doubts and critiques he expressed.

Accordingly, Maimonides' philosophical reservations did not lead him to adopt extreme skeptical or agnostic attitudes toward the basic structures of his metaphysical beliefs. They continued to hold cognitive significance for him, however scientifically suspect. The overwhelming thrust of the *Guide* is to construct a view of God that is logically consistent and philosophically persuasive, however undemonstrated. Though he may have signaled extreme skepticism on metaphysical issues to his most discerning readers,[7] Maimonides was not content with that position himself, and not only for reasons of political expediency. The structures of his metaphysical beliefs were wobbly at best, but he chose no other framework on which to hang his religious beliefs.

Qualified as it was, even Maimonides' version of creation and revelation can be seen as philosophically tenable. Were Maimonides to have accepted the futility of invoking philosophy's claims in matters metaphysical, it is unlikely that he would have dedicated so much of the *Guide* to discussing these issues. Nor would he have insisted on the message he said he wanted to convey to the addressee of the *Guide* and other sophisticates like him, to familiarize them with knowledge that could satisfy their souls and ensure them of immortality.

It is possible, of course, that while writing the *Guide* Maimonides became ever more convinced of the impossibility of attaining knowledge of metaphysics, yet could not bring himself to abandon the subject entirely, with its seductive claims. Perhaps it held a lingering fascination for him, and he thought it a worthwhile intellectual exercise personally, as well as instructive to his readers, however opposite the final message to the message he originally proposed. Then, too, Maimonides may have thought that disenchantment with metaphysics as the ultimate science could have opened the door for Maimonides' readers to greater appreciation of the role practical science and political activity, in its halakhic mode, played in striving for a happy life. This is the message of the *Guide* to not a few scholars today.[8]

However, reading the *Guide* as essentially a skeptical, agnostic, political, or educational treatise, shorn of its metaphysical claims, will not bring a person to the stage of transcendent joy with which Maimonides concludes the book. Doubting the sincerity of Maimonides' statement here and elsewhere that affirms the possibility of conjunction with the divine turns the *Guide* into a massive and unwarranted work of deception. Maimonides closes the *Guide* without sacrificing his belief in an impersonal though providential God, a being with deistic features in which divine will matches wisdom.

This is a difficult position to maintain, in Maimonides' day as in ours, but should be seen in terms of the scientific and theological options available to him. He could not bring himself to do away with the (angelicized) Agent Intellect,[9] or the "facts" of prophecy, however much he tried to naturalize them. Nor, given his commitment to and standing in his community and tradition, did Maimonides wish to sunder the intimate relation providence allegedly had to the Jews of biblical times, despite understanding it in nonliteral terms.

Maimonides, then, did not disparage theological tenets, though he recognized their limitations. His affirmation of the privileged status of Moses and the prophets of Israel need not be written off as purely theological, for much of it can be integrated with then-current theories of philosophical psychology. Added to this is the model that Ismāʿīlī prophetology afforded Maimonides, allowing him to be Moses' very own deputy, interpreting his revelations for public consumption.[10]

As intimated above, Maimonides took Neoplatonic emanationism as a given and did not subject it to critical examination. Maimonides was not taken, however, with the elaborate emanative schemes of Plotinus and Proclus, found in his day in the "Epistles of the Sincere Brethren," and in the theosophic literature of Ismāʿīlī authors. Rather, Maimonides mainly follows Alfarabi and Avicenna in insinuating emanation into an Aristotelian-based dynamic in which God may be said not only to move the world but to be the cause of its existence as well. Though Maimonides differs with his predecessors on the origin of this movement, he largely agrees with them on the mechanics, positing a concentric pattern of globes governed by heavenly intellects that think of motion, and by souls that energize it. This is a downward cosmic process that ends with the emergence of sublunar matter and an Agent Intellect that endows all the forms on earth, including and especially the specific form of human beings, which is their intellect.

It is at this level, between heaven and earth, that the emanative scheme to which Maimonides subscribed comes into bold relief, serving as the instrument of divine providence. Specifically, it is the Agent Intellect that acts as God's messenger, or "angel," impersonally bestowing on human beings that which is appropriate for them, as determined by their physical endowments and intellectual attainments. The beneficial impact of the Agent Intellect may, however, be blunted or effaced by the chance effects of physical or political circumstances over which the individual has no control. This may not be what an individual "deserves," though persons who have prepared themselves properly to understand the way nature expresses God's will and wisdom will accept whatever happens to them as part of a divine order that is ultimately good.

Maimonides' difficulty with the faith of his fathers lay in his conviction that certain metaphysical theses concerning God held by Aristotle and the Muslim philosophers he admired were true, and that they resulted in an essentially Aristotelian image of the divine that stripped God of a meaningful will and personality. Maimonides rather openly—and daringly—cedes God's personality, but is determined to retain His will.

This distinction may well appear suspect, given Maimonides' insistence that God's will, like His wisdom, power, and any other term that may be attributed to Him, is not separate from His essence, that essence being, moreover, purely one, so that the attributes we identify are our own projections. Long before Maimonides' day, however, the purity of this idea of God, in which theoretically He should represent Being only, had been "compromised" historically by the Neoplatonic belief that there emanates from the One/God forces that constitute ultimately the entire world in all its combinations of form and matter. This emanative process was consolidated under the rubric of a providential will, and that will was thought to function in both a universal and a particular fashion. Select qualified persons, such as philosophers, could receive communications from these emanations in their intellect, while prophets benefited from these emanations in both their imagination and their intellect.

Maimonides accepts this hybrid legacy of a Neoplatonized Aristotelianism and does not demur from viewing the divine will as directly responsible for the revelations bestowed upon the prophets in dreams, in conformity with the biblical account.[11] Presumably, Maimonides could reconcile this position with the more philosophically neutral image of the Agent Intellect, aka divine will, that he otherwise projects. Still, Maimonides' use of the divine will to explain prophetic dreams is the sort of action that gives his writing an unavoidably apologetic air.

We need to bear in mind that Maimonides was a man of his time, working with the constructs that science and philosophy gave him, accepting some, rejecting others. The widely accepted theory of emanation allowed him to treat the divine will as distinct from God's essence, though he knew it was not. It may be that Maimonides accepted the reality of a personal, providential deity, i.e., of the divine will, without fully explaining it (even to himself). This position would be consistent with other positions he holds, without proof of their validity.

Whereas Plotinus, followed by Alfarabi, regarded emanation as a rather neutral automatic procedure, however willed, Avicenna identified divine providence more directly with the God of Islam.[12] While God was understood to be (mostly) not understood, or understandable, and His being was understood to be unique and totally self-contained, His will was seen, without particular argument, to be omnipresent in nature and in human affairs.

A prophetic vision, as understood by the philosophers, is a communication, emanated mainly by the Agent Intellect, of certain abstract universal propositions that the prophet's imaginative faculty converts into particular sensory forms, constructed in the language and circumstances of the times. In this manner, the prophet personalizes, localizes, and popularizes universal truths. The revelations the prophet experiences derive from God, in that all true formulations of being emanate ultimately from Him, but they are mediated mostly by the Agent Intellect as well as by the prophet's rational and imaginative faculty. The prophet's intellect is able to receive the abstract formulations of the Agent Intellect, and his imaginative faculty is able to convert them into apposite narratives and symbols.

Avicenna speaks of emanations that also issue from the souls of the celestial spheres that impress concrete, particular images upon the imaginative faculty of a slumbering prophet.[13] The prophet understands them as symbols and representations of universal truths adjusted for his community. This view gives the celestial souls a function that is difficult to rationalize, extending their influence on earth beyond their commonly understood role of endowing the elemental mixtures of natural bodies, and personalizes their relation to a particular prophet, making him a passive receptacle of revelation.

Maimonides does not adopt this view, apparently believing that the Agent Intellect is sufficient to account for emanations that can be received by prophets both intellectually and imaginatively, awake and asleep, respectively. However, Maimonides does not dwell on the mechanics of revelation/emanation in dreams, giving the impression that he accepts the idea that the Agent Intellect can transmit particular imaginative forms as well as universal intelligible ideas. He has no philosophical warrant for granting that supernal intellect an imaginative faculty, however, and it would give the prophets a direct access through their imagination to the divine will other than the access Moses had, which was supposedly purely intellectual. Yet, as emerges from Maimonides' discussion of the degrees of prophecy in *Guide* 2.45,[14] it appears he believed that the prophet's imaginative faculty shapes the revelations it receives from the Agent Intellect.

Maimonides believes that the imagination did not enter at all into Moses' prophetic encounters with God. He considers that the revelations Moses received were devoid of the effects and artifices of imagination, whatever their source. This could be taken to mean (and was so intended) that Moses' prophetic utterances were the *ipsissima verba,* the very words, of God (as conveyed by His angelic agent). This belief, however, belies Maimonides' conviction that God does not speak and has no voice. Similarly, however specific its emanated form, the Agent Intellect does not possess a physical component with which to voice its intelligible message. To believe otherwise is to abandon the philosophical model Maimonides has embraced (however attenuated it became to accommodate prophetic experience), and replace it with a patently mythical presentation. Accordingly, Maimonides must have believed that it is really Moses' imagination that gives the intelligible forms received in his intellect a physical expression and a language in which to convey it. This process is similar to that which occurs when revelations are received by all other prophets, except that their imaginations are recipients of emanations either directly from the Agent Intellect or indirectly from their rational faculty. Maimonides says, however, that Moses' imagination is not involved in receiving revelations.

For Maimonides, Moses presented abstract universal ideas in popular language, the language of law and of historical deeds. He presented them as coming from God, which is part of Moses'—and Maimonides'—understanding of the divine will, an understanding that is necessary as well for the people's allegiance to the laws and to the society that keeps the law. Maimonides' account of Moses' prophecy is intended to stress its exceptional, unique, and never to be surpassed proximity to eternal, divine truths. Moses translated these abstract truths into the "language of men," but it is a discourse that Maimonides contends is as close to expressing the divine will as is possible, so that he can say it is the Torah (i.e., God) that speaks in human tongue. But the Torah is a human document, however divine its origin.

This view informs Maimonides' account of Moses' prophetic mission, which extends beyond the narrative of his life to include transmission of the entire Torah.[15] Though he does not spell this out, Maimonides considers Moses the (immediate) author of the *ḥumash,* the Pentateuch. This means that Maimonides understands Moses as serving more as an interpreter of God's will than as His secretary. The interpretation is excellent, but it is still an interpretation, in popular terms that often compromise the truth. Maimonides presents these compromises as deliberate, necessary to retain the people's essential fealty to God, and sanctioned by Him.

Maimonides actually presents God as acquiescing in the Israelites' habituated need to conceive of God falsely, and as condoning idolatrous practices borrowed from pagan, mostly Sabian rituals.[16] This is part of the divine scheme, Maimonides asserts, a "ruse" by which God defers to human nature but also transforms discredited practices and beliefs into proper understanding of Him.

In this manner, Maimonides gives voice to his own critical attitude toward many of the rituals and practices mentioned in the Bible. Given his image of God, it is unlikely that Maimonides believes in the religious efficacy of sacrifices and in the Temple ritual that surrounds them. For him it is all a carry-over from pagan practices, as are all the rituals meant as ways of entreating God, together with the carrot and stick of reward and punishment. Nevertheless, the cunning he discerns in the biblical adoption and adaptation of these practices elicits Maimonides' endorsement, and he believes in the contemporary relevance for the individual and the community of its hallowed rituals.

In his presentation of the reasons for the laws found in the Bible, as in his defense of the stratagems God allegedly adopts to accommodate the people's false beliefs, Maimonides offers a vision of God functioning as a hands-on ruler, a micro-manager who can be severe as well as kind, who commands the law and administers it. The impersonal God has become here very personal, very physical, responding to every situation in what seems to be an ad hoc, contingently derived, manner. It is difficult to reconcile this with the *Guide*'s earlier image of a remote, impersonal, and unchanging intelligence that acts upon mankind mainly through the Agent Intellect.

This is not, however, prima facie evidence of Maimonides' capitulation to tradition and abandonment of the emanationist mechanism through which God's will expresses itself. Maimonides may well have reckoned that just as the prophets were known to have received revelations in dreams from the Agent Intellect in the form of specific images (or so construed them), so Moses could have received intelligible universal ideas that he understood were to be interpreted as specific laws and directives, including the imperative to present God in human terms as a lawgiver and subtle, sagacious ruler.

Maimonides' account of the revelation at Sinai, and of the entire body of law and lore that composes the Five Books of the Torah, may thus agree with his metaphysics, however different they appear. Maimonides benefited from reading Alfarabi's writings in political philosophy and adopted for himself and for God the deceptions and disguises that that philosopher saw as incumbent upon a successful leader.[17] At the same time, Maimonides was convinced of the utility and spiritual benefits of observing the law.

Maimonides' apparent acceptance of a particular and personal providence in the guise of divine will enabled him to consent to the biblical narrative as given (before interpreting it), and to address each verse of Scripture as sacred, to affirm commandments and a history predicated upon an intimate relationship between God's emissaries/intermediaries, principally the Agent Intellect, and the Jewish people. Accordingly, Maimonides ascribes all of Moses' narrative to God, following the terms of the biblical narrative.

Maimonides had to be aware, however, that this separation of the (providential) will of God from His essence, the one in intimate relation with man and the world, the other totally aloof from everything, was incompatible with his understanding of God. He knew that the will of God was synonymous with His wisdom, which brooks no change and is therefore necessary, and that God's relation to the world is indirect at best, mediated by the celestial intellects and spheres. Yet it is this emanated mediation, together with an expanded notion of what emanation includes, that permitted Maimonides to contradict himself, or to appear to do so, distinguishing between God and His will. That distinction is often blurred in Maimonides' telling; in an application of the "gracious ruse" technique that he discerns in the Bible itself, he attributes the acts of the Agent Intellect (the chief emissary of the divine will) to God.

Maimonides gives the impression that God's will tracked the Israelites in their wanderings and that He provided them with personal governance. This is close to the traditional, biblical view of God's relation to His people. In Maimonides' (implicit) version, however, this providential will is a specific instantiation of a universal phenomenon, an expression of an essentially impersonal providence. This will/providence is personalized by the prophets and the people, who yearn for a relationship with God. The prophets' access to the Agent Intellect creates a sympathetic arrangement whereby it imparts suitable ideas and/or images to them. The Agent Intellect is both proactive and reactive in relation to human beings; the more they are conjoined to it, the more it provides them with an understanding of how to imagine and conduct their lives.

For Maimonides, the One is a Creator God whose will is evidently ubiquitous, in nature and human affairs. God communicates indirectly with human beings through emanations that are particular images as well as universal intelligible ideas. Though God remains impersonal and essentially unknowable, emanations willed by Him provide the personal touch otherwise lacking. Maimonides believed in the theory of emanation and accepted its extension into prophetic experience. This view undoubtedly expanded for him the parameters and significance of both religion and philosophy. It allowed him to personalize God indirectly and to rationalize the experience of prophecy.

More than benefiting prophets solely, the Agent Intellect, in Maimonides' opinion, assists the person willing (and able) to understand God's ways by continually emanating upon him or her ideas that form the universal concepts of science. The eager and talented student applies these concepts to ascend from the practical sciences to the theoretical, from physics to metaphysics, the "divine science." When the study is completed, the person knows (a portion of) that which is eternally within the Agent Intellect, and that person's perfected, acquired intellect may be said to conjoin or unite with it.[18]

Conjunction with the Agent Intellect was often conceived as contingent on complete mastery of the sciences, and particularly of metaphysics. The great difficulty of achieving this led Alfarabi (in one of his writings) to deny its possibility. Avicenna, on the other hand, believed that partial conjunction with the Agent Intellect occurred regularly, whenever one had a true cognition.[19] Maimonides, like Averroes, speaks of conjunction as a possibility for the very few. He posits it as an ideal toward which to strive.[20] Yet the logic that underlies the process of acquiring knowledge requires that any true cognition of a universal proposition be equivalent to identifying with the form of that idea, a form that is ultimately in the Agent Intellect. Having emanated originally from that universal intellect to the individual's intellect, the concept now "returns" to its origin when the individual intellect conjoins with it.

Still, most of the philosophers were opposed to seeing conjunction as a normative cognitive experience, or at least to labeling knowledge of some universal truth as a conjunctive experience. Labels aside, however, the satisfaction, bordering on profound happiness, that the philosophers promised those who achieved a respectable degree of knowledge shows that the process brought the benefits that conjunction promised.

For a true proposition, representing an eternally valid idea, allows the person who knows it to participate in eternal (intelligible) being, to the degree that the conjunction is maintained. As human beings are easily and necessarily distracted from thinking intelligible abstractions, the conjunction that endures and as such assures the person immortality is met with only at the moment of death, when other concerns disappear. This is the divine "kiss of death" that Maimonides understands a paradigmatic Moses, Aaron, and Miriam to have received.[21]

It is not completely accurate, however, to say that the person is assured immortality, since it is the person's rational faculty alone, among the faculties of the soul, that may achieve this status, and that at the price of divesting itself of all particular intellections and memories. That is, the person does not survive death other than as subsumed within that universal formal being represented by the Agent Intellect.

One does not need to die to have a taste of immortality, however, when it is understood as knowing eternal, universal truths, particularly since the living individual possessing that knowledge has already relinquished any claim to sole possession of that truth. Putting this immaterial, intellectual sense of immortality off to an after-death experience solely is, like the standard notion of conjunction, illogical. Doing so is attractive, nevertheless, for the comforting assurance it gives people that some part of themselves will endure after their death. That it is the impersonal rational faculty that remains is obscured by Maimonides' frequent invocation of "soul" for intellect.

In this he follows the practices of Alfarabi and Avicenna, though they, and particularly Avicenna, posit the existence of soul as a separate individualized substance with enduring feelings as well as intelligence. Surprisingly, Maimonides does not argue for this image of soul in the *Guide,* sharing with Averroes a more rigorous attitude toward immortality, one rooted more in the Aristotelian tradition.

Maimonides thus accepts the idea popularly known as monopsychism, which created a furor in Europe in association with Averroes' adoption of it.[22] Like Averroes, Maimonides also highlights the difficulty of attaining conjunction; it requires lifelong and nearly monomaniacal study, to be completed ideally only at death. He has thereby invested the pursuit of knowledge with the trappings of religious devotion, the satisfaction of knowing the truth with the unspeakable felicity of experiencing the divine presence.

Though reticent to dwell on the topic, Maimonides speaks of conjunction as a communion with God, and not with His agent. Likewise, his references to the intellect of a person may be taken as meant for the entire person; the immortality promised is highly personal. Maimonides does this both to hide his radical position from those who would be sure to oppose it were he more transparent and to express the truth as he saw it. That is, Maimonides believed that the Agent Intellect, as a divine immaterial being, stood in for an inaccessible God and that an enlightened individual would rejoice in knowing that "his" or "her" intellect would survive annihilation, however subsumed its identity. Moreover, Maimonides did not believe he was being irreligious in adopting in the philosophers' terms the philosophers' quest for transcendental being.

Maimonides thus sets the bar high for his reader, offering a vision of purely spiritual or intellectual immortality, shorn of particular cognitions and memories.[23] The addressee of the *Guide* is also expected to cultivate indifference to the evils and misfortunes that life holds, aware of their insignificance vis-à-vis that which counts, viz., true and eternal being. While not advocating full retreat from society, Maimonides poses the ideal of an internal withdrawal from meaningful engagement with other people, including family members. In this, he is borrowing a page from the handbook of mystics and pietists, who found meaning ultimately in sole communion with God. Maimonides has the same desire, tempered only by his knowledge of the logical impossibility of fully achieving this, and by his belief in the divinely ordained necessity of working toward establishing a good and just society. All this implies that a person is free to act as he or she wishes. This is a tenet of Maimonides' faith and of his philosophy, despite his avowal of strict, or nearly strict, causal relations that in one place compares human actions to those of animals bereft of intelligence.

Maimonides is both anti-anthropocentric and anti-anthropomorphic; he is against seeing mankind as the apple of God's eye, and against granting God that eye. Maimonides knows that the Bible (seems to) affirm both positions, and his first task in the *Guide* is to wean the reader off these erroneous assumptions. Maimonides' detoxification, as he sees it, of the Bible's anthropomorphic representations of God is exegetically brilliant, at once simple and exhaustive.[24] Following from his understanding of a God totally unique and eternally unchanging, Maimonides completely refashions the Bible's deity in that image. For him, all depictions of God in Scripture attest solely to His existence or providence. The providence is a necessary function of God's existence, an expression of His will and wisdom. Ultimately, both are refractions in the world of the one indissoluble source of all being that we call God.

Maimonides' idea of God is clearly dependent on the Greek philosophical tradition as transmitted by the *falāsifa* of Islam. However, they did not attempt a systematic overhaul of the Qur'ān's depiction of Allah as Maimonides did for the God of the Hebrew Bible, and they did not work as diligently to merge the philosophical canon with the scriptural. Maimonides has total confidence in the metaphysicians' teachings of God's unchanging and unaffected eternal nature, as well as in his belief in a One who, while beyond the being of this world, is responsible for it. The postclassical Greek notion of what perfection must entail for the one God, viz., omnipotence, omniscience, and omnibenevolence, in addition to eternal existence and undivided unity of being, replaced for Maimonides and other medieval philosophers the scriptural image of a questioning and demanding God.

Accordingly, Maimonides does not conceive of God in the terms in which the Bible presents Him and believes neither in the literal presentation of divine attributes, which entails multiplicity in the divine essence, nor in the Bible's literal presentation of God's appearance in history. Maimonides accepts the political necessity to endorse such positions, once qualified, but often proffers them without qualification. He was assisted in doing so by the conviction that the biblical narrative faithfully represented the divine will, as expressed through emanations correctly interpreted by the prophets.

Maimonides thoroughly examines the utility of negative predication (or "apophatic" discourse) of divine attributes, and believes he can salvage the Bible's positive locutions by interpreting them as negations of the privations of these attributes.[25] Accordingly, "God is good" means "God is not not-good," or "God is not bad." This presumably distances God from having any attributes at all, retaining thereby His purity of being, while not disavowing entirely what the positive attributes are meant to represent. Maimonides would have us believe that God in some sense possesses in His singular essence all the virtues that the positive attributes denote, but we cannot predicate them of Him without introducing multiplicity into His being. Hence, silence is the best way to praise God. It is an informed silence, however, and one that Maimonides breaks often in the course of expounding on God's nature, whether as intellect or as the emanating Necessary Existent.

As we have seen, one of the central tenets of Maimonides' belief is that God, whose perfect nature is unchanging, uncaused, and therefore unresponsive to anything, acts voluntarily (i.e., acts through His will) in relation to the world in general, and to human beings in particular. That involvement in the universe is exemplified paradigmatically in Maimonides' account of creation and of the revelation at Sinai.

Maimonides describes creation from nothing, ex nihilo, as a unique event, impossible to describe—or critique—in terms applicable solely to post-creation physics. It is a supreme manifestation of the will of God, acting in accordance with His mysterious nature. Maimonides would like the reader to accept the possibility of such a creation, though knowing that it extends the denotative range of possible events—all of which require antecedent actual existents—beyond that which philosophers would accept.[26]

Maimonides is also imprecise as to the meaning of the "nothing" after or from which the world emerged by divine fiat. Maimonides cannot mean that nonbeing actually existed, as a state of (non-)being, in opposition to and prior to the world that came into being suddenly. He must rather believe that there was absolutely nothing other than God originally and eternally, until the moment of creation. "Then," without really changing His mind (since God always intended it), God created the world.

Maimonides speaks of the "absolute privation" of being, i.e., of pure non-being, the complete opposite to that eternal state of being which Aristotle proclaims to be necessary. Maimonides must see this necessary nature of the world's existence as a threat to God's sole dominion and creative agency, depriving Aristotle and his followers of any meaningful use of the concept of God's will. Maimonides therefore has God exercise His will in creating the world as He does, however imperfectly we can understand it.

For Maimonides, this means that from its inception the world has been graced with a divine providence that is not mechanical or necessitated by external events. This does not mean, however, that God's will is not necessitated by internal realities, i.e., by His essential nature, in which God's will acts in complete accord with His wisdom, with which it is essentially synonymous. That wisdom is unchanging, and has been so eternally, Maimonides believes. This implies, though, that God has known from all eternity that He wanted to and that He would create the world; it existed in His mind, which is His being, eternally. Creation from nothing may thus be explicable philosophically, but the creation of matter remains a mystery, not the idea of matter as a substratum of form and principle of change, but the physical reality of it in relation to God.

For physical matter, as that which changes, is foreign to God's nature; it is impermanent and in itself purely potential. It cannot be known to God in its material individuation without introducing principles into His essence that contradict and violate that essence. It is difficult enough, though with ample philosophical precedent, to accept the notion that a purely simple One, whose essence is just existence, may yet be considered as containing in that unity of being a condensation of all possible forms in the world, as known through their species; it is too much to introduce absolutely unformed matter into the essence of God and have it emerge directly from His being. That is akin to the path Spinoza trod later.[27]

Maimonides is reluctant as well to go with Aristotle's or Plato's notion of an eternal, quasi-independent matter. Maimonides therefore adopts the Neoplatonic tradition that has matter emerging as the final stage of emanation, as far away from God's knowledge and creative energy as possible. Matter is so low in the scheme of things that it hovers over nonbeing, in that it is constantly in flux and causes accidents, calamities, and death. On the other hand, as the principle of potentiality and change, matter is not forced to conform to causal dictates, allowing human beings to express their will and break with predetermined causal necessity.

Maimonides presents creation as a sudden event, the beginning of a temporal-spatial world that did not exist before. This does not conflict, however, with the notion of an ideal world eternally in the divine mind. Plotinus and his followers thought that the emergence into physical reality was eternally necessitated by the overflowing power and goodness of the One, aka God. While Maimonides did not dissent from associating (in his own way) these attributes with the deity, he felt it possible, to preserve the notion of a God whose will is not overcome by necessity, to argue for a volitionally created physical universe.

Despite his refusal to entertain precreation narratives, Maimonides could have believed that the last stage of the classical emanative process, the formation of the realm of *physis* or Nature, came, by eternal "prearrangement," after and not simultaneously together with the upper hypostases of *nous* and *psyche,* Mind and Soul, God having always orchestrated nature's ultimate appearance as a sign of His providential largesse toward mankind. This of course assumes the presence of an eternal will in God that is more nuanced than that granted customarily by the philosophers, an assumption that Maimonides takes on faith.

Ultimately, however, Maimonides' creationist scenario turns out to be as necessitated as is Aristotle's, God's actions equally "constrained" by His nature. As a God of goodness and creator of all possible being, He had to create a world;[28] His wisdom and will, that is, His essential being, dictated it. Maimonides knows this, however ignorant of God's nature he claims to be. Still, insisting on creation does alter our perception of the deity and opens the door to seeing revelation in equally "miraculous" terms.

God is ultimately responsible for the creation of matter, in Maimonides stated view, whatever his reluctance to discuss this. Matter remains for him a threat—in the short run—to the dominion of form and the order of the good, that is, to God's providence. Maimonides does not want to cede the voluntary nature of God's creation of matter, as he may believe Alfarabi and Avicenna did in their adoption of the Neoplatonic model of emanationism. Maimonides does not believe that their protestations of a divine will have any more credibility than does that attributed to Aristotle, when paired with their belief in an eternal universe.

Maimonides, accordingly, is left with a doctrine of matter that challenges his understanding of God's nature, while providing him with a (partial) solution to the problem of evil. This paradox is a legacy of Neoplatonic thought, and Maimonides is attracted to it because of his desire to maintain a strong sense of divine will. He presents that will as "choosing" what it wants to do, as being uniquely able to change its mind, to initiate actions, and to know the future without affecting it. These are all activities that contradict the image of God that he has formerly presented as unchanging and unaffected, and leave the reader with two options: to believe either that Maimonides is dissembling, or that he has had a profound change of mind concerning what may be predicated of God.

Part of the difficulty with adopting the latter view is that Maimonides has invested considerable energy in debating with a (fictional) representative of *kalām* theology and wishes strenuously to present himself as a committed philosopher.[29] That entails accepting the universal meaning of terms and logical premises that the intellect has imposed on what is perceived to be a stable natural world, as well as the ultimately Aristotelian physics that observation has empirically confirmed, for the most part. Accordingly, Maimonides is against both the atomistic physics of the *mutakallimūn* and their imaginatively based notions of what it is possible for God to do. Maimonides realizes that without begging the question there is no way to resolve the impasse between imaginatively based premises and arguments based on intellectual/empirical premises, but he clearly leans toward the latter, philosophical stance.

Thus, when he says that God "chooses" what He wants to do, Maimonides does not intend to say that it is a free choice such as you and I might have. Maimonides cannot conceive of God as choosing any action but that which is the best choice possible, having known from all eternity what that is when a given scenario presents itself. This choice is free only in the sense that it is not compelled by anything outside of God's essence.

Similarly, when Maimonides says that God's foreknowledge of a possible event does not make it a necessary one, Maimonides does not believe that God follows a unique set of logical rules that upend the distinction between possibility and necessity, rendering any statement unintelligible, or that God could have the wrong knowledge of the outcome of the event in question, making its necessary nature, as foreknown, truly contingent. Maimonides may believe rather that the modal status of the proposition in itself remains possible until after the event that the proposition describes occurs, when its truth is necessary.[30] All along, though—actually, forever—God has known which possibility will be actualized. This is analogous to the "knowledge" possessed by a giant computer that contains the variant possibilities of every action that may occur, though not knowing which variant will actually be realized, owing to the inherent unpredictability of matter and of the human will.

Thus, when Maimonides says that God knows every particular being and event in the world, he must mean that God knows them insofar as they correspond to immaterial generic models.[31] Now, this is one of the philosophers' views that Maimonides recounts and apparently dismisses in *Guide* 3.16, just as he seems to discount the view that God knows nothing outside Himself, having no multiple cognitions. Yet Maimonides has in effect said just this when he asserted that God knows the world insofar as He knows Himself, that He knows the many as one. Nevertheless, Maimonides contrasts this latter view with one with which he identifies, that God "knows everything and that nothing secret is at all hidden from Him." That is, He knows everything worth knowing, having knowledge of real and permanent being, whenever and however instantiated.

These diverse positions can easily be conflated by subsuming the many cognitions in the one self-knowledge. Maimonides clearly, though, wishes to present God as involved in the world, however much he has asserted the deity's lack of affect and relationship. Maimonides wants to get away from Aristotle's self-contained, indifferent deity, and he relies on the Neoplatonic model of an ultimate One from whom emanations flow, emanations that connote will and knowledge. Perhaps Maimonides' covert sympathy with the philosophers' views presented can be deduced from his calling them "great men," *aqwām kubrā*.'[32]

Maimonides' understanding of Moses' dominant role in transmitting the Torah may temper his belief in the historicity of biblical claims, an issue to which he gives only lip service in the *Guide*. Similarly, he pays little attention in this book to the postbiblical historic past of the people Israel, and to the widespread consensus concerning its messianic future.[33] Maimonides is more of a historiographer than a historian here, identifying Sabian influences in the rituals and beliefs of biblical Judaism, and restoring a lost philosophical dimension to the Bible.

In this latter task, Maimonides probably saw himself as Moses' confidant, discreetly revealing to the philosophically initiated few the truths that Moses received, but that he transmitted in popular language that often cloaked their real meaning. Maimonides saw himself as coming to convert the popular language into universal propositions that would be intelligible to philosophically astute minds. Maimonides was thus Moses' deputy (his "legatee" or *wāṣiy*, in Ismāʿīlī terms) to the elite few.[34]

Maimonides wrote the *Guide* for this select audience, though he knew that many others would read it as well. He accommodates this larger, philosophically naïve group, with statements affirming a personal and historically interactive deity, though he warns explicitly against this belief. Maimonides is himself drawn to this traditional image of God and to the biblical text that conveys it. He follows Jewish tradition as well as Avicenna's affirmation of a divine will, pronounced also among Ismāʿīlī authors, who explicitly take their point of departure philosophically from their sacred scripture.

Maimonides' desired allegiance in the *Guide* is to philosophy, however, though he knows it is a theologically attuned philosophy. He knows that God's will is not essentially different from His wisdom, being an expression to us of that wisdom. As that wisdom is eternal and unchanging, so is God's will, appearances to the contrary as they may be. However, for Maimonides the appearance of God working His will in history and in a person's life is not a false impression, if properly understood. For him, everything that happens in the world can be traced, sooner or later, to the wise will of the Creator.

Following the literal text of the Bible, Maimonides often writes in a popular vein, personalizing God and His relation with the people Israel as well as with individual Jews. That has a definite political advantage, in assuring the masses of traditional Jews of his orthodoxy, and in securing their observance of the Law. That observance is necessary, in Maimonides' opinion; it is entailed by Moses' accurate construal of the divine will in political and legal terms. Furthermore, obedience to the Law creates the societal security and moral coherence in which philosophy can flourish and happiness, even supreme happiness, can be experienced. That is Maimonides' ultimate goal, for himself and his readers.

The popular presentation of religious beliefs thus has more than a political rationale, and Maimonides does not necessarily contradict himself in insisting upon exact conformity to the Law. He expends much effort to rationalize the particular edicts of *halakha,* to illustrate the Torah's sense of justice and compassion. As does the natural world, the Torah too bears witness to divine providence. Ultimately, though, and beyond the political sphere, Maimonides is convinced of the essential order and beauty of the world, and of the existence of a God whose majesty, providential will, and goodness, however impersonally emanated, he deeply experienced.

Today, we can dismiss the astronomy and celestial physics with which Maimonides struggled, the theories that supported emanationism and prophetology, and still warm to the concept of an ultimate source of the existence and continued being of the world, a source whose effects upon us we may personify as deliberate and wise. We still search for scientific knowledge, transcending personal subjectivities to join with what we view as universal truths. This can give us immense satisfaction, even if we may not believe that it grants us personal immortality; but neither did Maimonides. He considered the pursuit of truth, and the possibility of attaining it (to some degree) in every sphere of science, including metaphysics, a divine and blessed task, one that Judaism should embrace. He tried to lay out a road map for his people that would keep them together and ultimately allow for personal happiness and spiritual fulfillment. His map was accepted, the final destination, as he philosophically envisaged it, not.

Notes

Preface

1. Moses Maimonides, *The Guide of the Perplexed,* translated with an introduction and notes by Shlomo Pines, with an introductory essay by Leo Strauss. To be quoted as *Guide* for the pagination, and as "Pines" when quoting the translation given.

2. *Dalālah al-ḥā'irin le rabbenu Moshe ben Maimon,* ed. Shlomo Munk. To be quoted as "Munk," giving page and line number.

3. Cf. below, pp. 32–34, for clarification of these terms in Maimonides' day.

4. Not that the *Guide* is innocent of political considerations, but Maimonides had to be more circumspect than ever after its dissemination.

5. Cf. particularly Davidson, *Moses Maimonides: The Man and His Works* henceforth *MM;* and Kraemer, *Maimonides: The Life and World of One of Civilization's Greatest Minds,* henceforth *Life and World.*

6. For appreciation of Maimonides' masterful adaptations of Scripture, see Klein-Braslavy, *Maimonides as Biblical Interpreter;* Diamond, *Maimonides and the Hermeneutics of Concealment;* and now Stern, *The Matter and Form of Maimonides' Guide,* to be referred to as *Matter and Form.*

7. Edited by Yair Shiffman in 2001.

Introduction

1. Kraemer, *Life and World,* 39; Cohen, "The 'Convivencia' of Jews and Muslims in the High Middle Ages," 1–11.

2. As was common among Jews, Maimonides wrote Arabic in Hebrew letters, a dialect known as "Judaeo-Arabic." For a description of Judaeo-Arabic, see Blau, *The Emergence and Linguistic Background of Judaeo Arabic.*

3. Cf. Maimun b. Joseph, "Maimon: Letter of Consolation of Maimun Ben Joseph," 62–101; discussed by Ivry, "The Image of Moses in Maimonides' Thought," 122.

4. This is most striking in Maimonides' *Epistle to Yemen,* in Lerner, *Maimonides' Empire of Light,* 99–132; and cf. Lerner's discussion, 14–27.

5. Philosophically, the Karaites adhered to the views of the Muslim theologians, the *muta-*

kallimūn. Cf. Ben-Shammai, "Major Trends in Karaite Philosophy and Polemics in the Tenth and Eleventh Centuries," 339–59.

6. Maimonides, *Letters and Essays of Moses Maimonides* (Hebrew), ed. Shailat.

7. Cf. now Joel Kraemer's detailed study, "Maimonides' Intellectual Milieu in Cairo," 1–37.

8. *Guide*, p. 4. Cf. Munk, 1.24–28.

9. *Guide*, p. 15.

10. Whether Maimonides did or did not possess the foresight and talent to conceive a work of such immaculate style, it has been a premise of Maimonidean scholars (with the notable exception of Herbert Davidson) that he is to be taken at his word. Leo Strauss led the way in the past century in this pursuit, and his close reading of the *Guide*, pursuing its esoteric dimension, became a hallmark of his methodology.

11. Leo Strauss is the foremost esotericist of modern times in Maimonidean studies. Cf. "The Literary Character of the *Guide of the Perplexed*," in Strauss's *Persecution and the Art of Writing*, 38–94; and Strauss's introduction to the Pines translation of the *Guide*, "How to Begin to Study the *Guide of the Perplexed*," xi–lvi. For a critique of Strauss's approach, cf. Seeskin, *Searching for a Distant God*, 177–88.

12. Shlomo Pines has argued famously for Maimonides as agnostic on metaphysical issues. Cf. "The Limitations of Human Knowledge according to Al-Fārābī, Ibn Bājja, and Maimonides," 5: 404–31, and "Les limites de la métaphysique selon Al-Fārābī, Ibn Bājja, et Maimonide," 5: 432–46. For Pines, as for Strauss in "The Philosophic Foundation of the Law," 101–33, Maimonides is essentially a political philosopher, a view shared by Kreisel, *Maimonides' Political Thought*, 3.

13. Kasher, "Is There an Early Stratum in the *Guide of the Perplexed*?" 3:105–29; Manekin, *On Maimonides*, 5.

14. *Guide*, pp. 5, 6.

15. Stern, "Maimonides' Conceptions of Freedom and the Sense of Shame," 251 n. 51; "Maimonides on the Growth of Knowledge and Limitations of the Intellect," 174–88. This is also the burden of Stern's *Matter and Form*. He argues impressively that Maimonides' parables disclose a profound skepticism about the ability to have conclusive, scientific knowledge of metaphysical issues. The suspension of belief that this position entails appears contradicted, however, by Maimonides' endorsement of the philosophical and religious entailments of a supposedly discredited system. Stern views this endorsement as intended for the nonphilosophical masses.

16. Fox, *Interpreting Maimonides*, 294; Seeskin, *Searching for a Distant God*, 66–85; idem, *Maimonides on the Origin of the World*, 152, 194.

17. Cf. the English translation facing the Arabic original, in Al-Ghazālī, *The Incoherence of the Philosophers*, trans. Marmura.

18. *Maqāṣid al-Falāsifa*, ed. Dunyā. No English translation has been made of this work as yet. Al-Ghazālī wrote a number of esoterically oriented compositions based primarily on the *Maqāṣid* that evince greater sympathy with Avicenna's views than is often assumed. These works, called by their editor "Al-Ghazālī's Major *Maḍnūn*," offer a view of Al-Ghazālī as a philosophical theologian parallel to Maimonides. Cf. Al-Akiti, "The Good, the Bad, and the Ugly of Falsafa," 51–100.

19. Stern, "Maimonides on the Growth of Knowledge and the Limitations of the Intellect," 143–91; Stern, *Matter and Form*, 246, 311.

20. Through the centuries, however, many commentators have viewed Maimonides as successfully defending tradition in the *Guide*. See, for example, Heschel, *Maimonides*, 141–62.

Chapter 1

1. Not 1135, as frequently held. Cf. Davidson, *MM*, 9, and Kraemer, *Life and World*, 23.

2. Brockelmann, *History of the Islamic Peoples*, 202–9.

3. Maimun b. Joseph, "Maimon: Letter of Consolation of Maimun Ben Joseph," 71; editor's introduction, 11 n. 10.

4. *Maimonides Treatise on the Art of Logic; Maimonides' Arabic Treatise on Logic.* Cf. too Maimonides, *Maïmonide: Traité de logique*, trans. Brague.

5. Cf. Maimonides' letter to Samuel ibn Tibbon, as given in Kraemer, "Maimonides and the Spanish Aristotelian Tradition," 44. Maimonides' originality in this treatise is limited to his selection and organization of the material. Alfarabi's full name is Abū Naṣr Muḥammad ibn Muḥammad ibn Tarkhān ibn Uzalagh al-Fārābī.

6. This is in chapter 12 of the Arabic editions of the treatise. Cf. Davidson, *MM*, 314–22. Davidson also notes the lack of references to this treatise by Maimonides in his other writings, as well as its absence from Samuel ibn Tibbon's glossary of philosophical terms. One must weigh these arguments from silence against the coherence of the treatise with the rest of Maimonides' philosophical work, as well as against the nearly universal acceptance historically of Maimonides as its author. Additional considerations for accepting Maimonides as the author of the treatise are given now by Karin Almbladh in a forthcoming paper, "The Authorship and Textual Tradition of *Maqāla fī ṣināʿat al-manṭiq* Commonly Ascribed to Maimonides."

7. However, Kraemer, "Moses Maimonides: An Intellectual Portrait," 51 n. 48, claims that the juxtaposition of Moses and Jesus for purposes of exemplifying temporal priority was commonplace.

8. Some of the extant manuscripts feature superscriptions acknowledging God's presence in conventional Muslim terms, while others use a formula more recognizably Jewish. Maimonides used the former locution in his medical works, written specifically for Muslim patrons, the latter in his writings intended for a Jewish readership. Cf. Kraemer, *Life and World*, 499 n. 6.

9. Literally, "On the Science of ʿIbbur," which refers to the calculation of which lunar months should have thirty days, and which lunar years should have thirteen months. These adjustments are necessary to keep the lunar year synchronized with the solar year, upon which in turn the seasonal holidays of Succot, Passover, and Shavuot depend. Davidson, *MM*, 300, believes this treatise is also misattributed to Maimonides, as he does not refer to it specifically in his later writings on the subject.

10. Kraemer, "Moses Maimonides: An Intellectual Portrait," 19.

11. Davidson, *MM*, 296–99.

12. *Letters and Essays of Moses Maimonides*, 30–59; trans. and commented by Abraham Halkin and David Hartman in *Crisis and Leadership*, 13–90. See Soloveitchik, "Maimonides' Iggeret Ha-Shemad," 281–318.

13. Halkin and Hartman, *Crisis and Leadership*, 30. Davidson, *MM*, 506, believes Maimonides' distinction is itself disingenuous, contradicting both the rabbinic tradition in general and Maimonides' own writings on martyrdom in the *Mishneh Torah*. For this and other reasons, Davidson feels this epistle too may not be Maimonides.'

14. Cf. *Mishneh Torah* (henceforth *MT*), book 14 (Judges), Kings and Wars, 5.7–9, 5.12; a translation of 5.9 is found in Twersky, *A Maimonides Reader*, 218.

15. Though no longer in power, the Shīʿī theology of the Fatimids continued to resonate in Egypt and elsewhere, affecting Maimonides greatly. Cf. below, pp. 38–40. For Saladin's reign, cf.

Brockelmann, *History of the Islamic Peoples,* 225–31; for Maimonides' place in the larger scheme, see Cohen, "Maimonides' Egypt," 21–34.

16. As Bos says, Maimonides received the aphorisms of Hippocrates through Galen's commentaries upon them ("Maimonides' Medical Works and Their Contribution to His Medical Biography," 250). Cf. too Kraemer, "Moses Maimonides: An Intellectual Portrait," 37–40.

17. In addition to Shailat, *Letters and Essays of Moses Maimonides,* cf. Maimonides, *R. Moses b. Maimon: Responsa* (Hebrew). Joel Kraemer's translation of a selection of Maimonides' responsa is forthcoming with Yale University Press.

18. Cf. Ben-Sasson, "Maimonides in Egypt," 3–30.

19. In between these two majesterial compositions, Maimonides enumerated, in his *Sefer ha-Miẓvot* (Book of the Commandments), the 613 commandments that he believed constituted the totality of Jewish law. See Chavel, *The Commandments,* and the analysis in Davidson, *MM,* 173–85.

20. Above, p. xi.

21. Davidson, *MM,* 149–51.

22. Maimonides, *Maimonides' Introduction to the Talmud,* 181–83.

23. Twersky, *A Maimonides Reader,* 40.

24. Cf. Baron, "The Historical Outlook of Maimonides," in *History and Jewish Historians,* 109–63, and particularly 152. Baron explains (162) that Maimonides viewed biblical history "through the spectacles of rabbinic legend," but that he did not doubt the "fundamental historicity" of the events, as recorded.

25. Maimonides, *Maimonides' Introduction to the Talmud,* 193–96.

26. Twersky, *A Maimonides Reader,* 402–23.

27. Cf. below, pp. 34–35, 37–38, 47.

28. Twersky, *A Maimonides Reader,* 421, translates the tenth principle as stating that "God knows all that men do," whereas the Arabic states only that God "knows the actions of men," *yaʿlamu afʿāl al-nāṣ,* the precise nature of that knowledge left ambiguous.

29. Twersky, *A Maimonides Reader,* 411.

30. English translation by Raymond L. Weiss and Charles E. Butterworth, *Ethical Writings of Maimonides,* 59–104.

31. Maimonides is particularly indebted to Alfarabi's Aphorisms of the Statesman; see Davidson, "Maimonides' *Shemonah Peraqim* and Alfarabi's *Fusûl al-Madanî,*" 16–33.

32. Weiss and Butterworth, *Ethical Writings of Maimonides,* 79.

33. The Noahide laws, based loosely on Genesis 2:16, include prohibitions of blasphemy, idolatry, adultery, murder, robbery, and eating the limb of a living animal, and enjoin the establishment of a just system of laws and courts. Cf. book 14 of the *Mishneh Torah,* Kings and Wars, chapter 9; Twersky, *A Maimonides Reader,* 221.

34. Plato, *Republic,* book 4; Aristotle, *De anima,* books 2 and 3.

35. Cf. below, pp. 74, 80, 214, 220.

36. *Eight Chapters,* chapter 2; Weiss and Butterworth, *Ethical Writings of Maimonides,* 65. Ivry, "The Greek Tradition in Ethics and Its Encounter with Religious Moral Wisdom," 115–18.

37. *Nicomachean Ethics,* 4.3.

38. Cf. Daniel Frank, "Humility as a Virtue," 89–99.

39. Weiss and Butterworth, *Ethical Writings of Maimonides,* 83–95.

40. Below, p. 21.

41. Weiss and Butterworth, *Ethical Writings of Maimonides,* 93.

42. *Ha-kol ẓafui ve-ha-reshut netunah.* Twersky, *A Maimonides Reader,* 395, translates *reshut* as "authority." Josef Stern, "Maimonides' Conceptions of Freedom and the Sense of Shame," 234, renders *reshut* as "power" and does not believe it connotes free will or free choice.

43. Below, pp. 178–79.

44. Yale University Press has had an ongoing project of translating the *Mishneh Torah* into English since 1949, utilizing different scholars.

45. Cf. Davidson, *MM,* 189–203, for an informed discussion of Maimonides' work in relation to that of his predecessors.

46. Isadore Twersky has written a major study of this work, including a chapter on Law and Philosophy. See his *Introduction to the Code of Maimonides (Mishneh Torah),* 356–514.

47. Twersky, *A Maimonides Reader,* 35–227, offers translations of select passages from these books. Kraemer, *Life and World,* 326–56, summarizes Maimonides' teaching on key social and ethical issues in many of the books. Similarly, Davidson, *MM,* 160–65, highlights the extralegal positions Maimonides proffers in the work.

48. *MT,* Book of Knowledge, Study of Torah, 2.2. For Maimonides, the adult study of Talmud includes the sciences, and particularly metaphysics. See Study of Torah, 1.12.

49. Above, 16.

50. This is a "positive" view of Islam and Christianity from a Jewish perspective, but Muslims and Christians would not have appreciated the supporting roles Maimonides gave their faith. In any event, this section, at the end of Kings, chapter 11, was censored and did not appear in later versions of the book. Cf. Twersky, *A Maimonides Reader,* 226.

51. Maimonides' opposition to benefiting financially from rabbinical office is strongly expressed in *MT,* Study of Torah, 3.10.

52. Joel Kraemer translation in Ralph Lerner's *Empire of Light,* 99–132. Isaac Shailat's new edition of the Arabic text, together with the Hebrew translation of Samuel ibn Tibbon, is in Maimonides, *Letters and Essays,* 77–168.

53. Maimonides, *Epistle to Yemen,* ed. Shailat, 105; Kraemer's translation in Lerner, *Maimonides' Empire of Light,* 124. Subsequently, in the *Mishneh Torah,* Laws of Kings and Their Wars, 12.2, Maimonides inveighs against "calculating the end," referring to the rabbis' denunciation of such a practice (BT Sanhedrin, 97b).

54. Maimonides makes no mention of the kind of accommodation to conversion he and others made under Almohad persecution, probably because that was not realistic in the Yemen.

55. Kraemer, *Life and World,* 117.

56. Maimonides, *Treatise on Resurrection,* 154–77.

57. Lerner, *Empire of Light,* 178–82.

58. Cf. *Commentary on the Mishnah,* Sanhedrin 10.1. As Maimonides mentions in the *Treatise on Resurrection,* 157, he also affirmed belief in resurrection in the *Mishneh Torah,* claiming that its denial forfeits one's immortality. Cf. *MT,* Laws of Repentance, 3.5–6.

59. Maimonides, *Treatise on Resurrection,* 168. Maimonides also mentions the impression people received from his comment in *MT,* Kings, 11.3 that the Messiah, once present, would not interfere with the natural order, among other things not resurrecting the dead. Maimonides here explains (166) he meant that the Messiah would not resurrect people, but that God would.

60. Interestingly, Maimonides also cites a number of biblical passages that, he says, conclusively deny resurrection (*Treatise on Resurrection,* 169), but that he then claims posit a situation in which there is no need for miraculous intervention in nature.

61. Maimonides' position in his *Commentary on the Mishnah* is based, as he presents it,

on Sanhedrin 10.1, an affirmation of resurrection agreed to by the Amoraim of the Babylonian Talmud (Sanhedrin 90a ff.), as well as by all post-talmudic rabbis. In invoking the consensus—*ijmâ'*—of the community, Maimonides is using a Muslim judicial norm that grants validity to a proposition that is widely accepted.

62. There is some irony here, for Maimonides accuses his addressee in this treatise of reasoning in a *kalām* manner.

63. For Maimonides, resurrection at best is ancillary to the belief in the world to come, which he insists is a purely intellectual experience. While Davidson, *MM,* 534–35, recognizes the possibility that Maimonides did not believe literally in resurrection, the alternative, which he cannot accept, is that Maimonides would have been "simply lying . . . consciously misleading readers who looked to him for guidance." In creating this disjunction, Davidson ignores the seriousness with which Maimonides accepted Alfarabi's platonically inspired view, one that justified deception by a political leader.

64. Lerner, *Empire of Light,* 184.

65. Langermann, "Maimonides' Repudiation of Astrology," 123–58, offers a thorough analysis of Maimonides' reasons for rejecting astrology, and compares them with the astronomical views that he adopts.

Chapter 2

1. Chavel, *The Commandments.*

2. Twersky, *A Maimonides Reader,* 40.

3. *Sefer ha-Madda'* in Hebrew, which can also and perhaps more accurately be translated as "Book of Science," as Simon Rawidowicz noted. The *Mishneh Torah* is the only major work Maimonides wrote in Hebrew.

4. My translation, as elsewhere, unless cited otherwise. Cf. the rendition in Twersky, *A Maimonides Reader,* 43.

5. In the *Guide,* 2.1, p. 247 (see below, pp. 89, 109–10) Maimonides offers a modified version of Avicenna's proof for the existence of God as Necessary Existent, a philosophical proof that he doubtless felt was inappropriate for the readers of the *Mishneh Torah,* being foreign to their education.

6. This paragraph is omitted in Twersky's reader; cf. Maimonides, *Mishneh Torah: The Book of Knowledge,* ed. and trans. Moses Hyamson, 34a.

7. *MT,* Book of Knowledge, Basic Principles of the Torah, 1.6.

8. Ibid., 1:8–12.

9. Maimonides repeats this teaching in ibid., 4:12.

10. Ibid., 2:8. The angels/separate intellects of the spheres cannot, however, know God's essence.

11. Ibid., 2:9. The expression Maimonides uses is *u-lefi shehu' yode'a 'aẓmo . . . hu' yode'a ha-kol* (Maimonides, *Mishneh Torah: The Book of Knowledge,* ed. and trans. Moses Hyamson, 36a). This may more precisely be translated "He knows everything in accordance with His self-knowledge."

12. *MT,* Book of Knowledge, Basic Principles of the Torah, 2.10.

13. Ibid., 3.9. Maimonides commonly uses "angels" as a synonym for the intelligences of the spheres. Here, though, he places the knowledge had by stars and planets lower than that of angels, though greater than that of humans.

14. "Ibid., 4.8. Maimonides avoids using the term "intellect" here, calling it the "knowledge [*de'ah*] that is the form of the soul" instead. He also says here that it comes "from God from the heaven," not wishing to say that it comes via the Agent Intellect, as do all other forms (4.6). Maimonides here invokes God's statement in Genesis 1:26 that identifies intellect with the divine image and likeness (*ẓelem* and *demut*), the trope with which he begins chapter 1 of the *Guide.*

15. *MT,* Book of Knowledge, Basic Principles of the Torah, 4.10. *'Amoq* is the Hebrew here, which probably means both "profound" and "obscure," as does its Arabic analogue, *ghafla,* which Maimonides employs frequently in the *Guide.*

16. BT Hagigah 2.41.

17. *MT,* Book of Knowledge, Basic Principles of the Torah, 4.13. The Hebrew expressions Maimonides uses are *meyashvim da'ato shel adam* and *yishuv ha-'olam,* literally "settle the mind of man" and "settling of the world."

18. Below, pp. 212, 214, 220.

19. *MT,* Book of Knowledge, Basic Pinciples of the Torah, 7.1. Maimonides puts the Hebrew verb *menave'*, which I have translated as "grants prophecy," in what corresponds to the English present tense, implying that prophecy is not a past reality only.

20. *Guide,* 2.11. The Agent Intellect is also called the "Prince of the World" in *Guide,* 2.6, p. 264.

21. *Guide,* 2.37 and 2.45.

22. *MT,* Book of Knowledge, Basic Principles of the Torah, 7.6.

23. Ibid., 8.1.

24. Translated by Raymond L. Weiss in his and Charles E. Butterworth's *Ethical Writings of Maimonides,* 27–58. See too Weiss's *Maimonides' Ethics: The Encounter of Philosophic and Religious Morality,* 93–131. *De'ot* literally means "opinions" or "views," beliefs that are not based on logical or scientific proofs and yet are critical in establishing personal and societal norms. The character traits discussed are of this sort, and Maimonides is convinced of the validity of his opinions, for all their "nonscientific" dimension.

25. Maimonides puts this in *De'ot* 1.5 as *ve-halachta be-derakhav,* "and you shall walk in his ways," following Deuteronomy 28:9.

26. *De'ot* 4.1–19, given more extensively in Maimonides' *Medical Aphorisms.*

27. *De'ot* 3.2.

28. *De'ot* 2.2.

29. *Guide,* 1.36, p. 84; 1.54, p. 126.

30. *De'ot* 1.5.

31. Following Weiss's translation, Weiss and Butterworth, *Ethical Writings of Maimonides,* 46, and see 32. Cf. *De'ot* 5.13 and 2.3.

32. *De'ot* 3.2, 3.3. Cf. *Guide,* 3.51.

33. Charles E. Butterworth, trans., "On the Management of Health," in Weiss and Butterworth, *Ethical Writings of Maimonides,* 108.

34. Above, p. 17.

35. *MT,* Laws of Repentance, chapter 5. Twersky, *A Maimonides Reader,* 77–78; Maimonides, *Mishneh Torah: The Book of Knowledge,* ed. Hyamson, 86b–87b. Maimonides employs the phrase *reshut netunah* (literally "authorization [for free will] is granted"), echoing the rabbinic statement he quoted in the *Commentary on the Mishnah.*

36. Maimonides, *Mishneh Torah: The Book of Knowledge*, ed. Hyamson, 87b–88a. See above, p. 26.

37. Below, p. 179.

38. *MT*, Judges, 14.9; Twersky, *A Maimonides Reader*, 221–26.

Chapter 3

1. Altmann, "Maimonides on the Intellect and the Scope of Metaphysics," 108.

2. Major studies of this highly developed subject have been written by Harry Austryn Wolfson, *The Philosophy of the Kalam*, and by Shlomo Pines, *Studies in Islamic Atomism*. See too Corbin, *History of Islamic Philosophy*, 105–24, and the brief resumé of Richard M. Frank, "The Science of Kalām," 9–37. Wolfson has also written of the influence of *kalām* on Jewish thought in *Repercussions of the Kalam in Jewish Philosophy*, and see Stroumsa, "Saadya and Jewish Kalam," 71–90.

3. Cf. Averroës, *The Book of the Decisive Treatise Determining the Connection Between the Law and Wisdom, & Epistle Dedicatory*. Butterworth provides a brief biographical sketch of Averroes and analyzes the structure of the *Decisive Treatise*, xiii–xxxvii.

4. Kraemer, "Maimonides' Use of (Aristotelian) Dialectic," 123, believes that despite Maimonides' attempts to argue philosophically, using demonstrative proofs, "the *Guide* is preponderantly a dialectical, namely, a *Kalām* or theological book."

5. Thinkers such as Isaac Israeli, Saadia Gaon, Judah Halevi, and Abraham ibn Daud. Maimonides rightly considered the theology of the Geonim, his rabbinic predecessors, to be influenced by Muslim *kalām* (*Guide*, 1.71, p. 176). Cf. Stroumsa, "Saadya and Jewish Kalam," 71–90. Kreisel, "Judah Halevi's Influence on Maimonides," 97–121, lists the theological and philosophical work of Maimonides' Jewish predecessors with which Maimonides was explicitly or probably familiar.

6. For the Aristotelian corpus in Arabic, cf. Peters, *Aristotle and the Arabs*, 58–129. Davidson, *Maimonides the Rationalist*, 105–43, finds that Maimonides shows considerable familiarity with Aristotle's *Physics, On the Heavens*, and *Nicomachean Ethics* in the *Guide*, but that his acquaintance with Aristotle's *Metaphysics* was mediated, most probably by Avicenna and Al-Ghazālī.

7. Kraemer, "Maimonides and the Spanish Aristotelian Tradition," 40–68.

8. The *Republic* and the *Laws* were translated into Arabic in the ninth century, and chapters 15–19 of Alfarabi's *Views of the Inhabitants of the Perfect State* relate principally to the *Republic*. See Alfarabi, *Al-Farabi on the Perfect State*, 10. Alfarabi also wrote a summary of Plato's *Laws*, though the authorship of the summary has been contested. See Parens, *Metaphysics as Rhetoric*, xxviii–xxxiv. Averroes wrote a paraphrase of the *Republic* that is lost in Arabic but extant in later Hebrew translations. Cf. Averroes, *Averroes on Plato's Republic*, and Lerner's introduction, xiii–xxviii.

9. The *Timaeus*, or Galen's paraphrase of it, was translated in the ninth century and had marked influence on later writers. See D'Ancona, "The Timaeus' Model for Creation and Providence," 206–37.

10. Aristotle thought there were 55 or 47 such unmoved movers. Cf. *Metaphysics*, 12.7, 12.8.

11. Aristotle, in *Metaphysics*, 12.8.1074b 9, considered the identification of the first substances with gods, made by earlier generations, "an inspired utterance."

12. *De anima*, books 2 and 3.

13. Alexander of Aphrodisias seems to have been the first to systematize Aristotle's philosophy of mind. See below, p. 37.

14. *De anima*, 3.4, 3.5.

15. *De generatione animalium*, 2.3.736b28.

16. See above, pp. 11, 12.

17. Cf. the opening sentences of the introduction to the first part of the *Guide*, p. 5.

18. *Guide*, 2.5, p. 259. As Josef Stern has shown, Maimonides is following Alfarabi here in thinking of logic in relation to language formation and signification. Stern, "Maimonides on Language and the Science of Language," 174.

19. Kraemer, "Maimonides' Use of (Aristotelian) Dialectic," 120, concisely summarizes the functions of dialectic in the Aristotelian tradition. Hyman, "Demonstrative, Dialectical, and Sophistic Arguments in the Philosophy of Moses Maimonides," 41–51, concludes his analysis by emphasizing that "dialectical no less than demonstrative arguments have cognitive significance." Black, *Logic and Aristotle's Rhetoric and Poetics in Medieval Arabic Philosophy*, 105–8, 249, finds that the Muslim *falāsifa* (and hence presumably Maimonides) consider that propositions couched in rhetoric and even poetry also contain cognitive significance.

20. Cf. Aristotle's *Topics*, 1.1.100a25; *Rhetoric*, 1.1.1354a1, and elsewhere.

21. Maimonides, *Maimonides' Arabic Treatise on Logic*, 155–60 (English), 9–42 (Hebrew).

22. Literally, "unable to speak" (*ghayr mukhātab*), ibid., 55.

23. Ivry, "Revelation, Reason and Authority in Maimonides' *Guide of the Perplexed*," 324.

24. The most recent book in this vein is Josef Stern's *Matter and Form*.

25. Pines, "Translator's Introduction," lxiv–lxxiv. Pines believes it likely that Alexander is the source for Maimonides' claim that God exercised "wily graciousness" in ordering matters on earth. See *Guide*, 3.32; discussed below, p. 200.

26. Cf. Alexander of Aphrodisias, *The De anima of Alexander of Aphrodisias*, 51–120. D'Ancona, *Man's Conjunction with Intellect*, 57–89, has argued that Proclus and ultimately Plotinus are the sources of this doctrine.

27. The post-Aristotelian development of stages in the rational faculty is thoroughly discussed by Davidson, *Alfarabi, Avicenna, and Averroes on Intellect*, 9–33.

28. *Pace* Davidson, *Maimonides the Rationalist*, 57. Cf. Kraemer, "Moses Maimonides: An Intellectual Portrait," 25.

29. Cf. A. H. Armstrong's analysis of Plotinus's thought in *The Cambridge History of Later Greek and Early Medieval Philosophy*, 211–63. Proclus's philosophy is summarized by Rosán, "Proclus," 479–82. E. R. Dodds has edited and translated Proclus's *The Elements of Theology*.

30. Plotinus's *Enneads* appeared in Arabic principally as the *Theology of Aristotle*, and it and other (falsely attributed) Plotinian treatises have been edited by A. Badawi in *Plotinus apud Arabes*. They have been translated into English and set against Plotinus's original Greek text by G. Lewis in *Plotini Opera II*. Proclus's influential eighteen arguments for the eternity of the world, preserved by John Philoponus in his *De Aeternitate Mundi contra Proclum*, was partly known in Arabic translation, as Davidson states in *Proofs for Eternity, Creation and the Existence of God in Medieval Islamic and Jewish Philosophy*, 51. Proclus's entire book, including one chapter missing in Greek but preserved in Arabic, has now been translated by Helen S. Lang and A. D. Macro as *On the Eternity of the World*.

31. Cf. De Callataÿ, *Ikhwan al-Safa'*, 17–20, 74–77. For the encyclopedic writings of the Brethren, known in Arabic as the *Rasā'il ikhwān al-Ṣafā'*, as relevant to Maimonides, cf. Ivry, "Islamic and Greek Influences on Maimonides' Philosophy," 145–46. For Proclean influence on Al-Kindī, see Endress, "The New and Improved Platonic Theology," 553–70.

32. Plotinus, *Enneads*, 5.2.1, 6.9.6. In the Arabic sources as translated by Lewis, pp. 474, 487.

33. Plotinus, *Enneads*, 5.5.10, 5.5.13; trans. Lewis, 355–57.

34. Plotinus, *Enneads*, 3.1.3–5; trans. MacKenna, 164, 167, 180. Cf. Ivry, "Neoplatonic Currents in Maimonides," 118–26.

35. Plotinus, *Enneads*, 4.8.5; trans. Lewis, 239: "the souls enter this world of their own accord, and by the will of the creator, so that through them He may govern, beautify and adorn this world." See too 6.8.13, and the comments of Seeskin, *Maimonides on the Origin of the World*, 117.

36. Plotinus, *Enneads*, 5.2.1; trans. Lewis, 291–95.

37. Plotinus, *Enneads*, 2.4.5, 3.4.1, 3.9.3; trans. MacKenna, 107, 186, 252.

38. Plotinus, *Enneads*, 1.8.3, 1.8.7, 2.4.16; trans. MacKenna, 73, 107. See Rist, "Plotinus on Matter and Evil," 155ff.

39. Ivry, "Neoplatonic Currents in Maimonides," 127–39.

40. Madelung, "Aspects of Ismāʿīlī Theology," 53–65; Farhad Daftary, *The Ismāʿīlīs*, 144–255.

41. Shlomo Pines drew attention to the presence of Ismāʿīlī themes in Halevi and other philosophers in his monograph "Shīʿite Terms and Conceptions in Judah Halevi's Kuzari," 219–305. Cf. further Ivry, "Ismāʿīlī Theology and Maimonides' Philosophy," 271–99.

42. Walker, *Early Philosophical Shiism* 83–86; Al-Sijistānī, *Le dévoilement des choses cachée: Kashf al-Mahjūb*, 36, 50; Walker, "The Ismāʿili Vocabulary of Creation," 75–85.

43. Walker, *Early Philosophical Shiism*, 98–101; De Smet, *La quiétude de l'intellect*, 356–59.

44. Cf. the summary of Fatimid Ismāʿīlī doctrines in Corbin, *History of Islamic Philosophy*, 79–92.

45. Al-Kirmānī went even further than his predecessors, rejecting any intermediary between God and creation, while still denying causal agency to a totally unknowable God. See Al-Kirmānī, *Kitāb rāḥat al-ʿaql*, 171–75; De Smet, *La quiétude de l'intellect*, 110, 118–20; Walker, *Ḥamīd al-Dīn al-Kirmānī*, 85.

46. *Guide*, 2.25, p. 328; see below, p. 119.

47. Al-Kirmānī introduces the concept of emanation after the unique and inexplicable "origination" of Intellect, the first eternally created being. Walker, *Ḥamīd al-Dīn al-Kirmānī*, 91–98.

48. Pines, "Shīʿite Terms and Conceptions in Judah Halevi's Kuzari," 240–43.

49. De Smet, *La quiétude de l'intellect*, 37–83, 110–18, 343–78.

50. Ibid., 361–64, and cf. below, p. 142.

51. Charles Butterworth has translated much of this text in Parens and Macfarland, *Medieval Political Philosophy*, 36–55.

52. Cf. Miriam Galston's analysis of "Alfarabi and Religious Multilevel Writing" in *Politics and Excellence*, 43–47.

53. Alfarabi, *Kitāb al-milla wa nuṣūṣ ukhrā*, 46; Alfarabi, *Alfarabi: The Political Writings*, 97. In chapter 17 of *The Views of the Inhabitants of the Virtuous City* Alfarabi calls the representations or symbols of the truth *mithalāt*. See Alfarabi, *Al-Farabi on the Perfect State*, 278.

54. Alfarabi, *Kitāb al-milla wa nuṣūṣ ukhrā*, 47; Alfarabi, *Alfarabi: The Political Writings*, 98. See too Avicenna's *Al-Shifa: La logique* (vol. 6, *Al-Jadal*), 14.

55. Alfarabi, *Kitāb al-milla wa nuṣūṣ ukhrā*, 66; Alfarabi, *Alfarabi: The Political Writings*, 111.

56. Alfarabi, *Kitāb al-ḥurūf*, 131.

57. Ibid., 151, and see Mahdi, "Alfarabi on Philosophy and Religion," 6, 14.

58. Alfarabi, *Kitāb al-milla wa nuṣūṣ ukhrā*, 59; Alfarabi, *Alfarabi: The Political Writings*, 107.

59. Compare Maimonides' remarks about particular laws for which no cause can or ought to be found, in *Guide*, 3.26, p. 509, and see below, p. 200.

60. *Guide*, 3.27. See Berman's wide-ranging study of the congruence between Alfarabi's and

Maimonides' views on the relationship between philosophy, religion, jurisprudence, and theology, in "Maimonides, the Disciple of Alfarabi," 154–70.

61. Alfarabi, *Kitāb al-milla wa nuṣūṣ ukhrā*, 44; Alfarabi, *Alfarabi: The Political Writings*, 100.

62. As Pines notes, "Translator's Introduction," lxxxvi, Maimonides cites none of Alfarabi's "political" books in the *Guide*, despite their "strong influence" on him.

63. Alfarabi's views in this commentary are summarized by Pines, "The Limitations of Human Knowledge according to Al-Farabi, Ibn Bajja, and Maimonides," 404–7. See too Pines' French treatment of this topic in "Les limites de la métaphysique selon Al-Fārābī, Ibn Bājja, et Maimonide," 432–46.

64. *Guide*, 3.18, p. 476.

65. As detailed in the articles mentioned above in n. 63, Pines takes the denial of conjunction with immaterial substances, and hence of knowledge of metaphysics as concerns God and the immaterial intelligences, as allegedly expressed in Alfarabi's lost commentary on the *Nicomachean Ethics*, as the guidepost for interpreting Maimonides in a similar fashion. Davidson, "Maimonides on Metaphysical Knowledge," 3:49–103, has written a strong critique of Pines' interpretation; see too Altmann's response, "Maimonides on the Intellect and the Scope of Metaphysics," 110–29.

66. Galston, *Politics and Excellence*, 60–67.

67. Alfarabi, *Al-Farabi on the Perfect State*, 95–105, 199–203. Alfarabi's various statements about emanationism are discussed by Druart, "Al-Fārābī, Emanation and Metaphysics," 127–48.

68. Alfarabi explains the apparent lack of constancy in the emanations of the Agent Intellect as due to impediments external to it, including the lack of preparation of the person intended to receive the emanation; see his *The Letter Concerning the Intellect*, 220.

69. Alfarabi, *Al-Farabi on the Perfect State*, 221–25. Quoted in part by Kreisel, *Prophecy*, 243.

70. Alfarabi, *Al-Farabi on the Perfect State*, 245, 247.

71. Parens and Macfarland, *Medieval Political Philosophy*, 38–42.

72. For example, in his *Letter concerning the Intellect*, 220, Alfarabi has a person's intellect simply becoming "something closer" to the Agent Intellect; and in his lost commentary on the *Nicomachean Ethics*, Alfarabi denied conjunction with the Agent Intellect and immortality.

73. Cf. *Guide*, 1.74, p. 221; 2.9, p. 268; 2.24, p. 326; Langermann, "The True Perplexity," 159–71.

74. Cf. Ibn Bājja's *Tadbīr al-mutawaḥḥid*, partial translation by Lawrence Berman as *The Governance of the Solitary* in Parens and Macfarland, *Medieval Political Philosophy*, 98–104. See Stephen Harvey, "The Place of the Philosopher in the City according to Ibn Bājjah," 199–233.

75. *Guide*, 1.74, p. 221. Ibn Bājja, *Conjunction of the Intellect with Man*, ed. Fakhry, 155–73; trans. McGinnis and Reisman, 269–83. D'Ancona, *Man's Conjunction with Intellect*, 71–73, tellingly describes Ibn Bājja's doctrine of conjunction.

76. Cf. Ibn Ṭufayl, *Ibn Tufayl's Hayy Ibn Yaqzān*, 93–165, particularly 149. Political sections of the text, given as "Hayy the Son of Yaqzan," have been translated by George N. Atiyeh, in Parens and Macfarland, *Medieval Political Philosophy*, 106–22. See too Fradkin, "The Political Thought of Ibn Ṭufayl," 234–61.

77. McCallum, *Maimonides' Guide for the Perplexed: Silence and Salvation*, 6–9, 109–14, compares Ibn Ṭufayl's quest as an "isolate" for communion with God with Maimonides' politically nuanced approach.

78. See Dobbs-Weinstein, "Maimonides' Reticence toward Ibn Sīnā," 281–96, particularly 285; Warren Zev Harvey, "Maimonides' Avicennianism," 107–19; Steven Harvey, "Avicenna's Influence on Jewish Thought," 333–35.

79. Cf. comprehensive summaries of Avicenna's work in McGinnis, *Avicenna*, and Goodman, *Avicenna*.

80. See introduction, pp. 5, 6. Griffel, *Al-Ghazālī's Philosophical Theology*, 98, believes, however, that there is only a "very loose connection" between *The Intentions of the Philosophers* and the *Incoherence*.

81. See, though, Eran, "Al-Ghazālī and Maimonides on the World to Come and Spiritual Pleasures," 137–66. Al-Ghazālī's *The Incoherence of the Philosophers* treats many of the issues that Maimonides addresses in the *Guide*, resolving them often in similar ways. Cf. Ivry, "The *Guide* and Maimonides' Philosophical Sources," 68–70, and see below, pp. 101–2 n. 65.

82. Cf. Avicenna, *The Metaphysics of The Healing*, 29–34. See too the key passages in Avicenna's writings on this theme assembled by Hourani, "Ibn Sīnā on Necessary and Possible Existence," 74–86.

83. *Guide*, 2.1, p. 247; and see the nineteenth and twentieth premises in the introduction to the second part of the *Guide*, p. 238.

84. See, for example, Pines, "Translator's Introduction," xciv.

85. Avicenna, *The Metaphysics of The Healing*, 327, 363; the *Risāla fī sirr al-qadar*, quoted and discussed by Hourani as "Ibn Sina's Essay on the Secret of Destiny," 25–48. See, however, Ivry, "Destiny Revisited," 160–71.

86. Avicenna, *Al-Shifā', K. al-Ibāra*, 72; cf. too Avicenna, *The Metaphysics of The Healing*, 350–54; Avicenna, *Avicenna's Psychology*, 32–38.

87. Avicenna, *The Metaphysics of The Healing*, 9.6, pp. 339–47; below, p. 174.

88. Avicenna, *The Metaphysics of The Healing*, 327; McGinnis, *Avicenna*, 207; Acar, *Talking about God and Talking about Creation*, 131–49.

89. Avicenna, *The Metaphysics of The Healing*, 6.2, p. 203; Acar, *Talking about God and Talking about Creation*, 170–85. Janssens, "Creation and Emanation in Ibn Sīna," 470–77, describes Avicenna's struggle to reconcile creation and emanation; McGinnes, *Avicenna*, 196–202, discusses Avicenna's arguments for an eternal universe.

90. Avicenna, *The Metaphysics of The Healing*, 8.6 and 8.7, pp. 283–98; Avicenna, "The Salvation: *Metaphysics*, II. 18–19," in McGinnis and Reisman, *Classical Arabic Philosophy*, 216–19. Cf. Marmura, "Some Aspects of Avicenna's Theory of God's Knowledge of Particulars," 299–312; Acar, *Talking about God and Talking about Creation*, 94–101.

91. Avicenna, *The Metaphysics of The Healing*, 8.4, p. 274; 8.5, p. 282.

92. Above, p. 40, and see Walker, *Ḥamīd al-Dīn al-Kirmānī*, 36.

93. The emergence of the intellects and souls of the spheres is described in Avicenna, *The Metaphysics of The Healing*, 331.

94. Avicenna wrote on prophecy in a number of compositions, integrating it with his epistemology. Fazlur Rahman has translated book 2, chapter 6 of the *Kitāb al-Najāt* as *Avicenna's Psychology*, and cf. 35–37. Parallel material is found in Avicenna's chapter on the soul in his *Al-Shifā'*, and selected translations are in McGinnis and Reisman's *Classical Arabic Philosophy*, 199–205. See too Avicenna's remarks on prophecy in the metaphysics section of his *Al-Shifā', The Metaphysics of the Healing*, 364–74. Cf. also Avicenna's *Fī ithbāt al-nubuwwāt*, "On the Proof of Prophecies and the Interpretation of the Prophets' Symbols and Metaphors," 113–21. Cf. also Rahman, *Prophecy in Islam*, 20, 30–91.

95. Rahman, *Prophecy in Islam*, 36–39; Avicenna, "On the Proof of Prophecies and the Interpretation of the Prophets' Symbols and Metaphors," xiii; cf. too Avicenna, *Ibn Sīnā: Livre des directives et remarques*, 507, 514.

96. Avicenna, *The Metaphysics of The Healing*, 366.

97. In the *Al-Shifā'* chapter on the soul, in McGinnis and Reisman, *Classical Arabic Philosophy*, 204; in *Al-Najāt*, in Avicenna, *Avicenna's Psychology*, 36.

98. Pines, "Translator's Introduction," cii; Warren Zev Harvey, "Maimonides' Avicennianism," 117.

99. Warren Zev Harvey, "Maimonides' Avicennianism," 107–19.

100. Avicenna gives memory diverse functions, and adds an "estimative" faculty to the imagination to account for intuited responses of fear or joy that are triggered by sensory perceptions.

101. Rahman, *Prophecy in Islam*, 15. See too Davidson, *Alfarabi, Avicenna and Averroes on Intellect*, 85–87.

102. Avicenna, *Avicenna's Psychology*, 58–63; McGinnis and Reisman, *Classical Arabic Philosophy*, 195–99.

103. *Guide*, 1.74, p. 221.

104. That is, Averroes' *Faṣl al-maqāl* and *Kashf 'an manāhij al-adilla*; the former work, known as the *Decisive Treatise*, in Averroës, *The Book of the Decisive Treatise Determining the Connection Between the Law and Wisdom, & Epistle Dedicatory*, 1–33. Sarah Stroumsa has subjected the literary corpora of both Averroes and Maimonides to a thorough examination in "The Literary Corpus of Maimonides and Averroes," 223–41, and see p. 234 in particular.

105. Pines, "Translator's Introduction," cviii–cxxiii. For recent comparisons of select themes in Maimonides' and Averroes' writings, see Ivry, "Getting to Know Thee," 143–56, and Kogan, "Two Gentlemen of Cordova," 157–227.

106. Averroes, *Averroes' Tahafut Al-Tahafut (The Incoherence of the Incoherence)*, 264.

107. Averroes' views are presented largely by way of commentaries he wrote on Aristotle's psychological treatises, the *Parva naturalia* and the *De anima*, treating the latter work three times. Cf. Ivry, "Averroes' Three Commentaries on *De anima*," 199–216. Cf. too Black, "Conjunction and the Identity of Knower and Known in Averroes," 159–84.

108. *Guide*, 1.68, p. 165; 2.37, p. 374; 2.38, p. 377; 3.8, p. 432; 3.51, p. 620; 3.52, p. 629. Cf. Ivry, "The Logical and Scientific Premises of Maimonides' Thought," 73–77.

Chapter 4

1. *Guide*, p. 6.

2. *Guide*, p. 5. Cf. Arthur Hyman, "Maimonides as Biblical Exegete," 1–12.

3. Of course, Moses was a prophet too, but of a singular kind, his Torah traditionally differentiated from the books of the Prophets.

4. BT Hagigah, 11b, 13a; *Guide*, p. 7.

5. Pines, 23: "Instruction."

6. Munk, 19.14, *bi-ab'ad ta'wīl*.

7. Pines, 18, "the vulgar." Munk, 12.11, *al-jumhūr*.

8. *Guide*, 1.4, 1.23, 1.44, 1.45. The full implications of Maimonides' position, and its relation to Muslim and Christian theology, are brought out by Wolfson, "Maimonides on the Unity and Incorporeality of God," 433–57.

9. *Guide*, 1.11, 1.13, 1.15, 1.22, 1.23.

10. *Guide*, 1.26.

11. *Guide*, 1.11, 1.35.

12. *Mutassil* in Arabic (Munk, 15.18); *Guide*, 1.1, p. 23. Cf. below, p. 134.

13. Cf. Berman, "Maimonides on the Fall of Man," 1–15.

14. Maimonides besmirches the man's character as well as intellectual capability, and denigrates as well the value of books of history and poetry. Whatever the polemical or rhetorical dimension of this interjection, it is indicative of Maimonides' attitude to these nonphilosophical pursuits.

15. *Guide*, 1.2, p. 24. Cf. Kreisel, *Maimonides' Political Thought*, 71–75.

16. To be responsible for his disobediance and to deserve punishment, would not Adam have had to know from the start that it is bad to disobey God, and that it is bad to be bad? That is, would not Adam have had to be endowed with a practical intellect initially?

17. Cf. Klein-Braslavy, "The Creation of the World and Maimonides' Interpretation of Gen. i–v," 71–77.

18. Cf. chapter 10 below.

19. In BT Hagigah 14b, R. Aqiba is said to be the only one of four sages who was able to enter and leave a mystical garden or *pardes* in peace. Stern (*Matter and Form*, 81–94), regards this as a key parable that reveals Maimonides' belief in the spiritual peace that follows upon accepting scientific limitations.

20. Primarily *Guide*, 1.68 and 1.72.

21. Literally, "the Torah speaks as the language of man," *dibberah Torah ke-leshon benei adam*," *Guide*, 1.33. The expression is found in BT Yebamot, 71a and Baba Metsiʿa, 31b. Maimonides first uses this phrase in *Guide*, 1.26, seeing the Torah as accommodating its idea of God to popular comprehension, since people project human attributes upon the deity.

22. *Guide*, 1.35, pp. 80, 81; Munk, 54.6–9, 54.30.

23. *Guide*, 1.35, p. 80.

24. *Guide*, 1.36. Maimonides says such people "deserve destruction," *istiḥāq al-ḥalāk* (Munk, 57.6).

25. *Guide*, 1.46, p. 98; Munk, 66.10–13.

26. Cf. *Guide*, 1.54, p. 126; below, pp. 59, 60.

27. *Guide*, 1.34, pp. 76, 77; Munk, 52.7.

28. *Guide*, 1.34, p. 78; Munk, 53.13.

29. "Flashes" is Pines' translation of *talwīḥ* (Munk, 53.14). In his Hebrew translation of the *Guide*, Schwarz, p. 82, reads this as "hints," *remez*. In the introduction to the first part of the *Guide*, at p. 7, Maimonides refers to the lightning flashes that illuminate a prophet's mind and that can affect less endowed individuals as well. This is a metaphor that Avicenna as well as Al-Ghazālī employs.

30. *Guide*, p. 43; Munk, 29.9. As Maimonides says, "particularized privation" (as opposed to "absolute privation") is a concomitant of matter, the particular form that a given matter does not have but that it is capable of receiving.

31. Cf. *Timaeus*, 50D.

32. *Guide*, p. 13.

33. See below, p. 171.

34. *Guide*, p. 61. Munk, 41.17.

35. Maimonides himself says the issue will be treated later, alluding to *Guide*, 2.26. As noted above (pp. 39, 46), Shīʿī authors and Avicenna used *ibdāʿ* to describe the action of God as the *mubdiʿ* or "originator" (from nothing) of the world.

36. *Guide*, 1.47, p. 105. That God is best described as being an intellect does not mean that He has an intellect, for Maimonides. Cf. below, pp. 63, 64.

37. *Guide*, 1.49. Building on a midrashic view that identifies each angel with a single mission, Maimonides regards each angelic apparition as equivalent to a single idea.

38. Pines, 206; cf. below, pp. 79, 83.

39. Munk, 73.17, *muʿẓam man yanẓur*, let alone the majority of simple believers. Maimonides is addressing intellectuals, but his comments are intended for a wider audience, for all his attempt to ward off the uninitiated.

40. "Conviction" in Arabic is the same word (*iʿtiqād*) as "belief." The corroborative aspect of this statement is conveyed by the Arabic *innahu ka-dhalika* (Munk, 74.26), in the sentence that Pines, 111, translates: "belief is not the notion that is uttered, but the notion that is represented in the soul when it has been averred of it that it is *in fact* [my italics] just as it has been represented." A more literal translation of the last part of this sentence would read, "when it has been asserted of it that it is just like that according to which it has been represented."

41. *Guide*, p. 111; Munk, 75.12.

42. *Guide*, p. 112.

43. *Guide*, p. 113. Maimonides then refers to a demonstration of this that he will offer, which presumably is to *Guide*, 2.26.

44. *Guide*, 1.54, p. 124; see below, p. 59.

45. Following Aristotle, *Physics*, 4.11.219a1. Maimonides lists the interrelationship of time and motion as the fifteenth premise needed to establish the existence of God, in the introduction to the second part of the *Guide*, p. 237.

46. *Guide*, p. 118. This statement may be seen as emblematic of much of Maimonides' remarks throughout the book.

47. *Guide*, pp. 122f. Maimonides says at first that "it makes no difference" whether these attributes belong to the category of actions or relations, as long as what he has said about the latter category be borne in mind, i.e., that relations are imagined to exist, but do not.

48. Pines, "The Limitations of Human Knowledge according to Al-Fārābī, Ibn Bājja, and Maimonides," 99, views Maimonides' remarks in chapter 54 as a total denial of the possibility of any metaphysical knowledge of God, even for Moses. Where Maimonides seems to give Moses unique access to such knowledge, as at *Guide*, 1.38, Pines, 93, considers Maimonides as indulging in an unverifiable "philosophical theology."

49. *Guide*, p. 127; Munk, 87.5.

50. Munk, 84.24, *fāʿil afʿāl*. Pines, 124, translates this as "He performs actions," giving the impression that God acts directly, in an ad hoc manner. This is an impression Maimonides wanted to convey to those who did not follow him carefully, though his Arabic is sufficiently transparent to those who did to allow them to get his real understanding of the matter. At p. 125, Pines follows the Arabic more closely, though still equivocatingly, as "these are the actions proceeding from Him" (*al-sādirah minhu*, Munk, 84.27), translating as "proceeding" the term that in Arabic is often a synonym for (impersonal) emanation.

51. *Guide*, p. 123.

52. Thus, for example, Maimonides changes active verbs in the biblical account of God's response to Moses in Exodus 33:19 ("and He said," *va-yoʾmer*) to passive verbs ("and it was said to him," *wa-qila lahu*, Munk, 84:9), presumably but not necessarily, and certainly not literally, understanding the subject to be God. This substitution of the passive for the active voice is one Maimonides attributes in chapter 48 to Onkelos, an earlier exegete, to avoid biblical anthropomorphisms.

53. Cf. *Guide*, 3.17, p. 472, and see below, p. 164. Pines, 126, has Maimonides saying that

calamities occur to individuals "because of the deserts of those who are punished," translating *bi-ḥasab istiḥqāq alladhina ʿūqabū'* (Munk, 85.26).

54. Davidson, "Maimonides on Divine Attributes as Equivocal Terms," 37*–51*, considers Maimonides' treatment of these and other attributes to belie his designation of them as "purely" or "solely" equivocal.

55. *Guide*, p. 132, Munk, 90.3.

56. *Guide*, p. 132.

57. Munk, 92.23: *tufiḍu ʿanhu wujūdāt kathīra*. Pines, 136: "many other existents flowing from it."

58. So Pines, 133, translating *tasāmmuḥ fi al-ʿibāra*; Munk, 90.22 See Ivry, "The Logical and Scientific Premises of Maimonides' Thought," 81 n. 65.

59. Pines, 133, translating *al-tajammul*; Munk, 91.3, and see his translation of the *Guide*, Maimonides, *Le guide des égarés*, 1:237, *le sens collectif.*

60. Cf. Wolfson, "Maimonides on Negative Attributes," 195–230.

61. *Guide*, pp. 135, 136; Munk, 92.10–27.

62. *Guide*, p. 139; Munk, 95.5.

63. *Guide*, p. 144; Munk, 98.26.

64. Exodus 3:14. Literally, "I will be that which I will be," *ehyeh asher ehyeh.*

65. *Guide*, 1.63, p. 154.

66. Above, p. 45.

67. Or "active intellect," as Pines translates, *Guide*, p. 152; Munk, 104.21, *al-ʿaql al-faʿāl*. I prefer the term "Agent Intellect" to avoid confusion with the active intellect in a person when it acts as an intellect in act (*al-ʿaql bi'l-fiʿl*).

68. Alternatively, "the voice . . . was created," reading the Arabic *qawl* (Munk, 108.25) as the Hebrew *qol*, a reading favored by Michael Schwarz in his translation (Maimonides, *Moreh Nevukhim*, 1: 167). I give Pines' translation (158), though omitting the comma he chose to insert after "God."

69. Munk, 111.1.

70. Pines, "The Limitations of Human Knowledge according to Al-Fārābī, Ibn Bājja, and Maimonides," 93, considers it impossible, given the epistemological constraints on predicating attributes of God that Maimonides has enunciated, that this proposition could be intelligible; and the following analogy between God's and man's intellections "probably is not intended to prove anything."

71. *Metaphysics*, 12.7.1072b14 ff.

72. Above, p. 26.

73. *De anima*, 3.5.430a10 ff.

74. Cf. below, p. 94.

75. Alfarabi expressed the same idea; above, p. 43 n. 68.

76. *Guide*, p. 10.

77. Above, p. 3. My contribution to this industry: "Leo Strauss on Maimonides," 75–91. Cf. now Green, *Leo Strauss on Maimonides*, for a comprehensive review of Strauss's work.

78. Pines, 111; above, p. 57.

79. Wolfson, "The Terms *Taṣawwur* and *Taṣdiq* in Arabic Philosophy and Their Greek, Latin, and Hebrew Equivalents," 478–92.

80. Charles H. Manekin, "Belief, Certainty and Divine Attributes in the *Guide of the Perplexed*," 119–26.

81. *Guide*, p. 132; above, p. 61.

82. Stern, "Logical Syntax as a Key to a Secret of the *Guide of the Perplexed*" (Hebrew), 145, believes Maimonides does not consider abstraction of metaphysical concepts possible, given the limitations of our intellect and speech, captive as they are to the imagination. See Ivry, "The Logical and Scientific Premises of Maimonides' Thought," 80, for a response to this position.

83. Above, p. 25.

84. *Guide*, 1.52, p. 118; above, p. 59. Cf. now the analysis of Maimonides' treatment of divine attributes in Stern, "Maimonides on Language and the Science of Language," 198–207.

85. *Guide*, 1.61–64; above, p. 62.

86. Pines, "Translator's Introduction," xcv, believes it probable that Avicenna's adoption of negative theology gave it the "philosophic reputability" that allowed Maimonides to adopt it. Pines, "Shī'ite Terms and Conceptions in Judah Halevi's *Kuzari*," 295–97, traces the particular version Maimonides offers, that of "affirmation by way of negation"(*ithbāt min ṭarīq al-nafy*), to the Shī'i theologian Al-Kirmānī.

87. Cf. though Lobel, "Silence Is Praise to You," 25–49.

88. Stern, "Maimonides on Language and the Science of Language," 209, argues that privations of negations still affirm something of God, in that He "possesses a privation." Objections of this sort were made by Proclus and other late Hellenistic figures; De Smet, *La quiétude de l'intellect*, 79.

89. Above, p. 39.

90. Below, pp. 79, 83, 177.

91. Goodman contends, in "Maimonidean Naturalism," 67, that there are "virtual" possibilities, as opposed to actual ones, that allow God and the heavenly intelligences to exercise meaningful choice. "An event (pace Aristotle), is not to be called impossible *merely* [my italics] because it will never take place."

92. McGinnis, *Avicenna*, 182.

93. Above, p. 57. Cf. Janssens, "Creation and Emanation in Ibn Sīnā," 470–76.

Chapter 5

1. As the studies mentioned above, p. 32 n. 2, testify, the *mutakallimūn* were not all of one mind in their views, but Maimonides assumes that his readers would recognize his often unnuanced descriptions of *kalām* principles as authentic depictions.

2. Schwarz, in Maimonides, *Moreh Nevukhim*, 177 n. 7, cites *Guide*, 1.55 and 1.68, as sources for the view that God is without potentiality. Schwarz believes this to be an intentional contradiction on Maimonides' part.

3. See *Guide*, 2.12.

4. Or, more precisely, as containing spheres (*al-aflāk*) within spheres, or "globes" (*al-aqarr*, sing. *kurra*). Munk, 118.15; Pines, 172. Maimonides postpones further discussion of the heavens to *Guide*, 2.4, p. 257.

5. *Guide*, p. 172.

6. BT Hagigah, 12b.

7. *Guide*, p. 174.

8. Above, p. 21.

9. Averroes' view of monopsychism and related issues is discussed by Merlan, *Monopsychism*

Mysticism Metaconsciousness, 85–113. Cf. Ivry, "Conjunction in and of Maimonides and Averroes," 231–47.

10. Maimonides singles out the sixth-century philosopher John Philoponus and (anachronistically) the tenth-century philosopher Yahya ibn 'Adi. Pines, *Studies in Islamic Atomism*, 114, 117, feels that both Indian and late Greek thought, originating with Epicurus, are possible sources for *kalām* atomism. Alnoor Dhanani, *The Physical Theory of Kalām*, 97–100, summarizes Pines' view and finds further evidence of Epicurean influence upon at least the Basrian school of *kalām*.

11. Maimonides will repeat this crucial dependence of the one belief upon the other later in *Guide*, 2.25, p. 329.

12. *Guide*, p. 180: "The utmost power of one who adheres to a religious law and who has acquired knowledge of true reality consists, in my opinion, in his refuting the proofs of the philosophers bearing on the eternity of the world. How sublime a thing it is when the ability is there to do it!"

13. *Guide*, p. 183.

14. Though indebted to Muslim intermediary sources as well, Maimonides' ideas are based ultimately on Aristotle's *Physics, Metaphysics*, and *De caelo*; cf. Munk, in the commentary to his translation of Maimonides, *Le guide des égarés*, 1:354–59.

15. Above, p. 26.

16. As Pines comments in *Guide*, 2.9 n. 5, Maimonides translates both *kurra* and *falak* as "sphere," the latter term used here as well for "heaven." Freudenthal, "Maimonides on the Scope of Metaphysics alias Ma'ase Merkavah," 225, renders *kurra* as "globe" and *falak* as "orb," here and elsewhere.

17. Celestial matter would thus seem to have different properties when it composes the body of the sphere itself (transparency), and when it composes the stars and planets (luminosity).

18. *Guide*, 2.11, p. 273.

19. Maimonides refers to prime matter in *Guide*, 1.28, and see above, p. 57. He has yet to discuss this notion in any detail.

20. See above, p. 26.

21. *Guide*, p. 186.

22. *Guide*, p. 187.

23. *Guide*, p. 188. Munk, 1:364 n. 2, says Maimonides treats this issue in part 2, chapters 10 and 12.

24. *Guide*, p. 191.

25. *Guide*, p. 193.

26. *Guide*, 1.1, p. 23.

27. *Guide*, p. 192. Pines here, as well as elsewhere, calls emanation (*fayḍ*) an "overflow."

28. Though this may be an unintended error on Maimonides' part, writing "acquired" for Agent Intellect.

29. The diversity of *kalām* thought is well brought out in the extracts Pines brings in his *Studies in Islamic Atomism*. Cf. Michael Schwarz, "Who Were Maimonides' Mutakallimūn?," First Part, 159–209; Second Part, 143–72.

30. *Guide*, p. 201.

31. Schwarz, "Who Were Maimonides' Mutakallimūn?" Second Part, 175–83, finds little evidence in *kalām* writings for the atomization of time.

32. The *mutakallimūn* spoke of God as creating a certain quality and its contrary, rather

than the privation or nonexistence of an existent state. Schwarz, "Who Were Maimonides' Mutakallimūn?," Second Part, 143.

33. Schwarz, "Who Were Maimonides' Mutakallimūn?," Second Part, 169–72, does not find this premise held by the *mutakallimūn* of Maimonides' day or earlier.

34. *Guide*, p. 194.

35. *Guide*, p. 206.

36. Below, p. 84.

37. At *Guide*, 2.19, p. 308, Maimonides adapts this principle to the movements of the spheres.

38. Pines, "The Limitations of Human Knowledge according to Al-Fārābī, Ibn Bājja, and Maimonides," 96, believes that Maimonides' statements like this affirming immortality on the basis of conjunction with the Agent Intellect are part of his "philosophical theology" and not philosophically serious.

39. Maimonides could as well have mentioned Alfarabi's concurrence with this view, as mentioned in his *Al-Fārābī's The Political Regime*, 82; trans. Fillipowski, 43. I am indebted to Michael Schwarz for these citations.

40. *Guide*, 1.70, and see above, p. 74.

41. *Guide*, pp. 224, 225.

42. *Guide*, p. 224. In Pines translation, "if it is impossible for [a god] to exert an action upon the thing with which his activity has no connection," (*lā ta'alluq le-fi'lihi*); Munk, 157.2.

43. *Guide*, p. 226.

44. *Guide*, p. 229.

45. Translated by Pines as "Indwelling" here and elsewhere.

46. Pines, "Translator's Introduction," cxxvi.

47. Schwarz, "Who were Maimonides' Mutakallimūn?," First Part, 159–209; Second Part, 143–72, has subjected each of Maimonides' twelve *kalām* premises to critical examination and found sufficient confirmation of only half of them in the writings of the *mutakallimūn*.

48. Ibid., Second Part, 172.

49. *Guide*, p. 206. Schwarz, "Who were Maimonides' Mutakallimūn?," Second Part, 155, finds this premise, with its emphasis on an open-ended "admissibility" or "possibility," not particularly conspicuous in *kalām* texts, which prefer to concentrate on the related theme of God's "custom" or "habit" (*'āda*).

50. Cf. Ivry, "Maimonides on Possibility," 67–84.

51. *Guide*, p. 209; Munk, 146.10.

52. Maimonides follows Alfarabi in describing this stage of cognition. Cf. Kogan, "What Can We Know and When Can We Know it?" 123.

Chapter 6

1. Cf. Davidson, *Proofs for Eternity, Creation and the Existence of God in Medieval Islamic and Jewish Philosophy*, for Maimonides' proofs, pp. 197–201, 206–9, 240–48, 380–83.

2. Thirteenth premise, *Guide*, p. 237.

3. *Guide*, p. 240.

4. Aristotle, *Categories* 14, 15a14.

5. Aristotle, *Physics*, 3.1.200b26; *Metaphysics*, 11. 9.1065b5, and see *Guide*, p. 238, eighteenth premise.

6. *Guide*, p. 237, sixteenth premise. This establishes the basis for believing in the unity, or rather nonmultiplicity, of intellects after death.

7. *Guide*, p. 239; Munk, 167.18.

8. Munk, 167.29, *kulluhā qad tabarahanat burhān lā shaqq fīhi.*

9. *Guide*, p. 240.

10. Pines, 239, 240, translates *aulā* (Munk, 168.5, 168.24) as "most fitting" and *aḥrā* (Munk, 168.24) as "most probable."

11. *Guide*, p. 240; Munk, 168.23. I am indebted to Seymour Feldman for pointing this out to me. The ambiguity of the subject is due to the misleading demonstrative pronoun (*wa hadhhihi*) that begins the sentence quoted.

12. Cf. Klein-Braslavy, "The Creation of the World and Maimonides' Interpretation of Gen. i–v," 71.

13. *Guide*, p. 243. Maimonides calls the matter of the heavens a "fifth body." It is different from the bodies of the four elements in that the spheres and their bodies do not undergo change of any kind except in place, being always in motion.

14. Davidson, *Proofs for Eternity, Creation and the Existence of God in Medieval Islamic and Jewish Philosophy*, 240–49, offers a thorough analysis of Maimonides' proof from motion for the existence of God.

15. *Guide*, p. 246. Maimonides alludes to this proof at the end of *Guide*, 1.70, p. 175, calling it "the greatest proof through which one can know the existence of the deity."

16. This is a version of Avicenna's proof for the existence of a being necessarily existent by virtue of itself, discussed by Davidson, *Proofs for Eternity, Creation and the Existence of God in Medieval Islamic and Jewish Philosophy*, 281–98; Maimonides' construal (and misconstrual) of Avicenna's proof, 380–83.

17. *Guide*, p. 247. Maimonides words this argument in a way that makes it seem like a counterfactual past occurrence: if all possible existents were subject to generation and corruption, they would all have perished already. Now, this would be true in an eternal world through which all possible existents would have already passed (away). However, in a finite time-bound world possible existents may not yet have reached their end state as a species so as to require an external necessarily existing being. Maimonides thus here begs the question of the eternity of the world.

18. *Guide*, p. 248.

19. See below, pp. 100, 165.

20. *Guide*, p. 251.

21. Though Maimonides apparently believes, and wants the reader to believe, that as the Bible shows (when properly understood), the ancient Israelite community once possessed scientific knowledge of its own. See *Guide*, 1.71, p. 175; above, p. 74.

22. *Guide*, p. 254. Maimonides follows the opinion of Alexander of Aphrodisias in this, as he acknowledges.

23. Aristotle, *On the Heavens*, 2.2.2855a28–30; for Avicenna see above, pp. 46, 47 and n. 93.

24. *Guide*, p. 256. I have substituted "emanates" for Pines' "overflows."

25. Maimonides wants to distance God from the natural world, to avoid the mechanistic implications contained in Aristotle's image of the deity as an unmoved mover. It may be for this reason that Maimonides describes God as the "Necessary of Existence" at this point of his discussion.

26. *Al-khayarāt* (Munk, 178.19).

27. *Guide*, p. 260.

28. *Guide*, p. 263.

29. *Guide*, p. 263, and see *Timaeus* 28a ff., which Maimonides knew through secondary sources.

30. *Guide*, p. 266. Pines translates "choose," *mukhtār*, as "choose freely," following Maimonides in emphasizing the freedom to act that the angels, like God, supposedly possess.

31. Namely, Venus, Mercury, Mars, Uranus, and Saturn. The incorporation of the five planets in one sphere, or globe, was Maimonides' own contribution to astronomy. See Freudenthal, "Maimonides on the Scope of Metaphysics alias Ma'ase Merkavah," 225, and below, p. 152.

32. *Guide*, 2.10, p. 272. Langermann, "Maimonides' Repudiation of Astrology," 144, finds Maimonides' "fascination" with the number four "somewhat unusual."

33. *Guide*, p. 271. The theory regards the moon as responsible for the motion of the seas, and water in general; the sun for fire; the five planets for the various expressions of air; and the sphere of the fixed stars for the motion of the earth. The causes of each sphere's movements correspond to its component parts: the body of the sphere, its soul, intellect, and the "separate intellect which is its beloved."

34. *Guide*, p. 187. Maimonides does not specify here the particular provenance of the Agent Intellect in endowing the forms of all animated beings on earth. Cf. *Guide*, 2.4, p. 258.

35. See below, p. 105.

36. *Guide*, p. 274.

37. Munk, 191.27. Pines translates *khayarāt* interchangeably as "good things" and as "good effects," as above, n. 26.

38. Maimonides here is describing that emanation which is operative after that through which the world was created, which may be deliberately distracting from the pantheistic implications of the previous chapter.

39. *Guide*, 2.12, p. 279. Pines' translation: "He has caused to overflow to it everything in it that is produced in time." Maimonides describes God as the "efficient cause" of the world in His position as the source of the ubiquitous emanations that inform all being, though he has emphasized that they pass through intermediaries. Maimonides is careful not to call God the formal cause of being, though He is that too.

40. *Guide*, p. 280. The imagination, Maimonides says, "is really the 'evil impulse' [*yetzer ha-ra' ḥaqiqatān*]," so that the popular representations of God's actions are not just wrong, but morally reprehensible and equivalent to idolatry, as Maimonides defines it.

41. Langermann, "Maimonides' Repudiation of Astrology," 132, considers Maimonides' calling the action of the stars, or spheres, "emanation" (*fayḍ*, which Langermann terms "efflux") "strictly speaking . . . incorrect," as they are subject to the laws of physics.

42. Maimonides' own belief is a subject of much debate. Cf. the different interpretations offered by Klein-Braslavy, "The Creation of the World and Maimonides' Interpretation of Gen. i–v," 65–71; Fox, *Interpreting Maimonides*, 292–95; and Davidson, "Maimonides' Secret Position on Creation," 16–40.

43. *Guide*, p. 281. Pines renders "not from a thing" as "out of nothing."

44. Munk, 196.8, *bi-irādatahi wa mashi'atihi*.

45. *Guide*, pp. 282–84. Maimonides cites Plato's *Timaeus*, as well as Aristotle's report of Plato's view in *Physics*, 8.1.

46. *Guide*, p. 284.

47. Versions of Maimonides' arguments appear in the writings of many medieval authors; cf. Davidson, *Proofs for Eternity, Creation and the Existence of God in Medieval Islamic and Jewish Philosophy*, 13–29, 53–64.

48. *Guide*, p. 287.

49. *Guide*, p. 288; Munk, 201.10.

50. Stern, "Maimonides on the Growth of Knowledge and the Limitations of the Intellect," 189–91, finds that his unorthodox view of Aristotle as one who recognized the limits of metaphysical knowledge offered Maimonides a methodological paradigm of how to proceed as a philosopher.

51. Maimonides also quotes a passage from the *Topics* (1.11.104b15 ff.) in which Aristotle does appear to dismiss the argument for the eternity of the world, although Maimonides does not argue for this dismissal. Though Maimonides admires Alfarabi greatly, he faults the interpretation that that philosopher gave to this Aristotelian passage, since Alfarabi believed that Aristotle could not have doubted the eternity of the world.

52. *Guide*, p. 292; Munk, 203.16, *bi-hasab al-istidlāl min ṭabīʿa al-wujūd.*

53. Maimonides actually calls both positions "absurd," *shināʿa*, which may also be translated as Pines does in *Guide*, p. 294, as a "disgrace."

54. *Guide*, p. 294; Munk, 204.26.

55. *Guide*, p. 295.

56. *Guide*, p. 297.

57. Described by Maimonides in *Guide*, 2.14; above, p. 98.

58. *Guide*, p. 299. Maimonides quotes Alfarabi's *On the Intellect* for support here. See above, p. 43 n. 68.

59. *Guide*, p. 300.

60. *Guide*, 3.17, p. 474; below, p. 164.

61. Munk, 210.4; *Guide*, p. 301. Pines translates "essence" as "quiddity."

62. Munk, 210.11. The "being separate from matter," *al-mufāriq*, is of course God. The general thesis of an ostensibly changing yet essentially unchanging Will that Maimonides proposes for beings separate from matter holds only for the deity and the Agent Intellect. The other separate intellects of the spheres, though similarly without a material component, do not have a will that may be seen as varying in its expression.

63. Pines, in *Guide*, p. 303, as elsewhere, translates *akhtâra*, "he chose," as "chose freely." This is based on Maimonides' remarks in chapter 20; see below, p. 103.

64. Maimonides assumes that a purposive act must effect change in the purposed object, so that an eternally unchanging existent cannot be the product of a purposing will.

65. Davidson, *Proofs for Eternity, Creation and the Existence of God in Medieval Islamic and Jewish Philosophy*, 194–201, discusses Maimonides' use of the argument from particularization, and compares it to the arguments adduced by Al-Ghazālī.

66. Aristotle's *On Generation and Corruption* 2, chapters 3 and 4.

67. *Guide*, pp. 308 and 311; Aristotle's *Metaphysics*, 12.8.11074a15 ff.

68. Though Maimonides deviates from Aristotle and follows Alfarabi in discerning not one but two kinds of matter in the heavens. *Guide*, p. 309.

69. *Guide*, p. 314. Aristotle says in *Metaphysics*, 12.7.1072b16 only that the unmoved mover's actuality is pleasure.

70. Munk, 218.26.

71. In a section of his rebuttal of Avicenna's ideas that Maimonides may well have been

familiar with, Al-Ghazālī, *The Incoherence of the Philosophers*, 56–60, mounts a similar attack upon the philosophers' appropriation of will and choice to necessary divine agency.

72. As Munk comments in his translation of the *Guide*, 2.174 n. 1, the view that Maimonides attributed to Aristotle is really that developed by Alfarabi and Avicenna. Cf. above, pp. 43, 46.

73. *Guide*, p. 320; above, p. 37.

74. Munk, 224.5–7; *Guide*, p. 320.

75. An entirely different appraisal of this passage is found in Stern, "Maimonides on the Growth of Knowledge and the Limitations of the Intellect," 185.

76. Maimonides mentions Thābit ibn Qurra (ninth century), Al-Qabīsī (tenth century), and his near contemporary, Ibn Bājja (eleventh century).

77. Munk, 228.5; *Guide*, p. 326. Cf. Langermann, "The True Perplexity," 159–74.

78. *Guide*, p. 329.

79. Maimonides seems to disregard the Muslim philosophers' acceptance and endorsement of revealed law, coupled with their belief in an eternal world. Averroes, like Maimonides, even authored a comprehensive legal work, the *Bidāyat al-mujtahid wa-nihāyat al-muqtaṣid*, trans. by Imran Ahsan Khan Nyazee as *The Distinguished Jurist's Primer*.

80. *Guide*, p. 330. Cf. *Chapters of Rabbi Eliezer*, III.

81. Maimonides applies Moses' peroration in Deuteronomy 32:4,"The Rock, His work is perfect," to God's creatures.

82. Ecclesiastes 1:9, and see *Guide*, p. 344.

83. *Guide*, p. 345, referring to Genesis Rabbah and Midrash Qohelet.

84. Maimonides would have known paraphrases of this Aristotelian text as cited by Avicenna or others. Cf. Davidson's analysis, *Maimonides the Rationalist*, 116–24.

85. *Guide*, p. 349. The *midrashim* in question are Genesis Rabbah 3 and again, the *Chapters of Rabbi Eliezer*, III.

86. Avicenna, *The Metaphysics of The Healing*, 29.

87. Warren Zev Harvey, "Maimonides' Avicennianism," 113, has pointed out that Maimonides' proof for the existence of God conceived as a Necessary Existent assumes the existence of a physical universe, and thereby undermines the purely metaphysical nature of the proof as conceived by Avicenna. While Harvey believes Maimonides understood this, Davidson, *Proofs for Eternity, Creation and the Existence of God in Medieval Islamic and Jewish Philosophy*, 383, considers Maimonides unaware that he is misrepresenting Avicenna's position.

88. McGinnis, *Avicenna*, 135, believes that Avicenna thought the functions of the Giver of Forms corresponded with those of the Agent Intellect.

89. I once argued for consideration of this alternative, holding Maimonides to normative philosophical demands. Cf. Ivry, "Maimonides on Creation," 189–213.

90. See above, p. 38.

91. Among both Sunni and Shīʿī Muslims.

92. Munk, 178.12.

93. *Guide*, 3.51, pp. 621, 628.

94. In this chapter, Maimonides uses biblical citations to argue that the angels have will as well as choice. His identification of the separate intellects and spheres as angels allows us to attribute will to them also.

95. *Guide*, p. 274.

96. See above, p. 96, and compare the descriptions of these positions in Seeskin, *Searching for a Distant God*, 66–90.

97. *Guide*, p. 207, and see above, p. 79.

98. Maimonides may well have known that Muslim philosophers before him had made this very claim. Cf. Ben-Shammai, "Maimonides and Creation *Ex Nihilo* in the Tradition of Islamic Philosophy," 103–20.

99. Elsewhere, as in discussing the biblical tale of creation, Maimonides refers to the act of creation equivocally. See Klein-Braslavy, "The Creation of the World and Maimonides' Interpretation of Gen. i–v," pp. 65–71.

100. As Maimonides considers God before creation as not bound (voluntarily) by the laws and logic of postcreation physics, he does not feel that the creation of the world must follow immediately upon God's thought of it.

101. Dobbs-Weinstein speaks of the "essence" or essential pre-existential nature of prime matter, in "Matter as Creature and Matter as the Source of Evil," 222.

102. *Guide*, p. 285.

103. Roslyn Weiss, "Maimonides on the End of the World," 195–218, argues that Maimonides affirms the everlastingness of the world after its creation in order to endorse an Aristotelian view of a natural world that his denial of eternity *a parte ante* would seem to threaten.

104. Above, p. 103.

105. *Guide*, p. 319.

106. *Guide*, p. 320; Munk, 223.24, *idhā'āt al-shurūr*.

107. At *Guide*, p. 327 n. 12, Pines offers the version of this sentence that Maimonides' translator, Shmuel ibn Tibbon, had, a version that well may represent a revision of Maimonides' original statement. A forum on this passage was convened by Gad Freudenthal; I review the diverse interpretations given this passage in "*Guide* 2:24 and All That *(i)jāza*," 237–46.

108. *Guide*, p. 327. Munk, 229.1.

109. Cf. Langermann, "Maimonides and Astronomy," 1–11.

110. *Guide*, p. 328.

111. Cf. Averroes, *Averroes' Kitāb faṣl al-maqāl*, 50–62; and see the translated extract there from Averroes' *Kitāb al-kashf 'an manāhij al-adilla* dealing with allegorical interpretation, 78–81. See too the discussion in Ivry, "Ibn Rushd's Use of Allegory," 117–22.

112. Pines, 328, calls the esotericists "Islamic internalists," following the Arabic *ahl al-bāṭin*; he also refers to their "ravings" (*hadhayān*) as "crazy imaginings." Stroumsa, *Maimonides in His World*, 138–52, considers that Maimonides used this term in all his work to denote pseudoscientific assertions.

113. Maimonides adopts a different attitude entirely in his later *Treatise on Resurrection*; see above, p. 21.

114. Above, p. 101.

115. Manekin, "Divine Will in Maimonides' Later Writings," 207, posits that Maimonides could have conceived of an unchanging divine "novel will" that would rationalize miracles, though "whether this answer is philosophically satisfying is beside the point."

116. Above, p. 107.

Chapter 7

1. *Guide*, p. 360. Munk, 253.16. Actually, Maimonides refers to the "masses of pagans," *jumhūr al-jāhalīya*, as well as to "some" of the "common" Jews, *b'aḍ 'awām*. He is being careful not to

mention Muslims and Christians specifically, as well perhaps as to minimize the number of Jews who held this view, however widespread it was.

2. *Guide*, p. 364.

3. See *Guide*, 1.65, p. 158. The "created voice" of which Maimonides speaks is not a voice that God "has"; it is to be understood as part of the extraordinary sights and sounds at Sinai that are traceable ultimately to God, expressions of His will.

4. *Guide*, p. 167. See the seventh article of faith in the introduction of the *Commentary on the Mishnah* on Sanhedrin 10 (*Ḥeleq*), and the first book of the *Mishneh Torah* (*Yesodei ha-Torah*), 7.6.

5. Literally, "amphibolous" sense, *bi-al-tashkīk*.

6. At *Guide*, 3.39. Cf. Judah Halevi, *The Kuzari*, part 1, 47–78, particularly 73.

7. Above, pp. 34, 37, 38.

8. *Guide*, 2.12, p. 279. Emanation is the standard translation for the Arabic *fayḍ* that Maimonides uses, and see Munk, 260.20. Pines, *Guide*, p. 369, prefers to speak of an "overflow overflowing from God." He also calls the Agent Intellect the "Active" Intellect, both terms appropriate for the Arabic *al-ʿaql al-faʿāl*. I prefer referring to the Agent rather than Active Intellect, so as not to confuse it with the active intellect in man, known in Latin as intellect *in actu*, Arabic, *al-ʿaql bi'l-fiʿl*.

9. As we shall see, Maimonides exempts Moses from receiving emanations directly in his imagination.

10. Above, pp. 43, 47.

11. Cf. *Nicomachean Ethics*, 3.10.1182b2 ff., and see *Guide*, p. 371.

12. Pines, 372, "the perfect man who lives in solitude."

13. This is Alfarabi's conclusion as well, though he too is conflicted over the obligations the ruler has to himself and to his people. Cf. Galston, *Politics and Excellence*, 67, 92–94.

14. *Guide*, 2.37; Pines, 375: "and let his own perfection overflow toward them."

15. Cf. Avicenna's development of this theory, above, p. 47.

16. In this chapter Maimonides cites monasticism, pilgrimages, and "indulgence of appetites" as examples of improper religious behavior, thinly veiled criticisms of what Maimonides regarded as immoderate practices in Christianity and Islam.

17. This is directed more pointedly against Islam, without mentioning it by name and even refusing to call its legal system a *shariʿa*, religious law.

18. *Guide*, p. 381; Munk, 270.5. Cf. Aristotle's *Politics*, 1.2.1253a2–38.

19. *Guide*, p. 382.

20. That is, the prophet qua lawgiver, though the majority of the MSS utilized by Munk, 270.25, have *al-nabī aw wāḍiʿ al-nāmūṣ*, "the prophet or lawgiver," making it appear the two are not synonymous in this context. The medieval Hebrew translations follow a minority reading that mentions only the prophet. The Arabic I have translated as "lawgiver" is literally "the one who lays down the *nomos*," rendered by Pines as "the bringer of the *nomos*." The Arabic for "law" here, *nāmūṣ*, is clearly derived from the Greek. In some of his writings, Alfarabi refers simply to a "supreme ruler," but in his *Perfect State* this person, a philosopher-king, is also a prophet. Galston, *Politics and Excellence*, 100.

21. As depicted in Islamic sources by William Muir, *The Life of Moḥammad*, 511, 515; see though W. Montgomery Watt, *Muhammad at Medina*, 329–32.

22. *Guide*, 2.36.

23. Maimonides' designation of the separate intellects of the heavens as angels (*Guide*, 2.4, p. 258) is his way of imagining their natures in popular terms.

24. Cf. Kravitz, "The Revealed and the Concealed" (1969), 15.

25. These terms, which denote the same thing, are common in the Bible and rabbinic literature, which is probably why Maimonides introduces them without prior analysis. He does the same thing for the *Shekhinah*, which Pines translates as "Indwelling."

26. Cf. above, p. 127, the discussion of how Maimonides distinguishes political leaders from prophets and philosophers.

27. *Guide*, p. 398: "The second degree: It consists in the fact that an individual finds that a certain thing has descended upon him." Pines has "that a certain thing" for the Arabic "as though a certain thing" (*ka-anna*, Munk, 282.25). Without the qualification, Maimonides could appear to be saying that the Holy Spirit literally dictates these books, an anthropomorphic treatment of the Holy Spirit foreign to Maimonides' thought.

28. *Guide*, p. 403.

29. Maimonides begins his introduction to the first part of the Guide, p. 5, emphasizing the importance of understanding the language of the Bible.

30. *Guide*, p. 409. The designation of God as "First Cause" has Aristotelian overtones, but Maimonides immediately qualifies his use of the term, saying, "I mean God's will and choice" (*a'nī mashī'a lāhu wa-ikhtīyārahu*; Pines, "free choice"). In this Maimonides wishes to distance himself from what he regards as Aristotle's mechanistic, necessitarian approach to causality.

31. Cf. above, p. 78.

32. See below, p. 146, for a completely opposite reading of this chapter.

33. For Alfarabi, see Kreisel, *Prophecy*, 246; for Avicenna, above, p. 47. See too Macy, "Prophecy in al-Farabi and Maimonides," 185–201.

34. Above, pp. 63–65. The following discussion of the intellect is taken largely from my " The Logical and Scientific Premises of Maimonides' Thought," 73–76.

35. Maimonides' mention of the initial act of cognition as one of abstraction indicates the influence upon him here of Alfarabi, or possibly Ibn Bājja. Avicenna's influence is marked, however, in Maimonides' depiction of the subsequent stages of intellection. See, for a concise summary of the various positions of Maimonides and his predecessors, Kogan, "What Can We Know and When Can We Know it?," 122–28; and for a more extensive treatment, Davidson, *Alfarabi, Avicenna, and Averroes on Intellect*, 44–207.

36. *Guide*, p. 164; Munk, 113.8.

37. *Davidson, Alfarabi, Avicenna, and Averroes on Intellect,* 10, 11. Altmann, "Maimonides on the Intellect and the Scope of Metaphysics," 74, 75, assumes that Maimonides subsumed the intellect *in habitu* within the activity of the intellect *in actu*.

38. Alfarabi, *The Letter concerning the Intellect*, 117, 119; Altmann, "Maimonides on the Intellect and the Scope of Metaphysics," 77, and n. 136; Davidson, *Alfarabi, Avicenna, and Averroes on Intellect*, 50, 63, 69.

39. *Guide*, 3.8, p. 432.

40. These are the correspondences that Lawrence Kaplan also arrives at, for a number of reasons, in his article "Maimonides on the Miraculous Element in Prophecy," 233–56. Roslyn Weiss, "Natural Order or Divine Will," 1–26, has summarized and critiqued Kaplan's view; Davidson's, as expressed in his "Maimonides' Secret Position on Creation," 16–40; and the view of Warren Z. Harvey, "A Third Approach to Maimonides' Cosmogony-Prophetology Puzzle," 287–301.

41. *Guide*, 1.52, 1.53, 1.56.

42. *Guide*, 1.55.

43. Cf. Reines, "Maimonides' Concept of Miracles," 279.

44. *Guide*, p. 364.

45. Saadia's views on a "created voice" (*qol nivra'*) as well as "created speech" (*dibbur nivra'*) and "created glory" (*kavod nivra'*) have been summarized by Kreisel, *Prophecy*, 56–68. Schwarz (Maimonides, *Moreh Nevukhim*, 1: 379 n. 14) points out that *kalām* theologians taught that God created movements in the air that were heard as speech. The Shī'ī theologians regularly reified God's command (*amr*), some placing it at the top of the celestial substances they saw as intermediaries between God and man. Cf. Shlomo Pines, "Amr," 404–6.

46. *Guide*, 2.47, p. 407.

47. *Guide*, p. 366.

48. *Guide*, 2.37, p. 374: "men of science engaged in speculation." Munk, 264.13, *al-'ulamā' ahl al-naẓr*, i.e, theoretical scientists.

49. Maimonides' *Commentary on the Mishnah*, Seder Neziqin, 214; Kreisel, *Prophecy*, 177. Maimonides may be echoing here statements found in Alfarabi as well as in Avicenna that have the prophets occasionally receive direct emanations from the spheres that take the form of particular images, revelations that do not need to be transformed into popular speech by the imagination. Cf. above, pp. 43, 47.

50. Cf. Ivry, "Ismā'īlī Theology and Maimonides' Philosophy," 290 n. 72.

51. Cf. Maimun b. Joseph, "Maimon: Letter of Consolation of Maimun Ben Joseph," 24 (Arabic), 100 (English); Ivry, "The Image of Moses in Maimonides' Thought," 123.

52. BT Sotah 13b.

53. Seder Zera'im, 4.

54. Cf. the survey of sources in Ivry, "The Image of Moses in Maimonides' Thought," 124–31.

55. Bland, "Moses and the Law According to Maimonides," 49–66.

56. Ivry, "Ismā'īlī Theology and Maimonides' Philosophy," 296.

57. De Smet, *La quiétude de l'intellect*, 361. Al-Kirmānī, *Kitāb Rāḥat al-'Aql*, 301, 304.

58. Cf. Kreisel, *Maimonides' Political Thought*, 80, 81.

59. Above, p. 20.

60. This ideal was entertained by Ibn Bājja in his *The Governance of the Solitary*, and is also the ideal of Maimonides' contemporary Abū Bakr ibn Ṭufayl, whose fictional hero, Hayy ibn Yaqzān, flees society. See above, p. 44.

61. *Guide*, 2.37; Pines, 375: "men of science," translating *'ulemā'*, literally "learned men." For Maimonides, the philosopher was a man of science, as was the prophet too, though the latter had special cognitive gifts.

62. This term was commonly used to represent the mission of the Shī'ī leader or *dā'ī*, whose responsibility was to lead his people and try to convert others. Maimonides' mission is to counter such efforts and strengthen the faith of his people.

63. Strauss, "The Philosophic Foundation of the Law," 132, presents Plato's thought as the ultimate inspiration for Maimonides' political philosophy.

64. Alfarabi, *Alfarabi on the Perfect State*, 219–25.

65. Alfarabi, *Kitāb al-milla wa nuṣūṣ ukhrā*, 66. Cf. further above, p. 41.

66. Alfarabi, *Kitāb al-ḥurūf*, 151.

67. Avicenna's balancing of Islamic religious terms with his philosophical tenets, substantially similar to Maimonides' treatment of this matter, is well described by Janssens, "Ibn Sīnā's Ideas of Ultimate Realities," 253–69.

68. It is inconceivable to Maimonides that God speaks or appears; consequently, Maimonides follows the tendency of Onkelos in his early Aramaic translation of the Pentateuch to transform verbs describing God's actions from active to passive states.

69. *Guide*, 2.41, pp. 385–87.

70. Cf. Pines' excursus in his "Studies in Abul-Barakāt al-Baghdādī's Poetics and Metaphysics," 195–98; Altmann, "The Religion of the Thinkers," 35–52.

71. Pp. 132–33.

72. *Guide*, p. 410. Munk, 293.5–10.

73. Gellman, "Freedom and Determinism in Maimonides' Philosophy," 146–50, offers another reading of this passage that also rejects determinism.

74. Below, pp. 179, 181.

Chapter 8

1. *Guide*, p. 415; Munk, 297.20, *'alā mā 'aṣāhu an ẓuhira . . . bilā shaqq*, which Pines translates as "that which may have appeared to me as indubitably clear." Maimonides thus appears to be expressing ambivalence toward the extent of his "indubitable" knowledge, though he again insists upon it some sentences later.

2. Following Schwarz, in Maimonides, *Moreh Nevukhim*, 2:428, as supported in n. 11; Pines, 416, "conjecture and supposition."

3. *Guide*, p. 416. Maimonides intimates he is also deterred by the negative response to his teachings that he could anticipate; as he cryptically puts it, not teaching the subject explicitly "is imposed by opinion" (or judgment, *al-ra'y*).

4. *Guide*, 1.72, and see above, p. 75. In the notes to his French translation of the *Guide*, Salomon Munk evaluates the medieval commentators' views and offers his own interpretation of Maimonides' symbolism; see Maimonides, *Le guide des égarés*, 3: 7–44. In the notes to his Hebrew translation of the *Guide*, Michael Schwarz presents Munk's views together with those of Wilhelm Bacher and more recent scholars; see Maimonides, *Moreh Nevukhim*, 2: 428–40. Cf. now Davies, *Method and Metaphysics in Maimonides' Guide for the Perplexed*, 107–33; Kreisel, "From Esotericism to Science," 34–46.

5. Ezekiel 1:5–10. The term Pines translates as "living creatures," *ḥayyot*, is usually given as "animals," which fits better Maimonides' understanding of Ezekiel's psychology, as explained in *Guide*, 3.6, p. 427.

6. See Munk's translation, in Maimonides, *Le guide des égarés*, 3: 7 n. 1, and cf. *Guide*, 2.9 and 2.10. The outermost all-encompassing sphere mentioned in 2.9 is ignored here, probably because Maimonides cannot stretch his fourfold schematization any further, having already collapsed the five planets into one unit.

7. *Guide*, 3.2. Pines, 419, actually translates the equivocal term *ru'aḥ* as "air," following Maimonides in *Guide*, 1.40. The term is given as "spirit" in modern translations of Ezekiel 1:12.

8. *Guide*, 3.2, p. 417, and cf. Ezekiel 1:5 and 10:14. Samuel ibn Tibbon, followed by Munk (*Le guide des égarés*, 3: 7 n. 1), interpreted Maimonides' emphasis on the human faces of the creatures to signify that the spheres possess intellects.

9. *Guide*, 3.3, p. 422.

10. Ezekiel 1:15–21, repeated in 10:9–17.

11. *Guide*, p. 421, and cf. Ezekiel 1:19.

12. The commentators' identification of the wheels with sublunar matter is no doubt

strengthened by Maimonides' rejection of Jonathan ben Uzziel's interpretation of them as celestial spheres; see *Guide*, 3.4, p. 423. Nevertheless, as Munk mentions (19 n. 3), Isaac Abravanel (1437–1508) understood Maimonides to believe that the living creatures were the separate intellects of the heavens, the wheels were the heavenly bodies of the spheres, and the eyes in the wheels were the stars in the spheres.

13. Ezekiel 1:22–28, and cf. 10:18.

14. Munk, 23 n. 1.

15. *Guide*, p. 430.

16. *Guide*, 3.6, p. 427.

17. BT Ḥagigah, 13b.

18. Maimonides may here be making an exception for Ezekiel, as Maimonides regards the limit of cognition for most human beings as the Agent Intellect, the last of the separate intellects. See above, p. 135. Freudenthal, "Maimonides on the Scope of Metaphysics alias Ma'ase Merkavah," 228, believes that Maimonides deliberately omits specific mention of the separate intellects.

19. *Guide*, p. 426.

20. Munk, in Maimonides, *Le guide des égarés*, 3:33 nn. 2 and 3.

21. *Guide*, 3.7, p. 430.

22. *Guide*, p. 6.

23. *Guide*, p. 10.

24. Above, pp. 24–26, and see Kreisel, "From Esotericism to Science," 35.

25. Freudenthal, "Maimonides on the Scope of Metaphysics alias Ma'ase Merkavah," 225.

26. Ibid., 227.

27. See too Stern, *Matter and Form*, 295–301.

28. Kreisel, "From Esotericism to Science," 43 n. 65, finds that while Maimonides may here be expressing a new astronomical scheme, "he does not at all retreat from the Aristotelian view of the structure of the world."

29. Maimonides places Venus and Mercury above the sun and not below it, as was more common. Freudenthal, "Maimonides on the Scope of Metaphysics alias Ma'ase Merkavah," 225.

30. Altmann, "Maimonides' Attitude toward Jewish Mysticism," 200–219.

Chapter 9

1. *Guide*, p. 430, Munk, 309.27. The noun *'araḍ* (accident) in its verbal construction can be translated as "happens to," much like the Greek *symbebekai*.

2. Following originally Neoplatonic teachings. Cf. above, p. 39.

3. Adapting Solomon's remarks in Proverbs 6:26.

4. *Guide*, p. 432, my translation. In speaking of conjunction (*ittiṣāl*) with the "divine intellect," *al-'aql al-ilāhī*, and its emanative powers, Maimonides actually is referring to the Agent Intellect, the immediate source of emanated forms and the object of a person's quest for conjunction.

5. *Guide*, p. 433, Munk, 311.16.

6. *Guide*, pp. 431,432.

7. *Guide*, p. 433.

8. *Guide*, p. 436.

9. Psalms 97:2, 18:12; Exodus 19:9; Deuteronomy 4:11.

10. Cf. Aristotle's *Physics*, 8.4.255b24.

11. Isaiah 45:7.

12. Munk, 316.9; Pines, 438, "out of nonbeing," translating *'adam* interchangeably as "non-being" and "privation," as he comments in nn. 2 and 7.

13. *Guide*, p. 439.

14. Munk, 317.3 *yu'lamu yaqīnan*. Pines, 439, "it will be known with certainty."

15. *Guide*, p. 440.

16. Munk, 317.7, 317.8, *mukārana al-'adam*; Pines, 440, "matter always being a concomitant of privation." Pines also reads the preceding sentence as saying that God brings matter into existence "provided with" the nature it has.

17. Munk, 319.5.

18. As elsewhere, Pines, 443, translates *ikhtiyār*, "choice" (Munk, 319.17) as "free will."

19. See Pines, 444 n. 13.

20. Munk, 322.5; *Guide*, p. 446.

21. *Guide*, p. 449, and see Aristotle, *Politics* 1.8.1256b20; *On the Heavens*, 1.4.270a32.

22. Cf. Aristotle's *Physics*, 2.7.198a25, as Munk mentions, 86 n. 3.

23. *Guide*, p. 449; Aristotle, *Metaphysics*, 12.7.

24. Munk, 325.2, *amran 'aṣiran jiddan*. Note that Maimonides does not say that such knowledge is beyond man's attainments, just that it is very difficult.

25. Munk, 325.17, *al-'adam*. Pines, 451 as elsewhere, "non-existence."

26. This remark has to be balanced against Maimonides' view of the beauty and harmony of the universe as indicative of God's governance and goodness. His perfection, though not augmented by the universe, is manifested in it, so that the absence of beings would in some sense (from our viewpoint, as it were) detract from God's perfection. But that uses a human yardstick with which to measure God's being, and Maimonides is opposed to that in principle.

27. *Guide*, p. 452.

28. Munk, 328.18. Maimonides here mentions that the matter of the spheres, however superior to man's in that it does not perish, is yet obscure and dark, in comparison with the purely formal being of the separate intellects.

29. Munk, 329.25. Pines, 456, "terrifying."

30. See *Guide*, 1.73, Tenth Premise, p. 206; above, p. 79.

31. Munk, 333.3, *iftiyāt 'aẓīm*; Pines, 461, "a very great aberration." Maimonides cites Alexander of Aphrodisias's *On Governance* as the source for his summary of the philosophers' view. Pines, "Translator's Introduction," lxv, identifies this treatise with Alexander's *On Providence*.

32. This is the philosophers' view that Maimonides is repeating, though he too believes in the eternity (at least *a parte post*) of the world and thus in an ever-increasing number of particular things.

33. Munk, 335.15, *naẓim wa mudabbir*; Pines, 464, "someone who orders and governs them," thus giving the impression of a personal being. Maimonides may have wanted to give that impression, but he knew that Aristotle's First Mover, even if called God, was impersonal. Cf. Aristotle's *Physics*, 2.5 and 2.6; *Metaphysics*, 11.8.

34. Munk, 335.22, *al-ināya hiyya bi-ḥasab ṭabī'a al-wujūd*.

35. Ezekiel 9:9.

36. *Guide*, p. 469. Though Maimonides appears here to be affirming free will for human beings, his analogy between their will and that of other animals, who cannot, for Maimonides, choose to follow their will, as well as his attribution of the will of both man and other animals to the will of God, led Shlomo Pines to believe that Maimonides is here conveying his secret belief

in divine determinism. See Pines' excursus in his "Studies in Abul-Barakāt al-Baghdādī's Poetics and Metaphysics," 196–97. Though Alexander Altmann also believed that Maimonides held an esoteric belief in determinism, Altmann does not think this passage supports this view. See Altmann, "The Religion of the Thinkers," 42, and see above, p. 146. Rudavsky, Time Matters, 115–24, discusses both their views and the various responses, including her own, to them.

37. BT Berakhot, 5a. Maimonides finds that at least one and possibly more of the later Geonim have this view, which he attributes to the influence of the Muʿtazila.

38. Munk, 340.15, 340.16, *al-ināya al-ilāhīya innamā*; Pines, 471, "watches over."

39. Pines, 471, "is consequent upon."

40. *Guide*, p. 472. Pines reads this sentence as saying that it is "divine providence, which appraises all its actions," reading the verb actively as *qaddarat*, and noting that the word also means "determines." My reading puts the verb in the passive voice, as *quddirat*. This facilitates understanding that Maimonides is saying that the actions are appraised as befitting rewards or punishments, not that providence (or God) so judges them.

41. *Guide*, p. 472.

42. *Guide*, p. 474. Munk, 343.10, *maʿānī dhinīya.*

43. Aristotle, *Categories* 5; Maimonides, *Treatise on Logic*, chapter 10.

44. *Guide*, p. 475, "it is a light thing to kill [the ignorant and disobedient], and has been even enjoined because of its utility."

45. Munk, 345.6, *ayyu shai'*, literally "any thing." Pines, 477: "anything whatever."

46. Paraphrasing *Guide*, p. 479, which Pines translates more literally as "the circumstances of the human individuals, which by their nature are contingent" (literally, "possible," *mumkina*).

47. See *Guide*, chapter 16.

48. *Guide*, p. 480.

49. Munk, 348.4, *al-ʿadam al-maḥḍ*. Pines, 481, "an absolutely nonexistent thing," with a note giving an alternative reading of "absolute nonexistence."

50. Munk, 349.3, *mumkin mā*; Pines, 482, "a certain possible thing."

51. I use this locution since Maimonides does not want to claim that God is in any kind of relation to the world, though "position" is hardly more helpful.

52. *Guide*, p. 485. Maimonides' analogy between God and the artisan evokes Plato's concept of the demiurge; see *Timaeus*, 28a6.

53. *Guide*, p. 14.

54. *Guide*, p. 487, a distinction inferred from Job 1:6 and 2:1.

55. Based on Job 1:7, 2:2.

56. *Guide*, p. 488, "while Satan also has a certain portion, below them in what exists." Munk, 353.27, *wa huwa aiḍan lahu ḥaẓẓ mā fi al-wujūd dūnahum.*

57. Job 2:6.

58. BT Baba Bathra, 16a.

59. *Guide*, p. 494.

60. *Guide*, p. 495; Job 33:23

61. *Guide*, p. 496; Job 38–42.

62. Munk, 361.11, *mashhūr*; Pines, 497, "generally accepted."

63. *Guide*, p. 498; Deuteronomy 32:4.

64. To Maimonides, the adherents of this view are reduced to considering God's actions as frivolous, since they are performed with no end in sight (to us), being the product of a will that is unaccountable to anything else. Maimonides is thus opposing his understanding of a God who

acts (and must act) responsibly with regard to us to the Ash'arite view of a God whose nature and purposes remain (practically entirely) unknown to us.

65. *Guide*, p. 504; Munk, 366.20.

66. *Guide*, p. 505; Munk, 367.5.

67. Munk, 367.13; *Guide*, p. 505 (Pines translating *'adam* as "nonexistence" rather than "privation.")

68. Cf. Stern, "Maimonides' Conceptions of Freedom and the Sense of Shame," 254–66.

69. A succinct analysis of this subject is offered by Dobbs-Weinstein, "Matter as Creature and Matter as the Source of Evil," 217–27.

70. Funkenstein, *Theology and the Scientific Imagination from the Middle Ages to the Seventeenth Century*, 229, 230, puts it that Maimonides considered matter "the source of contingency throughout the universe" and a "principle of indeterminacy."

71. See above, p. 168, for the second negative portrayal of matter.

72. This is the thesis advanced by Pines, "The Limitations of Human Knowledge according to Al-Fārābī, Ibn Bājja, and Maimonides," 92, and "Les limites de la métaphysique selon Al-Fārābī, Ibn Bājja, et Maimonide," 215, though following Maimonides he speaks only of the impossibility of knowing God and the separate intellects. See too Stern, "Logical Syntax as a Key to a Secret of the *Guide of the Perplexed*," 149; *Matter and Form*, 191.

73. A different perspective is offered by Goodman, "Matter and Form as Attributes of God in Maimonides' Philosophy," 86–95.

74. Munk, 317.7, *Allāhu awjada al-mādda 'alā hādhihi al-ṭabī'a allati hiyya 'alayhā. Guide*, p. 440 (though I would prefer "according to the nature it has" rather than "provided with the nature it has").

75. Pines, 444, cites Galen, *De usu partium humani corporis*, 3.10. Maimonides may also be influenced here by Avicenna's view of the role of matter in explaining evil, and see above, p. 46.

76. Baron (*History and Jewish Historians*, 156) comments on the postbiblical period that "the general course of Jewish history appears to Maimonides . . . as an uninterrupted series of persecutions."

77. This is not to deny Maimonides' identification with and affirmation of Jewish history as given in biblical and talmudic sources in his other writings. Cf. Baron's comprehensive discussion, *History and Jewish Historians*, 114–63.

78. *The Kuzari*, 46–81.

79. Terms he expressed in his *Epistle to Yemen*; see above, p. 20.

80. Funkenstein, "Maimonides: Political Theory and Realistic Messianism," 131–55.

81. He seems to contradict this view in chapter 25; see below, p. 178.

82. Cf. Reines, "Maimonides' Concepts of Providence and Theodicy," 169–206, for a thorough analysis of Maimonides' arguments. See also Raffel, "Providence as Consequent upon the Intellect," 25–71.

83. *Guide*, p. 482.

84. Munk, 367.6, which Pines translates in *Guide*, p. 505 as "He, may He be exalted, wills only what is possible, and not everything that is possible, but only that which is required by His wisdom to be such."

85. See above, p. 89. Avicenna, *The Metaphysics of The Healing*, 140, expresses the commonly held philosophical view "that whose existence is impossible does not exist." Alfarabi, *Alfarabi's Commentary and Short Treatise on Aristotle's De interpretatione*, 96, mentions that some phi-

losophers "in antiquity" (viz., Stoics), but not in his own day, held that one can posit possible existence of what has never existed and never will.

86. *Guide*, p. 506; Munk, 368.1.

87. Manekin, "Divine Will in Maimonides' Later Writings," 218, offers an alternative reading of the sentence given above, n. 83, that removes the difficulty: "He, may He be exalted, wills only what is possible. There is nothing possible except what His wisdom requires to be such." Unfortunately, this translation forces the Arabic construction of the original sentence.

88. *Alfarabi's Commentary and Short Treatise on Aristotle's De interpretatione*, 92. Avicenna commented as well on the *De interpretatione*, and see above, p. 46.

89. Alfarabi, *Alfarabi's Commentary and Short Treatise on Aristotle's De interpretatione*, 93 (modified). Zimmermann here and below translates *millal* (the plural of *milla*) as "religion."

90. My translation; Zimmermann, in Alfarabi, *Alfarabi's Commentary and Short Treatise on Aristotle's De interpretatione*, 96, "From a religious point of view." Cf. Alfarabi, *Alfarabi's Commentary on Aristotle's Peri hermineias*, 100.

91. Alfarabi is more critical of the notion of divine foreknowledge of contradictory possibilities in Alfarabi, *Alfarabi's Commentary and Short Treatise on Aristotle's De interpretatione*, 246.

92. Cf. Schwarz, "'Acquisition' (*Kasb*) in Early Kalām," 355–87.

93. Above, p. 18.

94. See p. 26.

95. Above, p. 164; *Guide*, 3.17; Pines, 471, "nearer . . . to intellectual reasoning." Munk, 340.15.

96. Cf., for example, *Guide*, 3.17, Pines, 471, and my notes 38 and 40 above; *Guide*, 3.20, Pines, 482, my note 50 above.

97. *Guide*, p. 481 (slightly modified). Compare Gersonides, *Sefer Milḥamot Ha-Shem*, 25b; Gersonides, *The Wars of the Lord*, 2: 136.

98. Gersonides, *The Wars of the Lord*, 2: 117, 122. See the exposition of Gersonides' views by Feldman in Feldman, *Gersonides: Judaism within the Limits of Reason*, 90–97; and in Gersonides, *The Wars of the Lord*, 2: 226–30.

99. Cf. the thorough discussion and analysis in Eisen, *The Book of Job in Medieval Jewish Philosophy*, 48–77.

100. Pines, 356.

101. Cf. the views of Sara Klein-Braslavy and Yaakov Levinger, as given in Feldman, *Gersonides: Judaism within the Limits of Reason*, 368 n. 64.

102. This is Gersonides' understanding of divine omniscience as well, and see Feldman, *Gersonides: Judaism within the Limits of Reason*, 90. Gersonides believed that Maimonides did not hold this view; I believe he did.

103. *Guide*, p. 492; Munk, 357.14. "A certain knowledge" is *'ilm yaqīn*, a term often used to express fully demonstrated knowledge. Here, though, it is obviously not used in that sense, showing that for Maimonides one could know something convincingly without demonstrative proof.

Chapter 10

1. Heir to a political, halachically structured religion, Maimonides does not question the need for law to be comprehensively exacting in every aspect of life.

2. Earlier in his life, Maimonides identified these commandments in his *Sefer ha-Miẓvot*. Above, p. 14 n. 19.

3. *Guide*, p. 510; Munk, 371.17.

4. *Guide*, p. 511; Munk, 372.16.

5. Munk, 371.17, *ṣalāḥ an-nafs wa ṣalāḥ al-badan*, terms familiar in Hebrew as *tiqqun ha-nefesh ve-tiqqun ha-guf*.

6. "City" in Arabic is *madīna* (Munk, 371.25), the term for the Greek *polis*, and as such can stand equally for "state."

7. *Guide*, p. 511; Munk, 372.6; Aristotle, *Politics* 1.2.1253a2, and see *Guide*, 2.40 and above, pp. 128–29.

8. *Guide*, p. 511, "rational *in actu*"; Munk, 372.7, *nāṭiqan bi'l-fi'l*, the participial form conveying a state of being. This reflects Maimonides' feeling that the person is now totally identified with his realized active intellect. The ultimate results of this are brought out in *Guide*, 3.51 and 3.52, and see below, pp. 219–22.

9. *Al-baqā' al-dā'im*, Munk, 372.15

10. Munk, 373.9, *'alā al-tajmīl*; Pines, 512, "a summary way."

11. Literally "views," *arā'* (Munk, 373.11); "opinions," (Pines, 512).

12. Munk, 373.12, *fī ṣalāḥ al-aḥwāl al-madanīya*. Pines, 512, "for the sake of political welfare."

13. In sūra 2, verse 62; sūra 5, verse 69; sūra 22, verse 17.

14. Cf. "Sabianism," in *Encyclopedia of Islam*, 8: 672–75, and see Stroumsa, *Maimonides in His World*, 84–105.

15. At *Guide*, p. 520, Maimonides regards the Chasdeans and Chaldeans as other pagan groups with nonscientific "ravings," and names other books to avoid. The literature on Sabianism, and their purported religion, is, though, his main adversary.

16. Fenton, "Maïmonide et *L'Agriculture nabatéenne*," 303–35, has compared the *Guide*'s description of the contents of *The Nabatean Agriculture* with the recent critical Arabic edition of this work and found Maimonides' reports highly accurate.

17. *Guide*, p. 521.

18. Following the translation of *talaṭṭuf* given by Schwarz, in Maimonides, *Moreh Nevukhim*, 532 n. 2. Pines, 525: "wily graciousness."

19. Maimonides' example of anatomical perfection is drawn from Galen, as he acknowledges.

20. Pines, 527; Munk, 385.10, *al-talaṭṭuf al-ilāhī*.

21. *Guide*, p. 529.

22. Many scholars try to harmonize these facets of Maimonides' life and work, balancing statements in the *Guide* with those in the Code and *Commentary on the Mishnah*. Maimonides' conflicting remarks in the *Guide* on prayer, for example (above, pp. 188, 189), are interpreted within the larger scope of his other writings by Benor, *Worship of the Heart*, 86, 157.

23. Stern, *Matter and Form*, 337, believes that Maimonides in the *Guide* "unequivocally endorses apatheia" in relation to one's emotions and desires.

24. Munk, 389.16; Pines, 532, translating the verb *talaṭṭafa* as "employed a gracious ruse." The verb itself usually denotes showing kindness, its nominal form translating as gift, or benefit.

25. Pines, 534.

26. Cf. above, pp. 24–26.

27. Excerpts given in Twersky, *Maimonides Reader*, 74–76.

28. Pines, 542.

29. Twersky, *Maimonides Reader*, 51–64; above, pp. 28–30, and see n. 24.

30. Twersky, *Maimonides Reader*, 135–39.

31. Pines, 553.

32. Twersky, *Maimonides Reader*, 156–69.

33. Ibid., 190–211.

34. Pines, 558: "strange"; Munk, in Maimonides, *Le guide des égarés*, 3:312, "extraordinaires."

35. *Guide*, p. 562.

36. *Guide*, p. 563, "Thou shall not add (to the law) or diminish from it." Cf. Deuteronomy 13:1.

37. Twersky, *Maimonides Reader*, 171–88.

38. Ibid., 102–19.

39. Ibid., 87–100. Menachem Kellner has translated the entire book as the latest addition to the Yale University series of *Mishneh Torah* texts.

40. Pines, 574: "constant commemoration." Munk, 421.5, *tadhkār . . . da'īmān*, Maimonides using the verb associated with the widespread Muslim practice of *dhikr*, phrases and prayers recited individually or collectively (by Sufis) in "remembrance" of God. Cf. Al-Ghazālī's praise of *dhikr* in book 4 of his *Iḥyā' 'ulum-ud-Din*, 328.

41. Twersky, *Maimonides Reader*, 142–46.

42. Maimonides here ignores his exclusion of Moses' prophecy from this generalization. Cf. above, pp. 27, 141.

43. Twersky, *Maimonides Reader*, 140–50.

44. *Guide*, p. 591.

45. Twersky, *Maimonides Reader*, 152–54.

46. *Guide*, p. 595.

47. Pines, 597; Munk, 438.18.

48. Twersky, *Maimonides Reader*, 124–33.

49. Exodus 23:19, 34:26.

50. Twersky, *Maimonides Reader*, 99–100, 121–24.

51. Maimonides cites it as in book 9. *Guide*, p. 601.

52. *Guide*, p. 608. Maimonides' reading of the *Rhetoric* is forced. See *Rhetoric*, 1.11.1370a18–24, and *Nicomachean Ethics*, 3.10.1118b1–4.

53. Cf. above, p. 14 n. 19.

54. *Guide*, 3.27; Pines, 511; and see *Guide*, 2.39; Pines, 378.

55. "Sabians" is derived from the Arabic *al-ṣābī'un* and other variants of the name. Stroumsa, *Maimonides in His World*, 87–91, has summarized a century and more of scholarly investigation of the Sabians, their purported history and beliefs. Identified by scholars with various pre-Islamic groups, Sabianism appeared to Maimonides as a general term for idolatrous peoples extant from Abraham's day to his own. Stern, "The Fall and Rise of Myth in Ritual," 190, 202–16, sees Maimonides' indictment of Sabianism as aimed partially at beliefs in astrology and magic current among his contemporaries.

56. Stroumsa, *Maimonides in His World*, 102, rightly claims that Maimonides was "the first author to offer an explicit and detailed analysis of pagan influence on the development of monothesitic religions." The originality of Maimonides' "historical" approach to Jewish law was emphasized by Amos Funkenstein in a number of his writings; see "Maimonides: Political Theory and Realistic Messianism," 131–44.

57. Cf. Kreisel, "Intellectual Perfection and the Role of Law in the Philosophy of Maimonides," 34–37.

58. Funkenstein, *Theology and the Scientific Imagination from the Middle Ages to the Seventeenth Century*, 232, gives it as "cunning of God." Maimonides, Funkenstein points out, was not

the first Jewish writer to adopt the doctrine of accommodation as an explanatory principle of the law. See too Funkenstein's *Perceptions of Jewish History*, 144–47.

59. Above, pp. 188, 189. Maimonides' disparagement of petitionary prayer, however qualified (above, pp. 190, 195), and the apparent conflict it presents with his affirmative rabbinic writings on the subject and his negative theology, have been discussed by Fox, *Interpreting Maimonides*, 297–321; Benor, *Worship of the Heart*, 63–76.

60. *Guide*, 3.51, pp. 620, 621; below, pp. 210, 218.

61. Above, p. 41.

62. *Guide*, 3.28; Pines, 512; above, p. 188. While Maimonides describes these beliefs as politically necessary, rather than false, the implication of his remarks is clear. This chapter is subjected to a detailed analysis by Galston, "The Purpose of the Law according to Maimonides," 42–47.

63. Seen within the larger perspective of Maimonides' entire literary corpus, however, his understanding of the cunning of biblical law in the *Guide* can be viewed as integral to his view of an ever-increasing "monotheisation" of the world. Cf. Funkenstein, *Perceptions of Jewish History*, 149.

64. Munk, 391.18; *Guide*, 3.34, p. 535.

65. Cf., though, the analysis offered by Stern, "The Idea of a *Hoq* in Maimonides' Explanation of the Law," 116–21.

66. *Guide*, 3.41, p. 563.

67. Cf. Fenton, "Maïmonide et *L'Agriculture nabatéenne*," 318–20. These practices are for Maimonides intimately tied to astrological beliefs that he condemns explicitly in other writings.

68. *Guide*, 3.45, p. 577.

69. Munk, 406.21, *al-jāhalīya*. Pines, 554, "the Pagans," with a note "or: ignorant." Maimonides refers to the *jāhalīya* period of Arabic poetry and stories, before the advent of Islam and its laws.

70. Cf. Stern, "Maimonides on the Covenant of Circumcision and the Unity of God," 131–54, for a detailed analysis of Maimonides' attitude toward this rite.

71. *Guide*, 3.39, p. 553.

72. *Guide*, p. 558.

73. *Guide*, p. 563.

74. Munk, 318.13; Pines, 571. Maimonides views circumcision, however, as a moral corrective to nature. *Guide*, 3.49, p. 609.

75. Pines, 573.

76. *Guide*, 3.49, pp. 605, 612.

77. *Guide*, 3.46, p. 591.

78. *Guide*, 3.48, p. 599.

79. Stern, "The Fall and Rise of Myth in Ritual," 216, 220–25.

Chapter 11

1. Munk, 454.19, *shabaha al-khātima*, literally, "like a conclusion."

2. *Guide*, p. 619.

3. Munk, 456.4; *Guide*, p. 619. Pines, "The Limitations of Human Knowledge according to Al-Fārābī, Ibn Bājja, and Maimonides,"99, regards this statement and the following remarks Maimonides makes concerning the knowledge that Moses and the prophets have as part of Maimonides' "philosophical theology," at odds with his epistemology. As Pines says in "Les limites de

la métaphysique selon Al-Fārābī, Ibn Bājja, et Maimonide," 214, "il me semble que, dans l'esprit de Maïmonide, ces doctrines n'avaient qu'un raport ambigu et douteux avec la vérité des choses."

4. Munk, 456.11.

5. Cf. Exodus 34:28.

6. *Guide*, 2.45, and see above, p. 131.

7. *Guide*, p. 621.

8. Munk, 457.13; Pines, 621: "Thus it is clear that after apprehension, total devotion to Him and the employment of intellectual thought in constantly loving Him should be aimed at."

9. Later in the chapter, Maimonides distinguishes between normative love and passionate love, the latter such that "no thought remains that is directed toward a thing other than the Beloved" (Pines, 627).

10. Munk, 437.16. *Wuṣla* is a cognate of *ittiṣāl*, the term more commonly used for "conjunction" with the Agent Intellect, as at *Guide*, 3.8; Munk, 310.28 (Pines, 432, "union"); cf. above, p. 155.

11. Maimonides here as elsewhere has man uniting with a God he has elsewhere proclaimed is unaffected by anything or anybody. It is the Agent Intellect, God's "emissary" as it were, with whom the ultimate union is sought, and Maimonides' belief in the enduring nature of this intellect allows him to speak of it as divine. See below, p. 212.

12. *Guide*, 3.17, p. 474; above, p. 164.

13. Pines, 625. Munk, 461.7, *li-annahu ma'a allah wa-allah ma'ahu.*

14. Pines, 628, construes the subject pronoun of the sentence in Munk, 463.12, as referring to the person, "and he will remain permanently . . ." It could, however, as well refer to the intellect by itself, the previous subject given. Thus, we would read, "and it will remain permanently . . ."

15. At *Guide*, p. 629, Maimonides calls the emanating intellect that is the Agent Intellect a "great king," a term that at first would seem to denote God Himself.

16. Munk, 464.19, *al-infi'āl*; Pines, 630, "passion."

17. *Commentary on the Mishnah* on Avot, 5.6. Cf. Raymond L. Weiss, *Maimonides' Ethics*, 33–46.

18. Cf. *Guide*, 1.53 and 1.54; above, p. 59.

19. Munk, 466.8, *al-balāyā al-'aẓīmah al-iḍāfīyah.*

20. Altmann, "Maimonides' Four Perfections," 15–24, demonstrates Maimonides' indebtedness to Ibn Bājja for much of this chapter.

21. Munk, 466.22, *al-talaṭṭuf wa al-iḥtiyāl.* Pines, 632, "stratagems and ruses." It is remarkable that Maimonides uses the same word for the divine ruses as those ruses employed by people he considers evil.

22. *Guide*, p. 633. Cf. Maimonides' *Treatise on Logic*, chapter 8.

23. BT Shabbat, 31a.

24. Munk, 469.1; Pines, 635, "concerning the divine things" (*al-ilāhiyāt*). As stated before in a number of places, neither Pines nor Stern believes that Maimonides thinks this truly possible; cf. above, n. 3. Alfarabi expressed the same belief as Maimonides in his *Political Regime*, that bliss for human beings "consists in intellection alone"; cf. Galston, *Politics and Excellence*, 84.

25. Maimonides repeats the phrase used before in chapter 51; above, p. 212.

26. Jeremiah 9:22–23; *Guide*, p. 636.

27. Pines, 637, "assimilation."

28. Munk, 454.22. Pines, 618, "how providence watches over him."

29. *Guide*, 1.70, p. 174, and 1.74, p. 221; above, p. 80.

30. Stroumsa, *Maimonides in His World*, 59–70.

31. *Guide*, 2.24, p. 327; above, pp. 105, 118.

32. *Guide*, p. 619. Munk, 456.4, *al-'ulamā'*, literally, "the learned."

33. Averroes shares this more accessible view of conjuntion with Maimonides, as I have argued in "Getting to Know Thee," 149–56.

34. The Trinitarian belief of Christians, which Maimonides considered idolatry, would have posed a problem for him, however.

35. *Guide*, 2.40, p. 384.

36. Above, p. 129 n. 21.

37. The influence of Ibn Bājja's *Governance of the Solitary* (above, p. 44 n. 74) on Maimonides' view of how to reach ultimate happiness is, however, notable. Cf. Steven Harvey, "Maimonides in the Sultan's Palace," 48–50.

38. Munk, 457.4, 457.5, and 457.13. The various evaluations of *'ishq* in Jewish and Islamic philosophical and mystical texts are discussed by Stephen Harvey, "The Meaning of Terms Designating Love in Judaeo-Arabic Thought and Some Remarks on the Judaeo-Arabic Interpretation of Maimonides," 175–96.

39. *Avicenna's Treatise on 'Ishq and His Treatise on the Essence of Prayer*, discussed by Stephen Harvey, "The Meaning of Terms Designating Love in Judaeo-Arabic Thought and Some Remarks on the Judaeo-Arabic Interpretation of Maimonides," 184.

40. Warren Zev Harvey, "Maimonides' Avicennianism," 117–18, points out that Maimonides does not substitute *'ishq* for the intellectual contemplation of God, however much it may accompany it.

41. Cf. Affifi, *The Mystical Philosophy of Muḥyid Dīn-Ibnul 'Arabī*, 137–47.

42. Altmann, "Maimonides' Attitude Toward Jewish Mysticism," 200–219, delineates Maimonides' essential differences with the mystical traditions of his day.

43. *Guide*, p. 623.

44. Compare the striking parallels between Maimonides' goals for the perfect person and the Stoic ideals described by Pierre Hadot in *Philosophy as a Way of Life*, 81–125.

45. *Guide*, p. 624.

46. Blumenthal, "Maimonides' Intellectual Mysticism and the Superiority of the Prophecy of Moses," 27–51, emphasizes Maimonides' affinities with an intellectualized form of mysticism.

47. Munk, 460.9, *wa qad ẓuhira lī al-ān*, "it has become clear (or revealed) to me now"; Pines, 624, "has occurred to me just now."

48. *Guide*, 2.36, p. 372; above, p. 127.

49. Cf. references above, p. 48 n. 102.

50. Munk, 463.10–14; *Guide*, p. 628. Pines takes the pronoun that refers to the intellect in this passage to refer to the person who has the intellect, giving the impression of a personal immortality. Thus he translates, "After having reached this condition of enduring permanence, that intellect remains in one and the same state, the impediment that sometimes screened him (instead of "it") off having been removed. And he (instead of "it") will remain permanently in that state of intense pleasure . . ."

51. Above, p. 216 n. 29.

52. *Guide*, p. 629. Maimonides refers to it simply as "the intellect that emanates upon us [Pines, "that overflows toward us] and is the bond betweeen us and Him."

53. Above, p. 38.

54. Pines, 630; Munk, 465.4, *ʿalā mā huwa taʿālā ʿalayhi*, literally, "according to how He, the Exalted, (really, or essentially) is."

55. *Guide*, 3.51, p. 619; above, p. 216.

56. Pines, "The Limitations of Human Knowledge according to Al-Fārābī, Ibn Bājja, and Maimonides," 100: "The only positive knowledge of God of which man is capable is knowledge of the attributes of action, and this leads and ought to lead to a sort of political activity which is the highest perfection of man. The practical way of life, the *bios praktikos*, is superior to the theoretical." Cf., though, Altmann, "Maimonides' Four Perfections," 24; Stephen Harvey, "Maimonides in the Sultan's Palace," 66–72.

57. Benor, *Worship of the Heart*, 23, views this last chapter as providing a crucial shift in Maimonides' attitude toward the value of practical activity and prayer.

Conclusion

1. Above, p. 14.

2. *Guide*, p. 472.

3. Cf. Hadot, *Philosophy as a Way of Life*, 18–21, 83.

4. Above, p. 45.

5. Above, p. 38.

6. Above, pp. 102, 103.

7. As argued impressively by Stern, *Matter and Form*, passim.

8. Prominent among them being Leo Strauss and Shlomo Pines. Above, p. 3 nn. 11, 12.

9. Above, p. 92.

10. Above, p. 143.

11. Above, pp. 125, 126.

12. Cf. book 10 of Avicenna's *The Metaphysics of Yhe Healing*, 365.

13. Above, p. 47.

14. *Guide*, p. 402.

15. *Guide*, 2.33.

16. Above, pp. 100, 188.

17. Above, p. 41.

18. Above, pp. 216, 217.

19. Kogan, "What Can We Know and When Can We Know it?," 125.

20. Maimonides actually treats conjunction as an epistemological premise and does not explain it in detail, unlike his philosophical predecessors.

21. *Guide*, 3.51, p. 627.

22. Cf. Hasse, "Influence of Arabic and Islamic Philosophy on the Latin West."

23. Maimonides expressed himself in similar though more veiled terms already in his *Mishneh Torah*, Book of Knowledge, Laws of Repentence 8.3.

24. Above, pp. 53, 57.

25. Above, p. 61.

26. Above, p. 112.

27. Cf. part 1 of Spinoza, *Ethics*, 217–43.

28. God's goodness is given as a cause of the existence of the world in many classical and Neoplatonic texts, as noted by Davidson, *Proofs for Eternity, Creation and the Existence of God in*

Medieval Islamic and Jewish Philosophy, 61 n. 90. Proclus's argument for *jūd al-bārī'*, the goodness of the Creator, in his *Elements of Theology* 156.6, is extant only in Arabic.

29. Above, p. 79.

30. Above, p. 179.

31. This is the view Avicenna and Gersonides explicitly hold; above, p. 182. Acar, "Reconsidering Avicenna's Position on God's Knowledge of Particulars," 142–51, reviews the views of Michael Marmura and others on this question.

32. *Guide*, p. 463; Munk, 334.24.

33. Presumably Maimonides concurred in this consensus, as testified by his *Epistle to Yemen* (above, p. 20) and other writings. Cf. Funkenstein, *Perceptions of Jewish History*, 147–53.

34. Above, pp. 142, 143.

Recommended Readings

Chapter 1. A Concise Biography

Herbert A. Davidson. *Moses Maimonides: The Man and His Works.* Oxford University Press, Oxford, 2005.

Joel L. Kraemer, *Maimonides: The Life and World of One of Civilization's Greatest Minds.* Doubleday, New York, 2008.

Moshe Halbertal, *Maimonides*, trans. Joel Linsider. Princeton University Press, Princeton, 2014.

Joel Kraemer, "Moses Maimonides: An Intellectual Portrait," in *The Cambridge Companion to Maimonides*, ed. Kenneth Seeskin. Cambridge University Press, Cambridge, 2005, 10–57.

Chapter Two. The Mishneh Torah

Mishneh Torah, translations of books 2–14. Yale Judaica Series, 1949ff.

Mishneh Torah: The Book of Knowledge, ed. and trans. Moses Hyamson. Boys Town Publishers, Jerusalem, 1962.

Isadore Twersky, *Introduction to the Code of Maimonides (Mishneh Torah).* Yale University Press, New Haven, 1980.

Chapter Three. Maimonides' Graeco-Islamic Philosophical Heritage

Shlomo Pines, "The Philosophic Sources of *The Guide of the Perplexed,*" in the introduction to his translation of the *Guide.* University of Chicago Press, Chicago, 1963, lvii–cxxxiv.

Alfred L. Ivry, "The *Guide* and Maimonides' Philosophical Sources," in *The Cambridge Companion to Maimonides,* ed. Kenneth Seeskin. Cambridge University Press, Cambridge, 2005, 58–81.

Herbert A. Davidson, *Maimonides the Rationalist.* Littman Library of Jewish Civilization, Oxford, 2011, 53–84, 99–172.

Chapter Four. Wrestling with Language

Charles Manekin, "Belief, Certainty and Divine Attributes in the *Guide of the Perplexed.*" *Maimonidean Studies* 1 (1990), 117–41.

James Arthur Diamond, *Maimonides and the Hermeneutics of Concealment.* SUNY Press, Albany, 2002.

Mordecai Cohen, *Opening the Gates of Interpretation: Maimonides' Biblical Hermeneutics in Light of His Geonic-Andalusian Heritage and Muslim Milieu.* E. J. Brill, Leiden, 2011.

Sara Klein-Braslavy, *Maimonides as Biblical Interpreter.* Academic Studies Press, Brighton, MA, 2011.

Chapter Five. *Kalām* Claims and Counterclaims

Haggai Ben-Shammai, "Kalām in Medieval Jewish philosophy," in *History of Jewish Philosophy,* ed. Daniel H. Frank and Oliver Leaman. Routledge, London, 1997, 115–48.

Harry Austryn Wolfson, "The Kalam according to Maimonides," in Wolfson, *The Philosophy of the Kalam.* Harvard University Press, Cambridge, 1976, 43–58.

Majid Fakhry, *A History of Islamic Philosophy.* Columbia University Press, New York, 1970, 56–81.

Chapter Six. Philosophy Affirmed and Qualified; Creation

Herbert Davidson, *Proofs for Eternity, Creation and the Existence of God in Medieval Islamic and Jewish Philosophy,* Oxford University Press, New York, 1987.

Kenneth Seeskin, *Maimonides on the Origin of the World,* Cambridge University Press, Cambridge, 2005.

T. M. Rudavsky, *Maimonides.* Wiley-Blackwell, Chichester, 2010, 65–81.

Chapter Seven. Prophecy

Leo Strauss, "The Philosophic Foundation of the Law: Maimonides's Doctrine of Prophecy and Its Sources," in *Philosophy and Law: Contributions to the Understanding of Maimonides and His Predecessors,* trans. E. Adler. SUNY Press, Albany, 1995, 101–33.

Howard Kreisel, *Prophecy: The History of an Idea in Medieval Jewish Philosophy,* Kluwer Academic, Dordrecht, 2001, 148–315.

Chapter Eight. The Metaphysics of the Chariot

Daniel Davies, *Method and Metaphysics in Maimonides' Guide for the Perplexed,* Oxford University Press, Oxford, 2011, 107–33.

Chapter Nine. Providence and (Apparent) Evil

Charles M. Raffel, "Providence as Consequent upon the Intellect: Maimonides' Theory of Providence," *Association of Jewish Studies Review* 12, no. 1, 1987, 25–71.

Leonard S. Kravitz, "The Revealed and the Concealed: Providence, Prophecy, Miracles and Creation in the *Guide.*" *CCAR Journal* 16 (1969), 2–30; 18 (1971), 59–62.

Chapter Ten. Rationalizing the Law

Miriam Galston, "The Purpose of the Law according to Maimonides." *Jewish Quarterly Review,* n.s. 69, 1975, 27–51.

Lenn Evan Goodman, "Maimonides' Philosophy of Law." *Jewish Law Annual* 1, 1978, 72–107.

Josef Stern, "The Idea of a *Hoq* in Maimonides' Explanation of the Law," *Maimonides and Philosophy,* ed. S. Pines and Y. Yovel. Martinus Nijhoff, Dordrecht, 1986, 92–130.

Chapter Eleven. True Knowledge and Perfection

Ralph Lerner, "Maimonides' Governance of the Solitary," in *Perspectives on Maimonides,* ed. Joel L. Kraemer. Oxford University Press, Oxford, 1991, 33–46.

Bibliography

Acar, Rahim. "Reconsidering Avicenna's Position on God's Knowledge of Particulars." In *Interpreting Avicenna: Science and Philosophy in Medieval Islam,* ed. Jon McGinnis. Brill, Leiden, 2004.

———. *Talking about God and Talking about Creation: Avicenna's and Thomas Aquinas' Positions.* Brill, Leiden, 2005.

Affifi, A. E. *The Mystical Philosophy of Muḥyid Dīn-Ibnul 'Arabī.* Cambridge University Press, Cambridge, 1939.

Al-Akiti, M. Afifi. "The Good, the Bad, and the Ugly of Falsafa: Al-Ghazālī's Maḍnūn, Tahāfūt, and Maqāṣid, with Particular Attention to Their Falsafī Treatments of God's Knowledge of Temporal Events." In *Avicenna and His Legacy,* ed. Y. Tzvi Langermann. Brepols, Turnhout (Belgium), 2009.

Alexander of Aphrodisias. *The De anima of Alexander of Aphrodisias: A Translation and Commentary.* Ed. Athanasios P. Fotinis. University Press of America, Washington, DC, 1979.

Alfarabi. *Al-Farabi on the Perfect State.* Trans. Richard Walzer. Clarendon Press, Oxford, 1985.

———. *Alfarabi: The Political Writings.* Trans. Charles Butterworth. Cornell University Press, Ithaca, 2001.

———. *Alfarabi's Commentary and Short Treatise on Aristotle's De interpretatione.* Trans. F. W. Zimmerman. Oxford University Press, London, 1981.

———. *Alfarabi's Commentary on Aristotle's Peri hermineias (De interpretatione).* Ed. Wilhelm Kutsch and Stanley Marrow. Imprimerie Catholique, Beirut, 1960.

———. *Al-Fārābī's The Political Regime (al-Siyāsa al-madaniyya, also known as The Treatise on the Principles of Beings).* Ed. Fauzi M. Najjar. Arabic. Imprimerie Catholique, Beirut, 1964. Hebrew translation by Tsvi Fillipowski, Leipzig, 1843; reprint, Tel Aviv, 1970.

———. *Kitāb al-ḥurūf.* Ed. M. Mahdi. Dar Al-Mashriq, Beirut, 1970.

———. *Kitāb al-milla wa nuṣuṣ ukhrā.* Ed. Muhsin Mahdi. Dar El-Machreq, Beirut, 1968.

———. *The Letter concerning the Intellect.* Trans. Arthur Hyman. In Hyman and James J. Walsh, eds., *Philosophy in the Middle Ages.* Hackett, Indianapolis, 1973.

Al-Ghazālī. *Iḥyā' 'ulum-ud-Din.* Trans. Al-Haj Maulana Fazal-ul-Karim. Sh. Muhammad Ashraf, Lahore, 2000.

———. *The Incoherence of the Philosophers.* Trans. Michael E. Marmura. Brigham Young University Press, Provo, UT, 1997.

———. *Maqāṣid al-Falāsifa.* Ed. S. Dunyā. 2nd ed. Dār al-Ma'ārif, Cairo, 1960.

Al-Kirmānī. *Kitāb rāḥat al-'aql.* Ed. M. Ghālib. Dār al-Andalus, Beirut, 1967.

Almbladh, Karin. "The Authorship and Textual Tradition of *Maqāla fī ṣinā'at al-manṭiq* Commonly Ascribed to Maimonides." Forthcoming.

Al-Sijistānī, Abū Ya'qūb. *Abū Ya'qūb Sejestānī, Le dévoilement des choses cachées: Kashf al-Mahjūb.* Trans. Henry Corbin. Verdier, Paris, 1988.

Altmann, Alexander. "Maimonides' Attitude toward Jewish Mysticism." Trans. Gertrude Hirschler and Alfred Jospe. In *Studies in Jewish Thought,* ed. Alfred Jospe. Wayne State University Press, Detroit, 1981.

———. "Maimonides' Four Perfections." In *Israel Oriental Studies* 2. Jerusalem, 1972.

———. "Maimonides on the Intellect and the Scope of Metaphysics." In *Von der mittelalterlichen zur modernen Aufklärung.* J. C. Mohr, Tübingen, 1987.

———. "The Religion of the Thinkers: Free Will and Predestination in Saadia, Bahya and Maimonides." In *Religion in a Religious Age,* ed. S. D. Goitein. Association for Jewish Studies, Cambridge, MA, 1974.

Aristotle. *The Complete Works.* Ed. Jonathan Barnes. Princeton University Press, Princeton, 1984.

Armstrong, A. H., ed. *The Cambridge History of Later Greek and Early Medieval Philosophy.* Cambridge University Press, Cambridge, 1967.

Averroës. *Averroes' Kitāb faṣl al-maqāl.* Trans. George F. Hourani as *Averroes on the Harmony of Religion and Philosophy.* Luzac, London, 1967.

———. *Averroes on Plato's Republic.* Trans. Ralph Lerner. Cornell University Press, Ithaca, 1974.

———. *Averroes' Tahafut Al-Tahafut (The Incoherence of the Incoherence).* Trans. Simon Van Den Bergh. Luzac, London, 1969.

———. *Bidāyat al-mujtahid wa-nihāyat al-muqtaṣid.* Trans. Imran Ahsan Khan Nyazee as *The Distinguished Jurist's Primer.* Garnet, Reading, UK, 2000.

———. *The Book of the Decisive Treatise Determining the Connection between the Law and Wisdom, & Epistle Dedicatory.* Trans. Charles E. Butterworth. Brigham Young University Press, Provo, UT, 2001.

Avicenna. *Avicenna's Al-Shifa: La logique,* vol. 6, *Al-Jadal.* Ed. A. F. El-Ehwany. Organisme Général des Imprimeries Gouvernementales, Cairo, 1965.

———. *Avicenna's Psychology.* Trans. Fazlur Rahman. Oxford University Press, London, 1952.

———. *Avicenna's Treatise on 'Ishq and His Treatise on the Essence of Prayer.* Edited in Arabic and translated by M. A. F. Mehren as *Traités mystiques d'Abou Alî al Hosain b. Sînâ ou d'Avicenne.* 3rd fascicule. E. J. Brill, Leiden, 1894.

———. *Avicenna, The Metaphysics of The Healing.* trans. Michael E. Marmura. Brigham Young University Press, Provo, UT, 2005.

———. *Ibn Sīnā: Livre des directives et remarques.* Trans. Anne-Marie Goichon. Librairie Philosophique J. Vrin, Paris, 1951.

———. "On the Proof of Prophecies and the Interpretation of the Prophets' Symbols and Metaphors." Trans. Michael Marmura. In *Medieval Political Philosophy,* ed. Ralph Lerner and Muhsin Mahdi. Free Press, New York, 1963.

Baron, Salo W. *History and Jewish Historians.* Jewish Publication Society of America, Philadelphia, 1964.

Benor, Ehud. *Worship of the Heart.* SUNY Press, Albany, 1995.

Ben-Sasson, Menahem. "Maimonides in Egypt: The First Stage." In *Maimonidean Studies*, vol. 2, ed. Arthur Hyman. Yeshiva University Press, New York, 1991.

Ben-Shammai, Haggai. "Maimonides and Creation *Ex Nihilo* in the Tradition of Islamic Philosophy." In *Maimónides y su época*, ed. Carlos del Valle, Santiago Garcia-Jalón, and Juan Pedro Monferrer. Sociedad Estatal de Commemoraciones Culturales, Madrid, 2007.

———. "Major Trends in Karaite Philosophy and Polemics in the Tenth and Eleventh Centuries." In *Karaite Judaism*, ed. Meira Polliack. Brill: Leiden, 2003.

Berman, Lawrence. "Maimonides on the Fall of Man." *AJS Review* 5, 1980.

———. "Maimonides, the Disciple of Alfarabi." *Israel Oriental Studies* 4, 1974.

Black, Deborah L. "Conjunction and the Identity of Knower and Known in Averroes." *American Catholic Philosophical Quarterly* 73, 1999.

———. *Logic and Aristotle's Rhetoric and Poetics in Medieval Arabic Philosophy.* E. J. Brill, Leiden, 1990.

Bland, Kalman P. "Moses and the Law According to Maimonides." In *Mystics, Philosophers, and Politicians*, ed. Jehuda Reinharz, Daniel Swetschinski, and Kalman P. Bland. Duke University Press, Durham, 1982.

Blau, Joshua. *The Emergence and Linguistic Background of Judaeo Arabic: A Study of the Origins of Middle Arabic.* Brill, Leiden, 1981.

Blumenthal, David R. "Maimonides' Intellectual Mysticism and the Superiority of the Prophecy of Moses." In *Approaches to Judaism in Medieval Times*, ed. David R. Blumenthal. Scholars Press, Chico, CA, 1985.

Bos, Gerrit. "Maimonides' Medical Works and Their Contribution to His Medical Biography." In *Maimonidean Studies*, vol. 5, ed. Arthur Hyman and Alfred Ivry. Yeshiva University Press, New York, 2008.

Brockelmann, Carl. *History of the Islamic Peoples.* Trans. Joel Carmichael and Moshe Perlmann. Capricorn Books, New York, 1960.

Chapters of Rabbi Eliezer. Trans. Gerald Friedlander. Kegan Paul, London, 1916.

Chavel, Charles B. *The Commandments.* Soncino Press, London, 1967.

Cohen, Mark R. "The 'Convivencia' of Jews and Muslims in the High Middle Ages." dev.wcfia.harvard.edu/sites/default/files/CohenMarc_0.pdf. Also found in *The Meeting of Civilizations: Muslim, Christian, and Jewish*, ed. Moshe Ma'oz, 54–65. Brighton, UK: Sussex Academic Press, 2009.

———. "Maimonides' Egypt." In *Moses Maimonides and His Time*, ed. Eric L. Ormsby. Catholic University of America Press, Washington, DC, 1989.

Corbin, Henry. *History of Islamic Philosophy.* Trans. Liadain Sherrard. Kegan Paul International, London, 1993.

Daftary, Farhad. *The Ismāʿīlīs: Their History and Doctrines.* Cambridge University Press, Cambridge, 1990.

D'Ancona, Cristina. *Man's Conjunction with Intellect.* Israel Academy of Sciences and Humanities, *Proceedings* 8, no. 4, Jerusalem, 2008.

———. "The Timaeus' Model for Creation and Providence." In *Plato's Timaeus as Cultural Icon*, ed. Gretchen J. Reydams-Schils. University of Notre Dame Press, Notre Dame, IN, 2003.

Davidson, Herbert A. *Alfarabi, Avicenna, and Averroes on Intellect.* Oxford University Press, New York, 1992.

———. "Maimonides on Divine Attributes as Equivocal Terms. In *Tribute to Michael.* Tel Aviv University, Tel Aviv, 2009.

———. "Maimonides on Metaphysical Knowledge." In *Maimonidean Studies,* ed. Arthur Hyman. Yeshiva University Press, New York, 1992–93.

———. "Maimonides' Secret Position on Creation." In *Studies in Medieval Jewish History and Literature,* ed. Isadore Twersky. Harvard University Press, Cambridge, MA, 1979.

———. "Maimonides' *Shemoneh Peraqim* and Alfarabi's *Fusûl al-Madanî." Proceedings of the American Academy for Jewish Research* 31, 1963.

———. *Maimonides the Rationalist.* Littman Library of Jewish Civilization, Oxford, 2011.

———. *Moses Maimonides: The Man and His Works.* Oxford University Press, Oxford, 2005.

———. *Proofs for Eternity, Creation and the Existence of God in Medieval Islamic and Jewish Philosophy.* Oxford University Press, New York, 1987.

Davies, Daniel. *Method and Metaphysics in Maimonides' Guide for the Perplexed.* Oxford University Press, Oxford, 2011.

De Callataÿ, Godefroid. *Ikhwan al-Safā.'* One World Publications, Oxford, 2005.

De Smet, D. *La quiétude de l'intellect: Néoplatonisme et gnose ismaélienne dans l'oeuvre de Hamīd ad-Dīn al-Kirmānī.* Peeters Press, Leuven (Belgium), 1995.

Dhanani, Alnoor. *The Physical Theory of Kalām.* Brill, Leiden, 1994.

Diamond, James Arthur. *Maimonides and the Hermeneutics of Concealment.* SUNY Press, Albany, 2002.

Dobbs-Weinstein, Idit. "Maimonides' Reticence toward Ibn Sīnā." In *Avicenna and His Heritage,* ed. Jules Janssens and Daniel De Smet. Leuven University Press, Leuven, 2002.

———. "Matter as Creature and Matter as the Source of Evil: Maimonides and Aquinas." In *Neoplatonism and Jewish Thought,* ed. Lenn E. Goodman. SUNY Press, Albany, 1992.

Druart, Therese-Anne. "Al-Fārābī, Emanation and Metaphysics." In *Neoplatonism and Islamic Thought,* ed. R. Baine Harris. SUNY Press, Albany, 1992.

Eisen, Robert. *The Book of Job in Medieval Jewish Philosophy.* Oxford University Press, Oxford, 2004.

Endress, Gerhard. "The New and Improved Platonic Theology: Proclus Arabus and Arabic Islamic Philosophy." In *Proclus et la théologie platonicienne,* ed. A. Ph. Segonds et C. Steel. Leuven University Press, Leuven (Belgium), 2000.

Eran, Amira. "Al-Ghazālī and Maimonides on the World to Come and Spiritual Pleasures." *Jewish Quarterly Review* 8, 2001.

Feldman, Seymour. *Gersonides: Judaism within the Limits of Reason.* Littman Library of Jewish Civilization, Oxford, 2010.

Fenton, Paul B."Maïmonide et *L'Agriculture nabatéenne.*" In *Maïmonide: Philosophe et Savant (1138–1204),* ed. Tony Lévy and Roshdi Rashed. Peeters, Leuven, 2004.

Fox, Marvin. *Interpreting Maimonides.* University of Chicago Press, Chicago, 1990.

Fradkin, Hillel. "The Political Thought of Ibn Ṭufayl." In *The Political Aspects of Islamic Philosophy,* ed. Charles E. Butterworth. Harvard University Press, Cambridge, 1992.

Frank, Daniel. "Humility as a Virtue: A Maimonidean Critique of Aristotle's Ethics." In *Moses Maimonides and His Time,* ed. Eric L. Ormsby. Catholic University of America Press, Washington, DC, 1989.

Frank, Richard M. "The Science of Kalām." *Arabic Science and Philosophy* 2, 1992.

Freudenthal, Gad. "Maimonides on the Scope of Metaphysics alias Ma'ase Merkavah: The Evolution of His Views." In *Maimonides y su época,* ed. Carlos del Valle et al. Sociedad Estatal de Commemoraciones Culturales, Madrid, 2007.

Funkenstein, Amos. "Maimonides: Political Theory and Realistic Messianism." *Perceptions of Jewish History.* University of California Press, Berkeley, 1993.
———. *Perceptions of Jewish History.* University of California Press, Berkeley, 1993.
———. *Theology and the Scientific Imagination from the Middle Ages to the Seventeenth Century.* Princeton University Press, Princeton, 1986.
Galston, Miriam. *Politics and Excellence: The Political Philosophy of Alfarabi.* Princeton University Press, Princeton, 1990.
———. "The Purpose of the Law according to Maimonides." *Jewish Quarterly Review,* n.s. 69, 1975.
Gellman, Jerome. "Freedom and Determinism in Maimonides' Philosophy." In *Maimonides and His Time,* ed. Eric Ormsby. Catholic University of America Press, Washington, DC, 1989.
Genesis Rabbah. Trans. H. Freedman. Stephen Austen and Sons, Hertford, UK, 1961.
Gersonides. *Sefer Milḥamot Hashem.* Ed. Jacob Marcaria. Riva di Trento, 1560; reprint, Jerusalem, 1966.
———. *The Wars of the Lord,* trans. Seymour Feldman. 3 vols. Jewish Publication Society of America, Philadelphia, 1984–99.
Goodman, Lenn Evan. *Avicenna.* Routledge, New York, 1992.
———. "Maimonidean Naturalism." In *Maimonides and the Sciences,* ed. R. S. Cohen and H. Levine. Kluwer Academic, Dordrecht, 2000.
———. "Matter and Form as Attributes of God in Maimonides' Philosophy." In *A Straight Path,* ed. Ruth Link-Salinger et al. Catholic University of America Press, Washington, DC, 1988.
Green, Kenneth Hart. *Leo Strauss on Maimonides.* University of Chicago Press, Chicago, 2013.
Griffel, Frank. *Al-Ghazālī's Philosophical Theology.* Oxford University Press, Oxford, 2009.
Hadot, Pierre. *Philosophy as a Way of Life.* Trans. Michael Chase. Blackwell, Oxford, 1995.
Halevi, Judah. *The Kuzari.* Trans. Hartwig Hirschfeld. Schocken Books, New York, 1968.
Halkin, Abraham, and David Hartman. *Crisis and Leadership: Epistles of Maimonides.* Jewish Publication Society, New York, 1985.
Harvey, Stephen. "Avicenna's Influence on Jewish Thought: Some Reflections." In *Avicenna and His Legacy,* ed. Y. Tzvi Langermann. Brepols, Turnhout (Belgium), 2009.
———. "Maimonides in the Sultan's Palace." In *Perspectives on Maimonides,* ed. Joel L. Kraemer. Oxford University Press, Oxford, 1991.
———. "The Meaning of Terms Designating Love in Judaeo-Arabic Thought and Some Remarks on the Judaeo-Arabic Interpretation of Maimonides." In *Judaeo-Arabic Studies,* ed. Norman Golb. Harwood Academic Publishers, Amsterdam, 1997.
———. "The Place of the Philosopher in the City according to Ibn Bājjah." In *The Political Aspects of Islamic Philosophy,* ed. Charles E. Butterworth. Harvard University Press, Cambridge, 1992.
Harvey, Warren Zev. "Maimonides' Avicennianism." In *Maimonidean Studies,* vol. 5, ed. Arthur Hyman and Alfred Ivry. Yeshiva University Press, New York, 2008.
———. "A Third Approach to Maimonides' Cosmogony-Prophetology Puzzle." In *Harvard Theological Review* 74, 1971.
Hasse, Dag Nikolaus. "Influence of Arabic and Islamic Philosophy on the Latin West." In *Stanford Encyclopedia of Philosophy,* http://plato.stanford.edu/entries/arabic-islamic-influence/
Heschel, Abraham Joshua. *Maimonides.* Trans. Joachim Neugroschel. Doubleday, New York, 1991.

Hourani, George. "Ibn Sīnā on Necessary and Possible Existence." *Philosophical Forum* 4, no. 1, 1972.

———. "Ibn Sina's Essay on the Secret of Destiny." *Bulletin of the School of Oriental and African Studies* 2, no. 1, 1966.

Hyman, Arthur. "Demonstrative, Dialectical, and Sophistic Arguments in the Philosophy of Moses Maimonides." In *Moses Maimonides and His Time,* ed. Eric L. Ormsby. Catholic University of America Press, Washington, DC, 1989.

———. "Maimonides as Biblical Exegete." In *Maimonides and His Heritage,* ed. Idit Dobbs-Weinstein, Lenn Evan Goodman, and James Allen Grady. SUNY Press, Albany, 2009.

Ibn Bājja. *Conjunction of the Intellect with Man.* In *Opera Metaphysica,* ed. Majid Fakhry. Dār Al-Nahār, Beirut, 1968.

———. *Conjunction of the Intellect with Man.* Trans. Jon McGinnis and David C. Reisman in *Classical Arabic Philosophy: An Anthology of Sources.* Hackett, Indianapolis, IN, 2007.

———. *The Governance of the Solitary.* Partial trans. by Lawrence Berman, in *Medieval Political Philosophy,* ed. Joshua Parens and Joseph C. Macfarland. 2nd ed. Cornell University Press, Ithaca, 2011.

———. *Ibn Bājja's Tadbīr al-mutawaḥḥid.* Ed. Miguel Asin Palacios. Madrid and Granada, 1946.

Ibn Falaquera, Shem Tov ben Yosef. *Moreh ha-Moreh.* Ed. Yair Shiffman. World Union of Jewish Studies, Jerusalem, 2001.

Ibn Tufayl. *Ibn Tufayl's Hayy Ibn Yaqzān.* Trans. Lenn Evan Goodman. Twayne, New York, 1972.

Ivry, Alfred L. "Averroes' Three Commentaries on *De anima.*" In *Averroes and the Aristotelian Tradition,* ed. Gerhard Endress and Jan A. Aertsen. Brill, Leiden, 1999.

———. "Conjunction in and of Maimonides and Averroes." In *Averroes et les Averroïsmes Juif et Latin,* ed. J.-B. Brenet. Brepols, Turnhout (Belgium), 2007.

———. "Destiny Revisited: Avicenna's Concept of Determinism." In *Islamic Theology and Philosophy: Studies in Honor of George F. Hourani,* ed. Michael E. Marmura. SUNY Press, Albany, 1984.

———. "Getting to Know Thee: Conjunction and Conformity in Averroes' and Maimonides' Philosophy." In *Adaptations and Innovations,* ed. Y. Tzvi Langermann and Josef Stern. Peeters, Paris, 2007.

———. "The Greek Tradition in Ethics and Its Encounter with Religious Moral Wisdom: The Jewish Experience." In *Moral and Political Philosophies in the Middle Ages,* ed. B. Carlos Bazán, Eduardo Andújar, and Léonard G. Gbrocchi. Legas, New York, 1995.

———. "Guide 2:24 and All That (i)jāza." *Aleph* 8, 2008.

———. "The *Guide* and Maimonides' Philosophical Sources." In *The Cambridge Companion to Maimonides,* ed. Kenneth Seeskin. Cambridge University Press, Cambridge, 2005.

———. "Ibn Rushd's Use of Allegory." In *Averroës and the Enlightenment,* ed. Mourad Wahba and Mona Abousenna. Prometheus Books, Amherst, MA, 1996.

———. "The Image of Moses in Maimonides' Thought." In *Maimonides after 800 Years,* ed. Jay M. Harris. Harvard University Press, Cambridge, 2007.

———. "Islamic and Greek Influences on Maimonides' Philosophy." In *Maimonides and Philosophy,* ed. S. Pines and Y. Yovel. Martinus Nijhoff, Dordrecht, 1986.

———. "Ismāʿīlī Theology and Maimonides' Philosophy." In *The Jews of Medieval Islam,* ed. Daniel Frank. E. J. Brill, Leiden, 1995.

———. "Leo Strauss on Maimonides." In *Leo Strauss's Thought,* ed. Alan Udoff. Lynne Rienner, Boulder, 1991.

———. "The Logical and Scientific Premises of Maimonides' Thought." In *Perspectives on Jewish Thought and Mysticism,* ed. A. Ivry, E. Wolfson, and A. Arkush. Reading, UK, 1998.

———. "Maimonides on Creation." In *Creation and the End of Days,* ed. David Novak and Norbert Samuelson. University Press of America, Lanham, MD, 1984.

———. "Maimonides on Possibility." In *Mystics, Philosophers, and Politicians,* ed. Jehuda Reinharz and Daniel Swetschinski. Duke University Press, Durham, 1982.

———. "Neoplatonic Currents in Maimonides." In *Perspectives on Maimonides,* ed. Joel L. Kraemer. Oxford University Press, Oxford, 1991.

———. "Revelation, Reason and Authority in Maimonides' *Guide of the Perplexed.*" In *Studies in Jewish Philosophy: Collected Essays of the Academy for Jewish Philosophy, 1980–85,* ed. N. Samuelson. Philadelphia, 1987.

Jacobson, Howard. *The Finkler Question.* Bloomsbury, New York, 2010.

Janssens, Jules. "Creation and Emanation in Ibn Sīna." *Documenti e Studi sulla Tradiziione Filosofica Medievale* 8, 1997.

———. "Ibn Sīnā's Ideas of Ultimate Realities: Neoplatonism and the Qur'ān as Problem-Solving Paradigms in the Avicennian System." *Ibn Sīnā and His Influence on the Arabic and Latin World.* Ashgate, Aldershot, 2006.

Kaplan, Lawrence. "Maimonides on the Miraculous Element in Prophecy." *Harvard Theological Review* 70, 1977.

Kasher, Hanna. "Is There an Early Stratum in the *Guide of the Perplexed?*" In *Maimonidean Studies,* vol. 3, ed. Arthur Hyman. Yeshiva University Press, New York, 1992–93.

Klein-Braslavy, Sara. "The Creation of the World and Maimonides' Interpretation of Gen. i–v." In *Maimonides and Philosophy,* ed. Shlomo Pines and Yirmiyahu Yovel. Martinus Nijhoff, Dordrecht, 1986.

———. *Maimonides as Biblical Interpreter.* Academic Studies Press, Brighton, MA, 2011.

Kogan, Barry. "Two Gentlemen of Cordova: Averroes and Maimonides on the Transcendence and Immanence of God." In *Adaptations and Innovations,* ed. Y. Tzvi Langermann and Josef Stern. Peeters, Paris, 2007.

———. "What Can We Know and When Can We Know It? Maimonides on the Active Intelligence and Human Cognition." In *Moses Maimonides and His Time,* ed. Eric L. Ormsby. Catholic University of America Press, Washington, DC, 1989.

Kraemer, Joel L. *Maimonides: The Life and World of One of Civilization's Greatest Minds.* Doubleday, New York, 2008.

———. "Maimonides and the Spanish Aristotelian Tradition." In *Christians, Muslims and Jews in Medieval and Early Modern Spain: Interaction and Cultural Change,* ed. M. M. Myerson and E. D. English. Notre Dame University Press, Notre Dame, IN, 1999.

———. "Maimonides' Intellectual Milieu in Cairo." In *Maïmonide: Philosophe et savant,* ed. Tony Lévy and Roshdi Rashed. Peeters, Leuven, 2004.

———. "Maimonides' Use of (Aristotelian) Dialectic." In *Maimonides and the Sciences,* ed. Robert S. Cohen and Hillel Levine. Kluwer Academic, Dordrecht, 2000.

———. "Moses Maimonides: An Intellectual Portrait." In *The Cambridge Companion to Maimonides,* ed. Kenneth Seeskin. Cambridge University Press, Cambridge, 2005.

Kravitz, Leonard S. "The Revealed and the Concealed: Providence, Prophecy, Miracles and Creation in the *Guide.*" *CCAR Journal* 16, 1969; 18, 1971.

Kreisel, Howard. "From Esotericism to Science: The Account of the Chariot in Maimonidean

Philosophy till the End of the Thirteenth Century." In *The Cultures of Maimonideanism: New Approaches to the History of Jewish Thought,* ed. James Robinson. Brill, Leiden, 2009.

———. "Intellectual Perfection and the Role of Law in the Philosophy of Maimonides." In *From Ancient Israel to Modern Judaism,* vol. 3, ed. Jacob Neusner, Ernest S. Frerichs, and Nahum M. Sarna. Scholars Press, Atlanta, 1989.

———. "Judah Halevi's Influence on Maimonides: A Preliminary Appraisal." *Maimonidean Studies,* vol. 2, ed. Arthur Hyman. Yeshiva University Press, New York, 1991.

———. *Maimonides' Political Thought.* SUNY Press, Albany, 1999.

———. *Prophecy: The History of an Idea in Medieval Jewish Philosophy.* Kluwer Academic, Dordrecht, 2001.

Langermann, Y. Tzvi. "Maimonides and Astronomy: Some Further Reflections." In *The Jews and the Sciences in the Middle Ages.* Aldershot, Ashgate / Variorum, 1999.

———. "Maimonides' Repudiation of Astrology." In *Maimonidean Studies,* vol. 2, ed. Arthur Hyman. Yeshiva University Press, New York, 1991.

———. "The True Perplexity: The *Guide of the Perplexed,* Part II, Chapter 24." In *Perspectives on Maimonides,* ed. Joel Kraemer. Oxford University Press, Oxford, 1991.

Lerner, Ralph. *Maimonides' Empire of Light.* University of Chicago Press, Chicago, 2000.

Lobel, Diana. "Silence Is Praise to You: Maimonides on Negative Theology, Looseness of Expression and Religious Experience." *American Catholic Philosophical Quarterly* 76, no. 1, 2002.

Macy, Jeffrey. "Prophecy in al-Farabi and Maimonides." In *Maimonides and Philosophy,* ed. Shlomo Pines and Yirmiyahu Yovel. Martinus Nijhoff, Dordrecht, 1986.

Madelung, Wilferd. "Aspects of Ismāʿīlī Theology: The Prophetic Chain and the God beyond Being." In *Ismāʿīlī Contributions to Islamic Culture,* ed. S. H. Nasr. Tehran, 1977.

Mahdi, Muhsin. "Alfarabi on Philosophy and Religion." *Philosophical Forum* 4, no. 1, 1972.

Maimonides, Moses. *The Code of Maimonides (Mishneh Torah).* Book Two, *The Book of Love,* trans. Menachem Kellner. Yale University Press, New Haven, 2004.

———. *The Commandments: Sefer Ha-Mitzvoth of Maimonides.* Trans. Charles B. Chavel. Soncino Press, London, 1967.

———. *Dalālah al-ḥā'irin le rabbenu Moshe ben Maimon.* Ed. Shlomo Munk. 2nd ed. Azrieli Press, Jerusalem, 1929.

———. *Epistle to Yemen.* Trans. Joel L. Kraemer. In Ralph Lerner, *Maimonides' Empire of Light.* University of Chicago Press, Chicago, 2000.

———. *Le guide des égarés.* Trans. S. Munk. 3 vols. G.-P. Maisonneuve, Paris, 1960.

———. *The Guide of the Perplexed.* Trans. Shlomo Pines. Introductory essay by Leo Strauss. University of Chicago Press, Chicago, 1963.

———. *Letter on Astrology.* Trans. Ralph Lerner. In Lerner, *Maimonides' Empire of Light.* University of Chicago Press, Chicago, 2000.

———. *Letters and Essays of Moses Maimonides.* Ed. Isaac Shailat (Hebrew). Maaliyot Press, Jerusalem, 1987 (vol. 1), 1988 (vol. 2).

———. *Maïmonide: Traité de logique.* Trans. Rémi Brague. Desclée de Brouwer, Paris, 1966.

———. *Maimonides' Arabic Treatise on Logic.* Ed. and trans. Israel Efros. *Proceedings of the American Academy for Jewish Research* 34, 1966.

———. *Maimonides' Commentary on the Mishnah.* Ed. Joseph Kafiḥ. Mossad Harav Kook, Jerusalem, 1963–68.

———. *Maimonides' Introduction to the Talmud.* Trans. Zvi Lampel. Judaica Press, New York, 1987.

———. *Maimonides Treatise on the Art of Logic.* Ed. and trans. Israel Efros. American Academy for Jewish Research, New York, 1938.

———. *Medical Aphorisms, Treatises 1–5.* Parallel Arabic-English. Ed. and trans. Gerrit Bos. Brigham Young University Press, Provo, UT, 2004; *Treatises 6–9,* 2007; *Treatises 10–15,* 2010.

———. *Mishneh Torah* (Hebrew). New edition. Sinai Offset, 5 vols. New York, 1961.

———. *Mishneh Torah: The Book of Knowledge.* Ed. and trans. Moses Hyamson. Boys Town Publishers, Jerusalem, 1962.

———. *Moreh Nevukhim.* Trans. Michael Schwarz. Tel Aviv University Press, 2002.

———. *R. Moses b. Maimon: Responsa* (Hebrew). Ed. Jehoshua Blau. 4 vols. Rubin Mass, Jerusalem, 1989.

———. *Treatise on Resurrection.* Trans. Hillel G. Fradkin. In Ralph Lerner, *Maimonides' Empire of Light.* University of Chicago Press, Chicago, 2000.

Maimun b. Joseph. "Maimon: Letter of Consolation of Maimun Ben Joseph." Ed. and trans. L. M. Simmons. *Jewish Quarterly Review* 2, 1890.

Manekin, Charles, H. "Belief, Certainty and Divine Attributes in the *Guide of the Perplexed.*" In *Maimonidean Studies,* vol. 1, ed. Arthur Hyman. Yeshiva University Press, New York, 1990.

———. "Divine Will in Maimonides' Later Writings." In *Maimonidean Studies,* vol. 5, ed. Arthur Hyman and Alfred Ivry. Yeshiva University Press, New York, 2008.

———. *On Maimonides.* Thomson Wadsworth, Belmont, CA, 2005.

Marmura, Michael. "Some Aspects of Avicenna's Theory of God's Knowledge of Particulars." *Journal of the American Oriental Society* 82, no. 3, 1962.

McCallum, Donald. *Maimonides' Guide for the Perplexed: Silence and Salvation.* Routledge, London, 2007.

McGinnis, Jon. *Avicenna.* Oxford University Press, Oxford, 2010.

McGinnis, Jon, and David C. Reisman. *Classical Arabic Philosophy: An Anthology of Sources.* Hackett, Indianapolis, 2007.

Mehren, M. A. F. *Traités mystiques d'Abou Alî al Hosain b. Sînâ ou d'Avicenne.* 3rd fascicule. E. J. Brill, Leiden, 1894.

Merlan, Philip. *Monopsychism Mysticism Metaconsciousness.* Martinus Nijhoff, The Hague, 1969.

Midrash Qohelet. trans. Abraham Cohen. Soncino Midrash series. London, 1977.

Muir, William. *The Life of Moḥammad.* Revised by T. H. Weir. John Grant, Edinburgh, 1923.

Parens, Joshua. *Metaphysics as Rhetoric: Alfarabi's Summary of Plato's "Laws."* SUNY Press, Albany, 1995.

Parens, Joshua, and Joseph C. Macfarland, eds. *Medieval Political Philosophy.* 2nd ed. Cornell University Press, Ithaca, 2011.

Peters, Frank E. *Aristotle and the Arabs: The Aristotelian Tradition in Islam.* New York University Press, New York, 1968.

Pines, Shlomo. "Amr." In *Studies in the History of Arabic Philosophy,* ed. Sarah Stroumsa. Magnes Press, Jerusalem, 1996.

———. "The Limitations of Human Knowledge according to Al-Fārābī, Ibn Bājja, and Maimonides." In Pines, *Studies in the History of Jewish Thought,* ed. Warren Zev Harvey and Moshe Idel. Magnes Press, Jerusalem, 1997.

———. "Les limites de la métaphysique selon Al-Fārābī, Ibn Bājja, et Maimonide: sources et antithèses de ces doctrines chez Alexandre d'Aphrodise et chez Themistius." In Pines, *Studies in the History of Jewish Thought,* ed. Warren Zev Harvey and Moshe Idel. Magnes Press, Jerusalem, 1997.

———. "Shī'ite Terms and Conceptions in Judah Halevi's *Kuzari*." In Pines, *Studies in the History of Jewish Thought,* ed. Warren Zev Harvey and Moshe Idel. Magnes Press, Jerusalem, 1997.

———. "Studies in Abul-Barakāt al-Baghdādī's Poetics and Metaphysics." *Studies in Philosophy, Scripta Hierosolymitana* 6, 1960.

———. *Studies in Islamic Atomism.* Trans. Michael Schwarz. Ed. Tzvi Langermann. Magnes Press, Jerusalem, 1997.

———. "Translator's Introduction." *The Guide of the Perplexed.* University of Chicago Press, Chicago, 1963.

Plato. *The Republic.* Trans. Paul Shorey. Harvard University Press, Cambridge, 1953.

———. *Timaeus.* Trans. R. G. Bury. Harvard University Press, Cambridge, 1952.

Plotinus. *Plotini Opera II,* ed. P. Henry and H.-R. Schwyzer. English translation of Arabic by G. Lewis. Desclée De Brouwer, Paris, 1959.

———. *Plotinus: The Enneads.* Trans. Stephen MacKenna. 3rd ed. Faber and Faber, London, 1962.

———. *Plotinus apud Arabes* (Arabic). Ed. Abdurraḥmān Badawi. Cairo, 1955.

Proclus. *The Elements of Theology.* Ed. E. R. Dodds. 2nd ed. Clarendon Press, Oxford, 1963.

———. *On the Eternity of the World.* Trans. Helen S. Lang and A. D. Macro. University of California Press, Berkeley, 2001.

Qur'ān. *The Koran,* trans. N. J. Dawood. Penguin Books, London, 2000.

Raffel, Charles M. "Providence as Consequent upon the Intellect: Maimonides' Theory of Providence." *Association of Jewish Studies Review* 12, no. 1, 1987.

Rahman, Fazlur. *Prophecy in Islam.* George Allen & Unwin, London, 1958.

Reines, Alvin J. "Maimonides' Concept of Miracles." *HUCA* (Hebrew Union College Annual) 45, 1974.

———. "Maimonides' Concepts of Providence and Theodicy." *HUCA* (Hebrew Union College Annual) 43, 1972.

Rist, J. "Plotinus on Matter and Evil." *Phronesis* 6, 1961.

Rosán, Laurance J. "Proclus." In *The Encyclopedia of Philosophy,* ed. Paul Edwards. Macmillan, New York, 1967.

Rudavsky, T. M. *Time Matters.* SUNY Press, Albany, 2000.

"Sabianism." In *Encyclopedia of Islam,* ed. Kate Fleet et al., vol. 8. Brill, Leiden, 2007.

Schwarz, Michael. "'Acquisition' (*Kasb*) in Early Kalām." In *Islamic Philosophy and the Classical Tradition,* ed. S. M. Stern, A. Hourani, V. Brown. Cassirer, Oxford, 1972.

———. "Who Were Maimonides' Mutakallimūn? Some Remarks on *Guide of the Perplexed* Part I Chapter 73," In *Maimonidean Studies,* ed. Arthur Hyman, vol. 2. Yeshiva University Press, New York, 1991 (First Part); vol. 3, 1992–93 (Second Part).

Seeskin, Kenneth. *Maimonides on the Origin of the World.* Cambridge University Press, Cambridge, 2005.

———. *Searching for a Distant God: The Legacy of Maimonides.* Oxford University Press, Oxford, 2000.

Soloveitchik, Haim. "Maimonides 'Iggeret Ha-Shemad': Law and Rhetoric." In *Joseph H. Lookstein Memorial Volume,* ed. Leo Landman. Ktav, New York, 1980.

Spinoza, Baruch. *Ethics,* Part One. In *Spinoza: Complete Works,* trans. Samuel Shirley. Hackett, Indianapolis, 2002.

Stern, Josef. "The Fall and Rise of Myth in Ritual: Maimonides versus Nahmanides on the Huqqim, Astrology and the War against Idolatry." *Journal of Jewish Thought and Philosophy* 6, no. 2, 1997.

———. "The Idea of a *Hoq* in Maimonides' Explanation of the Law." In *Maimonides and Philosophy,* ed. Shlomo Pines and Yirmiyahu Yovel. Martinus Nijhoff, Dordrecht, 1986.

———. "Logical Syntax as a Key to a Secret of the *Guide of the Perplexed*" (Hebrew). *Iyyun* 38, 1989.

———. "Maimonides' Conceptions of Freedom and the Sense of Shame." In *Human Freedom and Moral Responsibility: General and Jewish Perspectives,* ed. Charles Manekin and Menachem Kellner. University Press of Maryland, College Park, 1997.

———. "Maimonides on Language and the Science of Language." In *Maimonides and the Sciences,* ed. Robert S. Cohen and Hillel Levine. Kluwer Academic, Dordrecht, 2000.

———. "Maimonides on the Covenant of Circumcision and the Unity of God." In *The Midrashic Imagination: Jewish Exegesis, Thought, and History,* ed. Michael Fishbane. SUNY Press, Albany, 1993.

———. "Maimonides on the Growth of Knowledge and the Limitations of the Intellect." In *Maïmonide philosophe et savant,* ed. T. Lévy and R. Rashed. Peeters, Leuven (Belgium), 2004.

———. *The Matter and Form of Maimonides' Guide.* Harvard University Press, Cambridge, 2013.

Strauss, Leo. *Persecution and the Art of Writing.* Free Press, Glencoe, IL, 1952.

———. "The Philosophic Foundation of the Law: Maimonides's Doctrine of Prophecy and Its Sources." In *Philosophy and Law: Contributions to the Understanding of Maimonides and His Predecessors,* trans. E. Adler. SUNY Press, Albany, 1995.

Stroumsa, Sarah. "The Literary Corpus of Maimonides and Averroes." In *Maimonidean Studies,* ed. Arthur Hyman and Alfred Ivry, vol. 5. Yeshiva University Press, New York, 2008.

———. *Maimonides in His World.* Princeton University Press, Princeton, 2009.

———. "Saadya and Jewish Kalam." In *The Cambridge Companion to Medieval Jewish Philosophy,* ed. Daniel H. Frank and Oliver Leaman. Cambridge University Press, Cambridge, 2003.

Twersky, Isadore. *Introduction to the Code of Maimonides (Mishneh Torah).* Yale University Press, New Haven, 1980.

———, ed. *A Maimonides Reader.* Behrman House, New York, 1972.

Walker, Paul E. *Early Philosophical Shiism: The Ismaili Neoplatonism of Abū Ya'qūb al-Sijistānī.* Cambridge University Press, Cambridge, 1993.

———. *Ḥamīd al-Dīn al-Kirmānī: Ismaili Thought in the Age of Al-Ḥākim.* I. B. Tauris, London, 1999.

———. "The Ismā'ili Vocabulary of Creation." *Studia Islamica* 40, 1974.

Watt, W. Montgomery. *Muhammad at Medina.* Clarendon Press, Oxford, 1956, reprint, 1962.

Weiss, Raymond L., and Charles E. Butterworth. *Ethical Writings of Maimonides.* New York University Press, New York, 1975.

Weiss, Raymond L. *Maimonides' Ethics: The Encounter of Philosophic and Religious Morality.* University of Chicago Press, Chicago, 1991.

Weiss, Roslyn. "Maimonides on the End of the World." In *Maimonidean Studies* 3, ed. Arthur Hyman. Yeshiva University Press, New York, 1992–93.

———. "Natural Order or Divine Will: Maimonides on Cosmogony and Prophecy." *Journal of Jewish Thought and Philosophy* 15, no. 1, 2007.

Wolfson, Harry Austryn. "Maimonides on Negative Attributes." In Wolfson, *Studies in the History of Philosophy and Religion,* vol. 2, ed. Isadore Twersky and George H. Williams. Harvard University Press, Cambridge, 1977.

———. "Maimonides on the Unity and Incorporeality of God." In Wolfson, *Studies in the History of Philosophy and Religion,* vol. 2, ed. Isadore Twersky and George H. Williams. Harvard University Press, Cambridge, 1977.

———. *The Philosophy of the Kalam.* Harvard University Press, Cambridge, 1976.

———. *Repercussions of the Kalam in Jewish Philosophy.* Harvard University Press, Cambridge, 1979.

———. "The Terms *Taṣawwur* and *Taṣdiq* in Arabic Philosophy and Their Greek, Latin, and Hebrew Equivalents." In Wolfson, *Studies in the History of Philosophy and Religion,* vol. 1, ed. Isadore Twersky and George H. Williams. Harvard University Press, Cambridge, 1973.

Index